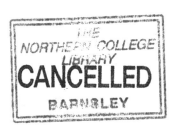

RULES OF DESIRE

BY THE SAME AUTHOR

Keep the Home Fires Burning:
Propaganda in the
First World War

RULES OF DESIRE

Sex in Britain: World War I to the Present

CATE HASTE

Chatto & Windus

LONDON

Published in 1992 by
Chatto & Windus Ltd
20 Vauxhall Bridge Road
London SW1V 2SA

A CIP catalogue record for this book is
available from the British Library

ISBN 0 7011 4016 X

Phototypeset by Intype, London
Printed in Great Britain by
Mackays of Chatham plc,
Chatham, Kent

Contents

For

Helen and Frances

and in memory of

Richard

Acknowledgements

This book has been researched and written over a period of nearly five years. Many people have helped and encouraged me on that long haul. Some have added fresh ideas, some have shifted me in new directions, many have helped with their insights, others have shown such interest as to make me feel it was all worthwhile if I doubted it, which I confess, when faced with mounting piles of research, I sometimes did.

Originally I planned a book on the politics of post-war sexual morals suggested by Professor Bernard Crick. It became clear there were several drawbacks. First, what was accepted as the startling change of the permissive sixties had roots reaching further back than the post-war years. The change was not brought about, as it had appeared, by youth protest; the people who carried through the legislative reforms and institutional changes were all by then approaching middle age. It was necessary to tease out what had earlier influenced *them*. Second, interesting though the politics of sex which focussed on parliament, politicians and lobby groups may be, they missed the heart of the matter – the personal experience of sex. The gap between private desire and society's rules seemed a more interesting area of discovery. So I opted for personal testimony as the starting point to plot the trajectory of political change.

I am extremely grateful to those who took time out of often busy schedules to read and comment on early drafts: Peter Copping, my old friend and mentor who from the start tirelessly steered me back to the main points; Tony Holden, Helen Haste, Phillip Whitehead and Neil Lyndon for their invaluable suggestions and support, and Faith Evans for her patience, her unwavering belief in the value of the book and her textual changes.

A number of people gave me their time for consultation and often lengthy discussion: Geoffrey Robertson, Michael Holroyd, Laurie Taylor, Peter Ackroyd (my Reading Room companion at the British Library), Tony Warren, who on a memorable train journey from Edinburgh inspired me to concentrate on the personal and encouraged me to carry on, Helen Buckingham, Leo Abse, Kenneth Robinson, Dick Taverne, and the late Alan Hancox who generously donated to me an invaluable censorship collection. I am also indebted to Carol Haslam and Jeremy Isaacs at Channel 4 who commissioned a series which gave me the chance to expand research, and to the members of 51% Productions (Veronyka Bodnarec, Sarah Boston, Jane Jackson and Rachel Tresize) with whom many themes were thrashed out early on. For their generous support at various times I am grateful to Udi Eichler, Peter Hadkins, Frances Haste, Hermione Lee, Diana Morant, Wendy Obermann, Sheila Pearson, Kathy Phillips and Chris Dunkley for the (long term) loan of his files.

I am particularly indebted to those who helped with the copious research and added their own views and experiences to my stock of resources: to Nick Mirsky for World War Two; Vivianne Howard for the 1950's and 1970's; Paul Wilmshurst for the 1980's; to Kate Southworth who chased up the references and Louise Allen whose typing rescued me when the computer lost the text.

Of the many sources I have used I wish to thank the librarians at the Imperial War Museum who never failed to give me new leads, the RAF Museum Hendon, the Fawcett Library, and the London Library who spent so much time on my behalf in the 'restricted' books section of the Librarians Room. Thanks also to the British Library and the Public Records Office; and to the following for permission to quote extracts: Pan Books Ltd for John Costello's *Love, Sex and War*, Scarecrow Books for R.C. Benge, *Confessions of a Lapsed Librarian*, and Faber and Faber Ltd, for John Osborne's *Look Back in Anger*.

Finally, I owe a special debt of gratitude to Jenny Uglow, my editor and Anne McDermid, my agent, and to my family – my husband for his unfailing support, and my children who always understood, gave me time and didn't mind that they could never use the word processor.

One

Introduction

Wed 5 May 1915 Midnight

My own beloved – how glad & grateful I am that you wrote your letter this morning, before we had our drive . . . I never saw you look more lovely, and there was in your divine eyes every now & again a soft & beatific radiance that I shall remember to my dying day . . .

You say, in your minimizing way, that it makes *you* happy to know that you help & sustain & inspire me. Darling – I owe you *everything*. Without you, where should I have been? or be now? . . .

For life, till death, you are the love of my heart, the joy & glory of my life. Your own.[1]

In 1915 Prime Minister Herbert Asquith was sixty-three years old and married. This was only one of the stream of letters in which he unburdened his heart to Venetia Stanley, a woman less than half his age with whom he had fallen obsessively in love. For three years, from 1912 to 1915, the statesman who steered Britain through a series of political crises into the First World War was consumed in his private life by an illicit passion for a woman who was not his wife but on whom he depended for daily comfort and ease. It was a highly charged, romantic and almost certainly unconsummated affair. It was also an impossible liaison. The depth of feeling lay more on his side than hers and they both realized she would eventually marry another man. When she did marry, partly to escape the developing complexities of the situation, their 'unique & divine intimacy' abruptly ended.[2]

David Lloyd George succeeded Asquith as Prime Minister in

1916. He was an altogether more passionate and flamboyant man than 'Old Squiffy', and since 1912 he had been conducting an affair with Frances Stevenson, his daughter's tutor. She had become his secretary on terms which, though 'in direct conflict with my essentially Victorian upbringing', she had accepted, already over-powered by his 'magnetism which made my heart leap and swept aside my judgement'.[3] The affair, and its accompanying life of constant vigilance and secrecy, lasted until Lloyd George even-tually married her in 1943 after his wife's death.

Both politicians made their private contract with the conven-tions governing the sexual code. Divorce was out of the question; it carried severe social and political penalties. Asquith appears never to have contemplated it. One of Lloyd George's first pres-ents to Frances was a book on Charles Parnell by the latter's mistress Kitty O'Shea. It was a message. Lloyd George believed that Parnell 'by marrying Kitty O'Shea Parnell had destroyed his own career and destroyed the Irish Party', and, he told her, 'no man has a right to imperil his political party and its objective for the sake of a woman. . . .'[4]

Both men benefited from the discretion which was observed about the private lives of public men. There was a more decorous code of conduct about intrustions into privacy by the press than now, and although illicit sexual behaviour may have been an open secret among colleagues, social proprieties dictated that it was simply not mentioned in public. With a rigid social code of moral conduct, divorce virtually impossible without scandal, and a com-paratively late age for marriage, 'immoral' behaviour by men was widely tolerated, although penalties on women were more severe.

Asquith was discreet. His known 'slight weakness for the com-panionship of clever and attractive women' (tolerated by his wife Margot as his 'little harem'[5]) camouflaged his deeper intimacy with Venetia even from close colleagues. This 'weakness' in a leading opponent of women's suffrage enraged the composer and suffragist Ethel Smyth, who protested to the Archbishop of Canterbury that it was 'disgraceful' that 'millions of women shall be trampled underfoot because of the "convictions" of an old man who notori-ously can't be left alone in a room with a young girl after dinner.'[6] But Ethel's complaint went no further.

There were other risks, for instance the threat of scandal engineered by political enemies. Although Lloyd George's affair and his other dallyings – he was known as the 'Goat' as well as the 'Welsh Wizard' – were widely rumoured, he had his protectors, who included newspaper proprietors. George Riddell, Chairman of the Newspaper Proprietors Association, personally warned Frances during a period of rising hostility to Lloyd George in 1916 to be 'very careful, as D's enemies are always on the watch . . . They would put poison in his cup', he told her, invoking Parnell again as the example of a scandal set up by his opponents to crush him.[7] Not long afterwards, an article about 'the beauty of D's family life!' by T. P. O'Connor appeared in the *Strand Magazine*, which excited Frances Stevenson's fury. 'He tells me that it is necessary – it is very useful to him in his public life . . . It amounts to hypocrisy.'[8]

There have always been people who believe they have a right to personal sexual liberty, and who feel that the promptings of desire and the demands of sexual passion override the rules society has erected in the name of social and moral order. For this they risk the penalties of public exposure, the punishment of social ostracism, or even personal destruction. At the beginning of the century people of all classes, and particularly the upper class, regularly found the means to get round the rigid rules of moral conduct, though it invariably condemned them to a twilight area of secrecy and duplicity. This gap between public and private morality then, as now, was called hypocrisy.

While some simply broke the rules, others worked to change the sexual ethic to fit human aspirations rather than religious imperatives or the dictates of conservative institutions. 'We must finally adapt our institutions to human nature', George Bernard Shaw decided in 1908, '. . . our present plan of trying to force human nature into a mould of existing abuses, superstitions, and corrupt interests, produces the explosive forces that wreck civilization.'[9] For the radicals of the late nineteenth and early twentieth century, the acknowledged gap between public and private morality was ethically offensive, socially disruptive and politically disastrous. They challenged a morality that castigated sexual desire as a subversive force, a terrifying passion which if not bridled would destroy the individual, the family and social order, rather than acknowledging it as a central force in human life, binding and enhancing social and personal relations. And they repudiated the morality which invoked God and 'Nature' to buttress the inequality between the sexes, which denied women rights and endorsed their sexual exploitation and their social inferiority.

Since the early years of the century, the individual's right to personal sexual freedom has been strengthened and the state's power to intervene in private morality in the interests of social order and stability has been reduced. This book is about how and why the rules governing sexual desire have been redrawn. For though sexual behaviour may not have altered that much, the loosening of external constraints has transformed personal and marital aspirations, the meanings ascribed to sex, and the boundaries within which people feel free to make sexual choices and discover their individuality. It also examines how far women's struggle to assert their natural rights to sexual equality has influenced changes and, on the other hand, to what extent the process of shaping new sexual and marital ideals has corralled women into new orthodoxies which still fall far short of equality.

I assume these changes are not to do with mysterious swings of some moral pendulum, but that people, institutions and professional practices interact with the effects of technology, ideology and economics to bring about shifts in moral norms. I have focused more on how mechanisms of external control – the church, the state and the law – operate to channel desire into the orthodox outlets of marriage and family, than on the matrix of other influences which make up learned understanding of sexual behaviour and mores. Parental controls, changing fashions in childrearing, medical and welfare practices, and education have all been harnessed to overt forms of social control. I have also explored the influence and background of individuals who have implanted new ideas into the culture or worked for change, and I have tried to link changes in sexual morals to the wider jigsaw of events and movements that have influenced society's changing concept of morality.

The book spans the period from the First World War to the present. The war accelerated a break with past conventions. By then, the major levers for change were already influencing beliefs and practices, but because they undermined orthodox morality, they had been resisted until new opportunities to explore sexuality opened up after the war.

By 1914 increased knowledge about sex was already undermining traditional beliefs. Scientific studies by sex psychologists round the turn of the century were beginning to infiltrate the culture and sex had begun to be detached from the divine. As psychology took over from God, some of the burden of sin and shame was lifted from sexual desire. Sex psychologists, notably Sigmund Freud and Havelock Ellis, instated sex as a central drive in the human make-up and a natural part of healthy relationships. Their work was harnessed to secular ideals which repudiated divine doctrine as the foundation for the social regulation of sexual desire, gradually changed the meanings of sex, and made possible more open discussion and wider dissemination of knowledge in an area hitherto shrouded in secrecy and taboo.

The technology of birth control, used extensively by the middle classes, was already influencing family size, but it was condemned as immoral by church, state and the medical profession. By separating sex from procreation, it offered new possibilities for eroticising sex; by releasing women from involuntary childbearing it opened up their choices; and it began to shape new marital ideals which acknowledged female desire and endorsed the mutual fulfilment of partners as integral to marital happiness. It was not until after the war, when birth control was seen as an agent for women's emancipation, that these ideals took root.

After fifty years of agitation against the subjection of women, the achievement of women's suffrage in 1918 symbolized an important stage in what had become by then a much wider struggle for sexual equality embracing every aspect of women's lives. The extension of women's rights has had a crucial influence on the sexual ethic.

As birth control relieved sex of the penalties of pregnancy, so medical advances in the treatment of sexual diseases gradually alleviated the stigma of sin and punishment associated with illicit sexuality. Disease began to be treated as an issue of public health rather than primarily a question of immorality – the physical manifestation of spiritual and moral decay. This assisted a more open public discussion of sex and altered attitudes to sex education. It lasted until AIDS. When sex was re-associated with death and disease, primitive concepts of moral retribution leaked back into public debate and encouraged stigmatization of 'deviant' groups, while influencing behaviour towards renewed caution and restraint.

Though the controls on sexual desire are now less rigid, the state still actively regulates behaviour, defines a code of morality, and has the power to employ more or less authoritarian constraints to marshal the population into a set of practices which conform to political and social ideologies. Institutions have been remoulded to fit ideals and expectations of freedom; a rhetoric of personal happiness, individual choice and personal responsibility now figures as the organizing principle of the sexual ethic. Yet the attempt by the Conservative administration in the 1980s to reaffirm 'family values' modelled on a conservative Victorian ethic threw into new relief the powers available to the state to intervene in private morality, even though the attempt met resistance and has so far largely failed. Although overt state control has diminished, the social control of sexual behaviour and desire has taken on new forms, using different methods of coercion. This book examines how these changes came about, and the conflicts, tensions, milestones, personal casualties, achievements and disillusionments along the route.

Two

Transition

Passionate Intellects

> She possessed a powerfully and physically passionate temperament which craved an answering impulse and might even under other circumstances – for of this I could have no personal experience – be capable of carrying her beyond the creed of right and wrong which she herself fiercely held and preached . . . For a brief period at this early stage of our relationship there passed before her the possibility of a relationship with me such as her own temperament demanded. But she swiftly realised that I was not fitted to play the part in such a relationship which her elementary primitive nature craved.[1]

This was how Havelock Ellis described the novelist Olive Schreiner, with whom he enjoyed an intense companionship for a year in 1884, shortly after the success of her first novel, *The Story of an African Farm*. Both were deeply interested in the 'sex question'; they talked about it incessantly. Ellis was to become a major sex psychologist, Schreiner was to spend much of her life seeking an enlarged understanding of women's personal and sexual identity in the interests of a progressive morality based on equality between the sexes.

Both were brought up in Victorian households and experienced the conflicts and tensions accompanying an ethic of sexual restraint. After suffering a religious crisis in youth, each emerged as a freethinker in search of a new spiritual ethic for personal relations. Havelock Ellis, born in 1859 (the year Darwin published

On the Origin of Species), was the son of a sea captain and a devout evangelical mother. He left England in his teens to teach in Australia, where, living in almost complete isolation, his spiritual crisis was induced by the simultaneous loss of his religious faith, the awakening conflicts of his sexual life, and a growing interest in science. Though he had lost 'the divine vision of life and beauty' associated with religion, he found that 'the scientific conception of an evolutionary world' was 'completely alien to the individual soul and quite inapt to attract love.'[2] On his return to England in 1879 he took up medical studies and later began a scientific documentation of sex, inspired by the aim to reconcile the sexual impulse to a new ethical order.

Olive Schreiner grew up in a strict, religious household from which all mention of sex or sexual attraction was sternly excluded. Her rejection of religion released a passion for intellectual ideas, and she became convinced that current social arrangements shackled women's freedom and that a new social and sexual order was needed. But though she openly confronted sex, she experienced continual internal conflict between her background, and the shame then associated with female sexual feelings, and her search for an intellectual ideal of companionate and equal relationships. Intensely aware of the sexual component of her nature, she was riddled with guilt at her feelings, which were constantly at war with her intellect.

The affair between Ellis and Shreiner was never consummated. He was passive and dispassionate by temperament, and uncertain of his potency; she was in turmoil recovering from a previous affair with a South African, Julius Gau, which had left her with an overpowering sense of guilt – after it she suffered lifelong and debilitating asthma. She had been striving 'to crush and kill all that side of my nature' and confided to Ellis in 1887, 'All that my sexual nature had to give I gave years ago.'[3] Their relationship, described by Ellis as an 'affectionate friendship' which was 'really even more intimate, than is often the relationship between those who technically and ordinarily are lovers',[4] gave them both an opportunity to intellectualize sex. Olive had a lasting influence on Ellis's views.

For Olive, the difficulty of reconciling sexual passion with an ideal of male-female equality debarred her from conventional marriage, which for her implied bondage. 'I *must* be free, you know, I must be *free*', she explained to Ellis, 'I've been free all my life.'[5] She wrote to her friend, the eugenicist Karl Pearson, 'All I know is that I am not a marrying woman; when it comes to the point my blood curdles and my heart is like stone.'[6] She abhorred the separation of woman's sexual being from her whole personality. 'A man thought', she wrote to Ellis, that when he 'touches a woman it is only her body he is touching, it is really her soul, her brain, her creative power. It is putting his fingers into her brain and snapping the strings when he draws her to him physically, and cannot take her mentally.'[7] But she also feared that true and equal companionship might be destroyed by sexual passion. 'Friendship between men and women *is* a possibility', she wrote. 'But is there not always a possibility of the consciousness of sex difference and the desires which spring from it creeping in, and spoiling the beautiful free frank relationship? – *No*, not when the friendship is true.'[8]

Her dilemma reached a crisis in 1885 when she joined the Men and Women's Club, a group which Karl Pearson, the charismatic and humourless Professor of Mathematics at University College London, had gathered around him to discuss new relations between the sexes. Pearson not only held the conventional view that women's inferiority was predetermined by their biological function of reproduction, he also firmly believed that intellect could triumph over bodily desires. A great admirer of Olive's intellect, he dictated that the terms of their relationship 'should and could only be the free open friendship of man to man' for he had already experienced the 'danger – perhaps evil' in male-female relationships.[9] By this Pearson validated her suppression of her sexual feelings; it was justified by their joint exploration of an intellectual ideal. 'It's just the absence of sex feeling that has drawn me,' Olive explained to Ellis.[10]

Olive chose to see this as a close relationship of intellectual equals, but when she suffered a physical collapse, her friend Bryan Donkin, a doctor who had read of the possible connection between sexual suppression and hysteria, suggested the cause was sexual love for Pearson. Olive was distraught. Though she felt for him more deeply than for anyone she had ever known, she was emphatic it was not 'sex-love'. She wrote to Pearson asking why, if he'd ever seen sex creeping into her thought or feeling for him, 'didn't you tell me of it, and crush it? See, I love you better than anything else in the world, and I have tried to keep far from you that nothing material might creep in between my brain and yours, and you have not understood me'.[11] Charlotte Wilson, a friend of both, blamed Pearson. She wrote acidly to him, 'I think that O. S. is well on the way towards crushing the emotional element in her . . . I consider that her energy is being wasted in the process – but, on your hypothesis, that hard schooling should be the way to rescue mental growth from the foes who would destroy it. In a few years she will be purely the woman of intellect – less than her best self I think – but a human being as you would have them be'.[12]

Olive retreated to Europe and then South Africa, where, at the age of thirty-nine she married Samuel Cronwright, who supported her writing, did not live with her all the time, and gave her freedom to pursue her own life and work. Intellectually, she never denied the importance of sexual passion in women, but her ideal of 'a labouring and virile womanhood, free, strong, fearless and tender'[13] developed from her belief that sexual union could only be successful when relationships were equal, when women had economic opportunity and financial independence and were free to choose their own destiny. Then it could be enjoyed as 'a sacrament to be partaken between two souls', as a union both physical and mental, in a marriage which was 'a fellowship of comrades, rather than the relationship of the owner and the bought, the keeper and the kept'.[14] Olive Schreiner had a powerful influence on many younger feminists: Vera Brittain thought *Woman and Labour* (1911) 'as insistent and inspiring as a trumpet-call summoning the faithful to a vital crusade'.[15]

Intellectual Passions

Olive Schreiner was a product of the guilts wrought by a society which cramped women's desire within a rigid code of passivity and denial. The conflicts this presented to women with any intellectual purpose beyond the domestic role allotted to them in an unequal marriage became increasingly difficult to ignore as women sought to enlarge their public space and extend their rights. Schreiner proposed an ideal that would reconcile women's sexual nature with their social emancipation. Beatrice Webb experienced a similar conflict between her passionate nature and her sense of higher purpose, but she resolved it by unequivocally choosing intellect above passion.

Born in 1858 and brought up in a wealthy family of liberal dissenters, in an intellectually stimulating atmosphere where her parents were hosts to the leading writers and philosophers of the day, the then Beatrice Potter learnt to 'reason on subjects which other girls have mostly been told to take on faith.'[16] Without formal education, she took to study as an antidote to idleness, and discovered a growing and 'restless ambition . . . for a life with some result'.[17] She had lost her religious faith in her late teens, but not her religious impulse. Motivated by a powerful sense of duty to wider humanity, she sought to channel the energy of religious belief into a new set of moral and philosophical principles which could regulate altruism. She found these principles in 'the religion of science', a reconstitution of politics and morality on a rational and scientific basis, and concluded that 'Social questions are the vital questions of today. They take the place of religion.'[18]

Beatrice had early discovered the conflicting claims of her own nature. Conscious of her own passion, her 'instinct and impulse', she had thoroughly internalized the Victorian ethic which suppressed sexual feelings as unseemly, especially in women. At sixteen she was chiding herself, 'You are really getting into a nasty and what I should call an indecent way of thinking of men, and love, and unless you take care you will lose all your purity of thought, and become a silly vain self-conscious little goose.'[19] She described later encounters with men as time spent 'unworthily', with 'the consciousness of having given way to a pleasure' which, she confessed, she lacked 'the necessary self-denial' to avoid.[20] '. . . I cannot maintain my reason as the ruler of my nature, but am still constantly enslaved by instinct and impulse.'[21] Her sense of purpose also led her to despise the conventional occupation of women in marriage.

This conflict between her ambition, her views on marriage, and her passionate feelings erupted in 1883 when she encountered Joseph Chamberlain, an influential and charismatic social reformer and a demagogue. He set her on a path of emotional turmoil which was to last for six years. She fell in love with him and there was talk of marriage within weeks. But when she came to assess marriage she was appalled at the prospects. He wanted someone 'to "forward" his most ambitious views',[22] he had 'a passionate desire to *crush* opposition to *his will*,'[23] he refused to allow division of opinion in his household, especially on the women's rights issue, he was a despot. Yet she felt 'great personal attraction' to him, and deeper feelings which she feared – '. . . passion, with its burning heat, an emotion which had for long smouldered unnoticed, burst out into flame, and burnt down intellectual interests, personal ambition, and all other self-developing motives.'[24] Struggling with her warring feelings she reasoned, 'If I married him I should become a cynic as regards my own mental life.'[25] Five weeks later, she was still unresolved: 'Once married, I should of course subordinate my views to my husband's, should, as regards his own profession, accept implicitly his views of right and wrong. But I cannot shirk the responsibility of using my judgement before I acknowledge his authority . . . I have not only no devotion to these aims, but have to twist my reasoning in order to *tolerate them*.'[26]

She turned down marriage, and threw herself into work, starting as a rent collector in London's East End. But she suffered deep depression: 'There is glitter all around me and darkness within, the darkness of blind desire yearning for the light of love. . . . I stand alone with my own nature now too strong for me.'[27] Her absorption in work had not killed her longing 'every day more for the restfulness of an abiding love', and she still instructed herself to 'check those feelings which are the expression of physical instinct craving for satisfaction; but God knows celibacy is as painful to a woman (even from the physical standpoint) as it is to a man. It could not be more painful than it is to a woman.'[28]

When Sidney Webb fell in love with Beatrice in 1890 she decreed that their only possible relationship was comradeship, the joining together of resources for the good of the commonwealth. 'I came out of that six years agony . . . like a bit of steel. I was not broken but hardened – the fire must do one or the other', she confessed to him.[29] It was her explanation of why she could not marry him. Personal happiness had become 'an utterly remote thing'; the only thing that counted was her commitment to serve the community.

In her diary she wrote, 'Personal passion has burnt itself out, and what little personal feeling still exists haunts the memory of that other man.' Marriage was now 'another word for suicide. I cannot bring myself to face an act of *felo de se* for a speculation in personal happiness.'[30]

Despite these obstacles, Sidney Webb persisted in his attempt to persuade her that it was possible to have a marriage in which she did not relinquish her self. Beatrice began to warm to him, but when she finally agreed to marry insisted, 'it is the head only that I am marrying!'[31] Marriage, she was persuaded, would be 'an act of renunciation of self and not of indulgence of self as it would have been in the other case.'[32] She 'shuddered' at the life she had missed – playing the unsuitable 'great role of "walking gentle-woman" to the play of *Chamberlain*.' By 1891 the Webbs were finding a happiness in each other and in their 'fellowship, a common faith and a common work'[33] which was becoming 'more complete and inspiring each day.' On their honeymoon, where they planned to study Irish trade unions, Beatrice wrote to a friend, 'We are very very happy, far too happy to be reasonable.'[34]

Where Olive Schreiner had tried and suffered in the attempt to weld sexual feelings to intellectual equality, Beatrice Webb moulded her intellect into an instrument for social progress, sacrificing her passionate nature. She then managed to integrate that rejection of sexual desire into a set of principles for the moral ordering of society: 'I cling to the thought that man will only evolve upwards by the subordination of his physical desires and appetites to the intellectual and spiritual side of his nature. Unless this evolution be the purpose of the race I despair – and wish only for the extinction of human consciousness.'[35]

Equality and Purity

The ethic of restraint which Webb redefined to fit her Fabian principles was shared by early feminists, who for fifty years had conducted a revolt against the edifices which supported their subordination. They had campaigned against the marriage laws which deprived them of legal rights, property and control over children, for the right to education and employment opportunities outside the home, and, since the formation of suffrage societies in the

1860s, for the right to vote. They saw the vote as the first condition of their emancipation from civic inferiority, abject dependence and confinement by 'nature' to the sphere of 'domestic affections'.

Some had also campaigned against the double standard of morality which enjoined purity on women while endorsing male licence. The seventeen-year political campaign to repeal the Contagious Diseases Acts, begun in the 1860s and led by Josephine Butler, focused attention on the sexual motive in the wider inequality between the sexes. Under the Acts, prostitutes could be forced to undergo medical examination on penalty of imprisonment if they were suspected of infecting men with disease. To the repealers, the laws were a violation of women's civil liberties. They protected men while penalizing women for the sins of male 'licentiousness', and amounted to the state's endorsement of 'vice'. The campaigners challenged the state's sanction of the belief that the 'natural' impulses of men could legitimately be expressed with no concern for the rights of women, and asserted that prostitution was a by-product of a morality that made women into sexual chattels through limiting their economic opportunities and endorsing their complete dependence on men.

Their solution was to press for the enforcement of a single standard of morality for men and women alike. This aim brought moral conservatives and religious puritans into a new alliance with feminists, which was welded in the aftermath of scandalous newspaper revelations about child prostitution by W. T. Stead, the crusading editor of the *Pall Mall Gazette*. In 1885 he published the results of his private investigation into the 'underworld' under the lurid title 'The Maiden Tribute of Modern Babylon' (with such sub-titles as 'Strapping Girls Down' and 'The Violation of Virgins'). This early example of campaign journalism not only delivered record sales for the paper, but provoked widespread moral indignation which was immediately channelled into a crusade under a newly formed pressure group, the National Vigilance Association, to purify the nation of 'vice'.

It signalled a new phase of pressure to extend the state's control over private morality. The immediate aim of Stead's exposure, to galvanise support for raising the age of consent to sixteen, was achieved with dramatic speed in the Criminal Law Amendment Act of 1885, which also made homosexuality a criminal act through Section 11 (the Labouchere Amendment). A series of measures to increase control over brothel-keeping, prostitution and soliciting followed, in which public pressure from the NVA was influential. They set a new agenda in the public debate with further campaigns to tighten controls over rape and incest and raise the age of consent to eighteen.

Feminists were prominent in the movement for social purity. Their claim to equal rights had never been at odds with their faith in religion and the family as the central planks of social stability, nor with their adherence to the Victorian ethic of sexual restraint. Many, though not all, came from evangelical or non-conformist backgrounds and, like Josephine Butler, drew strength from their religious convictions. Indeed, it was in religion that many found the language of resistance to patriarchial values – a language which endorsed the integrity and dignity of the human spirit and the individual conscience for men and women equally. Their struggle for equal rights did not conflict with their conviction of women's special mission of motherhood and their privileged position as guardians of the family and the domestic virtues.

It was not difficult therefore for them to enter into alliance with religious conservatives, who shared many of these beliefs. But while the NVA's early concern had been the protection of women and young girls, the initiative was rapidly seized by religious puritans who turned it into a force for repression and an instrument for stamping out immorality in all its forms. Their over-zealous activities – 'literally a hand-to-hand fight with the world, flesh and the devil' and 'an energetic legal crusade against vice in its hydra-headed form' as NVA's leader William Coote described them[36] – aimed to bear the flag of righteousness into all suspect channels of the body politic, to suppress literature, plays and all forms of public display with the faintest whiff of sex about them. The organization attracted rising hostility.

In 1894 *The Daily Telegraph* published one hundred and seventy-five letters protesting against 'Prudes on the Prowl'. Winston Churchill made his 'maiden' speech in the 'unvirginal surroundings' of the Empire, Leicester Square, where the vigilance activities of Mrs Ormiston Chant had forced the erection of barricades to defend the audience from prostitutes. Having pondered on 'the best traditions of British freedom' and 'the dangers of State interference with the social habits of law-abiding persons; and upon the many evil consequences which inevitably follow upon repression not supported by healthy public opinion', young Churchill joined fellow Sandhurst cadets to tear down the barricades, emerging into the street brandishing bits of wood. It appealed to his sense of drama, reminding him, he wrote, 'of the death of Julius Caesar when the conspirators rushed forth into the street waving the bloody daggers with which they had slain the tyrant', and even of 'the taking of the Bastille'.[37]

Some early supporters left the NVA, appalled at its repressive methods and disregard for individual liberties. Josephine Butler warned women's rights supporters in 1897 to 'Beware of "purity workers" as allies in our welfare'; they, along with others, were 'suffering largely from a species of moral atrophy – from a fatal paralysis of the sense of justice'.[38] She had distanced herself from attempts to coerce private behaviour from the beginning of her 'crusade' – 'convinced in my conscience and understanding of the folly, and even wickedness, of all systems of *outward repression* of private immorality, for which men and women are accountable to God and their own souls, not to the *State*.'[39]

Vigilance continued to influence the public debate about sex well into the 1930s. The single standard of morality remained the banner for feminists and social purists up till the First World War. It was appropriated by prominent prewar suffragettes as one tactic in the campaign to assert women's fitness to vote. Christobel Pankhurst adopted the slogan 'Votes for Women, Chastity for Men' in the belief that women were the superior moral force in politics. Only when they had the vote and took their place as independent, self-respecting, equal human beings would they have the authority to end the injustices women suffered through the exploitation endorsed by the double standard.[40] But by the First World War, younger feminists were countering this with a different conception of a new morality.

White Flowers and a Blameless Life

The suffrage campaign was the main focus of feminist political activity, but issues of women's personal emancipation had also begun to take on increasing importance. After Ibsen's *A Doll's*

House in 1879, the woman imprisoned in marriage, and the New Woman in rebellion against the constraints on her freedom made regular appearances on stage and in fiction. Though the New Woman was invariably punished or compromised in one way or another – with illness and death in Grant Allen's *The Woman Who Did* (1895) and with an unambiguous capitulation to conventional marriage in Thomas Hardy's *Jude the Obscure* (1895), or was otherwise neutered as an earnest and guileless blue stocking as in G. B. Shaw's *Mrs Warren's Profession* (written in 1893 but not published until 1898) – her presence in fiction was the vehicle for exploring the moral conflicts raised by women's changing aspirations.

Though women had begun to experience some enlargement of their freedom, their lives were still circumscribed by rigid rules. Women had entered higher education in increasing numbers since the establishment of the first women's colleges at Girton and Newnham in the 1870s and girls' secondary school education had expanded, but this had hardly eroded the belief that education would cause women to lose their 'femininity' and render them incapable of 'performing their functions as women'. More professions were opening up to women and employment opportunities expanded. There was a small but steady stream of qualified women doctors. By 1900 women were beginning to take over the typewriter and by 1911 they occupied one in five office clerk jobs. Nursing was feminized although it was refused professional status until 1919. With the influx of graduates, teaching became better paid at the higher levels and, with the expansion of secondary schooling after the 1880s, more working class women moved into the teaching profession; by 1911 there were 180,000 women teachers.[41] The unionization of working class women in Mary Macarthur's National Federation of Women Workers gave women a lever and a voice in the bastion of male trade union power.

Their freedom of physical movement was enlarged – bicycling, despite laments that it was 'beyond a girl's strength' and would 'destroy the sweet simplicity of her girlish nature', was particularly popular, as were active sports such as golfing, rollerskating and tennis. But middle class women were still closely controlled and their purity safeguarded. It was not sufficient, Dr Mary Scharlieb thundered at her young medical students, 'for each girl that she should possess the "white flower of a blameless life" '; it was also necessary that 'the white flower should be free from the slightest shadow which could in any way detract from its lustre.'[42] Chaperones were in constant attendance, even at Oxford colleges where, Mary Stocks recalled, there was an 'elaborate machinery for frustrating social contacts between male and female undergraduates'.[43]

Some women were beginning to challenge the constraints on their personal freedom as actively as they rebelled against the wider injustice of their political subordination. The suffrage movement became increasingly militant as the Women's Social and Political Union resorted to tactics of harassment, disruption and what Mrs Pankhurst termed 'the argument of the broken window pane', resulting in the imprisonment, force feeding and torture of members, and this stimulated a more acute awareness of the constraints on women's freedom in all areas. For many younger women, the vote was only one objective in a strategy for personal emancipation which must involve radical change not only in institutional controls but in the way women perceived themselves.

Rebecca West was brought up to believe a woman's place was in a career at the time of suffragette militancy, the Cat and Mouse Acts and failed suffrage amendments. She agreed with Emily Pankhurst that at the heart of men's opposition to women's progress was a sex antagonism 'so strong among men that it produced an attitude which, if it were provoked to candid expression, would make every self-respecting woman want to fight it . . . Women, listening to anti-suffrage speeches for the first time knew what men really thought of them.'[44] Her experience in the suffrage cause, she said, 'removed any inclination I might have had towards meekness'.[45] It bred in her 'a strong hatred, the best lamp to bear in our hands as we go over the dark places of life, cutting away the dead things men tell us to revere.'[46]

Rebecca West was one of the younger feminists who were exploring the personal issues of sexual equality. Their public platform, *The Freewoman*, set up by Dora Marsden in 1911, called for a New Morality. Though the vote would give women paper-and-ink equality, it would not tackle the fundamental issues of denial of women's passion or their personal subjugation which was woven into the social fabric. Women, in 'seeking the realization of the will of others, not their own . . . [had] almost lost the instinct of achievement in their own persons'.[47] They must claim responsibility, not protection, for themselves; claim passion and self-gratification, and relationships entered into on terms of equality. They must struggle to create conditions which enabled women to 'choose and follow a life work, apart from and in addition to their natural function of reproduction'.[48]

It was a new tone of voice, that of women who felt 'compelled . . . to recognize the disorder of living according to the law, the immorality of being moral, the monstrousness of the social code'.[49] Their frank discussion of free love and its implications for women's erotic freedom of choice, and their stress on personal development and self-realization marked a radical departure from the previous feminist position of support for a single standard of purity.

The younger feminists' approach to birth control was a further crucial shift. They saw contraception as an agent for female emancipation, which acknowledged that the separation of sex from reproduction could alter the definitions of women's sexuality and liberate women to take control of their lives. Older feminists had been either silent or actively opposed to contraception, seeing it as a pernicious device which only benefited men by relieving them of the penalties of fornication. In this they followed respectabel opinion. Though contraception was used increasingly by the middle classes from the 1880s it was banned as immoral by the church and condemned by most of the medical profession as actively injurious to physical and moral health, especially of women. It was alleged to be the cause of a variety of disorders, including cancer, sterility, nymphomania and 'mania leading to suicide', and was thought to degrade 'the finest moral instincts', leading to 'a bestial sensuality and indifference to all morality'.[50] One American doctor, however, had a different complaint: 'I do think that this filling of the vagina with traps making a Chinese toyshop of it is outrageous.'[51] Several publications dealing with contraception were successfully prosecuted for obscenity, among them the reissue by Charles Bradlaugh and feminist Annie Besant of Charles Knowlton's The Fruits of Philosophy in 1877.

When the suffragist leader Millicent Fawcett was asked to appear in defence of Besant and Bradlaugh, she refused, because of 'the objectionable character' of their publications.[52] Like many others,

Millicent thought that political espousal of Annie Besant's Neo-Malthusian views on population control in the interests of alleviating poverty might publicly identify the women's cause with a challenge to their duty of motherhood, quite apart from the association of contraception with immorality. Annie Besant lost custody of her daughter because it was thought that a woman of her views was an unfit mother.

On the eve of war, issues of sexual morality divided the women's movement along broadly generational lines. *The Freewoman* with its advocacy of women's sexual freedom was too much for older feminists. Mrs Fawcett received one copy, 'looked it through, thought it objectionable and mischievous, and tore it up into small pieces'.[53] Olive Schreiner thought it should be called 'the Licentious Male', since so many articles were written by men, and she objected to its frank tone, which she thought suggested promiscuity. 'It's unclean. And sex is so beautiful!' she wrote.[54]

New Moralists

Feminist supporters of the New Morality were part of a wider intellectual movement which had challenged a socially unjust and morally inequitable sexual ethic since the 1880s. This movement germinated among post-Darwinian scientific rationalists and free-thinkers who had lost their faith in religion as the foundation of ethics, but had not abandoned the religious impulse towards spiritual perfectibility.

One seedbed for radical theories was the Fellowship of the New Life, set up in 1883. Out of commitment to a new order based on service to humanity rather than God they evolved the principles of ethical socialism, which linked social improvement to ethical perfectibility. They sought 'a reconstruction of society in harmony with the highest moral possibilities' and lived by the principles they preached – a return to the Simple Life, the abandonment of superfluous luxury, the elevation of manual labour, the subordination of the material to the spiritual, and experiments in healthy living which would foster comradeship and enhance communion between people.

From this group, which fertilized the roots of Fabian socialism, evolved the basic principles of sexual libertarianism which were to influence most twentieth-century sex-reform movements: the application of rational and humane, rather than divine, principles to the organization and control of sexual morals; equality between the sexes; and the belief that to understand sex is to understand the self. These movements linked sexual reform directly to the wider transformation in the social power nexus. A hypocritical, conventional morality distorted human love and sexual relations, just as unjust and oppressive economic arrangements distorted social relations.

Edward Carpenter was the most influential exponent of the link between the personal and the political. A socialist active in Sheffield politics and a homosexual, who lived out his principles of simple living – market gardening, vegetarianism, sandal-making and writing – at his home in Derbyshire, he saw socialism not only as a political doctrine but a way of life. For him the personal took priority in all social relations; he had an almost mystical belief in a harmony possible through tenderness and communion between people. The key to regeneration, outlined in his book *Love's Coming of Age* (1896), was to restore feeling and sexuality to the centre of people's lives. Morality, custom and laws which denounced sex as unclean and saturated it in 'false shame', while enforcing the 'arbitrary notion' that the function of sexual love was limited to procreation and that any love not concerned with this must 'necessarily be of dubious character', had obscured the central importance of sexual union as a binding force in social relations and a 'symbol and expression of deepest soul-union'.[55] The institutional organization of sex which enforced women's sexual inequality and dependence in unequal marriage was another central distortion in the prevailing sexual ethic; equality was the only true basis for relationships. Society's attitudes to homosexuals, whom he identified as the 'intermediate sex' rendered them as oppressed as women and the working class.

Carpenter's views were not popular with all socialists. Robert Blatchford, editor of the *Clarion*, told Carpenter that the whole subject was 'nasty' to him and warned, as other socialists continued to do after him, that socialist identification with sexual questions would only retard industrial change.[56] But among many intellectuals, the prophetic and visionary qualities in Carpenter's writing and his emphasis on the personal – the 'universe of the senses' – were inspiring. E. M. Forster's novel *Maurice* owes much to a visit he paid to Carpenter and his working-class lover George Merrill in 1913; D. H. Lawrence read him and was acquainted with several supporters of his philosophy and way of life among Midlands socialists; the adolescent Robert Graves told him his later book *The Intermediate Sex* (1912) had lifted the scales from his eyes and crystallized his vague feelings.[57]

Havelock Ellis, another early member of the Fellowship, channelled his humanist quest into the scientific study of sex. Like Carpenter, Ellis believed conventional controls on sex were a central distortion of the truth of human nature. By penetrating the veils of ignorance, his work made possible more rational understanding and frank discussion of sex and established a scientific base for sexual liberalism. Though his work did not ultimately provide a framework comparable to Freud, who was working at the same time on the psychoanalytical study of sex, Ellis had a lasting influence.

He saw sexual passion not as a negative force – 'a fire that burns and consumes everything; like an abyss that swallows all, – honour, fortune, well-being', as Dr Krafft Ebing described it in his influential *Psychopathia Sexualis* (1886)[58], but as a positive force enhancing life. He acknowledged the centrality of the sexual impulse as a motivating factor in human development, recognized the importance of infant sexuality, and concluded that it was the denial and repression of the sexual impulse, not its expression, which wrought the greater damage to the development of an essentially healthy drive. He repudiated the rigid categorizations into 'normal' and 'abnormal' sex which previous experts – the physicians – had advanced to buttress the morality of marriage and family, and uphold the values of moderation, restraint, duty, thrift and conservation which informed other forms of commerce. Instead he asserted that there was wide variability in the expression of the sexual impulse and that normal and abnormal were merely points on a continuum of sexual variety. Both he and Freud probed and challenged the mechanisms of repressive cultural factors.

Ellis sought a spiritual regeneration: he aimed to change beliefs. He was critical of conventional morality and concerned to sweep away sexual myths and taboos. His studies gave him a firm base from which to propose reforms. An advocate of equality, he was critical of legal marriage founded on the dominance and possession of women by men. He once described it as a more fashionable form of prostitution in which women were underpaid. Neither her nor Freud repudiated the belief that the biological imperative of reproduction determined the differences between the sexes and their erotic responses. Though Ellis's theories accepted women's biological mission of motherhood, he was also responsive to wider debates about women's equality and, 'in accordance with our growing tendency to place the two sexes on the same level', was inclined to seek out similarities between the sexes and assess the influence of cultural factors on sexual responses. The view that women lacked sexual desire he repudiated as a Victorian myth – the product of cultural training which taught women to repress their sexual impulse as disgusting and sinful. He believed that cultural, more than physiological factors, played a part in female frigidity and male impotence, concluded that orgasm was remarkably similar in men and women (he noted women's ability to achieve multiple orgasms), and advocated women's right to enjoy their sexuality untrammelled by shame. Part of the 'problem' of female sexuality was failure in the art of love, which was largely a failure on the man's part to bring the woman to arousal, for, he believed, it was 'by nature' the man's part to give embraces, the woman's to receive – to be kissed into response.

Like most sexual progressives, Ellis's personal experience – his rejection of religion and his adoption of science as the key to an understanding of the human spirit – moulded his critique of the sexual code. In 1891 he married the writer and feminist Edith Lees with whom he attempted to live out his ideal of an 'ethical companionate marriage' in which partners had equal rights – 'a union of soul and body so close and so firmly established that one feels it will last as long as life lasts'.[59] This did not, however, include successful sexual relations; according to Ellis, they were 'relatively unsuited to each other, . . . relations were incomplete and unsatisfactory'. He attributed this to Edith's dislike of 'the mechanical contraceptive preliminaries of intercourse'. After a while sexual relations were discontinued altogether. 'Only one thing was left out', the prophet of sexual harmony concluded, 'yet so small in comparison to all that was left that we scarcely missed it.'[60]

Within two years Edith started a lesbian affair with 'Claire' which Ellis accepted. 'It is so wonderful to have married a man who leaves a woman her soul', Edith wrote to him. But Ellis then embarked on a series of affairs with powerful and independent women – the poet Hilda Doolittle and pioneer birth controller Margaret Sanger among them. Through them, he came to terms with his own sexual anomaly, urolagnia – sexual arousal at the fact or fantasy of women urinating, which he examined at length in his *Studies in the Psychology of Sex*. After Edith died from illness and nervous collapse in 1916, he started an affair with Françoise Delisle who, though twice married and separated with two children, had never been sexually aroused by either husband; she had not even seen them naked. Though alarmed at first by his lovemaking, with 'his hands and his kisses', she came to delight in the way that, she said 'my body, husbandless, yet spontaneously acclaimed its true rule at the guidance of this other soul: "Love, and do what you like".'[61] With her, Ellis reached full coital potency in his sixties.

H. G. Wells and Free Love

Where Havelock Ellis deployed science to change beliefs about sexuality, writer and Fabian socialist H. G. Wells used fiction – as G. B. Shaw used theatre – to propose a rational sexual order in which the state's power to intervene in an individual's private affairs was radically altered. Any society which compelled its citizens to live so at odds with the terms of their nature could, he believed, be neither sane nor prosperous; a revolution in morals was required, and socialism provided its rationale. For Wells, like Carpenter, socialism was not merely 'a petty tinkering with economic relationships', but a 'renucleation of society'.[62] The family, he argued, was 'an inseparable correlative of private pro- prietorship. It embodied jealousy in sexual life just as private ownership embodied jealousy in economic life.' Socialism should repudiate all forms of ownership and jealousy in personal relations. Women's emancipation was not a question of getting the vote, which he dismissed as 'that nagging ignoble campaign'; its first condition was complete freedom of their persons, sexual freedom of choice, access to birth control to replace 'directed and obligatory love and involuntary child-bearing',[63] and state support to further their economic independence, a system of state endowment of motherhood, and easier and more equal divorce laws.

Wells's attempt to 'sexualize socialism' by persuading the Fabian Society to adopt his theories for a new social contract failed when the 'old guard', appalled at the taint of promiscuity, defeated the younger members and the women who mostly supported Wells. But he established himself as a utopian and often visionary apostle of sexual freedom, and influenced a wider audience towards his theories through his fictional works and political polemics.

Wells elevated his personal revolt against Victorian morality into a set of theories for social organization which suited his own sexual temperament, satisfied his interest in utopian solutions and gave vent to his inclination to dissect (he was a biologist by training) the ironies and hypocrisies in social and personal conduct.

Wells rejected his mother's evangelism in favour of the scientific principles of his mentor, T. H. Huxley. Having been brought up to think of 'what was biologically the central element of his life, his sexuality, as something marginal and almost irrelevant to the central business of living'[64] he developed a lasting interest in 'unsolved sexual complexities' which he addressed with often surgical precision in life as in his work. Married twice, he found both wives sexually disappointing. His first marriage to his cousin Isabel was marred by what he later attacked as 'excessive artificial innocence . . . that "chastity" which is mere abstinence and concealment' in his wife, which fell far short of his romantic imaginative ideal of 'flame meeting flame'.[65] Although he admitted he was 'a very ignorant as well as an impatient lover', it was 'a profound mortification to me, a vast disappointment that she did not immediately respond to my ardours. She submitted.' After a brief lovemaking with an assistant which restored his faith in sex as something more than 'an outrage inflicted upon reluctant womankind', he embarked on 'an enterprising promiscuity'.[66]

In 1894, at the age of twenty-seven, Wells left Isabel for his young student Amy Catherine Robbins (whom he deprived of her name, rechristening her 'Jane'), but she, also 'innocent and ignorant of the material realities of love', failed to match up to his high ideal of 'Venus Urania', his 'Lover-Shadow', a complementary being who echoed his imaginative thirst for the fulfilment of his hopes and sensual desires. Much of his complex love life was elaborately explained by Wells as a persistent yearning for the embodiment of this shadow reflection of himself in flesh and blood – 'a lovely, wise and generous person wholly devoted to me.'[67]

Jane became the perfect manager of his life and domestic arrangements and she tolerated his many affairs. Happily she was never inclined to apply H. G.'s theories to her own life. She watched, and kept on being 'wonderful' in Wells's terms, that is 'she betrayed no resentment, no protesting egotism'[68] which might interfere with his pursuit of his 'Lover-Shadow'. His first experience of passionate love, an infatuation with Amber Reeves, the brilliant daughter of Fabian colleagues, caused him temporarily to modify some of his theories about sexual ownership; he experienced jealousy and 'fixation': 'When the sexual obsession was uppermost in me, all my theorizing about the open-living Samurai was flung to the winds. I wanted to monopolize her,' he wrote.[69] So much so that when she became pregnant and they decided the situation could only be resolved by marriage to her suitor, Rivers Blanco-White (since Wells never contemplated divorcing Jane), Wells refused to stop seeing her, believing they were 'sustaining some high and novel standard against an obtuse and ignoble world'. He always regretted the decision to part as a capitulation: 'We ought to have gone on meeting as lovers and saying "You be damned to the world." '[70]

Apart from this 'fever', Wells controlled all his affairs by dictating the precise terms and limits of commitment – that it should be fun and it should not impinge on his central relationship with Jane. He was excessively irked when any of his lovers demanded more of his life or displayed any jealousy. They could love him, but he cramped their love to the terms of his, not their, sexual desires. Though he could formulate theories for women's sexual emancipation, he retreated from them when they faced him with the completeness of their passion. 'I can't conceive of a person who runs about lighting bonfires and yet nourishes a dislike of flame,' Rebecca West chided.[71] Wells's affair with West, which began in 1913 and lasted ten years, was contracted on his terms –

'a matter of two people finding each other physically attractive and coming together to couple for coupling's sake. And it was not to last,' their son Anthony West wrote.[72] When she fell passionately in love with him, she wrote in despair: 'I have tried to conciliate you by hacking away at my love for you, cutting it down to the little thing that was the most you wanted', and added later, 'Your spinsterishness makes you feel that a woman desperately and hopelessly in love with a man is an indecent spectacle and a reversal of the natural order of things. But you should have been too fine to feel like that'.[73] Wells refused to see her; only after she capitulated to him did they resume the affair.

Much later, after Jane had died (in 1927), he fell in love with the eccentric Russian aristocrat and spy, Moura Budberg, who had been divorced three times and the mistress of a number of men including Gorky. Moura lived by emancipated ideals of women's erotic freedom – and the denial of sexual ownership – which corresponded closely with Wells's own theories. At the time, during the 1930s Wells was trying to disentangle himself from the irksome jealousies of his current lover, Odette Kuehn. He found in Moura for the first time a woman more committed to the ideal than he was. Wells's 'Lover-Shadow' was to have freedom, but not quiet as much freedom as Moura claimed. To his dismay, she resisted his control. She displayed no jealousy, treated him as a delightful sexual adventure, and, when he wanted to claim her as his own, defended her private person from the invasion of his ownership. She eluded commitment to him in much the same way, and on the same terms, as Wells had eluded possession by his various women.

He became 'suspicious and jealous', the 'ugly condition of mind' he had always denounced in his lovers. When he discovered she had lied about her movements he was baffled and angry: 'I was wounded excessively in my pride and hope . . . It was unbelievable. I lay in bed and wept like a disappointed child.[74] He had discovered that his theories did not fit the limits of his emotional needs. What he had really wanted, and what he had always been able to do when he was safely married to Jane – as the necessary condition of his imaginative sexual explorations – was to possess a home and a wife: 'I still dream of living with a wife, *my* wife, in a house and garden of *my* own . . . I wanted to feel a dear presence always in *my* home with me, . . . and see *my* own dear coming up the garden to *me*.' (my italics).[75]

Sex and the Nation's Collapse

Wells's radicalism was one stream in a current of dissent from respectability, convention and established principles of social order which, by the turn of the century, was building up to a sense of crisis about moral and social values. It was not caused only by the decline in religious belief and the changing nature of the relationship between the individual and the state. There was concern that rapid social change and technological advances were eroding moral standards, and that the 'woman question' and deepening ideological divisions were undermining traditional beliefs. Sexual morality was one arena for conflict. To progressives, social change was the cue to reorder moral priorities. For conservatives it signalled fragmentation which, at a time of economic uncertainty and growing international competitiveness, threatened not only the nation's stability but its survival.

Progressive ideas were not the only influence for change. The belief that the marriage and divorce laws were oppressive and inhumane, that they perpetuated unwarranted misery and exerted an adverse influence on social stability and public morality was shared by sections of the judiciary. When the president of the Probate, Admiralty and Divorce Division of the High Court publicly denounced the divorce laws in 1906 as 'full of inconsistencies, anomalies and inequalities almost amounting to absurdities', he paved the way for a Royal Commission to be set up to examine reforms. The Gorell Commission, reporting in 1912, recommended easier and more equal divorce (by extending the grounds to include adultery, desertion and incurable insanity, and removing the inequality whereby husbands could sue for adultery alone but wives had to prove cruelty in addition). But reform was blocked by the outright opposition of the Church of England who denounced it as a threat to Christian morality and the future of marriage.

Attempts to abolish the Lord Chamberlain's censorship of plays also attracted a wide spectrum of intellectual and liberal support after a series of plays by eminent playwrights dealing with controversial social and sexual issues were banned, including G. B. Shaw's *Mrs Warren's Profession*, Ibsen's *Ghosts*, and Granville-Barker's *Waste*. After intense public pressure, a Joint Select Committee was set up to look into stage censorship which reported in 1909. Despite Shaw's scathing condemnation of a system which stifled freedom and retarded the progress of ideas by putting the theatre at the mercy of the 'unenlightened despotism', the 'personal caprice, prejudice, ignorance, superstition, temper, stupidity, resentment, timidity, ambition and private conviction' of one man – an officer 'whose business it is to preserve decorum among menials',[76] the Committee did not recommend abolishing the Lord Chamberlain. Its proposals to make submission of plays optional satisfied neither the opponents nor the supporters of censorship and were not pursued.

Plays were not the only casualties. The obscenity laws were freely used to censor the portrayal of 'immoral' sexual themes. *Sexual Inversion*, the first volume of Havelock Ellis's seven-volume *Studies in the Psychology of Sex*, was prosecuted in 1897 as a 'lewd, bawdy, scandalous and obscene libel'. Though it caused no stir when it was first published in Germany, in Britain it fell victim to the combination of a general nervousness about the growing influence of progressive ideas and the moral backlash following the Oscar Wilde trial two years ealier. This had unleashed a storm of outraged protest against 'degeneracy' and 'unwholesome tendencies in art and literature', and generated calls for the renewal of 'intolerance' – 'a dash of wholesome bigotry into our art, our literature, our society, our view of things in general . . . without which a nation goes to collapse'.[77]

This 'dash of bigotry', increasingly evident in legal procedure, was also apparent in the influence wielded by vigilance activists. In 1887 Dr H. A. Allbut, a distinguished medical practitioner, was struck off the General Medical Council register after protests by the Leeds Vigilance Council for publishing a cheap and accessible edition of *The Wife's Handbook* which included advice about birth control. Bigotry was at work in the hostile response to writers who addressed the conflict between the claims of sexual love and the demands of social convention, especially when those conflicts centred on the New Woman. Thomas Hardy was no sexual radical, although his novels had frequently skirted round the accepted edges of public decency: several of his works were toned down at the request of editors because they dealt with 'those relations between the sexes over which conventionality is accustomed (wisely or unwisely) to draw a veil'.[78] *Jude the Obscure* (1895), in which Hardy aimed 'to tell, without a mincing of words, of a deadly war waged between flesh and spirit' and of 'the fret and fever, derision and disaster, that may press in the wake of the strongest passion known to humanity',[79] was received with almost unanimous hostility, called 'degenerate' and 'obscene', burned by the Bishop of Wakefield and banned from Smith's Circulating Library. After *Jude*, Hardy gave up writing novels and turned to poetry in the hope that 'I can express more fully in verse ideas and emotions which run counter to the inert crystallized opinion – hard as rock – which the vast body of men have vested interests in supporting.'[80]

H. G. Wells's *Ann Veronica* (1909), in which the heroine was 'allowed a frankness of desire and sexual enterprise hitherto unknown in English popular fiction', met a similar fate. It was denounced by St Loe Strachey, a pillar of moral rectitude, proprietor of the *Spectator* and a National Vigilance Association supporter as a 'poisonous book'. Its likely effect was to undermine 'the sense of continence and self-control in the individual which is essential to a sound and healthy state,' he thundered. 'Unless the citizens of the State put before themselves the principles of duty, self-sacrifice, self-control and continence, not merely in the matter of national defence, national preservation and national well-being, but also of the sex relationship, the life of the State must be short and precarious.'[81] *Ann Veronica* was banned from sale at the instigation of vigilance societies up and down the country, as indeed were many other works of literature. Arnold Bennett took stock in 1910: in the dozen or so libraries in Glasgow, for instance, he found the works of Richardson, Fielding and Smollett, Tolstoy's *Anna Karenina* and *Resurrection*, Hardy's *Tess of the d'Urbervilles* and *Jude the Obscure* and Wells's *Tono-Bungay* were all banned. 'The atmosphere of this island is thick enough to choke all artists dead', was his indignant comment.[82]

Conflict of Values

As civic and political turbulence intensified on the eve of the First World War so did friction over moral values. Though feminists were united in the political objective of obtaining the vote, divisions were deepening over the strategy for emancipation. While older feminists supported the enforcement of the single standard of morality, a younger generation of women began to place issues of personal sexual morality at the centre of feminist politics, and to explore the implications of women's sexual freedom as part of a strategy in which self-development, personal responsibility and independence, including financial independence, were central elements. A recognition of women's equal erotic rights – the right to enjoy their sexuality on similar terms to men – was beginning to emerge, which would displace faith in the single standard of sexual restraint for men and women alike as the solution to moral inequality between the sexes.

At the same time, the libertarian challenge to morality gained currency. It repudiated divine doctrine as the basis for social organization, and gave precedence to the individual's claim to personal moral responsibility and personal happiness over the controls maintained by the state in the interests of social stability. Scientific research into sex psychology was harnessed to these goals, and contributed to the emergent belief that to understand the sexual self was the key to personal happiness and fulfilment. But these were not readily accepted ideas, and were perceived by moral conservatives as fundamentally undermining to a stable society.

As these tensions crystallized the nation embarked on a war which would dramatically shake the foundations of the old order and sweep away many of the rituals and customs which had supported its values. But the initial response was to reinforce those values under the newly unfurled banner of patriotism.

Three

The First World War

Patrolling Women

The First World War dislocated British civilian life, disrupted domestic stability and cast the shadow of transience over personal relationships. It also gave young men and women new opportunities for independence and accelerated the erosion of old values and constraints. The 'national emergency' also required the state to take on responsibilities for the direction and supervision of a much wider area of national life – including sexual morals. This was justified in the name of patriotism, the efficient prosecution of the war, and the need to sustain the nation's fighting strength.

The government was initially cautious about intervening in personal freedom, although it soon relinquished *laissez faire* principles, in morals as in other areas, under pressure of 'the necessities of war'. Safeguarding the health and morality of the troops was deemed a matter of patriotic importance, and was used to justify a significant extension of controls over women. Several draconian measures had been canvassed at the outset. Lord Hamilton's recommendation in 1914 for the summary arrest of 'women of bad character who were infesting the neighbourhood of military camps' was turned down by the then Home Secretary, Reginald McKenna, though the Military Commander in Cardiff issued an order barring women from licensed premises between 7 pm and 6 am and prohibiting women 'of bad reputation' from going out of doors at all between 7 pm and 8 am. Five women sent before a military court martial were sentenced to sixty-two days imprisonment, despite one woman's plea that 'seven o'clock seemed so early – it seemed like a dream to me'.[1] This curfew, and attempts by the Plymouth Watch Committee to revive the infamous Contagious Diseases Acts, were stopped only after protests from women's organizations about the infringement of women's civil liberties.

Even so, after frequent military complaints about 'pests' and 'harpies' congregating round soldiers and diverting men from their patriotic duties, Defence of the Realm (DORA) regulations were extended in 1916 to make it an offence for any woman convicted of prostitution or vagrancy offences to remain in the vicinity of military camps. This method of dealing with 'vice' led one prominent activist, Damer Dawson, to protest, 'They talk as if men were innocent angels, helpless in the hands of wicked women . . . In the realm of morals we have not advanced beyond Adam who was tempted by Eve.'[2]

To begin with the government left moral supervision to voluntary and philanthropic organizations, who were quickly alerted to the 'grave moral dangers' threatened by war, especially to young women. While recruits had been sent to war armed with a personal exhortation from Lord Kitchener to exercise self-control and guard against temptation, women's duty, the Bishop of London warned, was 'to send out the young man in the right spirit, free from moral stain'.[3] This was rapidly deemed inadequate by vigilance organizations. According to the National Union of Women Workers, 'the girlhood of the country was thrown off its balance' by the excitement of war; large numbers of khaki-clad men had 'excited its imagination and aroused its patriotism', and this was 'unfortunately . . . expressed by foolish, giddy, irresponsible conduct'. The NUWW at once realized that girls behaviour 'might result in leading them into grave moral danger; and it determined to try to save them from their own folly'.[4]

The remedy was to set up part-time voluntary women's patrols 'to befriend and guide young girls'.[5] Patrols became a semi-official branch of the government's policing efforts, when the Home Secretary and most police authorities granted them official recognition and authorized their activities. By 1917, 2,284 patrols, some paid out of police funds, were patrolling parks, open spaces, railway stations and streets, not only befriending 'foolish girls and saving them from danger, and warning girls who behave unsuitably', but also saving men from 'women of evil reputation' as well as sorting out drunken soldiers 'by means of cups of black coffee laced with bicarbonate of soda which, after making them violently sick, left them sober enough to be entrained in due course.'[6]

Regular liaison was maintained with police and military authorities. For instance, when the army claimed young girls were using the excuse of collecting soldiers' washing to hang around billets, patrols ensured that only men or boys carried out this duty and reported any women doing it. They had seats used by couples for amorous purposes boarded up. One intrepid patrol watching a towpath in the depths of winter was 'astonished to find soldiers and girls sitting on seats far up the river on the terribly cold nights. Apart from the moral danger, the danger of falling into the river was great.'[7] Another seemed surprised that 'daylight and people about seem not to matter in the least. You come on a heaped mass of arms and legs and much stocking and they are too absorbed to know we are there'.[8]

These were not the only agents for moral policing. A rival organization, the Women's Police Volunteers, had been refused official recognition because they were tainted in the eyes of the police establishment by their leaders' prewar association with the suffragettes, and because their long-term aim was to promote women's recruitment and training on equal terms with men in the police force – an unpopular objective in police circles. The guiding light in the organization, which was set up in September 1914 and was later called the Women's Police Service, was Damer Dawson, a wealthy philanthropist, whose recreations were Alpine mountaineering and motoring. Her interest in saving horses had been transferred to rescuing women from white-slavery through the Vigilance Association; she was currently saving Belgian refugees. Dawson was joined by Nina Boyle, a member of the Women's Freedom League (a breakaway from the Pankhursts' Women's Social and Political Union, the WSPU), whose particular concern was the unfair treatment of women under the law, and by Mary Allen, whose arrest during a suffragette window-smashing demonstration had given her first-hand experience of that treatment. Together they resolved to set up an organization of trained women police who could deal with women's cases, paying particular attention to women's rights. One thousand and eighty women, almost half from private occupations and the leisured classes, with a tenth from working class backgrounds, were soon recruited.[9]

Their training, patrolling and police work were initially funded by voluntary bodies, sympathetic local watch committees and police authorities. In 1916, however, the Ministry of Munitions awarded them official recognition with a contract for a hundred trained and paid women to 'act as guardians' at their expanding munitions factories – checking the entry of women to the factories, supervising women going to and from work and dealing with complaints of harassment and annoyance to women.[10]

Apart from the semi-official patrols, the state had extended its powers of control over soldiers' wives by introducing measures in 1914 which penalized wives found guilty of 'intemperance' or immorality ('irregularily of conduct') by terminating their separation allowance – 15 shillings paid out by the state to supplement soldiers' pay. These penalties were portrayed as a form of paternalist correction for women 'deprived of the company and guidance of their husbands'.[11] Following an Army Council Memo, the Home Office in October 1914 instructed Chief Constables to set up consultation procedures with local army authorities and relief committees 'to ensure that relief shall not be continued to persons who prove themselves unworthy'.[12] This effectively put all soldiers' wives in receipt of allowances under surveillance. Police were authorized to enter and inspect any houses and ask questions relating to wives' behaviour. In Chesterfield, notices were hung in schools (where they would be read by children) giving details of cases of 'Cessation of Separation Allowances to the Unworthy', and urging school managers to report children coming to school in a neglected condition.[13]

The system put women at the mercy of secret reports and investigation without right of reply, with penalties exceeding those of ordinary law. Despite regular protests from women's organizations who argued that allowances should be regarded as wages to which soldiers' families should have an inalienable claim, the regulations remained in force throughout the war. There were some anomalies: when the government uncovered the vast extent of common law marriages, they agreed to pay the same separation allowances to common law as to legal wives, despite loud protest from the Archbishop of Canterbury among others that to put such women on the state's payroll was to endorse immorality. For the *Church Quarterly Review*, it was 'an outrageous insult to respectable and self-respecting womanhood'.[14]

Women police were increasingly used to enforce these extended controls, despite rising concern in their ranks that they were being used in ways which actually threatened women's civil rights. When they responded enthusiastically, eager to prove their worth, conflicts developed between protecting women's liberties and upholding social purity, at a time when the law was being more extensively applied to further the 'national interest'. At Grantham, for instance, where the local Watch Committee funded the first full-time woman police officer in November 1914, the commanding officer of the local military camp supported and praised women officer's work specifically because they were able to intervene in areas where the military police could not. He had given policewomen the right to enter any house, building or land within a six-mile radius of the camp, an entitlement they carried out in the belief it was a mark of trust in their abilities.[15]

The duties of the first Grantham woman police officer, Mrs Ethel Smith, a former sub-postmistress, including patrolling and rescue work, dealing with criminal cases involving women and children, with 'parents reporting misconduct of their boys with girls' (a hundred 'wayward' girls were cautioned in 1916), and rooting out 'fallen women' through regular visits to streets and houses and investigation of lodgers' documents. 'Husbands placing their wives under observation during their absence, husbands inquiring as to reported misconduct of their wives' was a routine part of her work.[16] In 1917, thirty women were investigated by Mrs Smith for alleged misconduct, and were either warned, or their separation allowances terminated.[17] In one case she reported, 'On visiting the house of a woman suspected of bad character, married, with seven children, whose husband is a soldier at the front, policewoman found a soldier in the house. The woman was alarmed and promised to send the man away directly after supper. The policewoman left, but returned to the house at 11 pm and, finding the man still there, drove him in front of them out of the house, cautioning him not to return'.[18] One young woman was investigated because, although without income, she was well supplied with money. Mrs Smith entered her lodgings in her absence and found them 'laden with costly clothing and the dressing table with aids to beauty'. It turned out that she was not a police case as 'she was only being kept by a man, which is not illegal'. Nevertheless, after she 'repented', she was despatched to a job as attendant in a rescue home.[19]

Criticism mounted that women police were adopting the very methods they had been set up to suppress. Nina Boyle resigned from the WPS in 1915 in protest at the way that women were being used to enforce police activity which, far from protecting women's rights, involved invasion of privacy, flexibility of the law of trespass and the erosion of their civil liberties. In 1917, another member, Hilda Nield, complained they were not using their powers 'to prevent petty tyranization over women in the work-shop, home and elsewhere', but to 'enforce illegal restrictions' and 'tyranize over other women's personal rights and privacy. Policewomen have done more than failed, they have done wrong. They have sown harmful seed instead of good'.[20]

Added to this was a rising chorus of complaint from the public about 'busybody' female patrols and 'interfering toads', who went about 'prying behind trees' and 'flashing torches in the faces of respectable persons sitting on seats in Hyde Park after dark', and from innocent respectable women accosted by patrols on suspicion of soliciting. 'Those who come back from France have earned a better title to our gratitude than that we should dog the footsteps of lovers upon a summer's night, or brand a man a criminal because he puts his arm round a girl's waist', protested the novelist Max Pemberton in the *Weekly Dispatch* in 1917.[21]

None of this prevented the steady expansion of female patrols and police work. By 1917, seven counties and twenty-four cities and boroughs employed policewomen on full-time duties and Special Patrols were working with the Metropolitan Police in selected areas of London. By 1918 Sir Leonard Dunning, Inspector of Constabulary, approvingly defined their role as 'the true guard-ians of the State in its public morals'. At a time of declining parental authority, women were to be used 'in the capacity of chaperones'; the duty 'for which her sex peculiarly fits her' was 'the maintenance of public decorum among girls'.[22] Women had won the right to participate in the police force – on very unequal terms – by proving their special capabilities in the area of moral policing.

Standards of Independence

The war had its most profound effect on women's lives as they moved out of the 'domestic sphere' into work and the mainstream of national life. It gave young women freedom from home constraints and the kind of financial independence women had aspired to before the war. But their absorption into the workforce also put new welfare responsibilities on the government, as large numbers of young women moved away from home for the first time into establishments under government supervision.

While young men enlisted, young women volunteered for war work. Gradually they replaced men in many occupations which they had hitherto been thought incapable of doing, although they usually worked for lower rates of pay. Women from the 'protected classes' who had never expected to be employed took up nursing, office jobs and munitions work, or joined the proliferating voluntary organizations geared to the war effort. Vera Brittain, after 'twenty years of sheltered gentility', volunteered for nursing and moved from home to live in London in the cause of duty. 'I picture to myself,' she wrote to a friend, 'Mother's absolute horror if she could have seen me at 9.15 the other night dashing about and dodging the traffic in the slums of Camberwell Green, in the pitch dark of course, incidentally getting mixed up with remnants of a recruiting meeting, munition workers and individuals drifting in and out of public houses. It is quite thrilling to be an unprotected female and feel that no one in your immediate surroundings is particularly concerned with what happens to you so long as you don't give them any bother.'[23] In such circumstances, one of the early casualties of the war was a young woman's obligatory chaperone. The chaperones too were hard at work for the war effort and, in the straightened conditions of food shortages, increased cost of living and uncertain transport, 'people who gave parties didn't want to feed and water them! And if they were elderly they didn't feel like having to walk home after late nights'.[24]

Working class women left home in large numbers to work in the expanding industries geared to war production. The number

38

of domestic servants declined sharply; it was considered unpatriotic to have an able-bodied woman serving you when she could be serving her country. Huge government-controlled munitions factories were set up, employing mainly women. In Coventry, of 16,000 new jobs created by 1916, 9,000 were filled by women. As much as half the workforce had moved from home to live in lodgings or newly built hostels around the town. At Gretna, where a vast complex employed 11,000 women, most moved into purpose-built hostels or lodgings around Carlisle. Over a third had been in domestic service, a fifth came from home, and the rest came from other factories or service industries.

Morals became a government responsibility on a new scale. It was now 'a national responsibility', the Home Office decided, to safeguard 'in every practicable way the health and welfare of workers who have left their homes by the thousands to take up work essential to the national interest'.[25] Reports from Coventry, for instance, recommended better hostel and recreation facilities to counter evidence of an increase in venereal disease and 'loose and immoral conduct in recreation grounds and dark streets' among women leading 'grey lives . . . separated from their homes and families.'[26] At Gretna, treasury funds were released for recreation facilities around the hostels, which were patrolled by women police after 1916, and women were shielded from temptation by the simple device of stopping late trains between there and Carlisle, except on Saturday, when the last train left at 9.30 pm.[27] New factory welfare superintendants were appointed to look after women's interests, including instruction in 'moral hygiene'. At the St Helen's Cable and Rubber Company, Lilian Evans issued a booklet of advice on personal hygiene and venereal disease, with the warning: 'Do not allow yourself to be hail-fellow-well-met with everyone. Maintain your womanly dignity always. Be true to your sex. It may be fun to "pick up" for a time, but the aftereffects are, all too often, very bitter and sad'.[28]

For women from sheltered backgrounds, being uprooted from home and family, meeting new situations in strange surroundings, and coping with the complex emotions raised by war was an enlightening experience. Olive Taylor was sixteen when war broke out. Isolated on a farm near the River Humber where she worked from 5 am to 10 pm, her only contact with the outside world was at Chapel on Sunday and Wednesday evenings. She left in 1916, aged 18, to work filling shells in a munitions factory near Morecambe Bay, where she took lodgings at 25 shillings a week (out of wages of 27 shillings) and 'slept five in a room and never got enough to eat'. Here she first found out 'to her disgust' how babies were made: 'It seems hard to believe . . . but women in the country had no idea of what was to happen to them when they married', she recalled. She was so horrified that she got herself the nickname 'Old Molly Never Had It'. In 1918 she joined the WAACs where speaking to soldiers within bounds was a serious offence leading to dismissal from the service. By now she was covering up for her friends illicitly meeting their boyfriends in trenches round the camp, and being treated to lectures, 'the sum total of these being to warn the girls that an awful disease could be caught through a kiss.' She had a sweetheart, a wounded soldier, who was 'exceptionally honourable.' Even with her enlarged experience, she was indignant to discover on a visit to Woolwich that WAACs 'were treated like scum and that we had been enlisted for the sexual satisfaction of the soldiers.' This, she complained, 'after the way we had worked so hard, and put up with so much deprivation for our country's sake was absolutely terrible. We were broken-hearted about it and never went into town again'.[29]

As women moved into previously male-dominated occupations, they gained a foothold in the services, also under government supervision. The various branches of the women's services were established during 1917 after a long struggle against the prejudices of the military establishment, and the Women's Land Army came into being at the same time. Questions of discipline and morality constantly cropped up. In the Land Army there were frequent complaints that young women were flouting the rules by staying out late. One woman was actually sent to prison for fourteen days' hard labour for this offence, even though the Land Army was not under army discipline. The Women's Army Auxiliary Corps *was* under army discipline and, while rules relating to women fraternizing with men in camp at home were strict, some latitude was applied in France. One new recruit was surprised to discover on her arrival that 'we could make friends with the troops, but were advised to choose carefully. I had not anticipated that this would be allowed.'[30] One motive, perhaps, was an appreciation of 'the advantage to soldiers of the possibility of frank and whole-some comradeship of women of their own race and the graver social dangers which such comradeship tended to avert' – such as low French life in the *estaminets*.[31]

Women's changing status and their new participation [with men] in the mainstream of national life gave rise to frequent outbursts of anxiety about morals. Rumours of immoral conduct among WAACs were so widespread by 1918 that the Ministry of Labour was pressed to set up a Commission of Inquiry. The rumours, attributed partly to jealousy and partly to the 'state of war' which 'tends to create a somewhat abnormal and excited mentality', were found to be grossly exaggerated. Among a WAAC strength of 6,023 in France in March 1918, there had been twenty-one preg-nancy cases, two of them married, and most had become pregnant before arriving in France, and twelve vencreal cases, several of long standing. This was considered not a bad record when large numbers of women came in contact with soldiers 'passing to and from the more electric atmosphere of the Line'.[32]

Similar fears had fuelled the 'war babies' scare of 1915, when Conservative Mr Ronald McNeill MP wrote to the *Morning Post* claiming large numbers of illegitimate babies were about to be born, especially in areas where troops were stationed. It was fanned by most newspapers into a wartime scandal about the collapse of morals among young men and women, but was aban-doned shortly afterwards as 'grossly exaggerated' when it was discovered that there was virtually no increase in illegitimate births in 1915, although there was a significant increase in the number of marriages. The illegitimacy rate did not begin to climb until 1916. By 1919 it was up thirty per cent on prewar years – the consequence, the Registrar General had soberly concluded, not so much of moral decline, but 'the exceptional circumstances . . . including the freedom from home restraints of large numbers of young persons of both sexes.'[33]

One side effect of the panic was an attempt by some philan-thropic organizations to ease the moral stigma of illegitimacy and encourage a more sympathetic attitude to the heightened emotional circumstances which led to women's 'downfall'. 'The children of our soldiers and sailors *must* be cared for', declared the War Babies and Mothers' League in 1915. 'In the majority of cases it is simply a matter of a young girl and a young man losing their heads when the man is going off to the Front'.[34] Although women's organizations extended their support for both mothers and children – Damer Dawson set up a war babies and mother's home, as did Mrs Pankhurst's WSPU which was abandoned when only five cases came forward – there was strong public pressure against condoning 'the steps which lead to their trouble' or making 'heroines of these poor girls'.[35] Any marginal improvement in attitudes to illegitimacy during the war was shortlived; one organization, the National Council for the Unmarried Mother and Her Child, survived but the punitive moral stigma persisted long afterwards.

Women's new financial independence was another cause for anxiety. Although women were invariably taken on at lower wages than the men they replaced, and the cost of living soon caught up with any advance they may have made, legends proliferated about new classes of affluent spendthrift women squandering their wages on trivialities in the absence of male financial guidance. The 'Boudoir Ladies' of Whitehall who had replaced male clerks were criticized for being only concerned that 'they should be beautifully dressed and well set up'; shops were allegedly catering for them with 'crêpe-de-Chine blouses, taffetas or velveteen dresses . . . and lingerie, such as the middle-class girl of a few years ago would never have dreamt of possessing'[36]. The popular press ran a spate of articles alleging munitions girls were all buying fur coats, while reports that working class women were using their unaccustomed spare cash on excessive drinking – although they proved wholly unfounded – were used to justify increased surveillance and to ban women from public places.[37] A new social phenomenon, 'Dining Out Girls' excited disdainful comment in the *Daily Mail* about 'the wartime business girl . . . with money and without men', who 'is seen any night dining out alone or with a friend.'[38]

These startling shows of independence were all very troubling. They went quite against the wartime spirit of austerity and self-sacrifice. Indeed, there were definite signs that women were determined to enjoy themselves and their enlarged freedom. One young woman, who like most of her set did war work during the day, 'used to dance almost every night . . . Sometimes at these dances there was a small band, often only a piano. The men looked so nice in uniform'. But hanging over it was the uncertainty of war. Life was 'very gay. It was only when someone you knew well or with whom you were in love was killed that you minded really dreadfully. Men used to come to dine and dance one night, and go out the next morning and be killed. And someone used to say, "Did you see poor Bobbie was killed?" It went on all the time, you see.'[39]

Though the war heightened emotional feelings and accelerated the decline of old taboos and conventions, there is little evidence of a dramatic breakdown in codes of sexual behaviour. Women could 'do much as [they] pleased'; but, as one woman recalled, many maintained their 'standard': 'the men were very careful of you if they thought you deserved to be looked after. I personally never dined alone with any of my men friends: we used to go about in fours or still larger groups'.[40]

Yet at a time when relationships could be conducted in an atmosphere free from the old constraints, but only in snatches on short leaves, the powerful grip of desire could become almost unendurable. Vera Brittain described such a meeting with her lover, Roland, on leave from the front in 1915: 'We sat on the sofa till midnight, talking very quietly. The stillness, heavy-laden with the dull oppression of the snowy night, became so electric with emotion that we were frightened of one another, and dared not let even our fingers touch for fear that the love between us should render what we both believed to be decent behaviour suddenly unendurable.'[41] Their affair was never consummated, and Roland was later killed.

Others described how the war intensified relationships. Bertrand Russell, then over forty, began an affair with Colette Malleson during 1915. The war 'was bound into the texture of this love from first to last', he recalled. 'The first time I was ever in bed with her, . . . we heard suddenly a shout of bestial triumph in the street. I leapt out of bed and saw a Zeppelin falling in flames.' In 'the harshness and horror of the war' Russell 'clung to Colette. In a world of hate, she preserved love . . . she had a quality of rock-like immovability, which in those days was invaluable.'[42]

Some commentators believed that conventions had broken down, for both men and women, under the strain of wartime existence. C. S. Peel later interpreted the atmosphere and the mood of the young: 'As the casualty lists lengthened, "Life is short, let us enjoy it whilst we may" became the motto of the young, and it was inevitable that this should be so. Men craved the sympathy which only women could give, they loved and married or merely mated, and in many cases a few weeks later the man was dead or lying maimed in some hospital. The mental strain, the desire to forget horrors and unhappiness, led to an increase of drinking, drugging, smoking, gambling and dancing.'[43] M. A. Hamilton recorded, 'Life was less than cheap; it was thrown away. The religious teaching that the body was the temple of the Holy Ghost could mean little or nothing to those who saw it mutilated and destroyed in millions by Christian nations engaged in war . . . Little wonder that the old ideals of chastity and self-control in sex were, for many, also lost . . . How and why refuse appeals, backed up by the hot beating of your own heart, or what at the moment you thought to be your heart, which were put with passion and even pathos by a hero here today and gone tomorrow?'[44]

Later evidence suggests that although female chastity suffered some onslaught during the war it was still only a minority of women who engaged in either petting or intercourse. But the numbers grew rapidly *after* the war. According to Eustace Chesser's later survey (with a bias toward middle class repondents), whereas only 19 per cent of married women who were mature during the war (i.e. born before 1904) had engaged in premarital sex, this went up to over 36 per cent of those who matured in the 1920s (i.e. born 1904–14) and increased only slightly (to 39 per cent) for those who matured in the 1930s (born 1914–24).[45] In other words, the incidence of premarital sexual intercourse almost doubled in the decade after the war and then the rate of increase slowed down.

Although the war did not dent faith in marriage, it altered some of its conventions and proprieties. There was a rapid increase in the number of marriages, particularly in the first year of war. There was also a steep jump in divorce – from 577 in 1913 to 3,100 in 1920.[46] This may indicate that the war accentuated the importance of immediate love and attraction. Many whirlwind love affairs with soldiers led to 'hasty' marriages, and sometimes rapid dissolution.

Parental control in the choice of partners waned, just as their control over their children's movements had diminished. Young people saw affairs more as the private concern of the lovers than a matter for family discussion. Vera Brittain vehemently wanted to preserve the privacy of her relationship with Roland from family and social interference. 'We foresaw a series of "leaves" ', she wrote, 'in which our meetings would be impeded by suspicion, and our love tormented by ceaseless expectant inquiries. . . . We did not want our relationship, with its thrilling, indefinite glamour, shaped and moulded into an acknowledged category; we disliked the possibility of its being labelled with a description regarded as "correct" by the social editor of *The Times*. Most of all, perhaps, we hated the thought of its shy, tender, absorbing progress being "up" for discussion by relatives and acquaintances.'[47] The break-down in conventions made it easier to dispense with the old forms and build relationships on different terms not only of privacy but of equality. Both Vera and Roland loathed the idea of an engagement ring – a ' "token of possession." . . . it seemed too typical of the old inequality.'[48]

The sense that the present counted more than an uncertain future, possibly no future at all, eroded the importance previously attached to a sound financial base to marriage: 'sound' marriages involved consideration of a future that was beyond the horizon. In addition, many women who had previously expected to be supported by their husbands had now experienced financial independence which changed their view of the economic basis of marriage.

When Roland was away at the front, Vera Brittain contemplated what the world would have called a 'foolish' marriage: 'now that the War seemed likely to be endless, and the chance of making a "wise" marriage had become, for most people, so very remote, the world was growing more tolerant. No one – not even my family now, I thought – would hold out against us, even though we hadn't a penny beyond our pay'.[49] She found it insulting that her father should think of asking Roland how he proposed to keep her, since she had every intention of earning her own living. The war had, she noted, 'already begun to create a change of heart in parents brought up in the Victorian belief that the financial aspect of marriage mattered more than any other. . . . it did break the tradition that venereal disease or sexual brutality in a husband was amply compensated by an elegant bank-balance.'[50]

The older generation tended to find this confusing. In January 1917, the *Manchester Guardian* remarked on the social mix-up of the wartime marriage market – 'the extraordinary jumble that has taken place in the ranks of Society through hasty war marriages . . . Young men and young women have married very much 'above' or 'below' their former station in life . . . Dukes' daughters are marrying social nobodies and finding it a delightful innovation, and bewildered parents have given up all attempts to control their children's matrimonial careers.' Apocryphal stories were told, such as the girl 'of notable family' who, asked who her fiancé's people were, replied, 'I haven't the slightest idea, but I am going to stay there next week and shall find out'. Another, asked by her new mother-in-law where she had met her son, rejoined, 'At a friend's. Why?' A despairing parent was allegedly to have remarked, 'But what can you expect . . . when any morning a strange flying man may fall into your garden and expect to be engaged to your daughter by evening?'[51]

Taboos in the Firing Line

The soldiers who fought the war were not only uprooted from the past, they entered a totally different world. After prolonged exposure to bombardment and slaughter conventions retained little meaning. 'To a soldier in the war it became second nature to live for the present,' wrote one soldier, Charles Carrington. 'When pleasures were few they were snatched and enjoyed with an intensity such as no civilian knew. Respite for a week or a day from the fear of death gave absolute enjoyment, for a week or a day. The future had for so long meant only a series of trips up the line, punctuated by short paradisal intervals of rest in each of which you laughed and drank in a company of whom some would probably be dead in a month, and the others in a year, that to survive the next tour of the trenches, to enjoy one more spell in rest-billets, perhaps to get one more week's leave in England, were all the ambitions and hopes that life could offer, the farthest rim of the horizon being bounded by "next spring offensive".'[52] Taboos broke down at the front. The world he'd left in 1914, where 'decent' women 'lived on a plane of such exalted virtue that the slightest allusion, however obscure or oblique, to the functions of the body was an insult', was a long way over the Channel. At the front, 'nothing prevented an approach to the other world of the women who "did", except a fastidious timidity.'[53]

By 1917, after two years at the front, Carrington's leave was a re-entry into a world bound by proprieties which he had long since abandoned. He experienced the feeling of growing estrangement from the home front which was common to soldiers. Though on leave in 1916, he, 'happily resumed my family life like a schoolboy home for the holidays', in 1917, his leave was spent 'mostly racketing round theatres and restaurants with soldier friends in London where – so far as I could see – the old taboos still prevailed. No doubt the social disruptions of wartime had encouraged promiscuity, but not in my quiet circle of friends. "Women who did" were still sharply divided from "women who didn't". The change had taken place in me, not in them, with the consequence that I found myself leading a double life. The quiet respectability of my family with its unaltered moral standards could in no way be related to the all-male society of the regiment, with its acceptance of death and bloodshed as commonplace events, and its uninhibited approach to women'.[54]

Robert Goldrich, an officer on active service in the Royal Navy, found that the war afforded a similar release. In 1915, aged nineteen, his spare time was spent stamp-collecting and writing letters to respectable girls at home, whom he was 'sweet on'. However, his diary of 30 September 1915 records, 'Heard from Sylvia, but am not going to reply as I have had enough of writing soppy letters to her.' On leave in 1916 he was taking daughters of military officers for walks along the towpath ('a little less icy this time') and 'making a little progress' with Dorothy before going 'to Rose Cottage for tea.'

By 1917, such inhibitions had all but evaporated. Shore leave was marked by considerable drinking with mates and varying success in picking up women: 'Journeyed down to Brighton & met the family. In the evening had a look at the front meeting one "Nancy" a lady & a very finely built girl. Did her a good turn on the beach & so home to bed very well pleased with Brighton.' Tuesday was spent 'on the pier this evening with Hunt & made arrangements to meet a rather charming girl at 7 pm to which end I equipped myself with a dozen "sixpennies". She failed me – damn her eyes! so I took a very nice girl to dinner at "Jimmie's" & spent a respectable evening until 11 pm when I fell across a little damsel whose name I forget and retired to 75 Middle Street with her. It appears she is of decent parentage of Russian extraction & ran away from home with an Army officer. He is in France and allots her the shekels. Only 17 (and a half) a very pretty lied (*sic*) with beautiful eyes & mouth & teeth & short (11") black hair. A very worthy bedfellow' (21 August 1917). On later shore leaves, in Glasgow and Belfast, the diary tells much the same story, with occasional breaks on to 'the path of virtue'. Once, he confessed, 'both the pilot and myself are sitting on the "stool of repentence" as we do not trust our sleeping partners of last night! However with prophylactics & the help of Allah we hope to pull through' (7 March 1918 Belfast). And later he explains, after a 'rotten debauch I lay low and was respectable for a bit – in fact until we sailed – as I was broke'.[55]

In France there were brothels behind the lines in all main towns. The French made them official, and insisted that the men queue up in orderly fashion, patrolled by French soldiers with fixed bayonets, and be inspected when they went in and when they came out. Blue-lamp brothels were for officers, red lamps for the 'other ranks'.[56] Charles Carrington recalled, 'Amiens and Boulogne swarmed with prostitutes and semi-prostitutes, some of them refugee girls from the devastated area, and some the riff-raff that is always to be found at the heels of an army. They did not lack custom from men who had not seen a woman's face for months, with the consequence that venereal disease was endemic in the armies.'[57] In the forward zone administered by British military authorities, no brothels were sanctioned.

The British Army had initially equipped their young recruits with no more than a message from Lord Kitchener, to be kept always in their Army Service Pay Book, warning, 'In this new experience you may find temptations both in wine and women. You must entirely resist both temptations, and, while treating all women with perfect courtesy, you should avoid any intimacy. Do Your Duty Bravely'.[58] The official view of a soldier's sexual needs was that self-control would solve the problem. In consequence

Britain was almost alone among the combatants in having no general instruction or preventative treatment for venereal disease in the first years of the war. Recruits were given lectures in moral hygiene during training. E. B. Turner had lectured to a million men by 1920: 'Whenever I spoke to them I always appealed to their patriotism and put it to them how much better they would be employed pumping lead into the Hun rather than lying in hospital having '606' (salvarsan) pumped into them'.[59]

In practice, information and precautions tended to depend on the initiative of commanding officers. Lower down the line, there was a more robust attitude. 'It is not reasonable to expect the youngsters to keep the trenches of England intact and their chastity inviolate at the same time,' declared Brigadier General Crozier, for whom free love in wartime was 'as inevitable as the rising and the setting of the sun.' Armed with these insights, he and his medical officer took steps to ensure that all men under his command were instructed and had access to disinfectants 'after indulgence', a facility he extended to women free of charge. 'My job', he wrote, 'was to provide food for cannon and good food at that', and to keep his troops up to scratch in every possible way. To those who might charge him with 'condoning or even encouraging vice', he simply argued 'war breeds vice and venereal'. He wrote proudly, 'our discretion in the boudoir had been admirable'.[60] His major headache was that, although he attempted to make free love safe from infection in the billets, there was no guarantee of protection for his soldiers in any district of London, from Whitechapel to Mayfair, where 'the peace-time barriers are relaxed "for the duration" '.[61] It was the civilians who were letting the side down.

By December 1914, there were 1,230 cases of venereal disease under British Expeditionary Force charge, by far the largest proportion of infectious diseases. Instructions that no VD cases should be returned home until clear of infection, which could take months, meant a huge accumulation of cases in hospitals in France.[62] At times, more soldiers were incapacitated by disease than by enemy action. By 1917, 55,000 soldiers were hospitalized with VD.

In view of the disastrous effects on troop strength and the efficiency of wartime workers, when the Royal Commission on

Venereal Diseases reported in 1916 on the extent of infection (at a conservative estimate 8–12 per cent of adult males and 3.7 per cent of females[63], its recommendations for immediate state action met with instant approval. It proposed swift measures to improve facilities, provide accessible and free treatment, and foster public education. The Commission represented VD as a pressing issue of public health, and for the first time wrenched it out of the region of secrecy and taboo by calling for state funds to tackle the problem, and a more frank approach by the public and authorities to penetrate the ignorance surrounding it. Even so, to suggest that the state should take responsibility for the consequences of 'immoral' actions was politically and ethically delicate. In practice, objections that the state might be appearing to condone immorality continued to inhibit the provision of universal treatment on the scale the Commission had envisaged. There were some advances. Public finance was made available for research, diagnosis and treatment for civilian and service personnel, and treatment by anyone except a registered medical practitioner was made illegal in 1917. An expansion of sex and hygiene education was initiated, mainly through the social purist groups already active in the field. But progress was slow at the front. No official army order was ever issued relating to universal preventative treatment, provision for self-disinfection was patchy, and it was not until July 1918 that hospitals were provided with up-to-date equipment for the uniform testing of syphilis (the Wasserman reaction).[64]

Undesirable Sin

The revelation of the damage wrought by 'avoidable disease' had one other effect. By 1916, with the nation's fighting strength being drained away by the death toll at the front, fears built up that its moral strength was being undermined at home. This provided the justification for a new spate of calls for more rigorous controls. Almost everything remotely 'immoral' was now condemned as a cause of incapacitation of His Majesty's troops by avoidable disease, and consequently a betrayal of the national interest in its hour of grave peril. As one observer put it, 'Sin', was 'denounced as undesirable in the interests of the national cause'.[65] The forces of social purity rushed to the banner of patriotism in their renewed efforts to control all those seeds of iniquity which had sprouted up to contaminate the minds and hearts of the fighting forces. These included not only prostitutes, but literature, all forms of 'frivolous' entertainment, theatre, music halls, the cinema, night-clubs and tea-shops.

Purity and cleanliness of mind were enlisted to the national cause. General Sir Horace Smith-Dorrien sounded the rallying call in autumn 1916 when he appealed to music-hall and theatre managers to 'place patriotism before their own interests' by 'elimi-nating anything that might be suggestive of vice'.[66] The Bishop of London, who had hardly ever been silent on the subject of moral decline since the outbreak of war, launched an offensive against 'the villains more mischievous than German spies, who ought to share their fate, who lie in wait to stain the chivalry of our boys, poison their minds and undermine their characters'. He was refer-ring to male pimps in Piccadilly – 'Shooting is not good enough for them' – but 'side by side as a male traitor to his country should be dealt with the writers of lecherous and slimy productions rank-ing as stage plays . . . [who have] the insolence to try and make money out of the weakness of our boys.' 'Our soldiers do not want their filthy innuendo,' he claimed, flying in the face of record theatre profits. 'It is the business of us middle-aged men who are not allowed to fight, and the women of London, to purge the heart of the Empire before the boys come back,' he admonished, as if 'the boys' had all been blameless while the decline was going on.[67]

The campaign to defend the country from the 'enemy within' was widely supported. Theatres and music halls were under con-stant attack for sensuality and 'indelicacy'; this put managers per-manently on guard against the possibility their licences might not be renewed. Literature was another target. The most prominent casualty early in the war was D. H. Lawrence, whose novel, *The Rainbow*, was successfully prosecuted for obscenity and publicly burned in November 1915. A crop of abusive reviews had alerted the National Purity League, which instigated the prosecution. Robert Lynd in the *Daily News*, warned readers not to venture into this 'monotonous wilderness of phallicism', the *Sphere* denounced it as an 'orgy of sexiness' by an author worse than Zola – who 'stood as a reeking symbol of pornography in the

British mind'.[68] In court the publishers, Methuen, offered no defence to the police charge that the book was 'a mass of obscenity of thought, idea and action throughout, wrapped up in a language which he supposed would be regarded in some quarters as an artistic and intellectual effort.'[69] After confessing they had 'acted unwisely in not scrutinizing the book more carefully' and declaring that they 'regretted having published it',[70] Methuen were fined ten guineas costs and the book was ordered to be destroyed. No publisher would take on a Lawrence novel until 1920, when *Women in Love* came out in a subscriber's edition four years after its completion. Most magazines, except the *English Review*, declined to publish Lawrence's work. He left England in 1919, looked back at 'her dead grey cliffs and the white, worn-out cloth of snow', and never returned to live permanently.

Cinemas, also enjoying a wartime boom, came under steady attack. There were 3,500 cinemas in Britain by 1914, and they were visited by half the population once a week, even though they were alleged to be dens of iniquity and a thoroughly pernicious influence on the young. Prewar cinemas had routinely employed supervisors to watch for offences against decency, but had abandoned them with the wartime labour shortage. Women's patrols sometimes filled the gap. In April 1916, F. N. Charrington, an old vigilance hand, started a campaign to clean up the cinema with a deputation to the Home Office to acquaint them with 'the grave moral perils to which young people were exposed',[67] and to call for more stringent censorship of film content. The Home Office did not institute a Cinema Censor, but local councils attempted to impose new restrictions over films 'injurious to morality and likely to incite crime'. Middlesex Licence Committee was keen on proposals to arrange lighting which would 'enable one to see clearly over the whole of the auditorium throughout the performance',[72] thus exposing indecencies which might take place under cover of darkness.

After a public outcry led by vigilance groups, a Cinema Commission was set up in 1916 to air grievances. However, contrary to expectations, allegations of indecency, except possibly in London's West End where prostitutes operated, were dismissed by Mr F. R. Goodwin, Chairman of the Cinematograph Exhibitors' Association as usually 'nothing more than the privileged manifestation of affection between the sexes'[73]. Vigilance workers who visited 248 cinemas had found no cases of indecency. This did not still the outcry, however, nor redeem the reputation of cinemas and, by 1918, women's patrols were still reporting shocking conditions at such places as the Rank Cinema, Finsbury Park, where 'couples were embracing each other all over the building, and were guilty of most unseemly behaviour.'[74]

Even so, behaviour in the back row was not as unseemly as that at some tea-shops. Hotel teas ' "caught on" tremendously . . . you sat in an immense hall or lounge, you saw much-talked-of people, you heard music, you watched tango-dancing, you were in ninth heaven as compared to most people's denuded home life, and in a celestial sphere as compared with a dug-out'.[75] But down in the City, there was a rash of convictions in the Tea-Shop Scandal. Kathleen Newton, proprietor of the Club Tea Room at Bishopsgate was convicted and fined for 'knowingly permitting disorderly conduct on the part of her waitresses' in the basement. And in another dimly lit and lavishly furnished salon de thé in Copthall Avenue, one room was divided by heavy curtains, and customers were served, often on the couch, by waitresses named Fifi and Pepi, dressed in low-cut blouses.[76]

Night-clubs were another target. After Lloyd George's enforcement of early pub closing hours in 1915, night-clubs flourished. By the winter of 1915 there were an estimated 150 premises in Soho alone, around which clustered legends of riotous behaviour and dissipation. Although soldiers were the main clients, they were also patronized by 'women and young girls of good reputation'.[77] After a campaign by the Bishop of London, backed by Northcliffe's The Times to tackle 'this scandal to our London life' where 'drinks were sold at preposterous prices' and hapless soldiers were preyed on by 'harpies of the underworld', an act was passed in 1916 to enforce earlier closing. Illegal after-hours club life, where patrons could listen to the new sounds of jazz and syncopation, nevertheless continued till the end of the war and after.

By 1917, the outcry against the 'moral conditions of the streets of London' had reached a crescendo in the press, reinforced by military complaints that prostitution was having a deleterious influence on 'our unfortunate soldiers'. 'Amateur prostitutes' were now the target for attack. Army sources in 1918 claimed only 28 per cent of diseased personnel were infected by professionals, the rest by the amateur 'flappers' and 'harpies' who amounted to a less detectable 'enemy in our midst'.[78] The press highlighted the theme of immoral women letting down the side. The *Weekly Dispatch* ran an article titled 'The Grave Sex Plague', claiming two women from the Waterloo Road had gone to a seaside resort and 'practically polluted a whole regiment'.[79]

The publicity paved the way for a new and more draconian Defence of the Realm Act passed in March 1918, which made it an offence for any woman suffering from VD to have intercourse with, or solicit or invite intercourse with any member of His Majesty's forces. Women could be detained for medical inspection, and imprisoned for up to six months (Regulation 40D). It led to immediate protest, since it was seen as an attempt to reinstate the Contagious Diseases Acts, with legislation which was unjust to women and imposed no penalties on men. The Women's Suffrage Societies, Women's Freedom League and the Association for Moral and Social Hygiene joined with the National Vigilance Association, the Women's Patrols, and Trades Councils up and down the country to campaign for its repeal. The *Daily News* described it as a 'hideous scandal' that men who laid the charges 'cannot possibly know that they are true; in any case, they are assured beforehand, first, that nothing can happen to them, and, secondly, that the woman, however innocent, will have, in order to clear herself, to submit to a filthily degrading ordeal. Could licensed injustice go further?' Half the charges brought against the women failed. By October 1918, there were 201 prosecutions and 102 convictions, in only fifty-one of which the defendants pleaded guilty.[80] Yet the regulations remained in force until after the end of the war.

There was no clearer indication of the moral panic and fever in 1918 than the Pemberton Billing scandal, when the potent combination of sexual licence and national betrayal riveted the public's attention. Pemberton Billing, MP, 'rather a flashy young man' with a flair for publicity, was, apart from being an inventor of aeroplanes, the editor of the *Vigilante* (formerly the *Imperialist*), which specialized in 'Hun-hating' and 'Hun-bashing' as proof of patriotism. He also ran the Vigilante Society which aimed to promote purity in public life and root out the German fifth column whose work was allegedly responsible for all the failures of the war. His associates in this enterprise were H. H. Beamish, who specialized in anti-Semitism and race hatred; Arnold White, editor of the *English Review*, who was convinced a Hidden Hand was manipulating people in high places, and had made several attacks on homosexuals and enemy aliens in this connection; and Captain Harold Spencer, who was invalided out of the British Army and its Secret Service, claiming darkly he had discovered many things hushed up by the authorities. In an article in the *Vigilante* in February 1918 entitled 'The Cult of the Clitoris', Pemberton Billing accused the dancer, Maud Allen, of perversion. His evidence was her participation in Oscar Wilde's *Salome*, which was being revived for private performance in a theatre owned by the *Sunday Times* drama critic, a naturalized Dane, Jack Grein. Maud Allen sued for libel.

When the case reached court in June 1918, the country was in a mood of almost hysterical anxiety about enemy aliens, 'traitors in our midst', after the successful German offensive on the Western front. In court, during a six-day trial which excited enormous publicity, Pemberton Billing made the sensational allegation that the German Secret Service had compiled a 'Black Book' containing the names of 47,000 British people who could be blackmailed because of their sexual perversity. The source of this information was German agents who had allegedly 'infected this country for the past twenty years, agents so vile and spreading debauchery of such lasciviousness as only German minds could connive and only German bodies execute.'[81] Billing claimed Captain Spencer had seen the Black Book in the *cabinet noir* 'of a certain German prince'. Pandemonium broke loose in court when he claimed that the name of Justice Darling, the judge at the trial, was on the list, as were those of the Asquiths (Herbert Asquith was the former Prime Minister), Lord Haldane (the former War Minister), and many other distinguished people in literature, politics and the diplomatic service.

The press had a field day. Justice Darling never regained control of the courtroom, and the trial was deplored in several quarters as a disgrace to British justice. *The Times* called it 'A Scandalous Trial', in which 'vague suggestions of vice and want of energetic patriotism have been publicly canvassed without the remotest prospect of proving or disproving them'.[82] Maud Allen, who was accused by Billing of performances calculated to appeal to moral perverts and practitioners of unnatural vices, lost her case by default, but was rehabilitated later when the frenzy died down.

For a time, however, the trial fed an unbalanced hysteria as the fortunes of the country passed through a critical phase. One soldier commented, 'I had been so innocent as not to know that sexual aberrations existed in society and can describe my experience only as being corrupted by what I read in the newspapers. Some morbid streak in me was strangely stimulated by these new suggestions at a time when my mind was off-balance'.[83]

The dramatic identification of sexual licence with national betrayal lasted only as long as the war. But the war had accelerated a breakdown in traditional constraints and taboos, some of which were never restored. The 'protected classes' of women were never so protected again. The war demolished the myth of female sexual apathy, since there had been so much evidence, and fear, of women's sexual activity, although it did not abolish the premium on the value of female chastity. It prompted closer scrutiny of the possibilities of equality in sexual relationships, particularly since women demonstrated their ability to equal men in so many areas of economic and social activity. And it also broke down the taboo on talking about sex, especially among the young. Discussion of the moral problems thrown up by war led many to conclude that ignorance was a root cause, and the remedy was to be found in sex education. Marie Stopes, the leading advocate of birth control, published *Married Love* in 1918 'while the war was still raging,' because 'I felt psychologically the time was ripe to give the public what appeared to me a sounder, more wholesome, and more complete knowledge of the intimate sex requirements of *normal* and healthy people than was anywhere available.'[84]

The end of the war meant a return to home front morality which seemed utterly alien to most soldiers after four and a half years in the trenches. 'When it came to be "after the war",' wrote one, 'you hardly knew what to make of it. Friends were parted. Life seemed large and empty. You had to earn a living. It was not easy to begin again, to take thought for the morrow when you had not expected to be alive for it.'[85] As one interpreter for the age wrote, 'What the war did most was to expose the fearful hollow of "authority". It had put a premium on obedience. Obedience was the king's mystical due, the country's right, the general's demand, the Church's everlasting exhortation and Lord Northcliffe's constant clamour . . . When, after the war, these leaders continued to ask for blind obedience and didn't get it, there was at first consternation and then an intense fury. A new morality campaign was put into action. The forces of reaction swept to the colours . . .'[86]

Four

Between the Wars

Erotic Rights

Marie Stopes described *Married Love* as 'crashing into English society like a bombshell . . . Its explosively contagious main theme – that woman like man has the same physiological reaction, a reciprocal need for enjoyment and benefit from sex union in marriage distinct from the experience of maternal functions – made Victorian husbands gasp.' Published in 1918,[1] the book proclaimed an emerging ideal of a companionate marriage in which the sexual fulfilment of both partners was integral to happiness, and it established Stopes as a pioneer in the transformation of the sexual ethic of the next two decades.

Marie Stopes's assertion of women's positive sexual desire repudiated the myth of female passivity. Women's submission to men's demands, she claimed, had distorted women's true sexual nature. Through prudery, the habit 'of using the woman as the passive instrument of man's need', and the custom 'of ignoring the woman's side of marriage and considering his own whim as marriage law', the male had 'largely lost the art of stirring a chaste partner to physical love'. Reciprocal sexual love was the path to the sublime happiness of mutal orgasm or, as she put it, 'the apex of rapture [which] sweeps into its tides the whole essence of the man and woman . . . vaporizes their consciousness so that it fills the whole of cosmic space'.[2] She recommended the 'restrained and sacramental rhythmic performance of the marriage rite of physical union' as 'a supreme value in itself', distinct from the impulse to maternity.[3]

Stopes was a rationalist and a proselytiser. She deployed the authority of science to divide sex from procreation, to enshrine mutual sexual pleasure, and to counter ignorance, particularily about female sexuality. She launched a campaign to make birth control respectable, not only for its contribution to marital happiness, but for its social benefits; it was the means that science had made available to alleviate the poverty and suffering women experienced through excessive and involuntary childbearing. She embarked on her work in the spirit of a moral crusade to improve women's lives, and to enhance the nation's wellbeing.

Three main themes converged in Stopes's work – the assertion of women's sexuality, the eroticisation of marriage, and the need to improve women's health and their rights in marriage and as mothers. These ideas transformed marital ideals in the interwar period.

Marie Stopes and Sexual Ignorance

Like Olive Schreiner, Marie Stopes had grown up within the late-Victorian ethic of restraint, and reacted against it by constructing a new theoretical basis for personal relationships. Her experience shaped her beliefs. Although she was not part of the radical socialist strand of libertarianism, and was, indeed, a political, and often a moral, conservative, she inherited a belief in women's independence and equality from her mother, Charlotte Carmichael, an early suffragist and the first woman in Scotland to take a university degree. From her father, Henry Stopes, an archeologist with an obsession for fossils, she acquired an interest in science, which she chose as the subject of her university studies, gaining her doctorate in 1905 at Munich where she had specialized in the study of plant life.

Yet in this apparently advanced household, sex was never mentioned and ignorance in a young girl was considered synonymous with righteousness. Marie took this ignorance into her marriage (after a week's courtship) to the Canadian botanist Reginald Ruggles Gates in 1911. The marriage was a disaster. It took her sometime to realize that it was not as it should be, but it was only after extensive reading of Havelock Ellis and Edward Carpenter at the British Museum reading room that she discovered that this was because her husband was impotent. The marriage degenerated from argument into abuse and after three years she left him and in 1916 had the marriage annulled on the grounds of non-consummation.

When she wrote *Married Love*, she was thirty-seven and still a virgin. She had decided, she said, that 'in my own marriage I suffered such a terrible price for sex-ignorance that I feel that knowledge gained at such cost should be placed at the service of humanity.'[4] After the book was written, she met and in 1918 married Humphrey Verdon Roe, a businessman with an interest in aviation, who provided the necessary finance to publish her book. She immediately set about putting theory into practice: 'The marriage is consummated, but naturally I haven't had it at its best yet,' she confided to a rejected suitor on the first day.[5] It improved, and the marriage went well for a time. Roe wrote tenderly to her: 'Fancy finding a glorious loving wife and all the other things thrown in, what a lucky man I am.'[6]

Married Love was an immediate and influential success. It sold 2,000 copies in the first fortnight, went through twenty-two reprints (406,000 copies) in five years, was later voted by American academics as among the twenty-five most influential books of its time, and continued to be used as a source of advice on marriage well into the 1950s.[7]

The postwar public was receptive to its message and willing to explore new sexual ideas with greater frankness. The war had fractured the moral status quo and eroded some of the rigid controls on sexual beliefs and behaviour, and women's position in society was in a transition. Those who had moved out of their families into the world of work during the war had experienced a freedom and independence which they showed little inclination to relinquish. After the war their rights and opportunities were extended in a temporary wave of government enthusiasm for principles of sexual equality. In 1918 women over thirty were granted the vote and the right to stand for parliament, although full enfranchisement of all women over twenty-one did not follow until 1918. In 1919 they gained the right to enter professions hitherto barred to them on grounds of their sex (The Sex Disqualification (Removal Act), which opened up new opportunities for careers, although in teaching and the civil service a marriage bar terminated a woman's career on marriage. Women entered the legal profession in small numbers (by 1921, there were twenty women barristers and seventeen women solicitors) and made some advance into the medical profession (the number of women doctors increased from 477 in 1911 to 1, 253 in 1921). Other legislation also reflected a shift towards equality: after 1923 women could sue for divorce on equal terms with men, and in 1925 they were given equal guardianship with fathers over children.

At the same time women's erotic rights were being reconsidered as sex psychology began to influence the way sexuality was defined. The works of Freud, Havelock Ellis and others were made accessible to a wider public. Freud, by connecting sexual repression with illness, instigated the removal of inhibition, and as his work was popularised, it became the rationale for a new sexual ethic which repudiated repression as a distortion of the natural development of the sexual drive, and authorised sexual release and fulfilment as the foundation of healthy relations between the sexes. Ellis encouraged understanding of the sexual impulse and its place in 'honest and open' personal relationships. The work of these two men was harnessed to the repudiation of the Victorian taboo on sex which had clouded sexual feelings with shame, guilt and sinfulness. *Good Housekeeping* the mouthpiece of a middle class readership, lauded the influence of the sex psychologists 'in convincing [women] that they had sex desires and that these desires were not wicked; that to repress them was as difficult and dangerous to women as to men, and that they needed no longer pretend that all they wanted was at most motherhood, when it was quite as natural for them to want loverhood.'[8] Women were no longer presumed to be sexual innocents. Similar standards could apply to women as to men.

These beliefs held particular appeal for the young, for whom the war had severed links with past conventions, and who were now in revolt against the values of their elders – the 'old order' which had sent the nations to a war which wrought such devastation on their generation. The war had left a deep legacy of distrust of moral authority and an uncertainty about the future. 'The beauty of living has gone out of the youngest generation,' Evelyn Waugh noted in his diary in 1921, 'I do honestly think that that is something that went out of the world in 1914, at least for one generation'.[9] The bitterness felt by the young at the maiming of their peers was sometimes acute. It generated, as social observer Irene Clephane diagnosed, a loss of faith in permanency and a sense of insecurity, which sprang 'from lack of any obvious object to be served by life, or any feeling of confidence in the people and the principles that were directing human society . . .' and it 'filled the imaginative with an almost unconquerable dread of the coming years.' It 'accentuated the impulse of the times towards casual sex relationships . . . and militated against the instinct of normal times to set up relationships having the intention of permanency as their basis.'[10] When he heard that two of his close friends were definitely to be engaged, Evelyn Waugh commented, 'It makes me sad for them because any sort of happiness or permanence seems so infinitely remote from any one of us'.[11]

Among the avant-garde the war had bred a cynicism about convention which found creative expression in art, music, literature, dance. For a time in the early 1920s the antics of the 'Bright Young Things', the sons and daughters of the mainly upper and upper-middle class, came to represent the new triumph of a cult of youth. They occupied a great deal of newspaper space as public attention focused on their hedonism, disregard for conventional behaviour, and alleged sexual licence. A determination to be eccentric, excessive and original appeared to be their distinguishing characteristics. Evelyn Waugh's diaries, among others, testify to regular drunkenness, and a certain amount of sexual licence and experiment among the young bourgeoisie, as well as an acceptance of sexual variety and delibertae flouting of conventions. A young woman in *Eve* magazine portrayed the spirit of revolt: 'Tired of shams, we have torn down the musty hangings which the Victorians erected. We talk of everything, we consider everything; we do not rule out one single emotion or experience as being impossible or improper to any person or set of persons. We are determined to let in the air – to ventilate every corner of our mansion . . .'.[12]

This new spirit of revolt and hedonism did not last beyond the 1920s and was confined mainly to the avant-garde and the bourgeoisie. Nor were feminist ideals of equality in personal relationships sustained. Even as women's positive sexuality and their right to reciprocal fulfilment was being newly acknowledged, countervailing social pressures were being operating to curtail women's economic independence, revive their 'femininity' and dependence, and send women back to the home and keep them there as nurturers of the future. By the 1930s women's positive sexuality was being shaped to fit the ideal of a marriage 'partnership', with distinctive role divisions based on the differences rather than the similarities between the sexes. The wife, as the popular magazine *Woman* warned newly weds in 1938, was to 'Be the Junior Partner Madam!'[13]

Mothers' Rights

There were some important changes in the 1920s. Birth control became respectable after a ten-year campaign pioneered by Marie Stopes. An equally arduous political campaign to establish it as a state responsibility and a right for all women was partially successful.

These moves were supported by feminists whose political drive, after the vote was won, had fragmented into single-issue campaigns on social questions – improved maternity care, extended welfare provision and family allowances. For birth-controllers, raising the standards of women's, and mothers' health, alleviating poverty and enlarging women's control over their lives were as important goals as enhancing their opportunities for sexual self-determination. The campaigners took differing approaches. The aim of the voluntary campaign, in which Marie Stopes seized the initiative, was to disseminate information and set up voluntary clinics which gave access to advice and facilities. These met an expanding need. Marie Stopes's first clinic, opened in 1921 in the Holloway Road, had a steadily rising attendance (it doubled each year, from 518 women in 1921 to 2,368 in 1923), and was followed by more clinics – twelve by 1930 – in mainly working class areas around the country. In 1922 the Malthusian League, the main group working in the field before the war, set up its first clinics in Walworth. Stopes's Society for Constructive Birth Control, established in 1922, was the next step in a strategy to attract influential support and propagate her ideas.

In 1924, another pressure group, the Workers Birth Control Group, began a campaign to make birth control a state responsibility as part of public health policy, and a facility available to women as of right. It was led by Labour Party women, and backed by other women's political organizations. Dora Russell, one of its feminist socialist leaders, saw birth control as an issue of women's right to control their lives. It should not be left to voluntary effort or to 'quacks, abortionists and non-medical people'.[14] Women had a right to decide how many children they should have, and to receive contraceptive advice as an integral part of the state's maternity and child health service. As a feminist, Russell also saw it as the prerequisite for equality in marriage: 'We were trying to set sex free from the stigma of sin,' she wrote. 'We saw it as an expression of the union and harmony of two lovers.'[15]

The initial stimulus to political action came in 1924 when the Labour Minister of Health, the Catholic John Wheatley, vetoed the provision of birth-control information at any of the recently opened Maternity and Welfare Centres. When it was discovered that the Battersea and Stepney clinics were providing information they were threatened with withdrawal of funds. After a health worker in Edmonton had been dismissed for giving advice in 1922, public demonstations in her support only provoked a further official ruling from the Ministry prohibiting any contraceptive information being given to any women under any circumstances at their clinics. In response, the Workers Birth Control Group launched a parliamentary lobby to change the ruling, and began an education and propaganda campaign.

Both the voluntary and the political campaigns were fought against entrenched opposition from the churches and the medical profession. The Church of England's condemnation of birth control as immoral had not abated; its 1908 Lambeth Conference Resolution which unanimously urged all Christians to 'discountenance the use of all artificial means of restriction as demoralising to character and hostile to national welfare' was endorsed in 1920 when the Conference called on 'principled men and women' to condemn 'such incentives to vice as indecent literature, suggestive plays and films, the open or secret sale of contraceptives'.[17] Not all Anglicans were so adamant. Dean Inge, Dean of St Paul's and an early member of the Eugenics Society, thought there was room for individual decision, although he refused to support Stopes openly. He pointed out later that of forty diocesan bishops, one had five children, two had two each, and the remaining thirty-seven had only twenty-eight children between them.[18]

The association of contraception with immorality and illicit sex occasioned much abuse against birth-controllers. At the opening of the Malthusian League's Walworth clinic, stones and eggs were thrown and men shouted 'whore' at the staff. When Marie Stocks and Chris Frankenberg opened the first provincial clinic in Manchester in 1925 (above a tea-shop which sold meat pies), huge protest meetings were mounted by Catholics who vilified the two women as 'middle class busybodies, attempting to introduce unnatural vices' and 'the kind of idle women who visit matinées and sit with cigarettes between their painted lips'.[19]

Though a few doctors supported the campaigners, the majority of the medical profession had hardly advanced on its prewar opposition, and this was now compounded by professional hostility to the leading campaigner. Dr Marie Stopes was not, they pointed out, a medical doctor but a doctor of science who was spreading spurious information unsanctioned by the medical profession. Medical objection and moral strictures were indistinguishable in the catalogue of disasters such doctors foretold. Dr Amand Routh, obstetric physician at Charing Cross Hospital, opposed all artificial methods of birth control (including prophylactics, despite being aware that twenty per cent of interine and neonatal deaths were caused by syphilis) on the grounds that they weakened 'moral resistance' and caused 'nervous exhaustion, inability to mentally concentrate' and 'pelvic troubles'.[20] Dr Mary Scharlieb, a distinguished gynaecologist and an unmarried Catholic, declared that people and nations who practised birth control and 'who therefore have no restraint in their sexual passions are likely to become effeminate and degenerate. The removal of the sanction of matrimony and the unhindered and unbalanced sexual indulgence that would follow would war against self-control, chivalry and self-respect'.[21] Dr Louise McIlroy, Professor of Obstetrics and Gynaecology at the London School of Medicine for Women, opposed mechanical methods as medically disastrous, 'unhygienic', a 'grave moral danger to the community' and 'repulsive to most individuals' for they involve 'manipulation of the genital organs' and 'turn the spontaneous impulse of the spiritual act into a premeditated physical performance.' Echoing the prewar feminist view that contraception only encouraged male 'vice', McIlroy countered any thought that women's freedom would be enlarged; instead it would bring them 'worse slavery in sexual matters, for they will remain the instruments of men's uncontrolled desires . . . Birth control does not mean sex control, but rather unlimited indulgence without its responsibilities and consequences'.[22]

Between them, the church and the medical profession colluded in the enforcement of ignorance in the name of morality, on the grounds that to spread knowledge about sex to the working class would weaken social controls and open 'the floodgates of immorality.' This attitude was condemned by Dr C. Killick Willard, Medical Officer of Health for Leicester, as 'something approaching hypocrisy'. The 'educated classes', he pointed out, were 'quietly and privately availing themselves of the knowledge and means . . . to escape from what they regard – and with good reason – as the evil of over-childbearing', and yet were joining in 'a conspiracy of silence to keep this same knowledge from reaching the poor who need it so much more.'[23] In 1922, Dr Halliday Sutherland, a Catholic convert and Commissioner for the Tuberculosis Services, attacked Marie Stopes as 'a doctor of German philosophy (Munich)' who was using the poor to make harmful birth-control experiments. Stopes sued him for libel. Although she lost the case, her nine-day trial focused public attention on the issue, publicised her views far beyond the confines of clinics, and, elicited widespread public and press support. When the Oxford Union passed a motion calling on the government to support birth control, Marie Stopes was greeted with tumultuous applause by undergraduates and presented by Evelyn Waugh (not yet a Catholic) with a large bunch of mimosa.

The Workers Birth Control Group's progress in the Labour Party was hampered by religious opposition and by socialist suspicion that eugenic arguments for birth control would be used to extend control over the working class. But there was also strong resistance to making such a controversial 'private' subject into a party political issue. The Labour women's organiser, Marion Philips, tried to deter the Group: 'Sex should not be dragged into politics,' she warned them, 'you will split the party from top to bottom'.[24] The party Executive agreed. The Labour Women's Conference in 1924 passed a resolution to make birth control part of maternity care funded by the state, but this was killed off at the Labour Party Conference when an Executive recommendation that the subject should not be an issue for party politics was narrowly carried.

The WBCG were convinced that it was, and they carried the campaign out into the press, local constituency parties and local health authorities. An attempt in February 1926 by Ernest Thurtle, MP for Shoreditch, to introduce a bill to enable local authorities to finance contraceptive advice was defeated, but progress was made in the House of Lords when a motion to withdraw the instructions which debarred welfare committees from giving contraception information at their clinics was passed by fifty-seven votes to forty-four. The Labour Party Conference then endorsed the House of Lord's decision, but since the party was out of power, nothing effective was done, and the decision was reversed by Conference the following year.

The practice of birth control spread steadily even though the circulation of knowledge was restricted and publication of accessible information remained a hazardous enterprise: Guy Aldred and Rose Sitcup, both socialists, were prosecuted for obscenity in 1923 for publishing Margaret Sanger's *Family Limitation* in a cheap edition. The desperate need for help, especially among the poor, was revealed in clinic experience and in Marie Stopes's enormous correspondence.

While many middle class women were interested in questions of sexual fulfilment, it was poverty and illness which prompted most working class women to seek help. Stocks and Frankenberg found that 'immorality' was far from the thoughts of the women who visited their clinic. What preoccupied them were involuntary childbearing and poverty. 'Many were surprisingly ignorant of their own physical make-up, and a good husband was often summed up as one "who seldom troubles me",' Stocks wrote. The message of *Married Love* and its plea for mutually satisfying sex was not uppermost in her clinic work for 'we had not as yet got beyond ensuring that the weekly, or even more frequent, "troubles" should at any rate have no disastrous consequences.'[25] One woman with five children living on a farm labourer's wage wrote to Stopes: 'If its wicked to prevent children from coming its also wicked to bring them into the world and not be able to keep them . . . I have five children. Three of them I had in just over 3 years. It seemed no sooner did I give in to my husband than I was in a certain condition [sic].'[26] Another wrote for advice 'knowing that another increase or more in our family would mean dire poverty and starvation'. She was a mother of four, the eldest ill, with a husband injured in the war.[27]

Clinics provided almost the only source of help. Doctors were not trained in birth-control methods, and were reluctant, although they produced among the smallest families of all, to give information to their patients. One mother of nine children, who nearly died producing a tenth, wrote to Stopes: 'Now the Doctor has advised me to have no more family but did not give me a remedy, please Dr, can you tell me what to do, I am terribly afraid.'[28] Many working class women were reluctant to ask the doctor: 'You daren't mention it to the doctor' and 'he would just tell you that was what married life was all about' were two typical responses in Lancaster.[29] Others took a fatalistic view, like Mrs Pearce, mother of six who 'never would take anything in them days. God had sent them and they had to be there.'[30] What information was available came by word of mouth. 'We were on the bus', one women remembered, 'and Harold knew the conductor and he asked Harold if we were married. He said, "Don't forget, always get off the bus at South Shore, don't go all the way to Blackpool." That was how they kept their family down. It was just that the men had to be careful.'[31]

By 1930 public pressures to make birth control a respectable issue of public health were succeeding, not least because the use of contraception was increasing steadily. Where in 1911 the least fertile section of the population had been professional people, by 1931 the lowest fertility was among clerical workers. There was a significant general reduction in family size, partly as a result of changes in material goals which encouraged the use of contraception. Where over a quarter of families had five or more children in 1900–1909, by 1930 this was down to 10.4 per cent while the proportion of those with one or two children increased from one third to a half in the same period.[34]

Under increased political pressure, opinion in the Labour Party was also shifting. In 1930 the new Minister of Health in the Labour

Government, Arthur Greenwood, issued a MOH Circular (153/ MCW) giving permissive, though limited, powers to local authorities to give contraception advice to nursing and expectant mothers 'in whose cases further pregnancy would be dangerous to health'. The newly formed National Birth Control Council set up their own clinics, starting in Plymouth in 1932, with grants and subsidies from local authorities. The provision of birth-control information expanded in a symbiotic relationship between local authorities and voluntary organizations, which lasted until the 1960s.

The Church of England also partly relented. In 1930 the Lambeth Conference voted by 193 to 67 to allow the use of contraception 'where there is a clearly felt moral obligation to limit or avoid parenthood, and where there is a morally sound reason for avoiding complete abstinence', but explicitly excluded its use 'on account of selfishness, luxury or mere convenience'. The resolution, the Archbishop of York confirmed, 'sweeps away the erroneous and harmful view that there is something necessarily evil in the functions of sex and proclaims they are a God-given factor in marriage.' [35] G. B. Shaw saw it as a case of the bishops giving way 'under the overwhelming pressure of accomplished fact'. The Roman Catholics, however, renewed their opposition, condemning the Anglican position as a departure from moral theology likely to lead to moral anarchy, and Pope Pius XI in his encyclical *Casti Conubi* (1930) condemned birth control as an offence against the laws of man and nature.

In a single decade birth control had passed from being a subject unmentionable in public to an acceptable issue of government health-care policy. Contraception spread from then on. Sixty-three per cent of couples married in 1930–34 and 66 per cent in 1935–39 used it, compared to 16 per cent of those married before 1910. About a third used artificial methods, and two-thirds used other means, mainly withdrawal.[36] The birth rate fell consistently through the interwar years. In 1900–1905 the average number of legitimate births per thousand married women had been 230.5; by the Second World War it was 105.4.[37]

Unmarried Sins

Although there was much fuller discussion of sexual issues in this period, powerful constraints, frequently backed by punitive sanctions, were used to control sexual behaviour. Any loosening of such constraints was a source of acute anxiety to the self-ordained guardians of public morality.

The young were still closely controlled. Fear of pregnancy and the premium placed on female chastity regulated sexual activity, although survey evidence indicated an increase in both petting and premarital sex. One survey found that petting increased from 7 per cent among those born before 1904 to 22 per cent among those born 1904–1914 (people in their teens and twenties during the 1920s), and an increase in premarital intercourse from 19 per cent for those born before 1904 to 39 per cent for those born 1914–24 (in their teens and twenties in the 1930s).[38] In another survey, only 4 per cent of the women questioned admitted to sex with men other than their husbands (Mass Observation put this at 10 per cent), although 40 per cent of men admitted to sex with women other than their future wives. Still another survey estimated that 50 to 66 per cent of men and 30 to 50 per cent of women had premarital sex during this period.[39]

Controls on the middle and upper class appear to have been less rigid than on the working class. Lord Jessel recalled how weekend parties provided an opportunity for intimacies: 'In those days the upper classes did not on the whole penetrate their girl-friends – just heavy petting, as I think it's called today, because I think they were frightened of having children ... They had big house parties and there were a lot of people going to the ladies' rooms. They did not sleep with them, but cuddled, and the man would have an ejaculation, that sort of thing'.

Lady Marguerite Tangye recalled similar weekend parties: 'if you were a bit attracted to someone you'd end up lying on the sofa with them when everyone had gone to bed. It just seemed a pleasant thing to do ... The mothers were there and sometimes they interfered but mostly they'd go to bed. They really expected all this to be going on, that's what everyone was paying for, for you to carry on with someone who had the right name and plenty of money and a nice country house. It was a market, so they weren't going to stop it . . . If you were very much in love you would think nothing of lying in bed with someone all night and talking to them'. The value put on female chastity survived: 'you knew or you sensed that you would be all right with them and they never went too far, but you led them on and it must have been very hard for them sometimes. I remember sitting in a car fooling about with one man and he said, "I must get out and run round the block," cool himself off, I suppose. And some of them would go to the Bag of Nails, which was a sort of quite smart brothel-type place.'[40]

Progressive ideas about sex filtered through only slowly. Parental control of working class women's behaviour was backed by the threat of social ostracism for transgressions. Ignorance was widespread among the working class, and sex was still obscured by secrecy and taboo. Unmarried sex was 'wrong', and it wasn't talked about by parents.

At dances, the main social activity of the time, proprieties had to be observed. Mrs Mulholland, whose brother organised regular dances in the Preston and Barrow area, remembered, 'M'brother was most strict, terrible, they had to dance so far apart. He wouldn't let them dance cheek-to-cheek. He'd separate them if they were too close, and say, "That is enough." And they knew.' Mrs McLeod remembers going to dances twice a week. She always had to leave early, and outside 'you would see three or four or five mothers all waiting for their daughters coming out', although it was only just around the corner from where they lived.[41]

Parents controlled their daughters' movements and their choice of partner and expected to meet their young men within the first few weeks. This did not stop courting couples meeting secretly, and petting, but the unspoken social controls on women who 'went the whole way' were strong. It was part of the code accepted by both sexes that women risked losing 'respect' if they gave in to male demands: 'it's always a battle and if the girl is crafty and uses her loaf she'll always avoid you accomplishing what you're after, sex or whatever', John Neary recalled. John Binns remembered: 'When you got the right girl you decided that no matter how hard you tried you would never get sex and that was a good thing . . . I think you looked down on them when they were too easy, when they let you have it too often.'[42]

The stigmatization of women who engaged in premarital sex as 'amateur prostitutes', which gained currency at the time, was one form of control. The penalties on unmarried mothers remained an even more effective deterrent, especially for the working class who were less able to disguise the consequences of mistakes. Women of all classes were packed off out of sight to have the child. The social shame brought on the family was severe; many women suffered rejection from their parents as well as intolerance and ostracism from the outside world. If they were well off, they might be sent to a nursing home and then the baby was adopted. If they could not afford this, they were at the mercy of institutions. Some voluntary or church organizations had a reputation for being as punitive as the workhouse had once been with regimes like those in prison, on which many of them were based. As illegitimacy was an indication of a woman's moral failure, these organizations saw their duty as moral reform. Arduous domestic work was considered the appropriate training ground. Under the Mental Deficiency Act of 1913, which gave local authorities powers to certify pregnant women who were homeless, destitute or 'immoral', many women were detained in reformatories or mental hospitals for long periods, often with little hope of rehabilitation, or even escape, as a draconian punishment for their moral lapse.

The illegitimacy rate throughout the period remained at a steady 4 to 5 per cent of all live births, but more premarital conceptions were covered up by marriage. In 1938–1939 the Registrar General estimated that 'one seventh of all children now born in this country are products of extramarital conceptions, or to go further, that nearly 30 per cent of all mothers today conceive their first born out of wedlock'.[43]

Some limited advances in sex education were made during the 1920s. The Board of Education in 1927 recommended sex education in schools, but it was discretionary. By the early 1940s only a third of secondary schools gave any formal instruction. The London County Council in 1935 recommended that schools should study the reproduction of flowering plants and the life history of frogs but thought 'class instruction in senior schools should not include mammals'.[44] Text books were coy on the subject. Furneaux and Smart's *Human Physiology* in Longman's Elementary Science Manuals dealt in 1931 neither with sex organs nor reproduction. In Thornton's *Human Physiology*, (Longman's, 1926) in 463 pages only one paragraph, 'Testes and Ovaries', was given to reproductive organs, hidden away in a chapter on 'The Liver and Ductless Glands'. There was no reference to the words 'uterus', 'vagina', 'menstruation' or 'sex'.[45]

Sex education was left to voluntary organizations, most of them offshoots of the social purity movement concerned to bind sex education to religious morality. But the standards did become less rigid and in 1921, the White Cross appointed a sub committee to revise its literature with the help of Ernest Jones, a prominent Freudian and some of the more heavily moralistic tracts (such as 'The Perils of Impurity') were withdrawn. In 1932 the Student Christian Movement came officially to the conclusion 'masturbation does no physical or mental harm' although Baden Powell's injunction to senior scouts in *Rovering to Success* remained influential: 'It cheats semen getting its full chance of making up the strong manly man you would otherwise be ... you are throwing away the seed that has been handed down to you as a trust instead of keeping it and ripening it for bringing a son to you later on.' The British Social Hygiene Council, a scientific rationalist group, promoted conferences, lectures and courses for parents, teachers, and youth leaders to encourage sex education through the 1930s. They and the Alliance of Honour were invited into schools to give lectures to the under 14s. One such lecture, on 'The Gift of Life', traced reproduction from the amoeba to the rabbit – a mammal at last. Another, 'You and Life', for older children, explained the male sex organs with mild warnings about masturbation, and the female organs, and with warnings against premarital sex.[46]

Public education in 'social hygiene' (i.e. VD), continued after the war, using the new medium of film. Educational propaganda films, like *Waste, Damaged Goods* and *Damaged Lives*, played to large audiences, though not usually in main cinemas as the films were not granted an official certificate.

The progress of enlightenment was slow. The proportion of married women who gathered from their parents that sex was something not to be talked about dropped from 76 per cent of those born before 1914 to 58 per cent for those born 1924–1934, the proportion whose sex education came from adults – teachers, doctors and others – went up from one tenth of those born pre–1904 to one fifth of those born 1924–1934. Those who got their information from books or pamphlets increased from 2 per cent to 17 per cent.[46] Other surveys showed the most common source of information for the majority was still friends and work-mates. Only 8 per cent of a 1949 Mass Observation survey sample learned about sex from a pamphlet, and only 11 per cent were told anything by their mothers, and 6 per cent by their fathers.[47]

Cleaning Up 'Vice'

Any diminution of constraints on moral conduct was viewed with concern by the guardians of public morality and social purists. The Home Secretary from 1924–1929, Joynson Hicks 'Jix', was a devout Churchman and patriot who had determined to 'impart cleanliness to some neglected corners', and seek 'a new birth of enthusiasm for a new cause founded upon a new belief in old principles'.[49] He was regularily satirised by the young for these efforts to put the clock back. One of his favoured targets for cleaning up 'vice' was night clubs, which were enjoying a boom among the fashionable young. Since he made no distinction between the reputable and disreputable, all night clubs were barri-caded against the possibility of a police raid which undoubtedly added to their glamour. The policy had limited success: 'One of the things which astonished him about night-clubs,' wrote one commentor, 'was that he expected them to be filled with whores and found them crammed with "society".'[50]

His office was responsible for banning the works of several authors and keeping publishers on their toes about risky publi-cations. There were, however, other social purists in prominent public office and these included Sir Archibald Bodkin, the Director of Public Prosecutions, a former member of the Council of the National Vigilance Association, and Sir Thomas Inskip, Solicitor General and Attorney General for most of 1922–1936, a fervent evangelical and an active supporter of social purity causes. The Public Morality Council was allowed discreet influence over public policy through most of the period. It was given regular access to the Lord Chamberlain and the Film Censor: The Bishop of London recalled how in 1936; 'Dear old T. P. O'Connor [Head of the BBFC] used to come down and have lunch with me when he had a doubt about a film.'[51]

With this alignment of power, the bounds of tolerance towards challenges to 'decency' were narrowly drawn, and there was a mounting list of obscenity prosecutions: in 1921 an anonymous psychoanalytical study, *A Young Girl's Diary*; in 1926 Shane Leslie's *The Cantab*; in 1928 Radclyffe Hall's *The Well of Loneliness*; in 1929 Norah C. James's *Sleeveless Errand*, in 1934 James Hanley's homosexual novel *Boy*, and Wallace Smith's *Betsie Cotter* – the last described by Sir Thomas Inskip as a book which 'deals with what everybody will recognise as an unsavoury subject – gratification of sexual appetite'.[52]

With the threat of the Old Bailey hanging over them, publishers proceeded with caution. Many books were expurgated – Richard Aldington's *Death of a Hero* (1929) was 'mutilated' before publication, and Sheila Cousins' *To Beg I am Ashamed*, an autobiography about prostitution, was withdrawn after a police visit. Authors increasingly resorted to publication abroad, and to the cat and mouse game of getting books through customs concealed in suitcases. James Joyce's *Ulysses* was first published abroad and with the establishment of the Obelisk Press (later the Olympia Press) by Jack Kahane in Paris, a publishing oasis was found for books already prosecuted and for works which authors knew in advance were too risky to run the gauntlet of the DPP and the Public Morality Council. These included most of Henry Miller's works, Frank Harris's *My Life and Loves* and Cyril Connolly's *The Rock Pool* as well as *The Kama Sutra* and *The Perfumed Garden*.

All these books posed a challenge to the Christian sexual ethic and the approved boundaries of public taste. D. H. Lawrence, already a casualty of the law with *The Rainbow* in 1915 was one of the more uncompromising opponents of the stifling influence of 'Victorianism'. Lawrence was expounding an ethic in which the human spirit would be released – through sexual tenderness and a mystic 'phallic consciousness' – from spiritual dreariness, alienation, the mechanisation of personal relations and the straitjacket of conventional morality which denied and distorted sex.

The 'grey ones' of 'Victorianism', declared Lawrence, had made sex the 'dirty little secret' through their hypocrisy and their 'pornography' – 'the attempt to insult sex, to do dirt on it . . . you can recognise it by the insult it offers, invariably, to sex, and to the human spirit.'[53] But what he saw of the new morality of the young also appalled him. Though they had advanced from 'fearing the body, and denying its existence', they 'go to the other extreme and treat it as a sort of toy to be played with . . . these young people scoff at the importance of sex, take it like a cocktail, and flout their elders with it. These young ones are advanced and superior . . . Why make a fuss about it. Take it like a cocktail!'[54]

Lawrence had only faint approval for those like Marie Stopes, who by being 'wise and scientific about it', merely 'disinfect the dirty little secret.[55] For him, sex was the 'source of all real beauty, and all real gentleness. And those are the two things, tendeness and beauty, which will save us from horrors'. His novels, and specifically *Lady Chatterley's Lover*, were an attempt to restore 'the other, the phallic consciousness, into our lives'.[56] 'You musn't think I advocate perpetual sex,' he explained to Lady Ottoline Morrell, 'But I want, with *Lady C*, to make an *adjustment in consciousness* to the basic physical realities.'[57] He worked, he told poet Harriet Monroe, 'direct from the phallic consciousness, which, you understand, is not the cerebral sex-consciousness, but something really deeper, and the root of poetry, lived or sung.'[58]

To a later generation still grappling with sexual guilt, Lawrence was to become the prophet of a religion of sexual release, and *Lady Chatterley* the seminal text for comprehending the mystical rapture of mutual simultaneous orgasm as a holy rite. To an even later generation of women, however, he became the representative of male phallic chauvinism with its solipsistic sexual possessiveness and fear of female sexuality. At the time, *Lady Chatterley's Lover* met with almost universal condemnation.

His publishers, Seckers, turned down a version he had already expurgated after they concluded, according to his friend and biographer Richard Aldington, 'that the book was a little ahead of the times, and were unwilling to risk the damages to their businesses which might be visited on them by the frenzies of the inhibited'.[59] When he brought out his own unexpurgated version in an edition of 1000 printed by a Florentine bookseller Guiseppe Oriolo, which he distributed to booksellers and subscribers, *John Bull* described it as 'the most evil outpouring that has ever besmirched the literature of our country'.[60] The first to cave in were fourteen booksellers who sent back their copies. The book was too much even for his more advanced friends, although David Garnett and Richard Aldington stood by him. George Bernard Shaw was mischievously supportive: 'Lady Chatterley should be on the shelves of every college for budding girls. They should be forced to read it on pain of being refused a marriage license. *But it is not as readable as* Ivanhoe or A Tale of Two Cities'.[61]

Lawrence's paintings were banned, charged with being 'gross, coarse, hideous, unlovely and obscene' after police raided his exhibition at the Warren Gallery in 1929, and the eighty-two year-old magistrate decided the pictures 'should be put an end to, like any wild animal which may be dangerous'.[62] It was, Richard Aldington wrote, 'an unhappy reminder of the survival of obtuse Philistinism, and a curious example of the authority of a state being used to support the religious prejudices of the Minister of the Interior.'[63]

As far as films were concerned Joynson 'Jix' Hicks, The Minister of the Interior, made his prejudices quite clear: 'No silly prating about the necessity of elucidating problems, or that "to the pure all things are pure", or that the claims of art must be satisfied, which we freqently hear, can change the moral law, or alter the fundamental facts of human nature', he proclaimed.[64] Although it was an independent body, the British Board of Film Censors appeared to take his views into account in structuring its role as custodian of the nation's morals. Unlike the Hays Code in the United States, the rules were never laid down, but broad principles applied against passing anything judged to undermine the conventional teaching of morality or bring the institution of marrige into disrepute.

If films give the impression of a stable, moral and virtuous society in these years, it was largely because of tight controls, and not only over overtly 'excessive' material. A long list of subjects – drunkenness among women, brutality to women, fights between women, prostitution, 'illegal operations', brothels, rape, confinements, girls made drunk or seduced, incest, white slavery – were prohibited altogether.[65] Complicated issues were trimmed in an attempt to fit accepted tenets of morality; while love triangles, for instance, may involve 'departure from virtue', distinction was to be made between 'errors caused by love' and 'the pursuit of lust' which was wholly unacceptable. The 'betrayal of young women' may be treated 'with restraint', but was unacceptable if it suggested the girl is 'morally justified in succumbing to temptation in order to escape sordid surroundings or uncongenial work'.[66] No 'glorification of free love' was acceptable, and objections were made to material which exonerated marital infidelity or the 'sacrifice of a woman's virtue', to 'first night scenes', couples in bed together, 'equivocal' bedroom and bathroom scenes and 'a growing habit with actors of both sexes to divest themselves of their clothing on slight or no provocation'.[67]

If in doubt about these matters, the Censor could be relied on to err on the side of caution, bearing in mind the need, dictated by their very function, to avoid trouble from vociferous moral and religious pressure groups who displayed a routine tendency to attack the serious rather than the frivolous portrayals of controversial moral issues. The result of this discreet approach to sex was an enhanced audience sensitivity to interpreting clues and reading beween the lines of those films which actually were dealing with sexual issues.

Ideal Marriage

Despite these public constraints, new ideals for personal relations gained ground, but only in relation to marriage: pre-marital constraints still applied. The companionate ideal shored up monogamy, but re-shaped it in line with the new emphasis on sexual fulfilment. The ideal was promoted by psychologists and marriage experts in proliferating marriage manuals which routinely repudiated the ignorance, shame and guilt associated with sex. 'The idea that there is anything wrong or 'nasty' in sex itself', Helena Wright asserted in *The Sex Factor in Marriage* (1930) was 'a man-made notion entirely untrue and evil in itself'; a successful sex relation was possible for all married couples as long as shame and inhibition were swept away. In the new model marriage, mutual fulfilment was the cementing ingredient in a partnership, which, described by Wright as 'the mating of two independent personalities', was in fact a team in which partners fulfilled complementary, rather than equal roles. The role separation followed accepted theories of the biological origins of sex difference in which man's active, and woman's 'natural', 'feminine' and 'caring' nature determined their sexual and economic status. Women's positive sexuality was now corralled into this ideal partnership.

The apex of sexual achievement was mutual orgasm, and each partner had a duty to bring the other to fulfilment. Sex, according to the manuals, could not take care of itself. It had to be learned, as an art. A new stress on technique appeared. Havelock Ellis was helpful, widely read, and accessible. Helena Wright's *The Sex Factor in Marriage* (1930) encouraged women to enjoy sexual expeience; the first condition was to know their own bodies, to which end she provided sympathetic instruction on how to give themselves to 'its fullest joy'.

By 1932 even the religious organizations were advocating the spiritual joys of mutual orgasm – in the White Cross League's *The Threshold of Marriage*, for instance, which sold over one and a half million copies. Theodore van de Velde's *Ideal Marriage*, (1930), which ran through forty-two editions with sales of 700,000 copies in four years, explained in frank detail physiology, techniques of arousal and alternatives and variations. He stressed his concern to promote 'normal' monogamous marital harmony and to 'keep the Hell Gate of the Realm of Sexual Perversion firmly closed', though this did not exclude discussion of the previously 'perverse' cunnilingus and fellatio – the 'genital kiss' which he authorised as part of Love Play.[68] This conservatism was not surprising; Edward Charles's *The Sexual Impulse*, though thoroughly endorsed with respectable references, was prosecuted for obscenity in 1935 for describing variations in coital positions, and in 1942, the eminently respectable Eustace Chesser's *Love Without Fear* was tried for obscenity (unsuccessfully) for making accessible and readable information he believed could alleviate the misery suffered through ignorance.

A sexual ideal which endorsed women's right to sexual fulfilment took a long time to gain any real currency. Janet Chance, a reformer who opened a sex education centre in 1929, found, 'in spite of all the apparent equality of outlook amongst the younger generation, passion in England remains a lopsided affair', in which women were 'not getting the best out of that relationship'.[69] Of ninety-three women at her centre, almost a third had come for advice because they never or only rarely experienced satisfaction, and though 'the subject of physical happiness in marriage' raised a 'pathetically eager response in working-women's meetings', it was 'often news to them that they might at all share the sex enjoyment of their husbands'. She pointed out that in most of the 20,000 letters received by the Divorce Law Reform Union from couples wanting to end their marriage, the reason given for failure was 'distaste of one of the partners for the physical marriage relationship'.[70] Sex remained a duty for women long afterwards, as Peggy Makins, *Woman* magazine's agony aunt, 'Evelyn Home', found: 'obviously some of the correspondents to our problem page found intercourse a bore or worse ... a whole lot of couples ... didn't enjoy love making much at all. At least, the man enjoyed it ('my husband is over-sexed' was a very much-used phrase), but the wife put up with it.'[71]

For manuals and moralists there was no question that the proper place for sex was lifelong marriage. A few reformers advanced alternatives to monogamy. In his influential *Marriage and Morals* (1929) Bertrand Russell proposed that now that women were free to chose when to have sexual relationships, able to control maternity, and were seeking 'equality in moral freedom', there was no justification for marriage to be based on sexual possession, and no reason why marriage should imply exclusiveness of affection. Adultery should be re-assessed. With the advance of women's equality, the marriage partnership should be based on complete equality, mutual respect and trust between partners; it should allow moral freedom to each partner to have affairs with other people 'provided the underlying affection remains intact', for, he claimed, 'unless people are restrained by inhibitions or strong moral scruples, it is very unlikely that they will go through life without occasionally having strong impulses to adultery. But such impulses do not by any means necessarily imply that the marriage no longer serves its purpose.' The doctrine he wished 'to preach' was, he argued, 'not one of license; it involves nearly as much self-control as is involved in the conventional doctrine. But self-control will be applied more to abstaining from interference with the freedom of others than to restraining one's own freedom.'[72]

He was not alone. Irene Clephane confidently claimed in 1935 'the idea that physical infidelity means the end – even the desire for the end – of an established relationship is dying fast among women – men have always known that it need imply no such thing. All men, even the chastest, and most women, pine, generally in the secret places of their hearts, for change, for something different in sexual experience.' Moreover, another sexual relationship may be just what is needed 'to save the existing relationship'.[73]

This is not widely accepted wisdom. When *Woman*'s first 'Evelyn Home', a Freudian psychiatrist (who chose the pen name because it incorporated Eve the temptress with the Home every woman was supposed to want), recommended in 1937 that a wife in love with somebody else's husband should go off for a short time with him alone, to relieve her feelings, it was instantly suppressed. The editor, Mary Grieve, exploded: 'This is a moral advice column . . . Any fool knows that you can't take risks with it . . . We could be prosecuted by the police for pornography if we published this.'[74]

Which is not to say that irregularities did not go on in private which were concealed from public view. Harold Macmillan's wife, Dorothy, for years conducted an affair with his friend and political colleague, Robert Boothby, which left a deep mark on this taciturn and emotionally reserved politician. Macmillan's training in the camouflage of privacy and his belief in the obligation to rein in private life to standards of public decorum played a crucial part in his reluctance to address early on the implications of the Profumo scandal in 1963 when he was Prime Minister. That he 'found it distasteful' to have to deal with gossip and innuendo which touched his private vulnerabilities was a blind spot in his political judgment which enabled the scandal to ripen out of control.

Bertrand Russell and Sexual Jealousy

Those who chose on principle to explore and live by ethical standards which flouted the sexual conventions of the day often found such a course painful. For Dora Russell it 'brought conflict and even tragedy into our private lives'.[75] Bertrand Russell set himself up as the apostle of a new morality. Brought up a Victorian aristocrat, he was an early member of the Fabian society when H. G. Wells was expounding his new morality, and a supporter of women's equality and birth control. His mother had been a suffrage campaigner since the 1860s, and he stood for Parliament in a 1907 by-election on that issue alone.

By the time he met Dora Black in 1916, he had behind him a failed marriage to feminist Alys Pearsall Smith and a number of affairs, including one with Lady Ottoline Morell who had 'gradually cured me of the belief that I was seething with appalling wickedness which could only be kept under by an iron self-control ... She made me much less of a Puritan, and much less censorious than I had been.'[76]

Dora Black was one of the younger generation of feminists for whom sexual equality in personal relations lay at the centre of the struggle for women's emancipation. When she met Bertrand Russell she had graduated from Cambridge, she saw a career ahead of her, was 'now desirous of spreading wings', and had 'deeply-cherished modern views' about marriage. She was 'afraid of entanglements, and was suspicious of the wiles of men who were forever scheming to drag women back into the legal, domestic and sexual bondage from which feminist pioneers were trying to escape and deliver their sisters.'[77] Legal marriage was 'not very important in sexual ethics ... one entered into a sexual relationship for love which was given and received freely. No other motive but such love ... was to be tolerated'.[78]

Russell, in his forties, clearly wanted to settle down to marriage and family, and faced her with a difficult decision. Although they held the same, unconventional views, Dora also detected that he was not unlike other men who 'could not divest themselves of the old notion that "to have and to hold"' a wife in economic dependence was the right and proper course for any man worthy of the name.[79] But they both objected to the marriage law which 'gave rights of property and possession of persons and, by treating infidelity as a crime, encouraged marriage partners to pursue one another with jealousy, suspicion, hatred and revenge masquerading as virtue and righteous indigation'. She and 'Bertie' agreed that 'husbands should not "possess" wives, nor wives husbands, parents should not "possess" their children'.[80]

They married after Dora became pregnant and conceded to Bertie's view that marriage was justified to provide a basis for stability in which to bring up children. Bertie's age, and the social ostracism which would ensure 'any academic work would have been closed to B. R. or myself, if we'd not married'[81] played its part. In their marriage they agreed to abide by their shared ethic. Marriage did not prevent either leading an active and often independent life. The crisis in their relationship came after Dora began an affair with journalist, Griffin Barry. Bertie accepted it as part of their code of personal freedom, 'not troubling about legal "matrimonial offences"' which Bertrand Russell had recently preached to a wider public in *Marriage and Morals*. Dora's love and affection for Bertie were undiminished, and she expected his to be the same: 'I had never felt that any "affairs" Bertie might have could shake the abiding nature of our close relation and trust in one another.'[82] Moreover, they had encountered sexual difficulties when they wanted another child: 'Bertie's severe Victorian upbringing and the intensity of his intellectual concentration had inhibited him sexually', she wrote, but both hoped this impotence in a man nearing sixty could be overcome by 'spontaneous, natural means' through a 'sufficiently strong attraction to some woman'.[83]

When she became pregnant by Barry, Bertie reassured her: 'Since I cannot do my part . . . there is no need to worry, you won't find me tiresome about it.'[84] It was, Dora later construed, a disguise – 'all part of that courtly behaviour towards his wife, which disdained marital bickering' and which enabled him to act with coldness and emotional detachment in crises. When she returned after the child's birth, he announced he had now transferred his affections to Margery ('Peter') Spence, a student employed looking after the children. Being very progressive, they adapted, and all (Bertie, Dora, Griffin and Peter) went on holiday together in 1931. When Dora became pregnant again by Griffin, despite the fact that Bertie made it 'plain that he did not want our marriage to break up, that his affection for me was deep and indestructible, the more so for no longer being sexual',[85] she reluctantly explored, then rejected, the possibility of an abortion. The day before the baby was born, Bertie informed Dora he now wished to live with Peter. When she returned home they had departed.

Dora's shock and the subsequent galling legal wrangles were exacerbated by her bitterness that Bertie had betrayed the moral code they had agreed to live by. Russell explained coolly in his autobiography that, although he had tried to respect his wife's liberty according to his creed, he found his 'capacity for forgiveness, and what may be called Christian love, was not equal to the demands I was making on it and that persistence in helpless endeavour would do much harm to me, while not achieving the intended good to others. . . . I was blinded by theory.'[86]

Dora, according to their daughter, Kathleen Tait, 'did not want to see that his nobility was inadequate to the demands she made on it, that, like any ordinary man, he was hurt and angered and wounded in his family pride by the arrival of cuckoos in the nest'.[87] Their experiment in trying to take account of passion as a current in life, ebbing and flowing, unconstrained and undiminished by the straitjacket of legal marriage had demanded they live without jealousy. But 'calling jealousy deplorable had not freed them from it'. Both found it 'hard to admit that the ideal had been destroyed by the old-fashioned evils of jealousy and infidelity'.[88] Russell could not crush his emotional possessiveness sufficiently to enable his wife to live according to his theories, nor, like that other apostle of sexual freedom, H. G. Wells, tolerate the extent to which women took hold of the freedom they had both advocated as a woman's right. In his autobiography (1968) Russell confessed wanly: 'I do not know what I think now about the subject of marriage.'[89]

Alternatives

Advanced theories about reform of sexual and personal relations were almost exclusively directed to a heterosexual marriage ideal. Though male homosexuality had received the attention of sex psychologists and the legislature, lesbianism remained almost completely unexplored and publicly invisible. In the 1920s, it became a public issue for the first time.

It had surfaced during the war in the sensational Pemberton Billing trial. After the war anxieties about 'perverse' lesbian sexuality filtered into public attitudes. The word 'spinster' acquired a pejorative meaning, and the negative image of the 'masculine' woman, which had been readily deployed to condemn women's rights activists, acquired an overt adverse sexual connotation. It was particularly potent since the depletion of young men had left a significant surplus of single women in the population. In a transitional post-war stage when sex roles were being re-defined, to brand 'masculine' behaviour in women as lesbianism with its threat of social censure and ostracism, was one way to reinforce sexual norms of femininity and masculinity. At the same time social pressures against women emulating men were mounting, for instance in women's magazines. Already by 1920, *Women's Life* was heralding a 'return of the feminine type', to the 'deep, very deep sea of femininity from which her newly-acquired power can be more effectively wielded', while another proclaimed, 'Miss Fluffy Femininity carries off the prizes'.[90]

In 1921 an attempt to extend the law to criminalize lesbians along similar lines to the Labouchere Amendment relating to homosexuals was defeated after Parliament was persuaded it was in the public interest to draw a veil over the subject. Lord Malmesbury, who accepted without question that women commonly shared bedrooms 'either for reasons of fear or nervousness, and the desire for mutual protection', thought it advisable to preserve the innocence of womankind from such vile suggestions; it was 'a very great mischief', Lord Desart warned, 'to tell the whole world that there is such an offence, to bring it to the notice of women who have never heard of it, never thought of it, never dreamt of it'.[91] Lesbians escaped criminal punishment because it was thought better that the female population should remain in ignorance of lesbian sexuality.

With greater openness about sex, came some willingness to acknowledge and explore 'abnormal' sexuality. In private, there was an acceptance of lesbianism and of the variations of women's love for their own sex which included sexual love. But when this was made explicit publicly, it was liable to be prosecuted for obscenity. Writer Vita Sackville West was one of those who discovered her own sexual ambiguity but chose to keep it private. Though familiar with the irregularities of aristocratic marital sexual behaviour – her mother was the product of an illicit affair between her grandfather and a Spanish dancer and she had witnessed her father, Lord Sackville, having a series of affairs – lesbianism and homosexuality were a closed book. The discovery of her duality was a revelation. Vita was not consciously aware of it until after her marriage. The passionate attachments she formed with girlhood friends were nothing out of the ordinary as far as she and probably the rest of society was concerned. Nor, when she married Harold Nicholson, a young Foreign Office diplomat, in 1913, did she know of his homosexual affairs.

They were happily married until Harold contracted a venereal infection which enforced their physical separation. When her close friend Violet Keppel, daughter of the Prince of Wales' mistress came to stay with her in Harold's absence, Violet discovered and brought out Vita's sexual ambiguity. Violet seduced her; she 'had struck the secret of my duality,' Vita wrote. 'I made no attempt to conceal it from her or from myself . . . it was all conscious on her part, but on mine it was simply the drunkenness of liberation – the liberation of half my personality'. She described it as an awakening – 'I hadn't dreamt of such an art of love. . . . She appealed to my unawakened senses'.[92] When they took off to Cornwall, Vita 'felt like a person translated, or re-born'. Yet she 'never thought it would last; I thought of it as an adventure, an escapade'.[93] The turmoil of her relationship with Violet lasted two years. It was a turbulent and passionate affair, which did not end until Vita finally decided she could not leave Harold.

Secure in her companionable marriage with Harold, she then fell in love with a succession of women, including Virginia Woolf, who wrote *Orlando* as a semi-open tribute in recognition of the duality, the mixing of the masculine and feminine in a personality, which Virginia Woolf recognized in herself. Her affairs were always passionate, and always discreet. 'She was never in the least tempted to become publicly known as a lesbian,' wrote her biographer, Victoria Glendinning. 'Not only did she have a traditional care for her "reputation" – and for Harold's – but the secrecy of her affairs added, for her, the element of adventure that she needed.'[94]

The privacy Vita maintained was not shared by other lesbians, who consequently lived in the shadow of social scorn. Radclyffe Hall made no pretence of her sexual orientation. Known by her friends and family as 'John', she conducted an open affair with Una Troubridge, whom she had detached from her husband, Admiral Troubridge, in 1915. Her flamboyant style contributed to the public image of lesbians at the time. 'She used to attend many first nights wearing a black military cape, with a high stiff collar and a man's stick. Her grey hair was cut and parted like a man's. Her entry into the theatre always caused a minor sensation,' Beverly Nichols recalled, adding: 'Radclyffe Hall was a very virtuous woman. She was brave, honourable, and deeply religious, and had it not been for that unfortunate accident of nature she might have ended up as a bishop or a field marshal'.[95]

Radclyffe Hall's novel, *The Well of Loneliness* (1928), an open attempt to portray the lesbian predicament, was prosecuted in 1928 for obscenity. In her view the time was ripe for 'a novel that would be accessible to the general public who did not have access to technical treatises', which treated lesbianism as 'a fact of nature – a simple though at present tragic fact' with 'sincerity and truth' and without 'camouflage'.[96] It was not a view shared by her publisher, Collins, who turned it down. Nor, when Jonathan Cape published it, was it a view shared by James Douglas of the *Sunday Express*, an 'unctuously moral. . . . champion of the muscular Christian',[97] who attacked it as 'a seductive and insidious piece of special pleading designed to display perverted decadence as a martyrdom inflicted on these outcasts by a cruel society', with the result that 'this pestilience is devastating young souls'.[98] The book sold out immediately.

When the Home Secretary ('Jix') threatened prosecution, Cape withdrew the book, but a copy of the Continental edition was seized, and the book prosecuted. It was found to be obscene and banned by the magistrate who complained that all the characters were attractive, and – even more serious – 'certain acts are described in alluring terms'.[99]

Male homosexuality avoided becoming a issue of major public concern in the period between the wars. There were few prosecutions to interest the popular press and male homosexuals were relatively unmolested by the police, though prosecutions began to go up in the 1930s due to increased police activity. (In 1938 there were 134 cases of sodomy and bestiality, 822 cases of indecent assault and 316 cases of gross indecency between males).[100] A public discretion was observed about the private lives of homosexuals who were in the public eye.

At Oxford University after the war, it was claimed to be a positive fashion to be 'queer' as part of the rebellion of the Bright Young Things against the moral order. John Betjeman exclaimed in a radio programme: 'But *everybody* was queer at Oxford in those days!'[101] Goronwy Rees, also up at the time, described how homosexuality was 'among undergraduates and dons with pretentions to culture and a taste for the arts at once a fashion, a doctrine and a way of life'. It was 'very largely the particular form which the revolt of the young took at the universities at that time'.[102] Evelyn Waugh's diaries reveal both the prevalence and acceptance of homosexual practices among his acquaintants. Brian Howard, writer and homosexual playboy, put his view in a letter to his mother: 'People should be left alone, dear. As long as children are protected, it really doesn't matter going to bed with a lamp-post. Napoleon and Lenin thought so, Rome and Greece thought so, the modern psychologists think so – and so do I. Certainly it isn't a virtue to be a homosexual. As society is now constituted it is excessively inconvenient. But it certainly isn't a vice.'[103]

By the 1930s, doctors were beginning to recommend psychiatric treatment for homosexual offenders instead of criminal sanctions. The author Lytton Strachey, a homosexual and member of the Bloomsbury Group, observed one undergraduate who received early treatment from 'a doctor from Freiburg': 'After four months and an expenditure of £200, he found he could just bear the thought of going to bed with a woman . . . Several other wretched undergraduates have been through the same "treatment". They walk about haggard on the lawn, wondering whether they could bear the thought of a woman's private parts . . . I shall certainly be badly in need of "treatment". But . . . I would rather receive it at the hands of P. Ritchie (the Hon. Philip Ritchie) than of the German doctor'.[104]

1930s – New Models

By the 1930s new marital ideals were being shaped by influences other than a concern for mutually satisfying sex relations. Social and economic pressures were pushing women back into the home. Social policies reflected a concern to improve health and the quality of marital and family life, and these were supported through an expansion of professional and welfare services which buttressed the modern companionate partnership as the normal domestic ideal.

Cumulatively their effect was to add status to women's role as housewife. Marriage was portrayed as a career for women, houswifery was elevated to a craft, the management of family and home became a professional activity demanding scientific skills to which women, by their nature, were deemed particularly suited. Women's recently acknowledged positive sexuality was tethered to a model partnership, not equal but complementary. Her sexual responsibility was part of a repertoire of skills indispensable to marital happiness – and team efficiency.

Women's opportunities for independence were undermined, and their 'proper place' as the pivot of the household reinforced by economic pressures. As their employment prospects diminished, their status as a reserve labour force was confirmed. Immediately after the war they were cleared out of wartime factories to make way for returning soldiers (three quarters of a million women had been dismissed by 1920). Social pressures against women 'taking men's jobs' shortly materialized into a more general hostility to women working. Married women's wages were derisively termed 'pin money', their right to work put in question. The Government deterred women from entering the work force by operating insurance policies which discouraged them from claiming unemployment benefit, and as unemployment rose, married women's benefit was cut on the grounds they should be supported by their husbands. Although, with a surplus of women over men, many single women had to support themselves, even their work was often viewed with derision, and they attracted pity as spinsters unable to fulfil their 'proper role' as women. By 1931 female participation in the work force was lower than it had been in 1911.[105]

Professional opportunities also diminished, after an initial post war expansion. In teaching and the Civil Service, areas which women had entered in large numbers during the war, a marriage bar was introduced after the war, enforcing a stark choice between a career and marriage. Some teaching hospitals had stopped training women doctors during the 1920s.[106] Attention was drawn to the BBC, which in 1927 had encouraged women's employment and rise up the career ladder, but by 1931 was being attacked by the *Manchester Guardian* for 'alleged evidence of anti-feminism.' The number of women producers was declining; as they retired they were replaced by men. Only one important post was held by a woman (Head of Schools) and only two women were left on the Board of Governors. The BBC, so the *Manchester Guardian* claimed, was becoming 'an exceedingly masculine institution' – which it remained until well into the 1970s.[107] By the mid–1930s feminist protest on behalf of equality was muted, and seemed to a younger generation old-fashioned, as the main drive of the movement fragmented and its political focus turned to issues on the broader canvas of European politics – peace, and the threat of fascism.

Government social reform initiatives further reinforced women's confinement within the family. Housing legislation was one area. After the 1919 Town and Country Planning Act, with a massive expansion in both municipal and private housing and slum clearance programme, a pattern of vast suburban estates was established, with homes paid for on mortgate loans, inhabited by the middle and upper working classes. The houses on these estates were designed for the modern, small, nuclear family; they had airiness and space, electricity, hot water and separate bedrooms, but they isolated non-working housewives in the home.

Health and nutritional policies reflected increased concern about maternal and child welfare and in particular the conditions in which children were nurtured. Revelations during the war of the inferior health of many recruits and of the appalling conditions in which many working-class women experienced pregnancy and childbirth, had boosted the impetus to improve health and welfare facilities. Though the infant mortality rate dropped in the inter-war years the maternal mortality and morbidity rates remained high. At the same time child-care and household manuals by psychologists, psychiatrists and medical experts proliferated, in a drive to educate women to become more skilled and professional mothers as part of their duty not only to their family but to the nation's future well-being.

Added to this, the growth of consumer industries and the rapid expansion of the electrical goods and home appliances market, helped confirm the housewife as the centre of an increasingly efficient household – not a domestic drudge but a professional manager with all the benefits which modern science could invent at her disposal. With the shortage of domestic servants (working class women after the war refused in large numbers to return to domestic service) housewives had to take responsibility themselves, further pinning them to the home.

This new image of the housewife was supported through the vastly expanded market in women's magazines. Sixty new titles were launched between 1920 and 1945.[108] Mainly aimed at the middle and upper working class they were influential agents for transmitting the new domestic ideal. *Woman's Own* was founded in 1932, *Woman's Illustrated* in 1936 and *Woman* in 1937. *Woman* was selling 3/4 million by 1939, the year that *Housewife* was launched. The focus on domesticity was unequivocal. *Women's Own* was launched as the new weekly 'for the modern young wife who loves the home . . . the home paper that makes every girl worth her salt want to be the best housewife ever . . . and then some.'[110] 'Happy and lucky is the man whose wife is houseproud . . . who likes to do things well, to make him pround of her and her children,' declared *Housewife*.[109]

Implicit in the pages was the message that only by proving her worth as the manager of the home would she remain attractive to her husband. The magazines dealt with sex in marriage, usually in the agony columns. Many stressed the importance of sexual fulfilment for both partners in line with current thinking in the more progressive sex manuals. But there was a different emphasis. Women were under obligation to be sexually proficient as another duty in the repertoire of the efficient housewife and mother. If a wife did not devote herself wholeheartedly and whole-time to the task of looking after her husband's welfare and sexual well-being, she stood little chance of keeping his love.

Feminists brought up on ideals of women's dignity and equality in personal relationships were dismayed. Vera Brittain spotted one article 'Keeping House for Him', where the 'career of the homemaker' was held up as 'the finest in the world'. Every wife, it declared 'is ambitious for her husband, and, when you come to think of it, a lot depends on her. She has to do with his smart appearance and if she is a cheerful, happy little woman as well as a careful manager, he will be able to go to work free of all home worries'. Vera Brittain was appalled at this subordinated new model wife, who lived life at second hand, took responsibility for the smartness and punctuality of her husband, shielding him from his own difficulties – in short playing 'the part of a first-class hypocrite' in order to solicit his love. It was she thought 'an employer and employee relation of the worst type'.[111]

Sex Law: i) Abortion

Concern to improve standards of health and the quality of marital life also figured in campaigns to liberalize the laws on abortion and divorce. In both areas, reformers argued, the laws were widely flouted, in danger of falling into disrepute, out of tune with the current standards and humane values, and promoted unnecessary hardship and suffering.

The abortion controversy was prompted by official concern about the role of criminal abortion in the persistence of disturbingly high maternal mortality rates, despite improvements in infant mortality and modern improvements in childbirth techniques. This link, made by the Ministry of Health in 1930,[112] was strengthened as more shocking evidence of the extent of illegal abortion accumulated. Marie Stopes was fully aware of the scale of demand; in 1932 she published in a letter to *The Times* the 'staggering facts' that 'in three months I have had as many as twenty thousand requests for criminal abortion from women who did not apparently even *know* it was criminal'.

Other women recalled how common abortion was. One from Preston spoke of the various methods used, including slippery elm bark – 'They pushed that up! I don't know what it did. They pushed needles up! Take washing-soda, quinine, all that sort of thing. But life isn't worth living if you are going to do that sort of thing.'[32] Mrs Hesketh's mother had nine children and sent her daughter to the chemist for potions – 'I remember that one of them was quinine . . . it must have been hell'. Mrs Dickinson 'tried to stop one or two, I took my salts (Epsom salts). . . . If you were weak and you hadn't had good food when you were young, it would work. There were one or two other things, hot baths and things like that . . . Everybody tried.'[33]

Professor Beckwith Whitehouse of the BMA concluded from the incidence of abortion among 3000 hospitals and private patients that there was a ratio of one abortion to every 4.7 births. Dr Harry Roberts surmised, in the *New Statesman and Nation* in

1932, that not less than 25 per-cent of all women in the country had at some time in their lives procured or attempted to procure an abortion.[113]

Pressure for law reform came from two main directions, the medical profession and women's organizations, with support from sections of the judiciary dealing with abortion cases who began publicly to express dissatisfaction with the law. The doctors' main concern was to clarify a vague and unsatisfactory law which rendered them vulnerable to prosecution. Abortion had been illegal since the 1861 Offences Against the Person Act, although doctors had performed it in extreme circumstances to save the life of the mother. The 1929 Infant Life Preservation Act had attempted to clarify their position but had not, in the view of the British Medical Association Committee which examined the law's operation, gone far enough. In 1936 the BMA put its weight behind support for law reform to clarify their legal position.

The main reforming pressure group, the Abortion Law Reform Association set up in 1936, was strongly influenced by its feminist leadership. Its primary aim was to bring those who resorted to abortion within the scope of proper medical care by statutory means. A second goal was to make abortion, like contraception, a woman's right, available to all women regardless of income, for in practice those who could afford it could obtain abortions, while those who could not resorted to back street and self-abortion, often with fatal consequences.

Until then, abortion had not been included in the feminist agenda, mainly for tactical reasons. Though many birth controllers had supported the legalisation of abortion, it was deemed unwise to make it an early campaign objective. One of Abortion Law Reform Association's founding members, Stella Browne, had long advocated legalised abortion on the radical feminist grounds that women had a right to control their own bodies. Abortion, like contraception, she argued 'should be available for any woman, without insolent inquisition, nor ruinous financial charges, not tangles of red tape. For our bodies are our own'.[114] There were more pragmatic arguments. Janet Chance, another founder, had run a Sex Education Clinic where she found evidence of considerably more abortions and attempted abortions than anyone cared to publicly admit. In one session with 40 women present, a secret

ballot revealed that of 21 women who had had at least one pregnancy, 16 had at some time taken pills or drugs or in some way
attempted abortion.[115] She was in no doubt that despair drove
women to the extreme measures they adopted, including external
violence, blows, kicks, violent abdominal massage, jumping from
a height, drug and self inflicted internal injuries from hair pins,
knitting needles and skewers.

Under pressure from ALRA and the BMA, the Government set
up the Birkett Committee to examine abortion. While it was
sitting, Aleck Bourne, consultant obstetrician at St Mary's Hospital, who was a member of the BMA's Abortion Committee and
ALRA's Medico Legal Committee, forced a judgment in 1938
which was to have considerable impact on the state of the law. A
fourteen year old schoolgirl who had been assaulted and raped by
a group of guardsmen in Wellington Barracks, was referred to him
for an abortion by Dr Joan Malleson, who ran the birth control
clinic in Ealing. Aleck Bourne was no radical: he observed her for
eight days to ascertain 'there was nothing of the cold indifference
of the prostitute in her' before agreeing to go ahead with the
termination. His declared aim was to get a ruling in court on the
legal status of abortion in this case. He took no fee, informed the
police of his intention to carry out an illegal operation and asked
them to 'take action'. They did, and he was charged with a criminal
offence.

Bourne was acquitted. The judgment was a landmark. It established that consideration of the physical and mental health of the
mother could be taken into account when abortion was performed
by a qualified doctor in consultation with his colleagues. This
position was endorsed in the Birkett Committee's recommendations a year later. The Birkett Report confirmed that the prevalence
of abortion was a threat to the nation's health when an estimated
110,000–150,000 abortions, 40 per cent of them criminally
induced, were carried out each year (this was widely thought to
be an under-estimate). 411 women had died in 1937 and 605 in
1938 as a result of abortion of all kinds. While not wishing to do
anything which would tend to lower the 'traditional and accepted
standards of sexual morality in this country', they recommended
the law be liberalized and clarified to make abortion legal if the
mother's pregnancy was likely 'to endanger her life or seriously

impair her health'.[116] No action was taken on these radical proposals as the war intervened.

Sex Law: ii) Divorce

Proposals for reform of the divorce laws to bring them into line with contemporary beliefs and practices and diminish the extent of deception surrounding divorce procedure also gained support. As divorce increased, so did dissatisfaction with the contradictions and sheer hypocrisy in the law. The number of divorces had shot up immediately after the war, and continued to rise steadily – from 3,280 divorces between 1911–1915 to 20,100 between 1931–1935.[117] As it was only necessary to prove adultery, the law was systematically flouted by those wishing to end their marriage, who were pushed into committing either adultery, or perjury to say they had, or who merely colluded in a single act of adultery, often in an hotel with a hired partner witnessed by a chambermaid. It was a system which reformers, led by Independent MP A. P. Herbert and supported by the Divorce Law Reform Union, believed was scandalous, was bringing the law into disrepute, and, far from upholding morality, was conducive to immorality. The present restrictions on divorce, it was argued, led to a great deal of unnecessary human misery which was offensive to any humane principles. Suffering would be considerably reduced if the 'empty husk' of a loveless and failed marriage were allowed to be shed in a decent fashion. And the current laws were also unjust since they discriminated between the rich and the poor, who could rarely afford the costs.

The result of A. P. Herbert's two year campaign was a Bill, introduced in Parliament in 1937 to extend the grounds of divorce to include cruelty, desertion for more than three years, and insanity. This was hardly more than had been recommended by the Gorell Commission back in 1912. Then the united opposition of the Churches had defeated the proposals. This time the Church of England opposition was muted. Times and values had changed and with it the Church's power to dictate morality in the increasingly secular society. With clear support for the Bill in Parliament, the Archbishop of Canterbury acknowledged the Church's dilemma: 'I came to the conclusion that it is no longer possible to impose the full Christian standard by law on a largely non-Christian population. . . . I could not as a citizen vote against the Bill, but I could not bring myself as a churchman to vote for it; and I announced I would not vote.'[118] The Act was passed with the overwhelming majority. Though it did not alter the basis for divorce, which remained the proof of a matrimonial offence, by broadening the grounds it diminished the State's powers to enforce the Christian standard, and it enlarged the area of individual moral choice. By then, with changed attitudes to marriage, there was widespread agreeement that this reform had strengthened rather than weakened the marriage bond.

The reform, however, did little to reduce the social stigma attached to divorce. Whatever liberal changes in attitude it might have reflected, these were not enough to enable the new King to marry the woman he loved – the twice divorced American Mrs Wallis Simpson. Edward VIII succeeded George V, who had exalted the monarchy 'into a kind of palladium of the domestic virtues'. The Government, under Stanley Baldwin was determined the monarchy should remain that way, and took the position that they were both the guardians of public morality and custodians of the institution of monarchy.

The Prince of Wales, over 40 in 1936, was known in private circles to have had a succession of affairs with married women before he met Mrs Simpson in late 1930. By the time he became King in 1936 his whole emotional, and increasingly his private social life was focused on her. Although gossip about them circulated in the foreign press, the British press published nothing. At the King's request, Lord Beaverbrook had engineered an agreement through the Newspaper Proprietors Association to keep the affair out of the papers.

Alarm spread in the Government as it became clear that Edward VIII intended to hold on tenaciously to his relationship with Mrs Simpson. A full blown constitutional crisis developed when the question of marriage was raised. To Baldwin and most of the Government, the idea that the King could marry a twice divorced woman was out of the question. She was unfit to be Queen. For the King to believe otherwise was a sign of a fatal flaw in his character and of a failure to distinguish between his private life and his public position. This confirmed growing doubts about his suitability to fulfil the role of monarch. Changing public standards did not apply to him, for as Baldwin countered to one of the King's supporters, though 'the ideal of morality and duty and self-sacrifice and decency certainly *has* gone down', the 'ideal of Kingship has gone *up* – in fact, never in history has it stood so high as now'. Divorce was no part of this ideal.[119]

When Baldwin and the Government dictated the limits of public tolerance and refused to sanction the marriage on any terms, the King was left with no choice but to abdicate. The country first knew of the crisis when the Press broke their silence on December 7th. The King abdicated on December 11th. To some, particularly the Americans, the affair seemed to be the Love Story of the Century; in Britain it was construed as a failure of character in the King, who was best got rid of: a newspaper cartoon showed a workman throwing down his tools, saying to his mate 'How can I do my work without the help and support of the woman I love?'[120] With the accession of George VI the emphasis 'went back to the family and to the old fashioned but still popular domestic virtues'.[121]

In the two decades since the First World War there had been significant changes in the control of sexual morals. Birth control which had been unmentionable in public became a repectable part of responsible family planning, as it was called in 1939. Its use spread steadily. Sexual repression was interpreted as the source of profound psychological disorders, which encouraged a new view of the meaning of sex in marriage. The sexual fulfilment of both partners was placed at the centre of a new ideal of marital partnership. Though the proper place for sex was marriage, some exploration of the legitimacy of extra-marital relations had been made. 'Abnormal' sex relations, continued to be outlawed in public, but a wider understanding of sexual variety made for tolerance in private. The pre-war ideal of the submissive protected and dependent wife was superceded by an ideal of women out in the world, with a degree of independence, and of a marriage of equality and mutual respect – until housework, house management and keeping a husband sexually happy was elevated into a profession which put women back in the home, servicing it efficiently.

Changes in State control reflected the increased influence of liberal and humanist beliefs. Law reforms diminished some inequalities between men and women and sanctioned secular deviations from orthodox Christian beliefs on morality. The church began to reconcile itself to new developments in science, such as the technology of birth control, and to changed views on the Christian teaching on sex, marriage and divorce. In an increasingly secular society where the hold of religion as the sole moral authority was weakening, a divided Church of England began to make compromises appropriate to changing conditions. The outbreak of the Second World War would consolidate those trends.

Five

Second World War

Uncertainties and Opportunities

Few escaped the impact of total war when the country mobilized all its resources to fight from 1939–1945. The war entered the fabric of everyone's lives, disrupted the continuity of family life and offered new opportunities, experiences and choices to individuals released from the normal sanctions on sexual behaviour. Expectations of courtship as well as the certainties of marriage and family life were tested under extreme conditions.

The first dislocation came when families were split up, often for very long periods. Men were called up first. By mid-1940 nearly 2,250,000 men – almost 15 per-cent of the male working population – had been enlisted in the Armed Forces, rising to a third – 4,500,000 men – by June 1944. Many were away for long periods. At least 250,000 men had served overseas for a continuous period of five years or more by the end of 1945. At the peak of the war effort, around 2,500,000 husbands were living away from their wives and families.[1]

Evacuation severed family relations on a vast scale. 827,000 schoolchildren with their teachers and helpers, 524,000 children under school age with their mothers, and 12,000 expectant mothers were moved out of major cities. 'It is an exodus bigger than that of Moses,' declared Walter Elliott, Minister of Health. 'It is the movement of ten armies, each of which is as big as the whole Expeditionary Force.'[2] By January 1940, when the expected devastation from the Luftwaffe did not materialize, three out of four evacuees had drifted back home, only to be uprooted again later that year when the Blitz started. With the threat of invasion after

99

Dunkirk, a further round of evacuations from the east coast and the major cities added to the disruption. These movements established a pattern of accommodation shortage and overcrowding in the receiving areas which was to last for the rest of the war.

Mobilization for industrial war production further fractured domestic life. War factories were relocated from cities to less vulnerable areas. Workers who were directed around the country stayed in hostels or billets, since plans to build accommodation for wives and families of munition workers foundered for lack of building labour and materials.[3] As a result of this redistribution London was left in mid-1943 with only 76 per-cent of its pre-war population (the East End was reduced by a half), Liverpool with 80 per-cent and Southampton with 67 per-cent. Small towns and the outlying areas of large cities where new war industries were set up or expanded found themselves inundated by strangers. Reading's population increased by a seventh. Oxford, which housed several government and civil service departments as well as its war industries, expanded its population by 27,000 and was, in 1940, 'swarming with disoriented hordes, the newly-acquired wartime population composed of evacuees, war workers, refugees, passing visitors and resident foreigners'.[4]

The mobilization and conscription of women further affected family relationships, as the majority of the female population was gradually absorbed into war work. Initially the Government relied on women volunteering for Forces, factory or civil defence work, but in 1941, when the labour shortage became acute, they introduced measures under which all women aged 16–49, with the exception of women with children under 14 and those already doing essential war work, were compelled to register, and could be 'directed' to essential war work. This was followed by the call-up in December 1941 of all women aged 20–30 who were given a choice of war work. By early 1942, with continuing manpower shortages in the Services, all remaining young women in non-essential jobs were put into uniform. After 1943, even 'grannies' (aged 46–50) had to register for war work – the only unpopular call-up in the war.

By 1943 women made up 57 per-cent of the total workforce. Nine single women out of 10, and 80 per-cent of married women aged 18–40 were in the Services, or working in industry or civil defence.[5] Women took over in almost all areas of industry and services. The pre-war movement of women into engineering, light metal and electrical industries was accelerated, and, despite some initial resistance among employers and trade unions to women taking over skilled work, they eventually replaced men in all essential industries – engineering, vehicle building, shipbuilding and aircraft production, in chemical and explosives, on the railways, buses and in the civil service. In almost all jobs women were paid less than – often as little as half – the rates paid to the men they replaced.

The sexual implications of women working alongside, or replacing, men caused some concern. It was expressed as a disguised form of the belief that the 'little woman' was not capable of doing the job. Herbert Morrison felt obliged to promise women fire-watchers – who could deal daily with incendiary bombs – that they would not have to serve in buildings infested with rats and mice. Alvar Lidell, BBC newscaster, claimed in 1943 there was no likelihood of a woman being appointed to his job because 'She might have to read bad news.'[6] It was not until 1941 that initial doubts about women's ability to remain 'tense and cool' when facing the same dangers as men on anti-aircraft batteries were finally dispelled. Auxiliary Territorial Service women had been put only with new male recruits to begin with – 'the point being that men who had known no other army life would not find the atmosphere of a mixed battery so hysterically unorthodox'.[7]

The sheer unfamiliarity of women working alongside men excited moral disapproval. Zelma Katin, who worked on the Sheffield trams, was aware that to many people, women in uniform working with men 'at once suggests immorality. . . . Numbers of passengers believe that the last act of a conductress and her driver or motorman each night before going home is the exercise of sexual intercourse'.[8] New female recruits on the shop floor met mixed reactions, including patronizing prejudice. It cannot have helped the first woman recruit to an armaments factory in 1941 that, as one man said, 'We looked at her, nine of us, for days, as though we had never seen a woman before. We watched the dainty way she picked up a file, with red-enamelled fingertip extended as though she were holding a cup of tea. We watched the way she brushed the filings off her overalls after every few strokes, the awkward way she opened and closed her vise, her concern for the cleanliness of her hands, her delicate, unhandy way with a hammer. . . . Behind her back we had great fun mimicking her; to her face we treated her with an almost desperate punctilio.'[9]

Single 'mobile' women were the first to be 'directed' around the country to essential war industries. Separated from their families and uprooted from familiar surroundings they encountered a wholly new life. From 1943, convoys of young women from the North of England, Scotland and Wales were moved to industries in the Midlands and South to be accommodated in lodgings or billets or in huge Ministry of Supply hostels which housed as many as 1000 war workers, some built together in groups of four or five. They not only led a more independent life, but they were also offered new opportunities. Large numbers of women were trained in skilled jobs which commanded higher wages than their pre-war occupations. Almost one million maids, nannies and dailies, for instance, were directed to war work where they could earn up to three times their previous wages.

The effects of mobility, of women in large numbers working outside the home, and the sometimes long-term separation of young men and women from their families added to the emotional and psychological tensions of war. They interrupted normal patterns of courtship and contributed to additional strains on marriage and family relationships.

A sudden increase in the number of marriages in the first year of war indicated one attempt to impose stability in increasingly uncertain circumstances. 1940 was a boom year. The marriage rate went up to 22.1 per thousand compared with 17.2 per thousand in 1938,[10] then stabilized by 1943 at a slightly higher rate than before the war. The pre-war trend towards young marriages continued into the war. Nearly three war brides out of ten were under 21. More couples cast aside considerations of long term financial security in favour of the immediate solace of marriage, often just before separation. A Camden Town jeweller sold thirty wedding rings in the first week of war where his normal sale would have been three or four.[11] One young RAF airman pointed out to Mass Observation in March 1940 that out of his class of airmen, four had married the previous December, three of whom had not even been engaged when war broke out.[12]

At a time when the sanctions on pre-marital sex were strong, a hasty marriage may also have been a response to what some men described as an upsurge of erotic impulse in the early excitement of war – a 'quickening of the tempo of the sex life of young people' leading to 'hurried marriage, friends getting suddenly engaged, boys and girls trying desperately for a good time on the argument that "next week may be too late".'[13] A married man of thirty-three described to Mass Observation how he 'distinctly experienced a heightened sexual stimulation' around the time of the outbreak of war, when, he reflected, his 'whole personality, acting under the influence of the supposed danger at hand, was more or less keyed up to expect and to meet this danger. . . . the primitive instincts thus aroused of self preservation and fear seem to touch off the other instincts also, such as sex, so that the individual experiences a general heightening of the whole personality which is almost pleasurable.'[14]

Weddings were often followed by almost immediate separation. The casualty rate among hastily contracted marriages was high. One Welfare Officer, Barbara Cartland, recalled a young woman from the Womens Auxiliary Air Force referred to her because she wanted a divorce after six months of marriage. She had lived with her husband for only a week before he was posted overseas, and wanted a divorce because she 'was disappointed. It wasn't what I expected.' Barbara Cartland gave her a two hour talk, pointing out that marriage had to be worked at, that you learnt from experience and, to the astonishment of the WAAF, that fulfilment in physical love did not come immediately, but only after practice; the first few weeks of marriage were often disappointing. The young woman agreed to give the marriage another chance, and compassionate leave was arranged for both partners.[15] Many other marriages contracted under the spell of passion but starved of opportunity for intimacy, or where the couples found they hardly knew each other, broke down.

Overcrowding – a permanent feature of the war due to acute housing shortage – was a continuing source of domestic tension, especially for young couples brought up in the 1930s to associate marriage with a home of their own. Many landed up with in-laws, which led to the awkwardness and discomfort revealed in one survey. 'There's no privacy,' complained Mrs J, 'there's always an audience. You have to restrain yourselves'. Mr L, living with in-laws, never felt at home. They had only their bedroom to retire to and 'everyone knows what is going on . . . I'm self-conscious,' he said.[16] It was not just the lack of intimacy: 'Having to live in a small space hemmed in by other people is another cause of things going wrong in the home,' one London woman pointed out. 'It is not only that working, housework and washing have to be done under uncomfortable conditions, but the atmosphere gets overcharged, restless, chaotic.'[17]

The strains on women of combining war work and keeping up a household began to tell after the first couple of years. The number of married women and widows in employment increased threefold, from 1 million before the war to 3 million in mid-1943. Many welcomed the return to work for the money and the company and the sense of their own worth it provided: 'The change of spending her days outside her own home, of making fresh contacts and seeing people, is actually welcomed by such women with something approaching an ecstasy with neither strain nor fatigue can spoil,' Mass Observation commented.[18] For others there was no choice. In the early years many wives of Service men said that the separation allowance was so low they were forced to go out to work to support the family.

As production schedules got tighter, and shift hours increased, the difficulties of fitting in running a home, with long travelling hours, queues and shortages and sheer tiredness, began to take its toll on women and on family relationships. Mass Observation warned of the dangers in 1942: 'While winning the war is the only big consideration . . . if the bonds of family and continuity are weakened beyond a certain point, the morale, unity and war effort of the country is weakened.'[19] In one family fully stretched by war work, the husband asked to start work at 8 a.m. instead of 7 a.m. because: 'He could not arrive any earlier since his wife had to be at another factory at seven, and he had to take their child to its grandmother who did not come back from her night shift until seven o'clock.'[20]

Working outside home could open up new opportunities – with some disturbing effects. Though her husband was working in a civilian occupation, Hetty Fowler found that when she went to work on the Ambulance Service in London their shifts never coincided and they rarely met. She described the sense of release which came with work where 'we were sort of thrown together in war and we all thought we hadn't much longer to live, so why not get what we can out of life. . . . I was just an ordinary wife and mother. But when you come out of your house and get among people, you're dancing with men, he thinks you're rather nice and you think well perhaps I am, but nobody's told me for years and you rather like it, you see, and you begin to see in yourself a different person – whereas you were just humdrum you began to try to make yourself look nice again. . . . It was nice that someone thought you were attractive. So of course when you got back with your husband he didn't think I was any more attractive, we were just the same – and it's not easy to take. But you can't say to him "I know a man who thinks I'm nice". You can't say that, can you, to your husband? Very strange, very difficult.'[21]

When husbands were away for long periods, working women developed a new independence and a new authority in the family, as well as an ability to cope on their own which had previously never been tested. Many women could earn better wages than before the war, and grew used to their financial independence. One group, interviewed by a welfare officer, expressed anxieties that this independence might alter the power within the relationship when their husbands returned. One woman who had got used to two wages thought: 'Things are not going to be so easy after the war and I, for one, am going to miss my "own money".'[22] Another, whose husband kept a shop and who, before the war, never 'interfered' with the business, had managed the shop, house, garden and been a Savings Collector. 'I only hope I'll have the sense to let him take over the shop again,' she reflected.[23]

For Service wives, separation and loneliness became a heavy burden. Even when men were stationed in this country, opportunities for leave were limited. On RAF stations during training and operations, though some pilots could live out, for others it was forbidden. 'This depends on the Commanding Officer,' wrote Richard Hillary, 'some believing the sudden change from night-bombing attacks over Berlin to all the comforts of home to be a psychological error, others believing it to be beneficial. In most squadrons the pilots live on the station, going home only on leave. It is always possible to apply for compassionate leave in the event of serious domestic trouble, and this is nearly always granted, though the 'passionate leave' applied for by some squadrons doesn't receive quite the same sympathy.'[24] Some wives of air crews were actively discouraged from living locally 'as it was considered their presence was far too much of an emotional strain on their husbands'.[25]

In their husbands' absence, wives who might never have thought of going out alone began to socialize with friends. The sight of unaccompanied women drinking together in pubs was one of the most striking changes in manners during the war. Dances improvised in halls up and down the country and organized by the Services – of British and Allied troops – were the most popular form of entertainment, along with cinemas which attracted huge audiences each week.

The period of greatest strain seemed to be the third year of war. A London probation officer found that 'many excellent young mothers have been unable to stand the loneliness at home, particularly when their husbands are abroad, with not even spasmodic leave to break the monotony'. Separation particularly affected hasty war marriages 'sometimes between comparative strangers, with a few days or weeks of married life, [which] have left both parties with little sense of responsibility or obligation towards one another.'[26] One welfare officer looked sympathetically on their loneliness, remembering 'a very young woman whose husband was abroad saying to me passionately, "I love my babies, but they go to sleep at six o'clock and I have no-one to speak to until the next morning. Sometimes I think I shall go mad, I'm so lonely".' She understood the women going out to dances, and the possibility of starting affairs. 'It is very easy to say what a woman should do or not do when she hasn't seen her husband for four years . . . I was often sorry for the "bad" women. They were young, their husbands were not fluent letter-writers – they started by not meaning any harm, just desiring a little change from the monotony of looking after their children, queuing for food and cleaning the house with no man to appreciate them or their cooking. . . . So often the new man was just an outlet for the pent-up feelings, the anxiety and misery the woman had been feeling about her husband.' She recalled one woman of twenty-two, pregnant by another man, who 'said to me through her tears: "I love my husband – I do really. You won't believe me, no-one will, but I've never stopped loving him. It wasn't me who did this to him – it was some fiend which got hold of me. Oh, I can't explain. I only want to die because I've let him down." '27

A twenty-four-year-old Manchester mother, whose husband was overseas, attributed her affair with an American serviceman to a sense of fear and the transience of everything around her: 'We lived in a world of uncertainty, wondering if we were going to survive from day to day. My husband was away in the RAF as an air gunner, and I'd conditioned myself to the fact that his lifespan was also limited and that our short, happy married life together was over. I lived in a vacuum of loneliness and fright as service in the Army, Navy, and Air Force claimed five of our personal friends whom I mourned as if they were my own family. When 1942 came in with the hit-and-run raids, I began to despair that the war was ever going to end.' In this frame of mind she met the American, Rick, at a dance, and formed a friendship. He brought extra food which she shared with her neighbours and friends – 'If they even wondered where it all came from, they tactfully never asked.' Her husband, whom she told about Rick, accepted it: 'He was delighted that I'd found someone to give me a break and that Rick seemed a really decent chap. So with my mind free of guilt, I began to come alive again . . . With Rick, I knew it was love, but for me it was attraction and the need to hold on to someone. So it happened that we finally made love.

'There was nothing cheap about our affair, and if Rick had my body, my heart was with my husband and somehow I didn't feel that I was doing anything wrong. Rick being a single man had fallen in love with a happily married woman, but he knew it was hopeless as far as I was concerned. I loved my husband too much to consider leaving him. Yet Rick and I were together for two years during the final stages of the war, until the evening when he was silent and withdrawn after he received orders to leave for Rome. We said our goodbyes at the garden gate on 31 May 1945. . . . Then my husband returned home and we tried to resume our old way of life.' They succeeded, and after the war her husband helped her to visit Rick in New York. Sailing back, she realized, 'My war romance had reached its finale.'28

The finale was different for the young Quintin Hogg, later Lord

Hailsham, when he returned home unheralded from abroad to discover his wife, Natalie, having an affair with a young French officer. She asked immediately for a divorce, which he reluctantly agreed to. It was a painful homecoming and a rude shock to his deep Christian belief in sacramental marriage as a lifelong contract of mutual fidelity. His experience disposed him towards a more tolerant view of marriage breakdown – difficult though this was to reconcile with the explicit teaching of the gospels – when he later had power to influence the direction of legal reform, although it led him to repudiate the notion that marriages break down because of faults on both side; he rarely had difficulty deciding where fault lay.[29]

For men serving overseas, wives' fidelity was a constant source of anxiety. Several men in one survey complained about their wives going out dancing when they were away. Mr L 'is very much against this as he knows married girls are fair game for other men, who make them drunk and "go ahead". He can't help worrying about it, especially as marital infidelity is one of the chief topics of Army conversation.'[30] When letter writing was the only contact between spouses, there was ample opportunity for misunderstanding and suspicions to flourish. The Army recognized this by stressing the importance of regular mail services in all theatres of war for, wrote a military psychiatrist in the Middle East, 'delay, irregularities or non-arrival of mail were potent causes of anxiety and depression even in the most stable personalities'.[31] Anxiety could spread like an epidemic. Mary Robertson, a nurse serving in Burma and Assam from summer 1944 recalled bringing in the mail one day: 'What excitement! They were all so thrilled. I could hardly wait myself to get back and hear their news. When I did return, it was to find a changed ward. The men just slouched about, or lay on their beds without speaking. I couldn't understand what had happened. . . . At last it came out. One of the men had heard from his wife that she wanted a divorce. Another wife wrote saying that she had a baby of a year old. The thoughtless cruelty of it. It seemed so unbelievably selfish. Why couldn't they have let their men come home first, for now all the others were wondering what reception they would get when they got home. It took a long time to get over it.'[32]

One of the shocks women's infidelity delivered was to the still widespread belief, revealed in one survey, that sex was something in which men indulged but women tolerated, with little value put on women's sexual satisfaction. 'A puritanical attitude was widespread. Sex is duty, and women are not trained to expect any particular pleasure,' concluded Slater and Woodside in their survey of 200 (mostly working-class) hospitalized soldiers aged 22 to 47 and their wives. Women praised men who were 'not too lustful', who 'wouldn't trouble you at all'. In both men and women they found 'a large proportion . . . dominated by the notion that for a woman to feel lustful would be an unseemly thing'. They also noted: 'A pattern of male dominance could be seen, and to some extent a general feeling of possessiveness and of "rights", not always agreed to. . . . Responsiveness in their wives was hardly expected, and there was some suggestion that where the wife was more sensually disposed than her husband, her "hot nature" was disapproved, and even feared.'[33]

In Birmingham the percentage of illegitimately conceived children born to married women tripled between 1940 and 1945. Almost one third of all illegitimate children in the last two years of war were born to married women. Over half the 520 mothers reported in 1945 had husbands serving in the Forces; the remainder were divorced, widowed or living apart from their husbands.[34] Since married women had to get their husband's consent for adoption, the illegitimacy was difficult to conceal. Many husbands accepted the cuckoos in their nest but for others it was a contributory, if not the main reason for divorce. The divorce rate soared. More men than women were petitioning for divorce by the end of the war. In 1938, just under 10,000 petitions were filed, of which 46 per-cent were by husbands. In 1945, 25,000 petitions were filed, 58 per-cent by husbands, and by 1947, of 47,000 petitions, 61 per-cent were filed by husbands. The percentage filed on grounds of adultery rose from 50 per-cent in 1938 to 70 per-cent in 1945.[35]

One reason for the increase in divorce was that the Forces actively assisted in dealing with matrimonial difficulties, and initiated various measures to enable easier access to divorce procedure. The Forces dealt with domestic difficulties on an ad hoc basis to begin with, but with the establishment and expansion of welfare services, they became more organized as the scale of the problem became apparent. The main priority was the morale of the fighting troops. 'One of the gravest morale problems,' declared a War Office history, 'was created by "the anxious soldier", the man who had been alarmed by reports from home about his matrimonial affairs or the well-being of his children. . . . Men with these anxieties unresolved would never make good soldiers.'[36] Anxiety and worry about home affairs was one of the principal causes of neurosis and absence without leave, according to the Officer's Handbook on *The Soldier's Welfare*.[37] The book encouraged officers to establish a confidante relationship their men, and provided points of guidance on letter writing – the principal and often only bond between soldiers and wives: 'Letter writing is not an easy habit with many men nor with their wives, nor are they very skilled in its practice. Some forget to write . . . others express themselves unfortunately, and so arouse unfounded jealousies and suspicions.'[38]

Compassionate leave was open to men with difficulties from the beginning, but as applications escalated, new procedures were adopted. By 1945 there were 419,000 Army applications compared with 16,000 in 1941. To decide whether it was warranted, an investigation into the soldiers' family circumstances was carried out chiefly by the Soldiers, Sailors and Airmen's Families Association with welfare officers, but also the local police, who were frequently asked 'to verify certain details submitted or to obtain other additional evidence'. Their involvement in soldiers' private lives was justified 'in view of the gravity of the manpower situation'. Funded initially through the Adjutant General's Department, the Welfare Service obtained the official backing of the Treasury with a grant-in-aid of £250,000 to deal with 'compassionate applications and other enquiries which might seriously reflect upon the morale of the troops'.[39]

The State extended its responsibility for Servicemen's domestic and matrimonial affairs when an Army Legal Aid Scheme was set up jointly by the Army and the RAF in July 1942 to assist soldiers, on the principal that 'the State owed an obligation to the serving soldier, whose problem had often arisen because he had been taken away from his home by the State'.[40] Under the scheme the basis of Poor Person's Certificate for legal aid was changed from a means test to a system where anyone below the rank of sergeant major could apply. Further amendments facilitated divorce: the Law Society established a Services Divorce Department to deal with cases initiated under the Scheme and there was a steady and increasing flow of cases through the Command Legal Aid Sections. Making legal aid and divorce more accessible to those who could not previously afford it led to an immediate rise in divorce applications. Of 175,000 legal aid cases dealt with up to the end of 1945, 140,000 were matrimonial cases, of which 94,000 were divorce applications. Just under 50,000 RAF and Army divorce cases were carried to their conclusion.[41]

The Forces welfare services also set up machinery for reconciliation, working with local welfare officers in cases of divorce, separation and requests for stoppage of family allowances. The investigating facilities of the Soldiers' Sailors' and Airmen's Families Association (S.S.A.F.A) were used though not, it was stressed, for making 'what are commonly called "discreet inquiries" ' leading to divorce proceedings, which were deemed not the War Office's responsibility.[42] Soldiers were not able to request that their wives' family allowances be suspended without going through this investigation and reconciliation procedure. On the other hand, the Army had powers to intervene in the moral affairs of soldiers' wives. Wives were penalized for 'serious misbehaviour amounting to public scandal' by having their family allowance discontinued 'whether or not the husband condones her conduct and even although he is willing to continue to make his qualifying allotment'.[43]

By the end of the war, the State, through its armed services, had taken on unprecedented responsibility for the matrimonial condition of a vast section of the population and intervened actively with reconciliation. Ironically, this involvement facilitated a massive increase in divorce by making it accessible to those who might not previously have been able to afford it. Though the war was undoubtedly a catalyst in the breakdown of many marriages, it must also have assisted in exposing already fractured marriages in which previously there had been no recourse to law.

Moral (And Not So Moral) Forces

For married and unmarried alike, the upheavals, separations and dislocation of war opened up new opportunities, widened horizons and presented people with unexpected choices in their personal lives. The tensions and psychological stresses on both the home front and the theatres of war drew out resources and exposed frailties often never so acutely challenged. Accepted tenets of sexual morality were as vulnerable to the conditions of wartime instability as most other aspects of normal life. But people responded to new opportunities in a variety of different ways.

The Armed Services were clear about their responsibilities in the field of sexual conduct. Their priorities were to maintain the morale of troops and keep as many as possible fighting fit. Their method of achieving this combined recommendations to continence with warnings against promiscuity which emphasized the dangers of venereal disease. Both men and women were given lectures on moral hygiene as part of basic training. For many it was the first experience of anything remotely like sex education. Care was taken to pitch the lectures at a level most likely to be effective. RAF guidelines stressed 'it should be remembered that the audience for the most part will consist of decent, clean living men, and that a bawdy approach to the subject will not be appreciated and may do considerable harm'.[44] It advised giving a clear clinical account of the signs of VD and the need for early treatment, while also warning against the danger of brothels and 'chance intercourse with "amateurs" ', and recommending that 'the sublimation of the sexual instinct by concentration on work, games and hobbies provides the only sure prevention against ultimate infection.'[45]

Some medical experts doubted that these warnings would have much effect on behaviour. Surgeon Vice Admiral Sheldon Dudley, with 38 years experience in the field, thought 'the large majority of adults have already formed their attitude towards promiscuous intercourse and rationalized their sex behaviour with any religious or ethical code they possess.'[46] Even so, care was taken to avoid the lectures becoming 'so boring, that personnel would treat the whole subject with contempt'.[47] Sex education was still a source of embarrassment even in the Forces. One senior Army medical

man recalled the first lecture he delivered: 'I . . . waded into sex
– masturbation, the lot; subjects then seldom voiced in public. I
could feel the temperature falling to sub-Arctic, except above my
collar where it was feverish. When I huskily announced that I was
finished. . . . Into the dead silence burst the roar of a bull-voiced
and popular subaltern, one year older than myself. "Well, doctor
– you've certainly taken a load off my mind." The laughter seemed
to raise the roof.'[48]

The Women's Services also had lectures as part of basic training,
which went some way towards enlightening the more naïve among
them. These were even more hedged around with warnings against
promiscuity. Dorothy Calvert of the ATS remembered: 'We had
cosy little chats on the actual discipline of the ATS, with the subtle
sort of inference that it would be best not to drop a clanger, like
a "bun in the oven" or a touch of the "clap", which on both
counts "good" little ATS would be better off without. Why didn't
they say straight out, "Thou shalt not fornicate?" What the devil
did they think we were, old girls from the whore's retreat or
something?'[49] Another ATS recruit remembered: 'We were examined for venereal infections when we joined the Army, and every
month at the medical inspection. Great moral emphasis was laid
on not having affairs with men. . . . Most of us had never heard
of VD or knew what it was, but like many others I developed a
discharge out of pure psychosomatic terror.'[50]

Troops serving abroad experienced long periods separated from
women's company with scarce opportunities for either sex or
domestic affections. Despite exhortations to continence, a proportion of troops returning from battle lines into civilian areas
tended to take up the available opportunities for entertainment
and sexual contact. The pragmatic approach adopted by the
authorities was largely determined by the need to control venereal
disease.

Condoms for prophylactic use were not made available free
until May 1942 (for troops abroad, not at home), and supplies
were haphazard.[51] In the early Middle East campaign bulk pur-
chases were made available to troops at cost price, but after a
windfall of 'many millions' of them captured from the Italians
they were issued free. After 1942 in most areas of war they were
readily available, despite home front protests that with a shortage

of rubber the available supplies were being diverted from production for contraceptives to production for prophylaxis to sustain the promiscuity of troops abroad.

Unlike the First World War, early treatment centres were set up in most units during the war. Early treatment packets were also distributed to troops from 1942, although this was not thought particularily effective, partly because of carelessness in their use, often because drunkenness had been a contributory cause of their infection in the first place, a claim made in 60 per-cent of infection cases.[52] ('Never drink till sundown' an Air Ministry pamphlet warned, it upsets the heat regulating mechanism and over-indulgence 'may lead to undesirable sex adventures'.)[53] Though pay was docked from men under treatment to begin with, because it was a disease contracted through the soldiers' own fault, this was repealed when it proved less a deterrent than a spur to concealment, which fostered the spread of the disease. But the emphasis in education about disease as a deterrent to incontinence remained. When penicillin began to be used after 1944, which reduced the side effects and cut down the length of treatment (of gonorrhoea to a few days, and syphilis from a year to ten days) there was official concern that its efficacy should not become 'so well-known that personnel treated the acquisition of VD with lighthearted contempt'.[54]

The official approach to brothels varied, depending on the theatres of war and the prevalence of VD. All troops going abroad were warned against the dangers of brothels and 'amateurs'. As in the First World War, blame for the spread of venereal disease among the troops was laid at the door of women. 'Remember that a very high percentage of native women in warm climates suffer from syphilis or gonorrhoea or both . . . the danger of being infected by such women is almost 100 per-cent. The "safe" house is a myth,' declared a pamphlet for airmen serving overseas.[55] Attempts to put brothels out of bounds had varying success. Some were sanctioned, and monitored by medical authorities. In the early days in France, although troops were debarred entry to certain houses and streets, two brothels in Rheims remained in bounds for certain hours in the evening, where preventive treatment centres were set up and no man was allowed to enter without a sheath. In some areas visited by medical Officer Aidan MacCarthy the authorities encouraged the use of brothels because of the high incidence of venereal disease outside. 'Typically, they attempted to bureaucratize them and a weekly check was made on every brothel by Service Medical officers, when the girls were examined and tested. . . . This brothel inspection job was very unpopular with British doctors, who viewed with dismay the prospect of visiting such "houses" in the cold light of morning.'[56] For one RAF doctor, it was a symptom of 'the curious crooked morality of the time. . . . we preached the painful symptoms and the dire consequences to those infected, while at the same time providing them with means of protection and even cleansing stations at strategic positions, to which they could resort after the event'.[57]

As the incidence of VD rose, the authorities resorted increasingly to closing brothel areas, and intensified propaganda against VD. Sustained efforts were made to organize amusements and games, although they were thought 'a poor substitute for the delights of the towns'.[58] In Italy, after a rapid rise in VD, particularly around Naples where a combination of sheer poverty and organized prostitution rackets drove many women 'to bargain their bodies for a bar of soap, a stick of chocolate or a packet of cigarettes', all brothels were placed out of bounds. The city was patrolled by military police who arrested 3,641 women in Naples alone for prostitution offences. The VD rate in the RAF rose to 45 per thousand in 1944.[59] In India and Ceylon, brothels were put out of bounds but were difficult to control. Cooperation with the civil authorities was not possible, although in Lahore, taxi drivers lost their licence if they took servicemen to brothels. The brothel area in Calcutta was large and had many entrances making it impossible to police. In Bombay, some houses with a slightly higher social tone were patronized by officers who treated them like a club, thus adding to the difficulties of policing. The 'Overlord' operation in 1944 was preceded by intensive propaganda against promiscuous behaviour. Although placed out of bounds at first, a policy of co-operation with civil authorities in liberated countries was adopted to regulate and inspect *maisons tolerées*.

When the main opportunity for sexual contact was the passing trade of brothels, many soldiers experienced a cluster of inhibitions. Some gave up sex more or less completely. A young major, R. C. Benge recorded: 'the sex part of my erotic life had become wholly sublimated. It was of course still *there* but its significance was peripheral.' For many, 'the usual release was a recount of past sexual exploits and future fantasies'. Benge had once 'foolishly stood in a queue in the boiling sun outside a brothel in Tunis. The man in front of me had a boil on his neck and my interest was extinguished.' Once, when he was out of the front line in a small town in Italy, a friend 'took me to an amateur establishment where there were very young ladies – in times of peace they would have been innocent and virginal students. We had fried eggs and wine and when the time came to retire to their back room Danny Lenihan was up and away, but I was not. I was, in any event, exhausted from the latest encounters with the enemy. Naturally the ladies were outraged, even though I offered them money. . . . Danny Lenihan was jubilant, but for me it was not a heroic adventure. In later life one comes to regret these lost opportunities – they were not real prostitutes after all; they were casualties of war.'[60]

In Germany as the Allies advanced, a non-fraternization order was issued in the full realization that it could not be enforced for very long. R. C. Benge experienced his first sexual relationship in Austria towards the end of the war: 'Officially we were still not "fraternizing", but for me as for everyone else it was difficult to be billeted with a family without any kind of intercourse.' He learnt German from the married daughter of the house whose husband was missing in action. 'Priggishly, I was determined that this relationship would remain strictly pedagogic and so, to begin with, it was. When I entered the war I had been, in spite of years of emotional involvement, almost virginal: my few sexual experiences had been inconclusive and unsatisfactory. I was afraid of women. Since then, there had naturally been no progress in my education; everything had been retarded. In some of these areas, therefore, I was still about eighteen or less. I disapproved of sex without love, etcetera.'[61] When she started an affair by joining him in bed one cold night, he did not resist: 'It was a mutually bene-ficial arrangement made possible because it could only be tempo-rary and involved no ultimate responsibility on either side.' His was not an isolated experience: 'within hours of the lifting of the official ban on fraternization, the valley blossomed with celebrating couples. The General responsible must have felt like a fairy godfather waving his magic wand'.[62]

For many soldiers, being removed for long periods from ordinary domestic affections produced a sense of detachment from normal feelings, which was a component in the unhinging of emotions produced by war. Writer Alun Lewis set his short story *Ward 'O'3(b)* in the claustrophobic confines of a hospital in South India in 1942, describing the experience of four patients for whom war had muted tenderness. The patients' memories of love and affection had become remote. Brownlow Grace 'had sent an airgraph to his parents and his fianceé in Shropshire telling them he'd had his arm off. Peggy sounded as if she were thrilled by it in her reply. Maybe she was being kind. He didn't care so much nowadays what she happened to be feeling.' Dad Withers, who had spent twenty-six out of the previous twenty-eight years overseas, dreaded his return home on discharge: 'What would it be like in the small Council house with five youngsters and his missus? She'd changed a lot, the last photo she sent was like his mother, spectacles and fat legs, full of plainness.' Weston had had an affair with a Frenchwoman, but been separated by the war. Because of a dream he'd had after the Dunkirk evacuation, he'd frantically tried to find her. When he failed, he lapsed into a detachment, seeking only the shadow of his former passion; 'I wanted to find her, I didn't care about anything else. And then something started in me . . . A French girl touched me on the street one night. I went with her. I went with a lot of women. Then we embarked for overseas. I had a girl at Durban, and in Bombay: sometimes they were French, if possible they were French. God, it was foul.'[63]

For R. C. Benge, the prospect of demobilization towards the end of the war, signalled a renewal of feelings of personal affection which had been 'sublimated' for years: 'Although at Gmund we were still in uniform our mental state was such that the Army receded into the background: as old soldiers we were beginning to fade away. The collective life was losing its meaning and long-forgotten tides of personal feeling returned. With almost unseemly haste I set up a domestic ménage with the Polish displaced person who later became my first wife . . . it was the most lasting consequence of my war and could not have happened otherwise.'[64]

Control of homosexuality was laid down in the regulations;

although it was officially outlawed in the armed services, some tolerance was practiced on the ground. According to Kings Regulations: 'Confirmed homosexuals whose rehabilitation is unlikely should be removed from the Army by the most expeditious and appropriate means.' The offence of indecency between males was dealt with by the Forces and carried with it the penalty of court martial. There was a steady rise in the incidence of offences, from 48 in 1939–1940 to 324 – the majority overseas – in 1944–1945, with a total of 790 courts martials for the whole period – about the same number as for fraud, mutiny, or falsifying an official document.[65]

Generally, only the most blatant indiscretion resulted in court martial. With manpower conservation a priority, alternatives were frequently found. An Army psychiatrist observed: 'it was often considered practical and realistic to post known homosexuals of good intelligence and proved ability to large towns, where their private indulgences were less likely to be inimical to the best interests of the service.'[66] It was also pointed out that 'sexual inversion does not necessarily imply a corollary of military uselessness' – many of the men had been mentioned in dispatches.

If handled carefully, punishment for discovery could remain at the discretion of individual commanding officers. George Melly, a Navy rating, and then a self-confessed homosexual, recalled one Christmas after a beery dinner 'I and Harry Wakefield fell asleep on the same bunk and were roughly awoken by a fiercely heterosexual Warrant Officer who had long suspected and resented my propensities. He put us on a charge but the Commander would have none of it. "Far too drunk to have done anything about it even if they'd wanted to," he commented dismissively. Our accuser reddened, and Harry and I . . . saluted, turned about and marched out of the room.'[67] One British major recalled the hushup of a court martial just before the Battle of El Alamein: 'A sergeant in our brigade was discovered masturbating with a private in a tent, and they were both put on a charge by the sergeant major. Our colonel, who was himself a homosexual, was absent, and so the case went right up to brigade headquarters. The brigadier, who had been a boy soldier promoted through the ranks and to whom nothing in army life was a surprise, dismissed both men with a reprimand. The colonel was absolutely furious that it had got as far as it did. "The battalion's been out here for two years, these two youngsters had never had home leave," he stormed afterwards in the mess. "Out in India when I was in the ranks, reveille brought every man tumbling out of everyone else's bunks. What the hell do they want the men to do for sexual relief, go down to the brothels in the bazaar, chase Arab women and catch syphilis?" '68

In his experience, Major Benge recalled, 'homosexuals were accepted without comment except for crude but kindly badinage – it was only obviously "effeminate" or passive types of homosexuals who were noticed at all. One reason for this tolerance was of course that we were "all in it together". Almost without exception they were good soldiers and naturally devoted to their comrades. During the fighting there was a simple law: one was either, within that military context, a good fellow or not. All other considerations were irrelevant or secondary and any prejudices brought about by social life in a particular place had disappeared. They were, therefore, accepted without reservation.'69 Many apparently sexual displays were, he suggests 'largely fantasy and a means of providing colour to an existence which would otherwise have been emotionally drab. For example, on the rare occasions when we rested out of the line, attempts would be made to set up a rudimentary officers' mess with all its ludicrous trappings . . . some of the batmen who were transformed into temporary waiters wore makeup and were given appropriate names. Just before ceremonial drinks were served – we used to drink copious draughts of vermouth out of a bucket – the officers would shout in unison, "We want Nellie" (or Diana or Lucy as the case might be). Then the ladies would flounce in with the potent brew in enamel mugs. It was the only kind of theatre we could manage, and quite therapeutic.'70

Homosexuality was viewed increasingly as a medical and psychiatric condition rather than a criminal problem. Men found engaging in homosexual activities could be referred for psychiatric examination, and many homosexuals voluntarily referred themselves for treatment, which could result in discharge or downgrading to medical category C2 or C3. An Army psychiatrist concluded that 4 per-cent of all military psychiatric cases admitted for war neurosis were 'conscious inverts'.71

Writer G. F. Green was court-martialled in Ceylon when, after leading a life of fairly blatant indulgence – 'a compound of drink, sex, benzedrine and cigarettes' – he 'had been found in his bed, all lights on, in the wrong place, at the wrong time, with someone whose company, in the circumstances, could only be regarded by military authorities as conduct unbecoming, to say the least.' Green, an infantry officer who edited a Forces newspaper had, a friend later commented, 'perhaps under the headiness of the East, flung himself into a period of self-indulgence, willingly and loving it, but with awareness of guilt and nemesis'.[72] He was sent to a military detention centre in Colombo where he remained for several months after a medical inspection (and relegation to category C2) and psychiatric examination. There he reflected on 'the continual risks I ran – the wooing of disaster' which at times 'represents itself actually as courage – it invariably seems to me at the time craven NOT to do the wild (and often ugly and "untrue") act. This is extraordinary and perverse.' He had, he thought, wanted 'to be a sort of martyr & have turned out merely a sort of criminal'. Although he had tried to make it 'seem more noble than squalid' he felt after his punishment that his homosexuality was a burden, that he was carrying 'the odium of disease' into the outside world.[73]

Passing Temptations

Young women at home had far more opportunities for social contact and they were less controlled by circumstances. Uprooted from stable, often sheltered, home backgrounds to live a communal life in camps or hostels, women encountered new experiences which could disturb or confirm their pre-war moral beliefs, and open their eyes to new possibilities.

For some it was a rapid education. Shirley Joseph, a recruit in the Women's Land Army defied 'anyone who has lived in a hostel for any length of time to be narrow-minded on any subject. . . . My companions said what they thought, and if I didn't like it, I could just lump it.'[74] Miss G. Morgan, at seventeen the youngest recruit in an anti-aircraft battery struck up a close friendship with a woman who 'cheerfully admitted to having been a prostitute before she joined up. Paradoxically, she took it upon herself to

be responsible for my moral education. Certainly I was in need
of a great deal of enlightenment on the facts of life because I was
completely innocent about such matters; so much so that I had
gone into the Army with a vague childlike idea that somehow or
other babies were born through the navel. If ever a young person
was at risk it was me and of all people it was the ex-prostitute
who set about remedying my appalling ignorance. She did this
with great delicacy and careful attention to her choice of language
for explanation. . . . The moral standard of her chats was high,
with the recurring theme of no sex outside marriage.' Her mentor
made no attempt to suggest she had reformed, for: 'there were
nights when she returned to the hut with her tunic and shirt in
disarray and her bra slung somewhere around her neck. She never
discussed these events and I was too polite or embarrassed to ask
her, but all the same I did wonder whether she had been acting
professionally or "just for the love of it".' Miss Morgan rapidly
adjusted to the mores of barrack life. When she returned home
on leave, she wrote, 'After experiencing just a couple of months
of communal life, I found that the girls with whom I had worked
before I enlisted were self-interested. We no longer spoke the
same language even, and there seemed to be a barrier between
us.'[75]

Communal life breached the barriers about talking about sex.
One WAAF commented: 'The main consequence of a lot of
women living together seems to be that, since everyone realizes
that everyone else's emotions, aims and actions are similar to their
own – conventional barriers and restraints are torn down and
conversation gets down to bedrock. . . . Not only in choice of
words, but also in choice of topic and depth of discussion is this
new candour created. . . . Here we've got to know each other well:
we're all in the same boat and we're all after the same thing. So
why kid each other?' The dominant topic was men – she reckoned
85 per-cent of conversation was about men and dances and only
15 per-cent about domestic matters. In 'The Great Man Chase'
she set down the points she and others looked for in an eligible
man – which were probably not that dissimilar to peace-time
attributes: that he should be high ranking, devoted, in love, never
be seen with another woman, should kiss well, but 'definitely
abstains from actual immorality. . . . We are frank to a high degree:

admit exactly what "he" did on the doorstep last night: are quite obvious in our ensnaring technique: BUT hesitate to admit defeat and pile on more love and stuff in the descriptions than represents the truth.'[76]

While women felt they could talk about sex and men, there is no clear indication that they engaged more readily in pre-marital sex. Some pressures peculiar to wartime clearly did incline women to go further than they would have done in peacetime, but many still observed the rules of courtship which postponed sex until marriage. According to one survey 58 per-cent of men and 34 per-cent of women from mainly working-class backgrounds had pre-marital sexual experience, though the authors thought 'the true figures may be nearer 75 per-cent and 50 per-cent'[76] and a later survey put the figure among mainly middle class women at 39 per-cent of those born 1914–1924.[77]

Many young women took advantage of the new opportunities and enjoyed the attentions of a number of men in the more fluid wartime atmosphere. A young woman scientist in London found it fun – 'so many nice lads – Norwegian, Polish, Canadian and of course the G.I.'s. We all made dates that we could never possibly keep, and had the time of our lives, never expecting the war could be such fun. There was no question of settling down with anyone, just the sheer enjoyment of dancing with soldiers of different nationalities in different styles. We re-cut our mothers' dance dresses, wore as much make-up as we could, and loved every minute.' A WAAF stationed near Newcastle remembered how they were 'all for having a good time . . . but we all disapproved of any girl who went "too far".'[78]

The dangers of war and the possibilities of separation heightened the sense of transience in relationships. People could be moved around the country or dispatched abroad with little notice. Civilians faced dangers from bombing, servicemen faced dangers from fighting, which made for an equality of awareness of risk and danger. One WAAF who went out with RAF pilots avoided long standing relationships: 'The war encouraged flirtations, although not all were "dirty weekends" because the girls were well aware of the stigma that went with pregnancy and being an unmarried mother.'[79] The constant proximity to death experienced by RAF men affected both men and women. One RAF tail-gunner working in Lancaster bombers recalled: 'While girls had a much stricter upbringing, they were sorely tempted when they knew what little chance their loved one had of returning unscathed. There was no doubt that wartime did make more opportunities, and caution was often not exercised under such stress. Equally quite a lot of us chaps would play on a girl's emotions by stressing the possibility of death, even though we as aircrew never believed it would be us who got the "chop".'[80]

For many, moving away from home and normal constraints brought new experiences and new choices. Sister A. M. Turner, a nurse serving abroad on a hospital carrier, recorded in her diary how she steadily drifted away from the boyfriend she'd left at home as she came into contact with an entirely new world. She left in June 1943 – 'Further and further away I am sailing from my Beloved. I wonder when and where we shall meet again.' Three months later she is still attached to him: 'And so to bed, to think and dream of my own Beloved, and I know full well he is thinking of me. I wonder when I shall be with him again.' But by then she had met and been charmed by Dr Gordon McCullough: '2pm. Lay in the deck chair with M as my companion. Very comfortable. He read me to sleep and kept the flies away from me. (14.8.43) Slowly an affair develops with 'Mac', who is married, but in the meantime she records visiting a Dutch gunboat: 'Had an interesting time with the First Officer. He wanted to kiss me and eventually he did.' She also records meeting an American Commander and being entertained on board ship, and having an unpleasant experience with 'E.M.O' who 'drank too much and would not take my no for an answer'. (23.8.44)

By August 1944 she is being courted by a new man, Bill: 'I fear he's getting fond of me. Shall have to talk to him. I'm too old for him. If only I was five years younger.' Now both Bill and Mac want to marry her: 'Mac came to stay the night. A bit awkward. I had already arranged to have dinner with Bill. Bill very kindly dropped out and left me with Mac. Mac is in love with me. Proposes we make a new life in a new work. Can I do it I wonder. I know I could be happy with Mac but it's such a big thing to encourage him to leave his family. I spend the night thinking about it.' (16.9.4) She agonizes for the next few days: 'Life is very difficult I wish I could have a straightforward love affair with no complications. I would love to be with Mac but!! . . . Bill asked me to marry him but I don't feel I can. He's too young for me. So we decided to continue as good friends.' Next day she decided to accept Mac's proposal despite his being married.[81]

Not everyone accepted that affairs could be transient – Vera Lynn's *We'll Meet Again* had a powerful resonance throughout the war – but many got hurt. One woman, Susan, who joined the WAAF after her brother got killed in Sicily in 1943, had a passionate affair with a New Zealander in the RAF. It lasted until he was posted to the Middle East shortly after they'd become engaged. He jilted her: 'The whole episode broke my heart, and in my desperation I had an affair with a young Polish sailor. He begged me to marry him after I was expecting a baby. But I could not bear to do anything of the sort, even though he warned me that such a decision would ruin my life.'[82]

The arrival of Allied and Dominion soldiers brought varied opportunities for social contact. By far the highest proportion were American G.I.'s while Canadians, Australians, New Zealanders, Poles, Belgians and French made up the total of 1,421,000 foreign troops stationed in Britain by spring 1944. Services entertainments and dances organized through American Forces clubs became the focus for social life in many areas.

G.I.'s brought with them a certain glamour as well as a ready supply of scarce commodities. Though G.I.'s were widely commended for their courtesy and charm, they also soon established a reputation for being fast and free, which led many a mother to warn her daughter to steer clear of them. The Home Office joined in the concern about the fate of young English women: 'the sudden influx of Americans, speaking like the films, who actually lived in the magic country, and who had plenty of money, at once went to the girls' heads. The American attitude to women, their proneness to spoil a girl, to build up, exaggerate, talk big, and to act with generosity and flamboyance, helped to make them the most attractive boy-friends.'[83] G.I.'s with their easy ways and ready gifts were a source of fascination in many a small town, especially black Americans, who had never been encountered before. A Somerset housewife described the small town of Wellington in 1942 as 'a seething mass of darkies now, followed by children who can't leave them alone . . . Our local girls are much attracted and

Bobbie's foreman saw three at the camp gate, looking longingly in. "They maids – prick mazed they be, prickmazed" was his comment.'[84]

One woman remembers how the G.I. invasion of Oundle when she was 16 affected her social life and horizons. She was recruited to serve refreshments at the weekly dances: 'By 1943 the G.I.'s were part of our community . . . Already their reputation for being wild, promiscuous and a threat to every female under seventy was well established. Nice girls should never be seen with one. But inevitably Johnny, Hank, Elmer, Chic and the rest became the only boys near our own age that we ever met. We served them steaming tea and wartime cakes and for the life of us we could not understand the terrible menace that our parents saw in them. We were incredibly naïve, brought up on sentimental Hollywood films and romantic fiction, but then so were these boys. Many of them had never been away from home before and were often as wary of us as we were of them. There *were* a hard core of drinkers and womanizers who kept the rumours flying but in fact they tended to go off to the bigger towns. . . . Eventually our parents must have relaxed their vigilance because we were allowed to go to the dances at the "Vic". Not the correct ballroom dancing we had learned at school! It was a slow cheek-to-cheek shuffle or an exciting jitterbug. These boys knew how to talk to girls, too. . . . It was thrilling to be told, "You look cute in that dress, honey", or "Gee, you smell sweet!" '[85]

As G.I's became part of the community, courtships flourished, despite widespread caution and disapproval. They provided opportunities and temptations, though not everyone appreciated their advances. Dorothy Calvert of the ATS recalled a group approaching her and a friend in Cheltenham: 'For a start we were not interested and gave them a few dirty looks, which was like casting pearls before swine. Then they started to make some very pointed remarks as to what they were after and did not bother to disguise the fact: we turned our backs on them. The next thing that happened was these Yanks threw a heap of notes at our feet, stating exactly what they wanted. Well that was the limit, we both got up, picked up the money, walked over to the blokes and . . . told them in good basic English what, how and where they could shove their money.'[86] But there was a natural diversity of responses. One woman journalist who spent the war working at the US Embassy in London believed: 'A girl could do what she liked. . . . I was young and reasonably attractive. I could have gone to bed with one every night . . . but once you put up the respectability sign you had no more trouble with the Americans than with the British. . . . I still had a perfectly wonderful social life. . . . This is not to say I remained unsullied throughout, but any sullying was done with co-operation on both sides.'[87]

Many courtships lasted, though as many more were broken off when the Americans and other Allied troops left to fight abroad. 100,000 women married allied troops, 80,000 of them G.I. brides who emigrated to America. An American estimate suggested they also left behind 70,000 illegitimate children.[88] And there were casualties on the way. Eileen McMurdo, who joined the ATS at seventeen, was posted to the Southern Command Signal office at Salisbury, where, at the American Red Cross Club, she met Bob, 'a tall, dark haired staff sergeant who worked as a quartermaster at the base . . . several years older than I and very much a man of the world.' On her nineteenth birthday he gave her an engagement ring and organized a large party. To get married, permission was needed from Bob's Commanding Officer. When, after a month, it had not come through, she rang the American base and was called for interview. The Commanding Officer 'suddenly banged his fist down onto the desk and with a look of anger on his face, said clearly and distinctly: "Damn all liars to hell." Startled at this outburst I looked at him with some surprise but before I could ask what on earth he meant, he said quite simply: "Here is the only way to tell you what I have to", and, reading from the file in front he quoted:

"Name, Robert Maxwell Manning. Dependants: Wife, Maria Dorita Manning. Child, Judith Mary Manning, born 1938." '

Later she reflected on how it had come about: 'in the loneliness of wartime separation from his family, Bob had attempted to fill the void in his life with something he must have known couldn't last and could only, in the end, bring pain to himself and others. Life had such a transitory quality about it in those days particularly in the services, when one could be posted away at a moment's notice.'[89]

Public concern about morals declining under the distruptive

influences of war focused, as usual, on the Women's Services, which acquired such a reputation for 'looseness' that the Government set up a Parliamentary Committee to investigate them. Letters and public protests from parents and churchmen about the alleged prevalence of pregnancies and venereal disease in their ranks led to questions in Parliament about conditions in the services, and the adverse effects the controversy was having on recruitment.

The Committee, set up in November 1941, concluded there was 'no justification for the vague but sweeping charges of immorality which have disturbed public opinion', and that rumours and gossip had been wildly exaggerated. Though it acknowledged there were 'emotional stresses due to war which lead to extramarital relationships', it pointed out the discipline of service life was 'corrective rather than an incitement to bad conduct'. The rumours could be explained by a combination of 'a certain bravado in much talk which takes place between young people about sex questions' and prejudice against certain services such as the ATS, who had a reputation for being 'a legion of Cinderellas, domestic workers of low degree among whom one expected and got a low degree of immorality'.

Attacks on the ATS originated almost wholly from male members of the Forces. At a time when ribald remarks such as descriptions of the ATS as 'officer's groundsheets', and 'Up with the lark and to bed with a Wren' had a wide currency in and out of the services, the Committee concluded: 'strictures, in particular from soldiers, sailors and airmen . . . carry weight out of proportion to their numbers and may be repeated, often with exaggeration, since no story loses in the telling'. The British, moreover, cherished 'a deep-rooted prejudice against uniforms', and a woman in uniform 'may rouse a special sense of hostility, conscious and subconscious, among certain people', and become 'an easy target for gossip and careless talk'. The Committee's Report dispelled rumours about illegitimacy rates among ATS women; their pregnancy rate was lower, at 15.4 per 1000 per annum, than the illegitimacy rate among civilians of a comparable age, which was 21.8 per 1000 per annum. Between 18 per-cent and 44 per-cent of these had been pregnant before they entered the Service.[90]

Servicewomen objected to the slur, but had to deal with the

consequences of their reputation. One WAAF who changed into civilian clothes at dances to stop men 'getting too fresh', commented: 'There was the attitude about girls in uniform, that they were easy, but they weren't any different from other girls.' Another sixteen-year-old WAAF described a visit to the camp cinema where 'an airman got very fresh and several of us younger girls had armed ourselves with hatpins for protection because we could hide them in the lapels of our uniforms. I had occasion to use mine. The lights came on when the airman screamed and clutched his bottom. Everyone stared at me. After that I was known as "the pin-up girl".'[91] Dorothy Calvert, recalled: 'The ATS were called some rotten names, and lots of civilians who did not know us thought that we were almost all whores, and to be on a gun site with a lot of men, well the "Holier than Thou" brigade used to have a field day. We were not saints, but we were not poor bloody nymphomaniacs either.' Because of their uniform, they were subjected to more advances. In addition to any number of passes and proposals, she recorded two sexual assaults arising from her being in uniform. On one occasion she had to fight off a man in a railway carriage, on another to escape an RAF policeman who lured her out of a railway station forecourt with an offer of help and tried to rape her. 'One thing was very certain, to get through one's service stint "Virgo Intacta" or in the same way as when you first joined up was almost impossible.'[92]

Redeeming Sins: (i) 'Fallen Women'

The war brought about significant changes in official attitudes to illegitimacy and venereal disease. Where previously they had been regarded as primarily moral issues they were increasingly viewed as social problems, to be tackled not by blame and punishment for sins, but through assistance founded in rational social policies. Since they were the consequence of wartime disruption, they were perceived as a government responsibility.

Though the illegitimacy rate went up during the war – and at the time it was construed as a sign of changing moral standards – in fact it was not necessarily an indication of increased promiscuity, especially among young people. Contrary to expectations, it was not mainly younger women who 'fell'. The proportion of irregular conceptions among the under–25s was actually lower than in peacetime. The largest increase – of 41 per-cent on pre-war levels – was among women aged 30–35; among women aged 25–30, it increased by 24 per-cent, and among women aged 40–45 it also went up – by a fifth. Between 1940 and 1945 there were over 100,000 more illegitimate births than in the previous six years, but as a proportion of all maternities, because the birth rate rose, the illegitimacy rate went slightly down during the war until 1945.[93]

The main difference compared with pre-war years was not in the number of illegitimately conceived pregnancies, but in the number of pregnancies not subsequently regularized by marriage. In 1938–1939 30 per-cent of mothers conceived their first child out of wedlock; for those under 20 the rate was around 42 per-cent. Pre war, 70 per-cent but in 1945, under 40 per-cent of these children were legitimized by marriage. The main reason for this is probably the absence of fathers due to the war. The rate of regularization by marriage went up again slowly after the war to 44 per-cent in 1946 and 56 per-cent in 1947.[94]

Before the war, provision for unmarried mothers was left almost entirely in the hands of voluntary organizations, mainly philanthropic bodies whose aim was moral reclamation. Now a more humane approach was beginning to emerge. In 1938 the Birkett Committee on Abortion had recommended a more tolerant attitude towards unmarried mothers as one step towards a reduction in the level of abortion, estimated at between 110,000 and 150,000 a year – 16–20 per-cent of all pregnancies. When war broke out, government policy on evacuation plans made no distinction between the married and unmarried. All expectant mothers were to be evacuated in their last month of pregnancy, and kept in accommodation for a month after it. This equality of treatment met with some resistance, not least from the body most concerned with the issue, the National Council for the Unmarried Mother and Her Child, which had traditionally made a fine distinction between 'deserving' and 'undeserving' cases. Though they agreed in theory with the 'official plan that all expectant mothers should have the same rights in this public scheme', they objected in practice to grouping together young married and unmarried women of 'good, or moderately good character, with the mothers of five or more illegitimate children and with prostitutes (married or unmarried)'.[95] Local authorities opposed the scheme because accommodation was in short supply and they found difficulty placing unmarried mothers and children in billets. On the other hand, when they remained in maternity homes they blocked beds for other patients.

As the numbers increased, the problems became more visible. Between 1939–40 and 1944–45 the number of women who approached the National Council for the Unmarried Mother and her Child for help rose from 932 to over 3,500, a minute proportion of the total. As the Services, government war factories and government evacuation plans all came into closer touch with the welfare problems created by the increasing numbers of unmarried mothers, support grew for the view that since wartime disruption had helped create the problem, the Government should take responsibility, and evolve a policy to deal with it.

A government plan set up in September 1941, for maternity provision for unmarried war workers, failed. It was so poorly publicized and so complicated to administer that by 1948 only thirty-six mothers had received any help at all under its auspices. A maternity scheme evolved by the Ministry of Health for unmarried ex-servicewomen, who were discharged after the third month of pregnancy, met with better response. This was supported with £25,000 of Treasury funds to help women either to return home, or be admitted to voluntary homes or into government-funded hostels, with back-up support from the Soldiers' Sailors' and Airmen's Families Association.

By 1943, with numbers increasing, continuing shortage of provision, increasing criticism of the inadequacy of voluntary facilities, and warnings rife about the danger of swamping resources, the Government initiated an inquiry into the problems arising from illegitimacy to be carried out by the Advisory Committee on the Welfare of Mothers and Young Children. The result was a Ministry of Health Circular of 1 October 1943, which made welfare authorities responsible for the care of unmarried mothers and their children and provided for the appointment of trained social workers with the duty of looking after the welfare of illegitimate children.

It was a significant change. That was the first time there had been any national policy on the issue, and it shifted illegitimacy from the realm of sin and punishment into an issue of public welfare, care and humane support. By March 1945, 339 authorities had submitted schemes to the Ministry of Health, and 50 had appointed qualified social workers. Adoption procedures were also streamlined after 1943, as adoption orders doubled from 26,000 between 1934–1938, to 55,000 between 1945–1947.[96] However facilities remained inadequate and patchy and there were further calls in 1945 to bring the care of unmarried mothers and illegitimate children into line with modern standards of social work and humanitarianism which were being defined under the provisions of the new welfare state. Though unmarried mothers were entitled to defined social benefits which replaced charity and poor law relief, including free maternity care, sickness benefit and maternity allowances, anomalies persisted. Up to the 1950s unmarried mothers were being admitted into institutions under the provisions of the Lunacy Act 1890 as social outcasts, not even permitted to take walks for fear of further pregnancies.[97]

What surprised many social workers was a new attitude of independence among unmarried mothers. Many decided to keep their children, not enter hostels, and discounted any sense of public shame. Mass Observation recorded one woman who deliberately chose to have a child out of wedlock: 'I have always wanted children – more than marriage and in spite of the inconvenience and difficulties I have had twins without being married. I fell in love with a man who was unfortunately married and having done so found it impossible to develope (sic) a satisfactory relationship with anyone else in spite of serious attempts to do so. I felt that a complete and conventional marriage with someone I could not completely love was less satisfactory than an unconventional but satisfying relationship with the man I loved. Having being (sic) convinced of this I decided that my desire for children coincided with my duty to have them. I persuaded my lover that I could manage it and I did.' She saw the children as 'the crown and harvest of our love'.[98]

Pauline Long also chose an independent course. When she got pregnant she moved from the ATS to being a cook in the Land Army: 'In this way I was able to get a roof over our heads and earn a living for us both. There was no other relevant way: 'service' was still more than a memory, and it was the only thing a 'bad girl' could do. My 'badness' of the time was based on left-wing politics, and I did not want to be dependent on a man, believed marriage was Bourgeois, and that women were equal (but different). The idea of abortion arose, but the backstreet stories were so horrific that I discounted the idea immediately. Anyhow even backstreet abortions required cash and I had none. The child's father was also a revolutionary and also believed in all my ideals so therefore he saw no reason to do anything for me, and indeed would not have known what he could have done'[99]

A more tolerant attitude to illegitimacy developed. Women in the forces whose companions fell pregnant tended to sympathize rather than disapprove. Miss G. Morgan remembered one girl in the ATS who got pregnant: 'Everyone did their best to make life less unhappy for her. She no longer had any dishes to do, and I think there was hardly a girl on the site who did not knit for the coming baby.'[100] A civil servant in her fifties told Mass Observation of the change by 1945: 'I know of one case of a girl having to resign from our office because she had "got into trouble". Other girls talked about her and the occasion quite freely, and the general attitude seemed to be that it was a great pity that she had been so foolish – but she was always a queer sort of girl – and there were sympathetic conjectures about how she would get another job. Years ago, when a similar thing happened, the girl concerned simply dropped out of office life – no-one even said openly why she left – she just went home on sick leave and never returned. I can remember one of her best office friends saying very seriously, "Oh, she was a *bad* girl", but apart from that her name was never mentioned.'[101]

Redeeming Sins: (ii) 'Social Diseases'

The State also extended its responsibility to the control of VD in the civilian population, but not until the middle of the war. Though the Ministry of Health had warned just before the war that the incidence was likely to rise, complacency about the steady fall in the diseases – a 45 per-cent drop in cases dealt with between 1931 and 1939 and the continuing belief that publicity about VD would lead to immorality had blocked initiatives to deal with it. When the Ministry of Health prepared advertisements warning of its dangers, the British press refused to publish them. Ministry plans for a supplementary treatment service were dropped, and the Treasury blocked grants for their plans to urge local authorities to provide additional treatment centres until late 1940, when 41 new centres were opened.[102]

Concern mounted as the figures rose. By 1941, syphilis had increased by 113 per-cent among male civilians and Servicemen, and by 63 per-cent among women; gonorrhoea had gone up by 90 per-cent among men and 81 per-cent among women. It was not until October 1942 that a campaign – 'the most intensive effort in the field of public education yet undertaken in this country'[103] was initiated by Sir William Jameson, Chief Medical Officer at the Ministry of Health, with a broadcast on the BBC immediately after the 9 o'clock news. (The BBC overcame its nerves: there had been pressure to re-schedule it to a quieter part of the evening for fear of protest.) Jameson set the agenda for the campaign. He dealt with it as a medical, not a moral problem. With the tone of a calm doctor talking medical sense, he circumnavigated his way to VD via tuberculosis; VD presented 'just the same sort of problem as any other infectious disease'. Secrecy was the danger, and it could not be dealt with 'by running away from it, by shutting our eyes to its existence, by refusing to discuss it, or by withholding from young people information regarding its dangers'. The response was favourable. 'He treated sex hygiene with the deftness and assurance of a bomb disposal expert,' wrote W. E. Williams in *The Listener*.[104] The campaign was launched four months later.

Government intervention was further extended under Defence Regulation 33B by which contacts cited by two or more VD patients as the source of infection would be required by persuasion or if necessary legal compulsion, to submit themselves for treatment. Justified by Ernest Brown, Minister of Health as part of his 'duty of keeping the nation fighting fit', the Regulation was passed by an overwhelming majority in the House of Commons and received widespread support outside. 'There are many freedoms for which we are fighting, but the freedom to spread venereal disease is not one of them,' declared Charles Hill of the Central Council for Health Education. Dr Edith Summerskill, who pointed out 'the effect of venereal disease upon the community is more disastrous than the injury inflicted by thousands of Nazi aeroplanes',[105] castigated the Government for not going far enough and for its drastic neglect of public education. There were opponents outside, who saw this as a repeat of the similar Regulation (40D) which had proved ineffective in the First World War, provided opportunities for wrongful accusation, victimization and the infringement of civil liberties, particularly of women.

Despite the Minister of Health's reassurance that it did not discriminate against women, between 8 January and 30 September 1943, 3,344 women were informed on, compared with 213 men. Of these only 4 men were cited as a source of infection by two or more people, compared with 228 women. The majority were persuaded to take treatment without recourse to law. The Regulation was legally enforced in the case of only one man and 95 women. The Services medical authorities were confident that the Regulation, 'As far as control of prostitutes was concerned in the United Kingdom . . . was of great value',[106] although the figures for treatment, compared with the scale of the problem, do not indicate that it had much impact.

Control of the 'new danger of "amateurs" ' concerned the authorities more than control of professional prostitutes. They were described in the official History of Wartime Medical Services as 'usually an unthinking pleasure-seeking girl who took little trouble over personal protections and was slow to realise that she had contracted an infection and equally slow to seek medical advice.' The belief that the culpable people and the targets for control of the spread of VD were women, was again evident. As a letter to The Times put it, 'Promiscuity is still accepted as inevitable in men and is even condoned, especially in wartime. But any such theory of inevitability demands the creation of a special class of women . . .'[107]

In this war the special class of women was the 'amateur prostitute' a euphemism much bandied about to describe behaviour which moralists found 'loose'. A particularly wide definition in an earlier study of prostitution in 1933 had classed as 'amateur prostitutes': 'girls from among his own social group whom he knows, or whose acquaintance he may readily make . . . Although he usually pays for his satisfaction, the payment takes the form of a gift, or a dinner, or a motor run; the episode appears less commercial and suggests more of passion and spontaneity than a similar episode with a professional prostitute . . . In addition . . . there may be no payment whatever, and the whole episode may be mutually desired and mutually satisfactory.'[108] In other words, any single women whose behaviour suggested she had intercourse outside marriage risked being branded an 'amateur prostitute'. One MP, Mr Muff, managed to encompass most of the Women's Forces in this category when he described to the House of Commons his visits to ATS, WAAF and WRNS camps: '. . . in the course of my duties in going to camps and seeing a collection of these irresponsible amateur prostitutes – they are nothing more or less – I have felt that I could take the law into my own hands and give them a jolly good slapping. But I have to leave it to the Home Office.'[109] The Americans, who had to deal with a large increase in VD among their ranks, at least put some of the blame on the men. They attributed the increase to the small use of station prophylaxis; when 'the vast majority of the sexual exposures were wholly uncommercial and on a friendly basis', soldiers were less impressed with the need for protection.

The public education campaign began in early 1943. After much wrangling over the use of explicit words – 'Sex organs', 'intercourse' – the Ministry of Health and the Central Council of Health launched a series of posters and advertisements. The press which carried the ads were more cautious than the Ministry about frankness. Mention of 'sex organs' 'pox' and 'clap' had been cut out in most papers, which prompted the *Daily Mirror* to make a bid for the liberal readership with a campaign for openness. The ads were 'frank, but not frank enough', it declared, because Fleet Street, 'with a delicacy of feeling not hitherto considered its predominant characteristic, felt perturbed'. It was essential that 'the facts be plainly stated . . . The best way to rid the nation of this nasty enemy is to subject it to a full frontal attack.'[110] '10 Plain Facts About VD' appeared in national newspapers in February 1943, followed by a poster campaign, aimed mainly at men.

The Churches continued to voice reservations. The Archbishop of Canterbury protested at a Health Conference in February that 'what was primarily a moral problem with a medical aspect was being treated as a medical problem with a moral aspect', and deplored the Army giving routine instruction in the use of prophylactics, implying 'that the authorities expected a considerable number to fornicate'.[111] David Mace, the Christian secretary of the Marriage Guidance Council, attacked as 'a melancholy reflection on our lack of moral fibre' the fact that 'all hope of eradicating venereal disease by a campaign to inculcate general continence . . . should have been virtually abandoned'.[112] The Services were unequivocal: 'As Service doctors our only duty is to keep as many men fighting as possible,' declared Surgeon Vice-Admiral Sheldon Dudley. 'Therefore, even if it is true that self-disinfection increases the amount of illicit intercourse by removing fear of the consequences, it is no affair of ours; and it is our duty, despite any personal feelings on the subject, to encourage the use of such measures if we honestly believe the amount of disease is reduced thereby.'[113]

The public, it turned out, welcomed more information, and were far from squeamish in their response. There was widespread demand for more specific information than was being provided. Mass Observation found: 'the lack of knowledge and atmosphere of secrecy surrounding the subject is greatly deplored, and many people believe the problem of V.D. will not be solved until it is regarded in the same light as any other disease'. One middle-aged married woman reported: 'During my life I have only heard vereal(sic) disease mentioned about 4 times . . . If they (my friends) thought I knew anything about it they would think I was a "dirty-minded" woman . . . Time and again in my general reading I came across accounts of obscure ailments, deformity, mental deficiency, blindness, barrenness, miscarriages, all put down to this mysterious disease. But from no one and from nowhere have I found out how one would recognise the first symtoms (sic) in oneself. . . . It is no use telling us to notify the disease at the first possible moment, when we don't know what to notify . . . as far as I can gather the first stage of venereal disease can be mistaken for a bad cold.'[114] The press advertisements had got through to the public more effectively than any previous government campaign – 77 per-cent had seen the ads and they were approved by the majority (94 per-cent of women, 67 per-cent of men)[115] Two fifths wanted more information; many thought the campaign was still too modest.

The medical pragmatists won; by the next year there was no question of restricting information for fear of inculcating immorality. A further 60,000 posters were distributed and a new film *Subject Discussed* was issued in cinemas throughout the country. 100,000 letters had been answered by the Central Council for Health Education by March 1944. New cases of VD reached a peak among men in 1942 and declined thereafter, (though the incidence in women continued to rise for the rest of the war.)[116] It was one more sign of the liberalisation of attitudes wrought by war, and a further stage in the shift in moral norms towards a more realistic appraisal of sexual dilemmas.

Though the war had disrupted normal domestic patterns of life, it had also opened up opportunities for knowledge and experience, and broadened moral horizons. While some clung to the pre-war moral standards, many found themselves in situations that enabled them to experiment and learn more about themselves, which could change the way they felt about the conventional constraints of sexual morality.

Many developments were accelerations of pre-war trends. The earlier age of marriage was already apparent in the 1930s. Where in 1938 one bride in six had been under twenty-one, in 1945 this applied to more than one bride in four. Despite an increase in illegitimate births, the numbers of conceptions outside wedlock did not increase proportionately, but a smaller percentage was legitimised by marriage. Figures available (all somewhat unreliable) indicate that the trend towards pre-marital sexual experience began before the war, frequently with intended spouses, and continued during it at about the same levels. The number of married women working was on the increase before the war mobilised them on a massive scale.

The most profound effects of the war were the consequence of the separation of families, which threw people back on their own emotional resources and cut them off from the constraining mores of a stable community. The increase in divorce was not only the result of wartime strains on marriage; making divorce cheaper and more accessible through the forces meant many already faltering marriages could be ended more easily.

Many women had experienced a new independence and author-ity in the family in the absence of their husbands. They had taken jobs not previously thought suitable for women and had emerged from the war trained in skilled work, capable of commanding relatively high wages. The war had demanded the energy to run two jobs – the family home and outside work and although many women, exhausted by long hours and shortages and queues welcomed the chance to return to the home, others felt bitter at being dispensed with so summarily as the men returned, and missed the financial and social opportunities work had given them. Mothers' experience of wartime independence was part of the inheritance on which their daughters, the young women of the sixties, were nurtured.

A more tolerant attitude to sex developed, partly as a result of the government and Services education campaigns, but also because people had encountered new situations which made for a more flexible view of the boundaries of permissible sexual behaviour.

At the end of the war, there were competing ideologies at work. On the one hand, there was a conscious attempt to restore faith in the values of Christian marriage and family life, in which sex was promoted as the welding element in monogamous marriage. But the dislocations of war brought about significant and largely pragmatic rearrangements of most aspects of domestic experience, which promoted reappraisal of those moral values. It was with an increasing awareness that the old certainties had been challenged, that it was a changed and changing world – socially and morally as well as politically – that the country moved through the immediate post-war reconstruction period.

Six

Reconstruction

Coming Home

The end of the war brought new problems of adjustment as the nation began to count the physical and psychological costs. Rebuilding family life and marital relationships after years of separation and fragmentation became a priority on the agenda of post-war reconstruction.

The anticipated return to 'normal' life was slower than many had hoped. Phased demobilisation avoided unemployment chaos but lengthened separation. Domestic circumstances did not become easier immediately. The housing shortage continued and people still lived in cramped and overcrowded conditions, often in hastily constructed accommodation while the Government pursued its priority housing programme. Rationing and shortages continued for several years.

Many servicemen found the return to family life problematic after the routine of an all-male society where personal responsibilities had merged with the collective military unit. Cut off from domestic and family values, sometimes for years, few men had had much contact with either women or children in a loving or affectionate relationship. One soldier, for instance, commented: 'I've had such a grand time with the chaps – they are a fine lot. We yarn or smoke and have a drink just when we like, and a chap need never feel dull or lonely . . . Nell is a good soul and the children are fine, only it's different and it rather scares me. One forgets one's manners in the Army and I may do things she won't like at first. If I get the blues sometimes she'll think I'm bored with her . . . and there'll be the bother of getting a job or a little shop and seeing I make enough money to go round. It almost makes me wish the war weren't over!'[1]

Many returned to a family which had survived self-contained without them, to children who had grown up in their absence and to whom fathers had become strangers, perhaps threatening strangers. They had to re-claim a place and authority in families where close bonds had developed between mothers and children, and re-establish their relationship with their wives, (which could mean turfing out young boys from the bed they had grown accustomed to sharing with their mothers). Some returned to find that their wives had been unable to stand the loneliness and had taken lovers. One welfare officer observed how men who 'had faced death and danger without flinching' were 'white faced and shaken at what had happened in their absence'.[2]

Training as soldiers did not fit well with re-entry into civilian life as fathers and husbands, as one soldier observed: 'They had to learn to do things they have been taught to hate and to unlearn many other things which were part and parcel of civilised life. Killing and the use of force are much discouraged in civilian collective life; here the use of force and the infliction of a maximum amount of death and damage on the enemy became a desirable aim . . . Now the process was once more reversed.'[3]

For women, too, there were more dislocations. Though many looked forward to the return to 'normal' life as a relief, and welcomed their husbands' return, others were reluctant to relinquish their independence. There was not much question that they would return home. Any potential unemployment problems were dealt with by encouraging women to give up their work and skills to make way for the men. Lauded though they may have been for their wartime participation in the economic life of the country, it was made fairly plain that women's continuation in work was no longer a priority, nor even a right. They were made redundant as the men returned.

Women responded in different ways. A Mass Observation study in 1944, *Will the factory girls want to stay put or go home?* found a quarter of factory workers polled answered 'yes' to the loaded question, 'Should women be allowed to go on doing men's jobs?' A further 28 per-cent said it depended on what happened after the war. The majority of those who wanted to remain were women who had worked before the war, mostly single or widowed women aged 35 to 50. Married part-time workers who had entered work during the war were also keen to remain. The most restless were single women under 25 who had unclear aspirations. Those most keen to get back to the home were the married women who had shouldered two jobs – factory and family – during the war.[4] According to a Ministry of Labour survey in 1947, two-thirds of 'unoccupied' married women had recently thought of getting a job, but nearly all had decided against it because of domestic responsibilities.[5] For other women, the return to the home was a reaction against the privations of war: 'People . . . really frowned on mothers working, because they had seen what the crèches and day nurseries had done during the war,' recalled one. Another woman, who had earned a high salary as a bomb inspector, gave up work to bring up the family, though she found it a bit strange not earning her own money: 'I'd seen little toddlers going to the nursery, in the blackouts on winter mornings. It didn't seem the way to bring up children to my mind, pushing them out into the cold with hats and coats and gloves on and handing them over to complete strangers. I wanted to bring my children up myself.'[6] Even so, some voiced reservations. One woman who had discovered her managing abilities in the war stated her anxiety: 'Sometimes I've wondered if I'm not going to find being a housewife a bit tame and too easy – though I keep saying I'll be glad of the rest', while an advice pamphlet pointed out: 'Many (women) will also feel that they are going back to a prison, unless they have some life away from sinks and brooms and washtubs.'[7]

There was no shortage of advice about the difficulties and tensions women might encounter on their husband's return. Couples often had to re-meet each other almost as strangers. If they found they had been changed by their experiences, the strain on marriage was acute, as 'Phyllis' recalled: 'When my husband finally came home we discovered we were two different people, so much had happened in those years apart. My husband, older than myself, was time-conscious, critical, and came back with the attitude of a regimental sergeant-major; I am sure he expected me to jump up and salute when he entered a room . . . I realised that settling down was going to be hard, but by this time I had two babies, quickly, and I was stuck. In a strange area, strange faces, and for hours on my own. He was finding it hard to get a civilian job and having to take orders after having had some measure of authority. I missed going to work and the companionship and intelligent conversation. After a while we settled to some sort of married life, but there were times when I thought that if there was a hell on earth, I was living it. I did not want a divorce, I could never have left the children.'[8]

Prisoners of war who had suffered acute psychological stress encountered particular difficulties, as a POW news sheet explained in a plea for understanding: 'You will find that we are moody. Also, don't be surprised if we just sit and think for an hour, or read a book without turning a page for an hour. We will not eat as much as we used to, but this is due to the natural shrinkage of our stomachs. We shall want to go to dances and parties, but in a great many cases you will find that we shall not be able to stand them for long. In many cases, we shall be rather shy of the opposite sex, not having been in contact with them for so long. That will soon right itself, but at first we may appear awkward through trying to remember our manners . . . Returning, we shall be like convalescents from an illness. As we get better, as all convalescents do, we will pass through a very irritable stage. You must forgive us our faults in this stage and try to help us through as much as you can.'[9]

Welfare officer Barbara Cartland was concerned to warn POW's wives 'not to expect too much at first . . . The wives were almost too excited at the prospect of seeing their husbands again to listen to me and it worried me to realise that they were all looking forward to a kind of second honeymoon.' She got nowhere with two padres who refused to help her warn them that 'privation and suffering do not make good lovers' but that with 'patience and returning health things will adjust themselves'.[10]

Men who had been on active service, a pamphlet *Living Together Again* warned, might behave strangely, and suffer 'nightmares, sleepwalking, talking or shouting' – the consequences of shock – and other forms of defensive behaviour. One ex-POW took to roaming the hills and wandering from inn to inn drinking with other men from the same camp. Though it was obvious he still loved his wife and children he was inclined to 'snap and be impatient' and then penitent. One day 'when Megan had told him to bring his friends home . . . the three of them suddenly grabbed the loaf and tore it to pieces'. Wives were advised: 'It is a hard task for those who love these men to get through the self-made barriers, but infinite patience, gentleness, and an exquisite tact, will gradually wear thin the resistance and enable the truly loving wife or sweetheart to get emotionally near enough to the man to deal quietly with his resistance.'[11]

There was also advice to women who might be anxious about their physical attractiveness. Godfrey Winn dispensed some reassuring advice to women who, looking in the mirror, had become 'conscious of the grey streaks in your hair, the tired lines, a thinness and a sagging that weren't there in the days of unrationed butter and eggs – and no queues. I dare say your first instinct is to try and cover it all up for him. Don't. Don't try to pretend that time has stood still for you, like the princess in the fairy story, waiting to be awakened with a kiss . . . when at long last it is all over, let your side of the picture be placed alongside his, with not a detail, not a sacrifice spared. It is a story not of sadness, but of riches.'[12]

Sex and Social Order

The future of marriage and the welfare of the family became priorities for government reconstruction as the foundations of the welfare state were laid. Concern that wartime dislocations might have more permanent effects on the stability of family life informed a range of initiatives to re-assert pre-war moral and marital norms, and re-define the code of sexual morality for post-war Britain.

Divorce cases were rising so fast that the administrative machinery could not cope with the demand. By May 1946, of 48,500 applications received through Command Legal Aid Sections of the forces, only 5,000 had been tackled. Pressure for more accessible divorce came from quite unlikely sources – *The Times*, for instance, which claimed that unless steps were taken soon to reduce the waiting time, 'the divorce lists are in danger of getting out of hand',[13] a concern echoed in the House of Commons by Mr Skeffington Lodge MP who warned that as many as half a million people could be involved in these 'tragedies', and 'the longer the delay in dealing with this matter, the more will the slime of unfaithfulness creep over our land.'[14]

The Government was responsive. The Denning Committee on Procedure in Matrimonial Causes in 1947 advocated that the State facilitate divorce procedure, but also proposed that the State take on new responsibility to intervene in support of marriage – by encouraging and funding 'marriage guidance as a form of Social Service', setting up reconciliation procedures through a Family Welfare Service, and attaching Welfare Officers to courts to look after children's well being.[15] These recommendations were all accepted. The 1949 Legal Aid and Advice Act was the most significant advance in divorce procedure so far; it enhanced equality before the law and made divorce accessible to those who could not previously afford it. It also led to an immediate temporary surge in divorce cases.

A further attempt to facilitate divorce by extending the grounds to include seven years separation with or without the partner's consent failed in 1951. Supporters of Labour MP Eirene White's Bill had argued that it was time to bring the law into line with the realities of marital breakdown, that the current law fostered immorality by encouraging an estimated 300,000 separated couples to enter into irregular unions, that it induced unnecessary and intolerable hardship, and was flouted on a large scale by arranged adulteries. But the Bill was opposed with renewed vigour by the Church of England, which saw it as an attempt to introduce a new principle of irretrievable breakdown (since no matrimonial offence needed to be proved by the clause), and protested that it looked dangerously like divorce by mutual consent, an exercise of freedom by partners which the Church opposed utterly. The Archbishop of Canterbury prophesied that any further extension of the grounds of divorce would bring about the collapse of family life – the bedrock of stable society – and would encourage marriage to be seen, not as a sacrament but as 'a contract which may more or less be easily broken'.[16] The Labour Government, which had a precarious majority and was anxious to avoid controversial Bills, referred it to a Royal Commission which did not report until 1956. By that time the tide of conservatism had sealed the impetus to reform.

State responsibility for shoring up marriage was handed over to voluntary bodies who became the recipients of government grants after the Denning Committee's recommendations were accepted. The Marriage Guidance Council, set up in 1937, the Catholic Marriage Advisory Council, set up in 1946, and the Family Welfare Association all received grants. The Home Office oversaw training, and the development of new counselling methods which drew on Army experience and employed psychiatrists and lay people.

For David Mace, the Christian secretary of the Marriage Guidance Council, the objective was to rebuild monogamous marriage and family life. The institution of marriage was under threat, he warned: 'the danger signal is showing, and it would be folly to ignore it. As we come home I want us to have our eyes wide open. That's all. Because there's a job of work to be done; a vitally important job of work – the rebuilding of family life.'[17] Mace developed a positive strategy for the promotion of monogamous marriage based on 'unselfish love and self discipline', a partnership in which men and women had 'complementary' not dependent roles, with children its 'natural fulfilment' – though contraception could contribute to the family's happiness and health. Sex was harnessed firmly to fulfilment in monogamous marriage as an integral part of marital harmony. Techniques had to be learned and worked at. The Council's first booklet *How to Treat a Young Wife*, in line with other manuals of the time, stressed the importance of the husband developing the full sexual potentialities of the wife. A 'good sex adjustment', Mace argued, 'means satisfying orgasm for both. Simultaneous orgasm is a desirable ideal.'[18]

Sex outside marriage was firmly proscribed in this reformulation of sexual morality. Mace and his contemporaries were adamant about the need to control the powerful 'animal' instinct: 'Beneath the surge of elemental emotion which sex lets loose,' Mace wrote, 'nothing will suffice to hold us steady save the stabilising emotional power of a spiritual ideal which commands our whole-hearted allegiance. The centrifugal forces of animal inpulse can be balanced only by the centripetal power of religious faith.'[19] He was echoed by the contemporary sex educationist, Edward Griffiths: marriage was the only outlet for 'the terrifically strong force or urge which rises up inside you . . . like a very powerful engine, and, like all engines, it can run amok if it isn't properly driven and controlled'. All distractions – masturbation, pre-marital sex, homosexuality – were as nothing to monogamous union, which was 'the natural fulfilment of our growth; it is for this that man is created; it is, if you like, the highest expression of man's activity and personality'.[20] It was within these persuasive constraints that the sexual rebellion of post-war youth germinated.

A re-definition of marriage and partners' roles was echoed through the activities of other official and semi official agencies. The Beveridge Report, the blueprint for the future Welfare State, designated marriage as the career for the vast majority of women: 'In any measure of social policy in which regard is had to facts, the great majority of married women must be regarded as occupied on work which is vital though unpaid, without which their husbands could not do their paid work and without which the nation could not continue.'[21] Even if they did paid work, it would be 'intermittent'; women were assumed to be dependent on their husbands in the vast majority of cases and they were to be treated for social security purposes 'as a team' – of breadwinner and housewife. The almost immediate closure of wartime nursery facilities, though not necessarily an act of conscious policy designed to push women back home, nevertheless endorsed the shift by depleting facilities which might encourage them to stay in work.

Over a range of Welfare State policies, the aim was to improve the conditions in which a traditional model of marriage could survive. Social security measures which supported families through mitigating the economic and social disadvantages of parenthood, and social policies which aimed to improve the care and protection of children were backed up by the development of increasingly professionalised agencies for family support. Social work, and particularly family case work, emphasised the needs of 'adjustment' to family norms. Despite some acknowledgement of women's changing position, the role of motherhood as defined by experts precluded any other occupation from women's lives. Motherhood is 'the essentially feminine function in society', claimed one in 1948: 'almost all intelligent women' agreed with this, and those who did not were 'normally deficient in the quality of womanliness and the particular physical and mental attributes of their sex'.[22] Experts on child care were on hand to endorse the crucial role of mothers' undivided attention in the early years of a child's development and affirm a new ideology of motherhood which pinned women firmly to the exclusive task of child care and nurture in the home.

Togetherness

These post-war goals did not conflict with new marital expectations among the young which revealed a shift towards sharing, coupledom and an ideal of 'togetherness'. One survey conducted between 1943 and 1946, found that whereas the older generation tended to look on marriage 'as a task, calling for renunciation and sacrifice . . . something which they had to shoulder willy nilly', the younger generation viewed marriage 'as a partnership, an opportunity for mutual enjoyment and activity'. In marriage, the researchers concluded, 'We are more inclined now than we used to be to demand a capacity for response between the partners, to look for intellectual and temperamental compatibility, as well as purely material welfare, in addition to the ordinary social and parental satisfactions'.[23]

This new mood did not dent the importance or 'seriousness' with which couples of all ages viewed the institution of marriage, as Geoffrey Gorer found in his early 1950s survey: 'It is marriage itself which is important, not, I think, love or sexual gratification.' He noted a strong inclination to keep the marriage alive despite personal unhappiness, and felt that stability depended more on how well husband and wife performed their respective duties than on how well they got on as a couple: 'contempt was felt for those couples who did not fit this complementary picture, particularly for couples where the wife 'wore the breeches' and the husband was 'hen-pecked'.[24] Both partners were, in Gorer's view, extraordinarily chaste and faithful: 'the high valuation put on virginity for both sexes is remarkable and I should suspect, specifically English'; half the married population had had no relationship either before or after marriage with any other person than their spouse.[25]

At the dawn of the post-war era, attitudes to sex remained ambiguous. Shame and sexual guilt were still in evidence. Slater and Woodside gained the impression sexual desires were 'thought of as being natural and inevitable, but at the same time not quite respectable, and are usually referred to with evidence of shame'. Sex was thought by many to be something men indulged in and women tolerated – on average twice a week. A third of women never or infrequently had orgasm, a fifth often or often enough and only a third always experienced sexual pleasure.[26] A Mass Observation survey in 1949 found only a third believed sex was indispensible in a relationship. It noted 'a suspicion that sex indulged in for its own sake is wrong, and, as such, is probably also unpleasant, harmful, and needful of control by accepted standards of morality'. Respondents revealed 'lurking anxieties and inhibitions', suggesting conflict between 'their acceptance of the natural inevitability of sex and . . . the tradition, possibly founded in religous asceticism, that *sex for its own sake is wrong*'.[27] Gorer found hardly any support for what he called 'therapeutic' arguments which equated sexual activity with physical and mental health and abstinence with physical or psychological damage – 'a rather more dangerous form of constipation', as he put it.[28] The double standard remained firmly in place; men were far more keen to insist on their wives' virginity than women were on their husband's chastity, but women also overwhelmingly colluded with the requirement for female chastity.

Material goals were changing in all classes as the country passed from austerity to economic boom. As small families became the norm, birth control was increasingly seen as the means to a better standard of living for working class couples. Large families, Slater and Woodside concluded, 'are firmly associated in their minds with poverty, hardship and the lowering of standards'. One woman, from a family of eleven children of whom seven survived into adult life, wanted about two or three, then 'I could give it things I never had'. Many who had not planned in the past were now taking precautions but while 80 per-cent had tried birth control, 'not more than 12 per-cent of all couples used any method (other than coitus interruptus) with consistency or persistence'.[29] Though the Royal Commission of Population in 1949 recommended comprehensive state provision of birth control facilities, this was ignored. Clinics flourished in the 1950s. There were 400 by the early 1960s (and for many newly weds they still had a slightly risqué air about them) but family doctors were still reluctant to supply information. One woman, Mrs. A, for instance, was told after the birth of a spina bifida child 'not to have another baby for some time, but no advice about birth control was given'. Slater and Woodside's 1940s survey concluded: 'As things are at present, it is left to the individual to find out about birth control as best he may. This is a system of *laissez-faire* which penalizes the uneducated working-class woman.'[30] By the late 1940s, 55 per-cent of all married couples used birth control, of which 40 per-cent used the sheath and 20 per-cent the cap, while just under 50 per-cent used withdrawal at some time in their marriage. However, only a quarter of social Class 3 (unskilled), had used mechanical methods, compared with 51 per-cent of social Class 1 (pro-fessionals).[31]

Even as these family and marital goals were being attained, there developed new challenges to the moral certainties which had underpinned the jigsaw of national renewal. As the post-war con-sensus fragmented from the mid-1950s, the old values were put under new pressure.

Seven

Protest
(1955–1963)

Domestic Tensions

As the country emerged from austerity into a period of unprecedented economic boom, the legacy of wartime priorities to conserve or do without, to put off till the future, was replaced by inducements to spend, to enjoy the fruits of accelerating affluence cushioned by the security of the welfare state. It was a gradual movement away from constraint towards release.

Outwardly the 1950s was a period of consolidation and stability. Increased material affluence permeated to all classes. Technological innovation and consumerism were yoked to the domestic companionate marriage ideal as the family became the focus of the expanding consumer economy.

But beneath this apparent stability, strong cross-currents of social and political conflict were forming. A crisis of authority developed as cracks in the mould of the post-war concensus widened. On issues of sexual morality, the tensions between taboo and licence became acute. Attempts to secure traditional moral standards came into conflict with social and economic trends pulling in contrary directions. The result was social division, ambiguities in practices and duplicities in behaviour. A succession of alarms swept the nation as the great hulk of tradition shifted and groaned under the pressure of rapid social change. The gap between private aspirations and public control widened. There was growing recognition of the need to reconcile public policy to diversifying private practices, beliefs and aspirations if moral crisis and widespread social disruption was to be avoided. The question of how far the

State had a legitimate right to control the private realm of sexual morals became a key area of political dispute.

As the Church's influence continued to decline, the libertarians' challenge on behalf of personal freedom gained ground. Their identification of sexual morals with social justice rather than sin was in tune with wider concepts of equity embodied in post war welfarism. The stress on individual liberty and moral choice rather than divine imperative chimed with a new emphasis on the pursuit of personal fulfilment and achievement which the consumer society and the meritocratic state were simultaneously promoting.

On a broader canvas, the moral and political certainties of the past were undermined. The Cold War heightened international instability, the hydrogen bomb became the arbiter of the future, and Britain began its turbulent and divisive retreat from its place as a world imperial power. From being an outward looking power, certain of its political and moral values, the nation began to look inward and examine itself, to scrutinise the nature and extent of its decline, and to seek prescriptions for renewal.

Even so, marriage patterns remained outwardly stable as companionate marriage solidified into an unchallenged domestic ideal. Marriage was popular. More people got married then ever before and they married younger. By 1961 808 women per thousand aged 21–39 were married compared with only 552 per thousand in 1931 (and by the mid–1960s, 95 per-cent of men and 96 per-cent of women were married by the age of 45). The average age of marriage dropped from 27 for men and 24.5 for women married between 1946–1950, to 26 for men and 23.5 for those married ten years later, and it continued to fall. White weddings were the natural outcome of courtship and, on average, two years engagement. Parental assent in the choice of the partner was part of the ritual, and defiance of parental veto was still the occasion for considerable drama. Almost all young couples remained at home until they got married when, as the housing shortage eased, they expected to set up in a separate home. The trend towards smaller families continued, with couples taking advantage of increased affluence to improve standards of living and the technology of birth control to plan families.

One index of stability was the steady decline in divorce. After the post-war peak and the effects of the 1949 Legal Aid Act worked their way through the system, the numbers fell from 34,000 in 1953 to a low of around 23,000 in 1958, after which they began to climb slowly again in the 1960s.[1] The public stigma attached to divorce had not diminished, as the Church of England signalled decisively when it intervened to prevent Princess Margaret marrying the divorced Captain Peter Townsend in 1955. Divorce, in the words of one divorcee, remained 'a grave social misdemeanor, agonizing, suspect and against the moral grain'.[2] The Morton Commission on Marriage and Divorce which reported in 1956 did little to alter this. It was set up to examine reforms which might extend the grounds for divorce to include seven years separation, introduce a new principle of irretrievable breakdown, or retain the matrimonial offence system. But it emerged with a confusing, divided and inconclusive report; although half the members favoured the seven year separation clause, the majority supported the retention of the matrimonial offence system. Nothing was done, and though the subject was given a public airing, the Commission's report precluded any further discussion of reform for the next decade.

Beneath this façade, other pressures were moulding different, conflicting expectations. The domestic ideal of lifelong marriage as a partnership of breadwinner and housewife still put women at the centre of the home and family. Social policy, backed up by social scientists, psychologists, welfare agencies and a range of other influences dictated that marriage was women's career; the 'normal' adjustment to their 'natural' role, moulded by nature and biology, was to be the 'feminine' dependent wife, coerced back into the sphere of caring and the affections by the promise of social status as housewife. 'Women are born to love,' Monica Dickens explained in *Woman's Own*, they are 'born to be partners to the opposite sex, and that is the most important thing they can do in life . . . to be wives and mothers, to fix their hearts to one man and to love and care for him with all the bounteous unselfishness that love can inspire'.[3] Motherhood – already the crown of women's achievement – acquired specialist status, as welfare and psychiatric expertise was harnessed to support family norms. For instance, in what seemed progressive thinking at the time, child psychiatrists, notably John Bowlby, stressed the crucial influence on a child's future development of mothers' undivided attention in the early years. This further riveted women to the domestic sphere at the expense of their autonomy.

Yet as women's role was narrowly defined, opportunities outside the home were simultaneously opening up. The economic boom stimulated women's participation in the economy as earners as well as consumers. Married women's return to paid, mainly part-time employment in growth industries was the biggest single increase in the labour market from the mid-1950s. In 1947 18 percent of married women worked outside the home; by 1957 this had risen to one in three; by 1962, over half of all women workers were married women.[4] They returned to work, according to surveys, to improve the family's standard of living, but interest in their work, boredom at home and the need for companionship and stimulus also played a part.[5]

As consumers, women were the target of advertising which reinforced their role as housewives; technology which would transform domestic routines was sold through imagery identifying success, sexually and as wives and mothers, with ownership of the dazzling array of new inventions which tumbled onto the market at an alarming pace – transistor radios, long playing records, processed and frozen foods, bri-nylon and crimplene. The campaigns hit home. The number of families owning a vacuum cleaner doubled, fridge ownership trebled and washing machine ownership increased tenfold. Consumerism was reinforced by the always conservative women's magazines which not only catered almost exclusively to the housewife but actively discouraged careers outside the home.

Contradictions multiplied. The flood of consumer goods and labour-saving devices to all classes undermined women's role as the full-time pivot of the household by potentially reducing the amount of time spent on housework; earlier marriage and smaller families had already reduced the amount of time spent on full time child care. But while women were encouraged to go out to work both by the demands of the economy and by their own need 'to use the time and energy no longer absorbed by the demands of home',[6] they encountered a wall of social censure. 32 per-cent of husbands in one survey expressed unqualified disapproval of married women working, only 23 per-cent expressed unqualified approval.[7] Married women's work was denigrated as a threat to family values, a break 'with long-established patterns of family life, and with the values and beliefs supporting them'.[8] Monica Dickens dispensed her cheery wisdom to readers of *Woman's Own*: 'Ask any man if he'd rather his wife worked or stayed at home and see what he says,' she wrote in 1961, 'he would rather she stayed at home and looked after his children, and was waiting for him with a decent meal and a sympathetic ear when he got home from work . . . You can't have deep and safe happiness in marriage and the exciting independence of a career as well . . . Men don't want to talk about a woman's work. They want to talk about their own.'[9]

When a series of alarms about juvenile delinquency hit the country in the mid-1950s, working women were blamed for a new social problem – 'latch key kids'. In a society which refused to acknowledge poverty, and insisted that women's wages were supplementary, 'pin money', and not essential to family income, these 'misfits' were allegedly the products of women (mainly working class women) putting material advance and acquisitiveness above the needs of their children. In was not till 1962 that social scientists produced research showing that women's work was a positive contribution to family welfare. They refuted the imputation or selfishness, and found no evidence that women who worked harmed their children or contributed to juvenile delinquency.[10] Even so, male disapproval of wives working persisted – 32 per-cent of husbands in 1965 still opposed it, 6 percent on the grounds a woman's place is in the home.

The pattern of dual-earner families established in the 1950s was one of the most enduring agents of change in domestic relationships. The stigma attached to working women lessened. This was 'not a passing phase', the *Daily Mail* confirmed, but 'a permanent feature of modern society. A job outside the home is meeting deep-seated needs which are now felt by women in general.'[11] The ideology of the separation of roles remained the norm, but the changing economic basis of family relationships was putting new stress on the complementary ideal.

Seductive Duties

Discrepancies also developed over sexual ideals. Sexual fulfilment for both partners was, by the fifties, widely recognised as the bonding ingredient in deepening love and 'togetherness'. But 'scientific' sex inquiries exposed a widening gap between the moral standards endorsed by society and actual behaviour.

The first large scale surveys of sexual behavior by Alfred Kinsey in America were milestones. *Sexual Behaviour in the Human Female*, his second report published in 1953, exploded several myths about female sexuality. From his study of 6000 American women, Kinsey concluded that far from being sexually unresponsive, women were physiologically remarkably similar to men in their sexual responses, and were capable of responding sexually as readily as men and in a greater variety of ways. While men reached their sexual peak between ages 15–20, women reached theirs in their late twenties and it continued well into their fifties. Women's behaviour, however, was more inhibited by psychological factors and social controls; frigidity, which had decreased with each generation since the First World War was, he claimed, largely a man-made phenomenon. The most frequent cause of lack of sexual fulfilment was men's failure to understand women's sexual responses. Sexual factors were estimated to be the cause of problems in three quarters of marriage breakdowns.[12]

In this and in *Sexual Behaviour in the Human Male* (1948) Kinsey contributed to a different way of perceiving sex. By concentrating on objective study of 'outlets', he distanced himself from moralizing; he also laid stress on orgasm as the measurement of sexual achievement, a preoccupation which informed the discourse about sex from then on. By recording behaviour formerly divided into moral categories of 'normal' and 'abnormal' as neutral points on a spectrum of variety in human behaviour, he opened up discussion of variety in the expression of sexuality.

Kinsey also revealed that moral norms were flouted by women on a wide scale. When virginity and fidelity were held up as the moral standard, nearly half his sample had experienced sexual intercourse before marriage, a large proportion with the intended spouse, and more than a quarter had been unfaithful after marriage. Several newspapers in Britain refused to publish these 'shocking' findings, and in Doncaster attempts were made to ban the reports as obscene.

The Kinsey Reports became the agents for renewed discussion and frankness about sex. They also helped endorse the importance of mutual sexual fulfilment in marriage. Women's sexual aspirations had already been raised. Three quarters of women in Eustace Chesser's mid-1950's sample had believed before marriage that they should be passionate and enjoy marital sex.[13] He noted a change over half a century from it being shameful for women to admit to pleasure in sexual intercourse, to it being shameful to admit they do not experience orgasm. Its achievement, Chesser observed, was 'felt by many women to be a "right" in itself'. More women were seeking advice about sex; three-fifths of young married women had read books on sex and marriage, compared with a half of those born in the first decades of the century.[14]

If the goal of successful marital harmony was to be measured, as it increasingly was, by mutual orgasm, then there was potential for shortcomings. Half Kinsey's female sample had experienced orgasm in the first month of marriage, and 75 per-cent within the first year. The remaining quarter may take up to fifteen years to achieve it. In Britain, Chesser found a only quarter of his respondents always achieved orgasm, around a third frequently, a quarter sometimes and 15 per-cent rarely or never, while fewer than half his survey recorded a great deal of 'satisfaction', just over a third a fair amount, and one-fifth little or none.[15]

These shortcomings were compounded by cultural myths equating femininity with submission and romantic illusions about married 'togetherness', for which the sexual analogy was simultaneous orgasm. Sexual failure was still largely blamed on women, whose duty it was to keep husbands sexually happy on penalty of losing him. Sex was the bait to fidelity. Conflicting messages from experts added to the confusion felt by many women. There was the 'surrender school' exemplified by Dr Marie Robinson, whose book *The Power of Surrender* (1959) sold over a million copies. Passivity, and complete psychic dependence were apparently the necessary conditions for fulfilment. The excitement of women's orgasm came *'from the act of surrender'*; there was 'a tremendous surging physical ecstacy in the yielding itself, in the feeling of being the passive instrument of another person, of being stretched out supinely beneath him, taken up will-lessly by his passion as leaves are swept up before the wind'.[16]

An alternative to surrender was for women to shoulder the entire burden of sexual 'adaptation' in marriage. Maxine Davis, author of the best-selling *The Sexual Responsibility of Women* (1957) chided women for expecting sexual pleasure to be delivered on marriage like breakfast on a plate. They had to work at it, to get to know themselves, and every little detail of their husbands' sexual make-up: 'A man's sexual nature is so dissimilar from her own that a wife has to give it full attention for a long time in order to understand it with her reflexes as well as her brains,' she wrote. A wife should not expect similar 'adaptation' from her husband: 'The best a wife should hope is that her husband wants – as he usually does – to meet her half-way, and even then more likely than not she will have to put up road signs to enable him to reach that common ground.' And if she should fail, her 'paramount' and 'imperative' responsibility was 'to find out exactly which part of her emotional clockwork is out of gear, have it repaired and put into smooth running order as soon as possible'.[17]

In the new ethos, sexual success had become 'a duty like every other success demand in America,' anthropologist Margaret Mead observed. It was one more item in a lengthening agenda of wives' obligations and accomplishments necessary to keep the home together, the husband faithful and 'togetherness' intact. No wonder women were beginning to feel the pressures. Deeper confusions were developing. Women were expected to enjoy sex in the same way as men, from the simple act of copulation. If they didn't achieve 'mature' vaginal orgasm, they were, according to Mead, labelled frigid by both psychiatric practice and social pressures which failed to take into account the nature of female sexuality. There was no reason to believe that 'climactic responses to simple copulation are "natural" to all women, or even to any large proportion of women'. New demands were being put on women, with no corresponding development of a philosophy and practice in sex which encouraged men to learn varieties of evoking women's climactic behaviour – 'technique, even if learned, is to a degree learned unwillingly and despised'.[18]

If this left many women stranded, it put men under obligations which could be equally confusing. One writer recalled: 'At the center of that religion of marriage was a cult every bit as hallowed as that of the Virgin: the cult of the orgasm, mutual and simultaneous. It descended to the young people of my generation from both Lawrence and Freud as the Inner Mystery, something they all aspired to, a sign of grace. Because of it I had impossible expectations of my marriage, my sex life, myself. I was an absolutist of the orgasm before I had had enough experience to ensure even sexual competence.' When sexual success failed to materialise, loneliness set in. 'The subject was unmentionable and humiliating. Even my wife and I never talked about it. It seemed too private, too laden with guilt, too insulting. As a result, it not only became the main source of our devastating loneliness, it also became such an obsession that, although I thought continually about sex, I no longer associated it with enjoyment.'[19]

The tensions between taboo and license were exposing ambiguities which by the early 1960s fuelled new moves to re-order sexual priorities.

Secret Sex

The controls on pre-marital sex came under pressure: constraints on young people loosened in other areas and allegiance to traditional values gradually eroded. By the late 1950s the gap between public standards and private behaviour was threatening disruption.

In 1953 Kinsey had revealed considerable deviation from moral norms among women. Half his sample of American women had sex before marriage, 3 per-cent before the age of 15 and a fifth between ages 15 and 20. One of his more shocking conclusions (for moralists) was that women who had pre-marital sex had a two to three times better chance of achieving sexual fulfilment earlier in marriage, which looked uncomfortably like advocacy of pre-marital sex. His 'Biggest Bombshell' was the revelation of the extent of petting. 95 per-cent of women who married young had petted, 17 per-cent to the point of orgasm. Four out of ten had engaged in petting by the time they were 15, and 81 per-cent by the age of 18, with no difference between those of different backgrounds. Nor was it new; 76 per-cent of women born before 1900 had experienced petting as had 90 per-cent of those born in the next decade. Girls who didn't pet were less likely to marry, he concluded.[20]

A similar picture emerged from Gorer's early-1950s' British attitude survey. A third of his sample supported pre-marital experience for men and just under a quarter pre-marital sex for women, with men more in favour of women's pre-marital sex than women; 38 per-cent of men and only 14 per-cent of women approved of pre-marital sex for women.[21] Sexual experience was justified to avoid ignorance, maladjustment or clumsiness on the honeymoon and for its future effect on married life. Chesser's survey confirmed the gap between morals and behaviour; more than 2 out of 5 married women and 30 per-cent of single women had sexual intercourse outside marriage, three fifths of married and half single women before the age of 21. Two out of 10 first had intercourse when they were under 18.[22]

By the early 1950s, the link binding sexual love to marriage was loosening, at least among the avant-garde. Playwright John Osborne recalled his youthful and heavily supervised courting of Renee which consisted of 'snatched pelvic felicities during the Quickstep' and fumblings on the doorstep or the front room couch, until, after a due amount of time and attention, he found himself 'being encouraged by Renee and her mother to willingly buy her an engagement ring, a solitaire diamond, if that it was, for £12 from Bravingtons.' Both titillated and alarmed by these events, he realized his 'doggy, lecherous, sentimental feeling for Renee' was 'fired by a wholly selfish desire for comfort and flattery', and began looking for an escape route from this prospect of married 'lower middle-class gentility'.[23] He made his escape and embarked on a passionate affair with a married woman.

In this social code, marriage was not infrequently contracted to legitimate sexual desire. Designer and painter Jocelyn Rickards recorded her almost unconscious association of being in love with getting married. She came to live in London from Australia in the late 1940s and began an affair with philosopher Freddy Ayer, who was 39 and divorced. She 'managed to keep out of his bed' until one evening, she found herself 'not only in his flat but in his bed, bedded, and smiling all over my face. A few days later, when we were walking in Green Park together, I was so obviously happy that Freddie asked why I wasn't able to say I loved him. I laughed and said I loved him, but didn't think I wanted to get married. Oh, naïve Jocelyn, who ever mentioned marriage?

I was then still so innocent I believed that if two normal people fell in love, and there was no just cause or reason why not, they married. I regarded myself as abnormal for not wanting to do so. On his side, no man was ever more pleased to hear that I was not hell-bent on marriage.'[24]

Powerful constraints were put on young people throughout the 1950s. In a climate of renewed puritanism, the virginity ideal – and the double standard – were reinforced by strong social and cultural controls on girls. In this sexual code the 'dangers' of sexual experiment, the damage to a girls reputation of becoming, as the commercial epithets put it, 'shop soiled' or 'second hand goods' were sternly proclaimed. One woman brought up in the late-1950s recalled: 'a girl who slept with more than one man became a slag. Women's magazine agony columnists therefore unanimously counselled the defence of virginity at all costs. He'd lose his respect for you if you gave in, and if he really loved you, he'd wait until you were married. The assumption was that women didn't have uncontrollable feelings.'[25] Boys made the running, girls were under obligation to say 'no', to be the moral gate to 'uncontrollable' male passions, at the risk of losing their 'reputation' or, if they actually enjoyed it, acquiring the tag 'nymphomaniac', a pejorative term which has fallen out of use recently.

In a society becoming increasingly eroticized, in which sexual love and fulfilment was placed at the centre of the morality of marriage, the justifications for cordoning off sex within marriage were beginning to lose their meaning. Furtive and secretive petting was part of the common experience of adolescence, in Britain as well as America. Yet it was taboo, an illicit secret which the young kept hidden from their parents. The secret formed one agent for revolt.

For adolescent girls sexual experiment was an enjoyable high-risk area. As one recalled: 'we wanted to dabble in the whole sea of sex and emotions, although we were by no means ready to wade in and get our feet wet then'.[26] Virginity was still important but: 'What ... was to hold *us* back, coming from delightfully exploring our bodies with boys, when we knew it would be all right if you didn't go all the way? Our mothers never discussed the practical problems of "snogging" with boys. They just loaded the responsibility on to us, as it had been dropped on to them, but unfortunately it was not so easy to tell right from wrong as it had been in the thirties.'[27]

A few sexologists and social scientists were beginning to re-assess the sexual code in the light of changing behaviour, and face the discrepancies and contradictions revealed by research. Sexual maturity was reached earlier – girls reached the menarche by 13½ compared to 16–17 a century earlier, boys reached full growth by 17 compared with 23 around the turn of the century,[28] and their behaviour was a manifestation of these changes. 93 per-cent of Kinsey's male sample had reached orgasm by the age of 15 through masturbation, heterosexual or homosexual activity. 99 per-cent of unmarried men and an almost equal number of women engaged in petting – sexual activity which was frowned upon by the Church and respectable society. The justifications for adolescent restraint were losing their power, sexologists Peter Fletcher and Kenneth Walker argued in 1955; it was increasingly difficult to sustain an ethic in which the 'spiritual integrity' of sexual love came into being only after a marriage ceremony; the taboos on pre-marital sex demanded revaluation.[29] These were lone voices, but harbingers of change.

Other contradictions were incubating confusions. A more equal education system was widening the gap between generations while it narrowed the divisions between the sexes. The 1944 Education Act had extended educational opportunity within a selection system based on innate ability, which enhanced girls' opportunities and expectations of equal achievement with boys, even though some divisions between the 'natural' interests of girls and boys (girls – marriage and motherhood; boys – jobs and career) remained. Some observers saw this equality as a potentially disrup-tive factor, stimulating among girls new goals incompatible with prevailing definitions of 'femininity', and with the designation of marriage and motherhood as their appropriate life ambition. Girls were being given 'too much freedom of movement as a child to stay placidly within the house as an adult', Margaret Mead warned. To accommodate this duality, she observed, the girl 'learns to disci-pline and mute an ambition that her society continually stimu-lates'. The burden of adaptation fell on her as she learned that she 'must display enough of her abilities to be considered successful, but not too successful; enough ability to get and keep a job, but without the sort of commitment that will make her either too successful or unwilling to give up the job entirely for marriage and motherhood. "Two steps forward and one step back" is the dance call-she must obey.'[30]

Sexually it was a similar story. While girls learnt to be assertive in the classroom, they learnt to be submissively 'feminine' in sexual encounters; if they weren't quite getting the message intelligence was incompatible with sexual attraction, then they were being warned it was a positive liability, a threat to male pride, a passion killer, to display too much intelligence in the tender arena of adolescent love. It was hardly surprising that the fruitless attempt to reconcile these internal dilemmas became one catalyst in the erosion of their allegiance to the moral code.

That allegiance was further undermined by teenagers' cultural separation from their elders. The distinctive style and values of 'youth culture' were moulded as much by economic market forces as by young people themselves. Teenagers commanded public attention in a new way. There were more of them than ever before by the early 1960s, and they carried new social weight as a group. They were better off than their parents had been for as wages rose generally through the 1950s, the differential between adult and apprentice wages narrowed; adolescent wages rose at twice the adult rate. With more disposable income they became a significant segment of the consumer market. They were targeted with luxury items catering to teenage tastes, which helped reinforce and unify a distinctive cultural identity. In films, music, lifestyle, youth culture was identified with rebellion against parental and society's constraints.

Pop music, soon a mass entertainment industry became the centrepiece of youth culture. Rock and roll replaced jazz as the vehicle of subversion against sexual constraint. Bill Haley's *Rock Around the Clock* generated mass youth hysteria as rock and roll ignited British culture in 1955. Elvis Presley's arrival in 1956 was a breathtaking experience for young teenagers. He had been banned in parts of America as obscene, for rolling his hips, suggesting the sexuality of youth people had wanted to ignore or obliterate. 'He had the voice of the sorcerer,' recalled one fan. 'He was subversive, sexy and his music was very good. He was the first great singer whom one's parents hated. That was very important. We used to track him on Radio Luxemburg as if trying to receive allied messages from beyond enemy lines.' Jeff Nuttall interpreted the impact: 'Most of all he was unvarnished sex taken and set way out in the open . . . he was the incarnate spirit of the fast lay and his audience of adolescents responded, not only sexually but also with some gratitude, for here was someone who was acting out in the open something that was still a secret from the adults. He broke the secret and made himself a god all over the world.'[31] Elvis was followed by a parade of rock heroes, who engaged the commitment of adolescents with songs which expressed the pain and sexual torment (and fun) of adolescent love – the tensions between license and taboo.

'Youth' became an urgent social problem, their behaviour, attitudes and lifestyle viewed as a threat to established values. With its 'rebellious, anti-establishment overtones', and its 'alternative and self-supporting system of values and status', one disapproving social commentator observed, modern youth culture 'erodes moral restraints and lowers resistance to delinquent temptations'. It undermined the protestant values of hard work and rewards which underpinned stability. The rapid rise of working class pop stars from obscurity to fabulous wealth exemplified this disgraceful trend: they 'capture the imagination of the under-achievers, because they symbolize the fantasy of a meteoric rise to the top without visible effort or conventional virtue.'[32]

The alleged adolescent embrace of 'sex and violence' constituted in the eyes of alarmists a dual attack on social order, which was the more perplexing in the society which had 'never had it so good'. The rise in juvenile delinquency was one symptom of the breakdown of order. Widely publicized outbreaks of gang violence magnified the sense of moral crisis by identifying sections of youth – the more exotic and independent, such as teddy boys and mods and rockers – as the carriers of social pathology. The crisis deepened as 'deviant' behaviour spread from the 'underprivileged' working class to the middle class. Mods, it was pointed out, came from affluent backgrounds. The 'beatniks' – dubbed 'layabouts' – who trudged between London and Aldermaston in protest against the bomb from 1958 were largely middle class. Young people from homes where parents could provide them with all the benefits of affluence were found in one early-1960s' survey to be 'an unstable lot' who were 'drifting . . . aimlessly from one job to another.' Their behaviour was 'unsettled'; they 'rejected parental injunctions and affected to despise the trappings of conventional respectability'. They showed 'a preference for middle-class luxuries without middle-class effort'. Their 'favourite activity' was 'going to private teenage parties where sexual licence, rowdyism, heavy drinking, and sometimes illicit drugs, could all be indulged'.[33]

To allegations of widespread promiscuity were added reports of the increase in illegitimacy and veneral disease. Yet young people's sexual behaviour remained remarkably conservative during the period. By the early-1960s, according to one survey, only a third of boys and one in six girls had experienced sexual intercourse by the age of eighteen, though most had experienced petting. The majority (86 per-cent) of the experienced girls had intercourse with steady boy friends or fiancés, while just over half (56 per-cent) of the boys were in a steady relationship. Only 5 per-cent of all girls had had more than one partner, though boys were more prone to casual relationships. Nearly half the boys, and less than a quarter of the girls, were in favour of pre-marital sex. Two thirds of the boys wanted to marry virgins, but only a third of girls (38 per-cent) were against their boyfriend having sexual experience.[34]

Teenage illegitimacy figures were grist to alarmist fears. Though the rate among girls aged 15–19 accounted for 18.6 per-cent of all live births in 1960, compared to 17.8 per-cent in 1938 (it increased to 20.5 per-cent in 1962), because there were more young people, the actual numbers increased from 12,463 in 1938 to 52,125 in 1960 and 67,774 in 1962.[35] Reports of a rise in venereal disease were construed as another index of decline. While there was an increase, mainly in gonorrhoea, which was proportionately higher among young people, it came after the post-war drop to all time low in 1954 of half of the pre-war figure. The overall incidence did not catch up with pre-war (1932) figures until 1960.[36], while the incidence of syphilis fell so dramatically after the war that, worldwide, it could be classified as a rare disease.

The panics in the late 1950s were symptoms of fractures in the social fabric which widened as challenges to established values multiplied. Sex was politicised as alarm about sexual morals was bracketed with a wider crisis in values, in which indictment of the materialism and the alienating effects of a mechanised consumer society figured prominently. Sexologist Alex Comfort concluded that the 'real crisis' of teenage morals 'affects not the teenager but his elders, who find themselves increasingly defending an ethos which they are beginning to recognize as unworkable'.[37] An official report on youth in 1960 found teenage behaviour a symptom of a wider malaise; a feeling that 'society does not know how to ask the best of the young, that as a whole it is more concerned to ask them to earn and consume ... One cannot indict the young for the growth of delinquency without also indicting the older generations for apathy and indifference to the deeper things of the heart.'[38] Writer J. B. Priestley interpreted the mood: 'the young, less addicted to self-deception (the great English vice) than their elders, began to feel dissatisfied and restless, the best of them clearly uneasy in the consumer role allotted to them, unable to find ecstasy among toothpastes, chocs and after-shave lotion'.[39]

Anger and Lies

The message of dissent came from a number of different directions. The rebellion of young intellectuals against conformity, authority, cultural stagnation and 'outworn' political and personal values was one influential strand. It was, according to novelist Doris Lessing, a protest against the vacuum of moral ideals – 'a confusion of standards and the uncertainty of values' which distinguished the period and its literature. It surfaced prominently in the work of various writers loosely grouped under the heading 'Angry Young Men'.

Though not so young, the products of wartime deprivation and post-war austerity, and of National Service which detached them from family and future into a training which appeared to have no ultimate point, the Angry Young Men refined truculence and disillusion with authority into an art form. Their anti-heroes were welcomed as the new heroes of the age – 'churlish, curmudgeonly and denigrating', as one critic described John Wain's main character in *Hurry On Down* (1954).[40]

They were seized on by critics and the public as the representatives of innovation, a new mood and a new breed. When John Osborne's *Look Back in Anger* was put on at the Royal Court in 1956, its protagonist Jimmy Porter was greeted by the *Observer*'s critic, Kenneth Tynan as 'post war youth as it really is, the instinctive leftishness, the surrealistic sense of humour . . . the casual promiscuity, the sense of lacking a cause worth fighting for'. T. C. Worsley in the *New Statesman* found in Porter's soliloquies 'the authentic new tone of the Nineteen Fifties, desperate, savage, resentful and, at times, very funny'.[41]

Although they attacked the entrenched values of the time, they were puritan in their attitudes to sexual morals. Both John Osborne and John Braine in *Room At the Top* used the sexual conquest of middle class women as the passport for their heroes to escape from their backgrounds. For Braine's Joe Lampton, marrying the rich man's daughter succeeded in breaking down the class barrier. For John Osborne's Jimmy Porter, that conquest is the fuse for the anger he splays over the stage. The central drama is played out at the expense of Alison, Porter's middle-class wife. Detached from her background, she becomes the object of his brutalising polemic, which is made to seem dramatically justifiable because she represents for him everything about the strangulating, lifeless and soulless middle class which he loathes, and which has unmanned him. As with almost all the writers in the group, Osborne expresses male anger and male aggression. The deepest seam of rage in the play is hostility to women.

The play is a sexual battleground. Jimmy's sexual passion confronts Alison's constrained coolness, and his only way through is to victimise her for the frustration of his passion, to blame her by identifying her with the impoverishment of feeling which permeates every aspect of social organisation. To Alison, Jimmy embodies 'vitality': 'Everything about him seemed to burn, his face, the edges of his hair glistened and seemed to spring off his head, and his eyes were so blue and full of the sun'. The only time Alison burns is with pain at the loss of their child, when she abases herself as Jimmy's victim – 'This is what he's been longing for me to feel,' she says, 'I'm in the fire, and I'm burning, and all I want is to die! . . . But what does it matter – this is what he wanted from me!' It is her emotional detachment and her implied sexual coldness which provokes his brutality.[42]

To a generation in search of symbols of cultural regeneration *Look Back in Anger* acclaimed the priority of passion and feeling over good taste, of anger over artificial and deadening constraint. That it also betrayed a deep mysogyny seemed irrelevant. It appeared to represent a rougher, more honest version of the truth, social as well as personal. The work of other intellectuals across the spectrum of film, theatre and literature challenging established values and transforming the rules of the genre, created an invigorating sense of a coherent cultural movement.

Intellectual protest was soon identified with wider dissent on more overtly political issues. The Suez crisis of 1956 (which provoked the first important post war divisions in the country and signalled the turbulent retreat from Empire) and the establishment of the Campaign for Nuclear Disarmament the next year, were signs of fracture in the political consensus. Both were seen as having significant moral overtones. Suez was a failure of the Government's moral as well as political authority. CND, the nursery of political commitment for thousands of young people, focused on the Bomb as a potent issue of morality.[43] The threat of nuclear catastrophe framed a backdrop of insecurity which put in question the values of the consensus. It was this uncertainty about the nuclear future and the decline in the nation's international status which was, according to the official inquiry into the condition of Britain's adolescents, 'felt to lie immediately behind the small stage of many an adolescent's activities, like a massive and belittling backcloth'.[44]

CND supporter Jeff Nuttall spoke for the young when he described the threat of the Bomb as a decisive break with any previous norms of morality: 'No man was certain any more of anything but his own volition so that the only value was pragmatic. Moral values, thought absolute, were now seen to be comparative, for all social entities around which morality had revolved were now called into doubt. . . . Even Nature had come to mean poisoned stratosphere, contaminated rain, vegetables and milk that made men breed monsters.' It was a break with the past full of pretences and lies – about the bomb as much as about sex – which provoked rejection: 'Dad was a liar. He lied about the war and he lied about sex. He lied about the bomb and he lied about the future. He lived his life on an elaborate system of pretence that had been going on for hundreds of years.'[45]

Private Liberties and Public Duties

The overt political challenge to the institutional control of sexual morals came on the issue of how far the State could legitimately intervene in what was increasingly seen as the realms of private behaviour. This key debate of the 1950s, which polarized opinion for the next decade, was precipitated by controversy over the operation of the homosexuality laws after an intensified Home Office and police effort to 'clean up vice'.

Homosexual activity between consenting adults in private had been a criminal offence since 1885. Though scientific understanding of homosexuality had been enlarged through research, no attempts had been made to alter the law. Kinsey's 1948 Report had uncovered the extent of homosexual activity; it concluded that 4 per-cent of American males were exclusively homosexual throughout their lives, 8 per-cent were more or less exclusively homosexual for at least three years between ages 16–65 and 37 per-cent of the total male population had at least some overt homosexual experience to orgasm between adolescence and old age.[46] This tallied with British research which showed that around 1 in 25 males, i.e. 4 per-cent, were homosexual, an estimated 650,000 men.[47] Kinsey's treatment of normality and deviance not as fixed absolutes but as points on a wide spectrum of sexual variety gained currency. As experts began to reassess the medical and psychological definitions of homosexuality, doubts formed in other quarters over whether criminal sanctions were the appropriate means of control. The Church of England was in the forefront when they set up a Committee in 1952 to look into whether homosexuality, though a sin in the eyes of the Church, should remain a crime under the laws of the state.

It was the Home Office's law enforcement policy which triggered a full scale public confrontation. Law enforcement had in practice varied widely across the country, depending on the zeal of local Chief Constables, until the Home Office initiated a policy to tighten up on 'vice' in the early 1950s. This policy is attributed to anxiety in the aftermath of the defection to Russia in 1951 of the spies, Burgess and Maclean, both homosexuals, which began an identification of homosexuals with spies as scapegoats of Cold War paranoia. America, in the grip of McCarthyism, identified homosexuals as security risks and carried out a purge of known homosexuals in the security services. In three years from 1947 to 1950, 192 cases of homosexuals were handled by the US government departments; in the next seven months, there were 382 cases.[48] It was known that senior police officers had been sent from Scotland Yard to confer with the FBI.

With the appointment of the new Metropolitan Police Commissioner Sir John Knott-Bower in 1953, new directives were issued by the Home Secretary Sir David Maxwell Fyffe to make sentences stiffer and more uniform. His views on homosexuals were quite plain; they were 'exhibitionists and proselytisers, and a danger to others, especially the young. So long as I hold the office of Home Secretary, I shall give no countenance to the view that they should not be prevented from being such a danger.'[49]

The result was an increase in prosecutions in 1953, supported by a particularly vitriolic chorus from sections of the press, notably John Gordon of the *Sunday Express*, in which homosexuals and homosexuality were excoriated as, variously, a 'cancer', a 'spreading fungus', a 'disease', and 'an unsavoury and repulsive subject'. In October 1953, police activity reached its height with the prosecution of a series of public figures. William Field, Labour MP for Paddington North was convicted on charges of importuning on the evidence of two police officers. Nobody had actually been picked up by Field and he denied the charges, but resigned in October – 'a heavy price to pay', as his colleague Ian Harvey wrote, 'for a wink and a smile'.[50] Actor John Gielgud was fined for persistently importuning, but on his return to the theatre was given a standing ovation by the audience. Author Rupert Croft-Cooke was convicted of committing acts of gross indecency on the evidence of two naval ratings who had spent the weekend with him. Croft-Cooke denied the charges, but despite testimonies of his exemplary character from Lord Kinross and Compton Mackenzie, he was sentenced to nine months imprisonment, after which he left Britain to live in Morocco.

The sensational trial of Lord Montagu of Beaulieu, charged with indecently assaulting a 14 year old boy-scout at a beach hut on his estate, was the culmination of the campaign and the point at which the tide began to turn in favour of reform. The boy scout, who, with others, had been guarding the treasures of Beaulieu during the Bank Holiday weekend, had been invited by Lord Montagu and a film director, Kenneth Hume, for a swim. When Lord Montagu reported a missing camera to the police, the boy-scout was called in for questioning and made the allegations. Though Lord Montagu was cleared of the charge of committing an unnatural offence, the jury disagreed on a second charge of indecent assault, and a re-trial was ordered.

This time Lord Montagu and two other men, Peter Wildeblood, diplomatic correspondent of the *Daily Mail*, and Michael Pitt-Rivers, Montagu's cousin, were further charged with conspiracy to incite unnatural acts and acts of gross indecency. The case rested on the evidence of two airmen, John Reynolds and Edward McNally, who admitted having been involved in twenty-four other homosexual affairs, but were granted immunity for turning Queen's evidence. The trial, which lasted for eight days in March 1954 and received sensational press coverage, resulted in the conviction of all three men. Montagu was sentenced to prison for twelve months, Wildeblood, who had confessed to being an 'invert', and Pitt Rivers, were both sentenced to eighteen months. As Reynolds and McNally left the court, the large crowd outside, which had waited daily, Wildeblood's defence counsel suggested, to see 'the crucifixion of a human being', booed and jeered Reynolds and McNally as they covered themselves with a travelling rug in the back of the car. For Peter Wildeblood, the public exposure had one side effect: 'I was able, at last, to move out of a false position and take up a true one. There was no further need for pretence; I could discard the mask which had been such a burden to me all my life.'[51]

The trial triggered profound concern about the homosexuality laws. The exposure of several disquieting aspects of police procedure in dealing with homosexuals – searching premises without a warrant, the use of witnesses who were granted immunity, the use of police *agents provocateurs*, and mounting evidence that homosexuals were a group particularly vulnerable to blackmail became a just cause, in the view of sections of the press, for an immediate and full inquiry into the state of the law. In Parliament

Sir Robert Boothby was among those who had been convinced by events that the duty of the State was 'to protect youth from corruption and the public from indecency and nuisance. What consenting adults do in privacy may be a moral issue between them and their Maker, but . . . it is not a legal issue between them and the State'.[52] It was a view influentially endorsed by the Church of England in its interim report *The Problem of Homosexuality*, (1954). This advocated separating the sin from the crime and criticized a law which uniquely interfered in the private actions of consenting adults, and which failed to act as a deterrent while encouraging blackmail, police corruption and the social isolation of homosexuals.

Within a month the Home Secretary announced that a departmental committee would look into the law relating to both homosexuality and prostitution. The Wolfenden Committee reported in 1957 with unequivocal support for decriminalizing homosexual activity between consenting adults in private. In a statement of principle which became the blueprint for libertarian legislation, it declared that the function of the law was to preserve public order and decency, to protect the citizen from what was offensive or injurious and to provide safeguards against corruption and exploitation of others. It was not the law's function 'to intervene in the private lives of citizens, or to seek to enforce any particular pattern of behaviour further than is necessary to carry out the purposes we have outlined'. There must remain, they decided, 'a realm of private morality and immorality which is, in brief and crude terms, not the law's business', but the personal and private responsibility of the individual, which they could be expected to carry out without the threat of punishment by law.[53]

This important statement of principle was an explicit departure from previous belief that the State had a duty to intervene in private morality to protect the order and stability of society and its institutions. It triggered a public debate which polarized opinion between paternalist defenders of the State's controlling powers, and libertarian defenders of the right of individuals to enlarge their freedom of choice. It energized a campaign to reform the homosexuality laws, deemed by supporters to be unjust, inhumane, conducive to more social evil than they prevented, out of tune with humanitarian concepts of social justice and out of step with modern scientific understanding of sexual behaviour, which victimized a group of men by condemning them to a life of duplicity, secrecy and constant fear of prosecution.

Although seven national newspapers supported reform, and public opinion moved steadily in its favour (polls showed over 40 per-cent of the public in support[54]) the Government resisted. The Home Secretary, R. A. Butler, under pressure from paternalist opinion in the Conservative Party, argued that public opinion was not in favour of change. The Government, he said, could not risk offending the 'natural moral sense' of a very large section of the population by any alteration of the law which might imply approval or tolerance of 'a great social evil', for the constraints of criminal law carried even more weight at a time when religious and ethical restraints were weak.[55] The task of persuading Parliament and public opinion towards reform passed to a lobby group, the Homosexual Law Reform Society, set up in 1958 and supported by a group of mostly Labour MP's. They kept the issue in the forefront of public attention, although it was another decade before they had any success.

The liberal defence of individual rights in the Wolfenden Committee's recommendations on homosexuality were nowhere in evidence when it came to prostitution, the subject of the other half of their Report. Applying the same principle, that the law's function was to preserve public order and decency and protect the public from corruption, exploitation and what is offensive, they recommended increasing the penalties on soliciting and prostitution, and paid little attention to individual liberties.

Prostitution had been included in the brief in response to rising concern about the ineffectiveness of the soliciting laws and the increased visibility of prostitution. Several local councils and morality organizations had sent deputations to the Home Secretary demanding action to clean up the streets. The Bishop of London led one in 1951, and various petitions from residents in affected areas added to the pressure. Convictions for street offences had risen steadily – from an annual average of 2000 in the early years of the war to nearly 12,000 by 1955. Much of this however was the consequence of increased police activity and did not reflect an increase in the number of prostitutes. In the West End Central

Division of the Metropolitan Police District in 1953, the 6,829 prosecutions involved only 808 prostitutes.[56]

Several scandals had brought organized prostitution to public attention. In 1950 Duncan Webb of the *People* published an exposé of the notorious Messina Gang who had been known to run a prostitution racket for years – a state of affairs, Webb declared, mobilizing a form of racist paranoia, 'that would disgrace one of the licentious ports of the Middle East'.[57] The five Messina brothers, of Maltese extraction, had run a chain of brothels, starting in Egypt, and then in London, before and during the war. It was lucrative business. One prostitute who was set up by brother Gino, estimated she earned £150,000 for him during the fifteen years she was on the streets. He set her up in a flat and controlled her completely, dictating that she must sleep with him when he demanded, have no more than ten minutes with each client, and deliver all her earnings to him. When Gino was imprisoned in 1947 for assault, rumours began to circulate about the brothers' activities. In the House of Commons it was alleged that they earned £500,000 a year, owned a firm of West End estate agents and controlled up to twenty women.[58] But they were not caught until 1951, when Alfredo Messina was convicted of living on immoral earnings and bribing a police officer and was sentenced to two years in prison.

The alarm over the visibility of prostitution occurred at a time when there was simultaneous concern to shore up marriage and the family. Prostitution represented the antithesis of ordered, contained female sexuality. Its visibility was condemned as a possible source of corruption of marital ideals, not to mention innocent young men, and the prostitute herself was vilified as an outlaw and a threat to social and moral values – a 'reproach to our society', as R. A. Butler, Home Secretary condemned her, who chose an occupation which 'gives her both freedom from irksome routine and the means of earning much more than she would earn in regular employment'[59] (a legitimate aim, one would think, in a later economy, but not in the 1950s). It was her visibility, with its threat to stable values, which was used to justify further controls over women.

Hence the Wolfenden Committee's brief was not with organized prostitution, nor the private morality or immorality of prostitutes, which they believed was the concern of the Churches and social welfare institutions, but with activities in the course of carrying out their occupation which were offensive to public decency. They recommended tightening control over prostitutes by increasing penalties for soliciting, facilitating the police work by no longer requiring the need to prove annoyance and enabling them to arrest women without warrant on suspicion 'with reasonable cause' of soliciting, and increasing magistrates powers over tenants or occupiers using premises for prostitution. The objective was to clear the streets. The risk that this would encourage closer organization of the trade and increase opportunities for the exploitation of prostitution was less judged injurious to public morality than the presence of prostitutes on the streets.[60]

The Government showed no hesitation in endorsing these proposals in the Street Offences Act of 1959, despite criticism that the removal of requirement to prove annoyance was a gross infringement of women's liberties, and that the law was 'archaic, harsh, and unjust to women'. It increased penalties on women while the clients, men, went unpunished. It endorsed, according to the Archbishop of Canterbury, 'the old-fashioned view . . . that men have every right to a reasonable supply of prostitutes and should not in any way be restrained from resorting to them'[61], and it confirmed the sexual confusion of a society which tolerated prostitution as a social necessity, but subjected the prostitute to serious disabilities and treated her, not as a public benefactress but as a 'degraded woman of vicious character'. Doubts were expressed in Parliament about the wisdom of dealing with it by driving it underground. The proposals, suggested Anthony Greenwood, MP, 'would not cure the disease; they would merely conceal the symptoms . . . it would facilitate the work of vice rings and might well produce a new crop of touts battering on prostitution'. This consideration did not trouble Dr A. D. Broughton MP who declared, 'It is better, I think, if we have a festering sore, to keep it covered and out of sight rather than have it exposed, a revolting sight to decent people and a possible cause of infection among the young.'[62]

The immediate aim of cleaning up the streets was achieved. Convictions for soliciting dropped from nearly 17,000 in 1958 to 1,100 in 1962, although few would argue that prostitution itself had declined so rapidly. Off the streets, organized prostitution and call-girl arrangements flourished, as the Conservative Government was to discover to its cost during the Profumo scandal of 1963.

Filth, or Sacred Sex

The struggle between libertarians and paternalists was joined again over the obscenity laws, when opinion polarized around the key questions of how far the State should legitimately intervene in freedom of publication, and whether the law was so far out of step with public beliefs and standards of frankness about sex that it was in danger of falling into disrepute. The conflict was again precipitated by the zealous activities of the Home Office exceeding what was seen by an influential section of the intelligentsia as the boundaries of permissible State control, which led to orchestrated attempts to reform the law.

In the early 1950s, public concern over sexual frankness in anything from Sunday newspapers to imported, 'pornographic' publications, was kept alive by vigilant public morality bodies and by the Churches. Their efforts were backed up by the Commissioner of the Metropolitan Police who had instituted a drive against pornography in 1949 which resulted over the next few years in the destruction of around 100,000 publications with such titles as *A Basinful of Sin, Academy of Love, Shameless*, and *Soho Street Girl*. Serious literature had not been immune, but a 1949 attempt to prosecute Norman Mailer's *The Naked and the Dead* as obscene was blocked by the Attorney General, Sir Hartley Shawcross. He made plain that it was not his intention to 'seek to make the criminal law a vehicle for imposing a censorship on the frank discussion or portrayal of sordid and unedifying aspects of life simply on the grounds of offence against taste or manners', and asserted there should be 'the least possible interference with the freedom of publication'.[63]

It was a very different regime in 1954. Reputedly on the advice of the recent Interpol Conference which concluded that pornography was the cause of sex crimes, the Home Office launched a campaign against 'obscene and licentious publications' in which the distinction between serious literature and pornography was blurred. In what appeared to some to be a witchhunt by the Home

Office – which was coincidentally cleaning up homosexual 'vice' – four reputable publishers found themselves in the dock at the Central Criminal court charged with publishing obscene libels.

Three books – *The Image and the Search* by Walter Baxter, *The Man in Control* by Arthur Barker, and *September in Quinze* by Vivian Connell had been brought to the attention of the Director of Public Prosecutions after a publisher in a pornography case had defended himself by inviting comparison between his products and these examples of serious literature. The DPP decided to prosecute. Two more books, Stanley Kauffman's *The Philanderer*, and Margot Bland's *Julia* were prosecuted independently in the Isle of Man after police received a complaint that they were available at Boots Circulating Library. The High Bailiff reluctantly convicted both, but imposed only a nominal fine of £1 and expressed regret that though the public might regard modern books with a different eye from their fathers the law had not changed.[64] The DPP, on hearing about these, decided to prosecute them as well.

The cases immediately alerted publishers and intellectuals to the vulnerability of literary freedom under the arbitrary censorship laws. Secker and Warbug decided to take a stand and opted for trial by jury in *The Philanderer* case. They were fortunate in being tried by a liberal judge, Mr Justice Sable, whose respect for writers who felt it their duty to portray 'the realities of human love and intercourse' was evident when he directed the jury to consider whether 'the act of sexual passion' was 'sheer filth', and whether the standard of censorship should be determined by what was suitable for a fourteen-year-old schoolgirl. Though Secker and Warburg were acquitted (or, as C. H. Rolph a leading expert put it, the judge 'declared that it is not dirty for men and women to go to bed together, or even record in print the fact that they do'[65]), the fate of the other books exposed considerable uncertainty in the law. Publishers were left with no clear indication of whether or not they were publishing an obscenity. *Julia* was convicted by a magistrate, *September in Quinze* was convicted at the Old Bailey, it took three trials to acquit *The Image and the Search*, and *The Man in Control* was acquitted after only fifteen minutes of the jury's deliberations.

Several writers mounted a press campaign to protest against a

law which 'threatened to . . . establish a police censorship of literature' and forced authors to 'write under the shadow of the Old
Bailey if they failed to produce works suitable for the teenager'.[66]
Their unease was channelled into a campaign by the Society of
Authors and the Publisher's Association to change the law to
safeguard literary freedom. The trials also provoked public comment on the gulf which had opened up between official censorship
standards which denounced literary representations of sex as cor-
rupting 'filth' and a more general frankness about sex accepted by
the public. The 'frank discussion of topics regarded as unmentionable by our grandfathers' was, Frederic Warburg maintained in
his defence, as much a part of life as of literature.'[87] Graham
Greene described as 'Manichean nonsense' the attitude that 'seems
to condemn any description of man's sexual nature as though sex
in itself were ugly'.[68] J. B. Priestley commented: 'You would
imagine from all these complaints that sex can only be discovered
in print, whereas there is so much sex in most people's heads that
a writer would have to work very hard to put any more in it . . .
This talk of "sheer filth" and corruption of the young appears
to me very silly.'[69] Marghanita Laski confessed herself 'stupidly
confused' on the meaning of corruption. It could be, she suggested,
that reading books may 'lead to adultery, but a far more usual
cause, I think, is attractive members of the opposite sex . . . Or is
it that these books make people want to copulate, like war and
music and the time of year? But if that were so, we'd surely start
by banning war.'[70]

The law reform campaign orchestrated by A. P. Herbert published proposals in 1955 which were introduced as a Bill under
the Ten Minute Rule in Parliament by Roy Jenkins MP (also
a Committee member) in March. This failed but when it was
reintroduced as a Private Members Bill two years later, it received
a more favourable response and was referred to a Select Committee
under Sir Patrick Spens. The Spens Report came out in support
of the Herbert proposals in March 1958.

Although the Home Secretary, R. A. Butler, was more sympathetic to reform than his predecessor, he perceived that the problem
was how to frame a Bill which would protect literature but strengthen the law against pornography. The Obscene Publications Act,
1959, was the result of much compromise. It replaced the common

law offence of obscenity with a test of whether, taken as a whole, the article would 'tend to deprave or corrupt', and added a provision for defence that its publication was 'for the public good on the grounds that it is in the interests of science, literature, art or learning or other objects of general concern'.

The Act was welcomed in 1959 as piece of progressive legislation which improved the safeguards on literary and artistic freedom. But as the boundaries of permissible expression shifted over the next two decades it became the battleground for endless legal wrangles and satisfied neither libertarians nor paternalists.

The immediate test of the law came with the DPP's decision in 1960 to prosecute Penguin Books for publishing D. H. Lawrence's *Lady Chatterley's Lover* in a 3s 6d paperback edition to complete their publication of Lawrence's works. The thirty five men and women experts who were now able, under the new law, to come to the defence of the book (and indeed, Lady Chatterley, for it sometimes appeared it was she who was on trial) made this, as one commentator observed, 'the most expensively-mounted and high-powered course on D. H. Lawrence that money has ever been unable to buy'.[71] It was the opportunity not only to justify freedom of expression about sex; it also illuminated contemporary views on the positive meaning of sex in relationships, for rarely had sexual intercourse been talked about in so much detail in a public place.

From the outset prosecuting counsel, Mervyn Griffith Jones, excelled himself as the embodiment of an old order. He condemned it as a book 'of little more than vicious indulgence in sex and sensuality' which 'may tend to induce lustful thoughts in the minds of those who read it', which 'sets upon a pedestal promiscuous and adulterous intercourse' and 'sets out to commend sensuality almost as a virtue'. The jury were invited, in an ill-advised phrase which echoed through the trial, to ask themselves if it was 'a book that you would have lying around in your own house? Is it a book that you would even wish your wife or your servants to read?'[72] The book contained no moral teaching; moreover, he pointed out, it contained 'thirteen episodes of sexual intercourse', twelve of them 'described in detail leaving nothing to the imagination' and it 'abounds in bawdy conversation..' and four letter words. 'The word "fuck",' he declared, 'or "fucking" occurs no less than thirty times. I have added them up . . . "Cunt" fourteen times; "balls" thirteen times, "shit" and "arse" six times apiece; "cock" four times; "piss" three times, and so on.'

It was one way to analyse a work of literature, though not one which commended itself to the Defence counsel, Gerald Gardiner, or the thirty five experts, who preferred see the book as, in Gardiner's words, 'a passionate and sincere work of the moralist in the puritan tradition, who believed he had a message for us in the society in which we live'. Far from favouring promiscuity, he claimed, Lawrence 'contrasted the unsatisfactory and futile nature of promiscuous relations with a normal and healthy relationship of people in love, which should bind a man and woman perfectly together'. There was the question of adultery; he rather objected to statements made about Constance Chatterley 'as though she were a nymphomaniac'. From a legal point of view, a book was not obscene merely because part of its subject matter was a relationship between people who were not married or who were married to someone else, for if that were so, 90 per-cent of English literature would be obscene. There were minds, he suggested, 'which would describe Anthony and Cleopatra as a play about adultery, as "the story of a sex starved soldier copulating with an Egyptian queen" . . . minds which are unable to see beauty where it exists and doubt the integrity of purpose in an author where it was obvious.'[72]

The parade of witnesses expressed almost unqualified approval for the author's philosophy and purpose, and for his celebration, of sex. Dame Rebecca West introduced the view that the book was an allegory for a culture which had become sterile: 'the love affair with the gamekeeper was a calling, a return of the soul to the more intense life that he felt when people had had a different culture'. This provoked Griffith Jones to exasperation at the elevated plane of learning which marked the distinguished witnesses: 'I ask you, is that typical of the effect that this book will have upon the average reader . . . ? Are they really going to see an allegory in the thing . . . One wonders . . . whether one is talking the same language', a view echoed by the judge, who instructed the jury 'not to get lost' in the higher realms of literature, education, sociology and ethics. The prosecution kept insisting the jury remember the book was being sold for 3s 6d, which seemed to exclude the possibility of allegory.

Richard Hoggart, author of *The Uses of Literacy* and Senior lecturer in English Literature at Leicester University prompted even more astonishment by declaring the book was 'highly virtuous and, if anything, puritanical'. Asked for clarification, he explained it was 'a moral book' expressing 'the enormous reverence which must be paid by one human being to another with whom he is in love and, in particular, the reverence towards one's physical relationships'. It was a view endorsed by Dr John Robinson, the Bishop of Woolwich, who was in no doubt Lawrence was trying 'to portray the sex relationship as something essentially sacred . . . as in a real sense an act of holy communion'. Having delivered this banner headline, he went on to describe Lawrence's 'quite astonishing sensitivity to the beauty and value of all organic relationships' and the book's positive ethical value in stressing 'the real value and integrity of personal relations; that sex is not just a means of using other people but a means of respect for them'. Pressed by the judge to comment, as a man of the church, on whether it portrayed 'the life of an immoral woman', the Bishop decided it portrayed 'the life of a woman in an immoral relationship, is so far as adultery is an immoral relationship' and affirmed, in another banner headline, that it was 'a book that Christians ought to read'.

This precipitated an immediate rebuke from the Archbishop of Canterbury who wished to dissociate the Church with the utmost speed from the Bishop's views and re-assert the immorality and sinfulness of adultery: 'The good pastor will teach his people to avoid both the fact of and the desire for sex experience of an adulterous kind and fornication also,' he warned, regretting that the Bishop's participation in the trial was 'a stumbling block and a cause of offence to many ordinary Christians'. The Bishop was unrepentant, and launched into print the following week to point out Lawrence's views on 'the sacredness of sex' had much to teach Christians. The Church, he claimed 'has had an unhappy record in this matter, for which it has to make amends'.[73] For the Bishop, this was just the opening salvo.

The trial lasted six days, during which no book by anyone had probably been better read in public to such rapt attention, and nowhere had the meaning of sexual intercourse been so exhaustively examined. The publishers were acquitted. And so, in a way, was Lady Chatterley, for as the *Sunday Observer* remarked: 'We also remembered the persistence with which both judge and prosecution had hammered it home that Lady C. was an immoral woman, that she had had sexual relations before marriage, that she had committed adultery under her husband's roof; as if these charges somehow disqualified her from participation in serious literature. Indeed, there were long periods in the trial during which an outsider might well have assumed that a divorce case was being heard.'[74]

The judgment provoked an immediate outburst in the House of Lords. Several of their Lordships wondered what terrible floodgates had been opened, and where it was all leading to. Speaking to a motion asking the Government to 'take such steps as are possible to ban for all time writings of this nature, particularly those of the author of this book', The Earl of Craven launched into picturesque assault: 'We have opened the gate to any book which presents lust and unfaithfulness in what some concupiscent minds will call art ... The Christian virtues of our ancestors are being violated in order to fill the ever-bulging pockets of unscrupulous publishers with gold filched from the virtues of our children ... What is the result? Purity is sacrificed on the altar of promiscuity as woolly-headed intellectuals pour their vociferous sewage into the ears of the public.'[75] The steam was taken out of this rearguard action by other Lords pointing out that the time to have objected was during the passing of the Obscene Publications Act, and this was now the law of the land which they had passed without division. The motion was defeated.

Libraries and bookshops around the country dealt cautiously with the book. Swansea Libraries Committee bought a copy to be available on request only; young girl assistants would not be able to handle it, and if other woman assistants objected to it, they could refuse.[76] A bookshop in Bromley, Kent prohibited the sale to schoolchildren unless they had a note from parents. In Yorkshire an enterprising butcher displayed the book in his shop window alongside the parsley and lamb chops. Half the booksellers were reported to be following W. H. Smith's example of keeping it off the shelves and selling only on demand. Several important bookshops refused to sell the book at all. The regional librarian at Eastwood, Lawrence's birthplace, reported only seven requests for it; the current bestseller there was *Saturday Night and Sunday Morning*.[77]

In Edinburgh, Miss Agnes Cooper, 62, a former missionary in the Belgian Congo, bought a copy and set fire to it on the pavement outside the shop. She said she had not read the book but 'was convinced it was evil'.[78] In a Midlands Girls school on the day of acquittal the thirteen-year-olds class, which had followed the trial as part of current affairs, wrote 'Congratulations Lady C' across the blackboard. A former pupil recalled the trial had been: 'an open forum to discuss eroticism, sensuality, and, in the words of the Bishop of Woolwich, "quite astonishing sensitivity for the beauty and value of all organic relationships" . . . While the trial continued our excitement was about the idea of the book, that sex was not a taboo "dirty" subject . . . it wasn't the titillation of reading rude words that fascinated me, as my father drily dismissed it. It was the revelation that sex for a woman could be an incredible physical experience, not just an artificial, romantic, airbrushed ecstasy, guilt ridden surrender in sordid circumstances. We wouldn't be lying back, thinking of England.'[79]

A New Morality

By the early 1960s, the tide was turning as support gathered for measures which would loosen State controls over private morality and individual choice. Members of the Labour opposition began to put sexual morals on the agenda as part of a bid to capture the libertarian electoral terrain. Roy Jenkins MP proposed the concept of a 'civilized society' to identify the Labour Party with the removal of restrictions on personal liberty, and rally 'those who want to be free to lead their own lives, to make their own mistakes, and to decide in an adult way . . . the code by which they want to live'. The Labour Party, he argued in the *The Labour Case* (1959) should foster a climate of opinion 'favourable to gaiety, tolerance, and beauty, and unfavourable to puritanical restriction, to petty-minded disapproval, to hypocrisy'. His targets were the 'brutal and unfair' laws on homosexuality, the 'fantastic' powers of the Lord Chamberlain to censor plays, the divorce laws which 'involve both a great deal of unnecessary suffering and a great number of attempts . . . to deceive the courts', and the 'harsh and archaic' abortion laws.[80]

For Anthony Crosland MP these goals held electoral appeal as part of a programme of modernization, and as issues of social justice. As material conditions improved, 'an ethical, idealistic appeal, such as a true socialist party should always make,' he wrote, may be 'more in tune with the temper of the country'.[81] Reform of the laws governing sexual morals may be as important a goal as material advancement, for 'if we really attach importance to the "dignity of man", we must realize that this is as much affronted by a hypocritical divorce law . . . as by the refusal to establish a joint production council in a factory'. The time would come he suggested, 'when divorce-law reform will increase the sum of human welfare more than a rise in food subsidies'.[82]

Although these proposals never became official policy in a party still hesitant to bring controversial and divisive 'private' issues to the centre of the political stage, they changed the terms of the sexual debate. Reforms were identified on the left as issues of liberty, social justice, and progress. 'If we can not only abolish material poverty, but begin to reduce the poverty of human relationships, we shall in the end enrich not only private life but the vitality of the community as a whole,' echoed Anthony Arblaster in the left-wing *Tribune*. Progress was not merely material advance – '*real* progress is measured in terms of the enrichment of human lives'.[83]

It was an astute initiative, for by 1962 there was widespread support for a new morality, and for a change in institutional controls. Reith lecturer G. M. Carstairs condemned popular morality as 'a wasteland, littered with the debris of broken convictions', and questioned whether a sexual morality which appeared to consist entirely of sexual restraint was tackling the moral problems raised by social change. Moral norms were shifting rapidly, especially among the young. Chastity no longer seemed 'the supreme moral virtue'; young people, seeing sexual relationship as a source of pleasure, were 'turning our own society into one in which sexual experience, with precautions against conception, is becoming accepted as a sensible preliminary to marriage'; they saw marriage as 'a mutually considerate and mutually satisfying partnership' – in marked contrast to 'the unromantic compromise between sensuality and drudgery which has been the lot of so many British husbands and wives in the past 60 years'.[84] In 1963 social commentator Alan McGlashan diagnosed the national judgement as 'ambiguous and vascillating' on any sexual issue: 'we half-enjoy the new freedoms, but carefully maintain institutions, based on a now discredited moral code, to punish ourselves remorselessly for doing so'.[85] These were just preliminaries to a more concerted onslaught.

The tension between license and taboo which dominated the 1950s was moving towards some sort of resolution. The State's right to control individual morality had been challenged, and sexual reforms had reached the political agenda as issues of social justice and personal liberty. Young people were seen as the catalysts of change in the search for a new morality because conventional values of sexual restraint no longer commanded their allegiance. They were to remain the agents of change during the next decade.

Eight

Release

'We're not hung up on sex like our parents were. Sex used to be a dishonest activity that one indulged in with stealth. Now it's considered a normal part of a relationship. People accuse us of being immoral, but in fact we have a very strong moral code – a genuineness in our approach to each other. It's our parents' generation that's obsessed with sex, not ours.'[1]
'Girl' student interviewed in *The Sunday Telegraph*, 30 Nov, 1969

Sex was politicised in the 1960s. From lurking as an often unspoken factor behind a range of social anxieties, it became the pivot of profound political division. Between the Profumo Affair of 1963 and the onslaught on established authority which fuelled the convulsions of 1968–69, a major shift of allegiance occurred. The Profumo Affair embroiled the Government in sexual scandal and unlocked the outrage about declining moral standards which had built up during the 1950s. By the early 1970s society had shifted towards a pluralistic morality, in which the State's power to dictate morality was reduced, the individual's power to make moral choices strengthened and an ethic of individual choice, which asserted the priority of the personal over external constraints, commanded the allegiance of a wide spectrum of public opinion.

The shift was made possible because key institutions charged with custody of public morals – Parliament, the church, censorship authorities and broadcasting organizations – steadily abrogated their powers to intervene in private morality. Motivated partly by pragmatic considerations of how best to retain their authority at a time of changing standards, and partly by a commitment to pluralistic values, they were also responding to public pressures, in particular from the younger generation.

As the political currency of sex changed, so did its commercial currency. From being private and secretive sex became suddenly public, available and accessible. In an affluent consumer society which lauded the values of individual choice and instant gratification, it became a marketable commodity on a new scale. Sex came out in the open – on the billboards, in the pages of the daily press. As the boundaries between private and public sex crumbled, the sexual bargain changed. Sex could be dissociated from the social ceremony and emotional baggage which had hitherto pegged it to love and marriage as the foundation of social stability. Now the bargaining counters – promises of love, commitment, fidelity – became disposable items, optional clauses in a new sexual contract in which the priority, sexually and commercially, was to 'spend'. This was one kind of freedom.

It was freedom bought at an uncertain price by women, whose full participation in the contract had been guaranteed by the intervention of the Pill. Infallible contraception broke the carefully maintained link between female sexuality, reproduction and domesticity which had been the central mechanism for controlling women. It promised women not only freedom but sexual equality. But as women were released to experience sex as part of personal self-discovery, and saw themselves reflected on the billboards as eroticized, de-personalized *objects* of desire, they saw how unfree and unequal they were. The process of re-negotiating women's sexual rights, of establishing their own terms for equality proceeded from this recognition.

Other freedoms fought for in the 1960s – the right to make personal sexual choices without the constraint of discredited rules, the right to explore private sexuality without guilt, to liberate the consciousness for pleasure, and the freedom to be explicit in literature, film and theatre – were all subversive claims in a society still bound by traditional restraints. But in the early 1960s the ethic of individual choice which was to blossom with a general loosening of constraints over sexual behaviour, was seen as a regenerative force, if also a source of acute and sometimes dramatic social tension.

'A Woman of Easy Virtue and a Proved Liar'

The Profumo Affair of 1963 could have been just another piece of Fleet Street gossip. But in the heightened atmosphere of the time, it became the occasion for an orgy of moral outrage which left the Conservative Government's moral authority in tatters and almost certainly contributed to its downfall. It brought other anxieties to the surface: about the gap between public and private morals; about the decline of restraint and discipline in national life; about the private conduct of public men, and about public hypocrisy. And it linked sex with spying in the most potent cocktail of subversive activities possible at the time.

The story itself was relatively unremarkable. In 1961, John Profumo, the Minister for War in Macmillan's Cabinet, had a brief affair with Christine Keeler, a nineteen-year-old ex-model and showgirl. They met at the swimming pool at Cliveden, Lord Astor's country mansion, through the auspices of Stephen Ward, a fashionable society osteopath with whom Keeler was at the time sharing a flat. The affair was elevated beyond a subject for mere gossip by Ward's association with Captain Eugene Ivanov, the assistant naval attaché at the Russian Embassy, with whom, it was subsequently alleged, Keeler also shared her bed (though this has been doubted ever since).[2]

In 1963, the country was in the grip of acute anxiety over spies. It had just emerged from a period of critical international tension over Berlin and the Cuban Missile crisis, followed by a round-up of spies which had caused some embarrassment to the Government and security services. The latest case of John Vassall, a former junior clerk in the Foriegn Office in Moscow was to have crucial repercussions in the Profumo case. Vassall claimed he was blackmailed into spying after being found in compromising homosexual relations with men sent to trap him. He was convicted and imprisoned for espionage. But a press campaign of rumour and innuendo picked up the theme of subversive sex when it linked Vassall in a homosexual relationship with Thomas Galbraith, the Civil Lord of the Admiralty, (for whom Vassall had worked as secretary). Galbraith denied the allegations, but offered his resignation to Macmillan, who accepted it in a decision he soon regretted as 'a serious mistake'.

The Tribunal set up to look into the handling of the Vassall affair cleared Galbraith of any improper association and conduded the rumours had been without foundation. This not only confirmed to Macmillan the error of accepting his resignation, it also left the Government suffused with confidence that rumours could be proved baseless. There was another repercussion. When two journalists were imprisoned for not revealing their sources, it opened a wound of bitterness in sections of the press which was still smarting when the Profumo affair broke.

By early 1963, even as the Tribunal was sitting, rumours were circulating round Fleet Street that a 'call-girl', Keeler, had shared her bed with both the Minister for War and an attaché at the Russian Embassy. The press, armed with accumulating evidence, waited at bay, not wishing to follow a French newspaper's example and be sued for libel by Profumo. The rumours had already reached government and security service circles, Ward and Keeler had been investigated, Profumo, questioned by government officials on a number of occasions had denied the affair, and MI5 had been consulted and reported back that there was no breach of national security. This justified a degree of equanimity in the Government's handling of these rumours.

The Opposition had also been alerted. The lugubrious Labour MP George Wigg (who had recently suffered a minor humiliation at Profumo's hands) was in no doubt there were security implications. He had been keeping a dossier on the affair since January and was now awaiting an opportunity to bring it to public attention. It came when Christine Keeler disappeared before the trial of a West Indian boyfriend on a charge of attempting to shoot her, giving the press the pretext to run a story on her as the 'missing model'. As the House of Commons was debating the Vassall case, Wigg used the protection of Parliamentary privelege to challenge the Home Secretary to deny the rumours surrounding Christine Keeler, which may, he suggested, cover matters which 'infringe on the security of the State'.[3] The fuse was lit. Next day, after a 3 a.m. confrontation with senior government officers, Profumo delivered a statement in the House of Commons denying that there was any 'impropriety whatsoever in my acquaintanceship with Miss Keeler'. This dispelled any lingering doubts among those who ardently wished it to be true. Macmillan registered his support. He sat beside him on the Government Front Bench and clapped him on the shoulder. 'The boil has been lanced,' declared the *Daily Telegraph*.

It was not until June 5th that Profumo confessed he had lied to the House of Commons and the dam burst. Revelation followed revelation in the press. Everyone at all involved whom the press could get to talk published their accounts. The world was riveted.

In Britain, outrage knew no bounds. National security had become the lever to prise open the meatier topic of sexual immorality. Security fast diminished in relevance as a chorus rose to condemn the Government for the collapse of morality on every front. Profumo was the immediate target. His lie had caused profound shock: 'the decencies of public life have been outraged,' Lord Preddie fumed. He had offended the proprieties governing the private behaviour of public men, and many took a stern view. 'People who cannot regulate their own lives have no business regulating the lives of others,' thundered John MacCallum Scott from the Reform Club. 'Men who choose to live in adultery, men who are homosexuals or men whose moral influence is against the highest interests of the nation . . . ought not to be appointed to serve our Queen and country,' Conservative MP John Cordle echoed. No rattling skeletons in cupboards were audible through this barrage of righteousness, and few heeded the Warden of All Souls, John Sparrow's caution against 'any Puritanical crusade in Parliament or the press' for 'every party has, as it has always had, its stock of dirty linen'. For sexual reformers, the unfolding drama chiefly illuminated the hypocrisy and double standards surrounding sexual morals: 'Given that the Government is committed to traditional sexual morals, the least that can be expected is that they should try to live up to them, even if no-one else does,' Anthony Arblaster crowed.[4]

The attack soon shifted from Profumo to an indictment of the government's entire record. The *Sunday Telegraph* had already accused the Government of contempt for those struggling 'to maintain standards of behaviour against the current tide of license and laxity',[5] when *The Times* in an editorial entitled 'It *is* a Moral Issue', stimulated an onslaught on the whole tone of successive Tory governments. By their appeal only 'to immediate self interest' where 'nothing else . . . mattered compared with the assertion that the nation had never had it so good', they had, the leader alleged 'brought the nation psychologically and spiritually to a low ebb'.[6] Scores of letters came by return to indict the Government for presiding over the country's moral decline, encouraging worship at the shrine of materialism, and fostering an 'enervating and sometimes noxious atmosphere', distinguished by 'triviality, vulgarity and irresponsibility, indifference to or disbelief in any kind of standards'.[7] As the tide of opinion turned away from the Government, Lord Hailsham exploded on BBC Television: 'A great Party is not to be brought down because of a scandal by a woman of easy virtue and a proved liar', while in the *Sunday Times*, William Rees Mogg cautioned that even a scandal 'had to be brought back into proportion. The life of England does not really pass through the loins of one red-headed girl'.[8]

The most damaging condemnation was of Macmillan's handling of the affair. He had never confronted Profumo personally, and though he heard about the rumours in February, they were dealt with by his private secretary Timothy Bligh who referred them to MI5. With a patrician sense of proprieties and a natural inclination to believe his colleague's public and private denials, strengthened after the Galbraith incident, Macmillan had a profound distaste for scandal and rumour. The 'raffish, theatrical, bohemian society, where no one really knows anyone and everyone is called "darling" ', in which Profumo moved, was alien to him.[9] He found the whole thing, according to close colleagues, deeply distasteful. 'In the old days you could be absolutely sure that you could go into a restaurant with your wife and not see a man that you knew having lunch with a tart. It was all kept separate but this does not seem to happen these days,' he recorded later.[10] It was a matter of public decorum: 'Profumo does not seem to have realized that we have – in public life – to observe different standards from those prevalent today in many circles,' he wrote.[11] His personal reticence and his patrician sense of proprieties intensified by his own experience of his wife's affair proved politically costly.

In the House of Commons, as national security returned to the agenda, he faced a blistering attack on his political competence. Opposition leader Harold Wilson studiously focused on the security risks to avoid any suggestion of using sexual scandal for political gain – all other issues were 'not appropriate for party politics' in this 'very sad affair,' was his consistent claim.[12] But he did not fail to emphasis how the disclosures had 'shocked the moral conscience of the nation', had linked a government minister with 'a sordid underworld network, the extent of which cannot be measured', and taken 'the lid off a corner of the London underworld of vice, dope, marijuana, blackmail and counter-blackmail, violence, petty crime'. Macmillan's dignified and frank reply, asking for the 'sympathetic understanding and confidence' of the House and the country, for he and his colleagues had been 'grossly deceived . . . but we have not been parties to deception' was insufficient to turn the tide. Both confidence and sympathy had been undermined. Macmillan's personal authority was in question. Looking 'bowed and dispirited' as he confessed he did 'not live much among young people myself', he seemed to dramatize the gap between the older and the younger generations, adding force to the bitterest attack, which came from his own backbench. 'We cannot just have business as usual,' declared Nigel Birch. 'I myself feel that the time will come soon when my Right Honourable Friend ought to make way for a much younger colleague.'[13]

Amid the wave of indignation, the popularity of the Conservative Party dived. The Labour lead in the opinion polls reached twenty points, the highest ever recorded since polls began. The *Financial Times* index dropped seven points. Attempts to contain the damage were ineffectual as the drama ran its course.

Sacrifices were needed. Profumo was outlawed, his career ruined. Keeler was imprisoned for six months for perjury. Ward, the agent of the affair was convicted on charges of procuring and living off immoral earnings in a trial described then, as later, as a travesty of justice. The trial amplified the sense of widespread corruption, as witnesses, including Christine Keeler, Mandy Rice Davies and two prostitutes testified to lives of promiscuity, drug-taking, being kept as mistresses, picking up and servicing middle-aged men with sexual favours, of whipping and two way mirrors and unusual sexual practices. Ward, confident of acquittal because, although he had many dealings with women, he had never lived off immoral earnings, claimed that most of the witnesses lied, a claim confirmed by later evidence which showed they had been subject to police pressure. He took an overdose of sleeping pills before the verdict was announced and died shortly afterwards.

'This is a political revenge trial,' he had told a journalist friend. 'Someone had to be sacrificed and that someone was me.' Many legal experts were 'affronted by the case'. Lord Goodman described Ward as 'the historic victim of an historic injustice'.[14]

By the time of the Denning Report into the affair, which attracted vast queues outside HMSO on its day of publication in September, the scandal was all but over. Denning's report was a whitewash, but a spicily written one from as eminent a judge. It exonerated the Government in most respects, although it criticised Macmillan for failing to take seriously rumours of Profumo's adultery and then discharging his responsibilities accordingly.

The episode left an uneasy feeling that an overwhelming surge of public moral righteousness had banished all sense of proportion or justice which survives to this day. But in undermining the moral authority of the Government, it helped shape a mood receptive to calls for national regeneration. This was exploited by the Opposition, whose rhetoric of social reform and modernization harnessed to the 'white heat of technology' bore fruit in their election victory the following year.

Public Decencies

By then signs of the break up of moral consensus were multiplying. Old taboos were challenged, new meanings for sex were proposed, attitudes to sex became more flexible. Across a range of social and political issues, the liberal intelligentsia, youth and the dissident middle class were signalling a repudiation of established authority and entrenched cultural values. It became increasingly difficult to sustain traditional authoritarian moral positions when a political rhetoric which offered liberal tolerance, social justice, social mobility, innovation, and a libertarian concern with personal freedom as the keys to progress and modernization was now capturing the allegience of progressive opinion in all classes. These ideals began to transform key institutions in national life.

Not least the church. When the Bishop of Woolwich in *Honest to God* (1963) advocated that Christian morality be re-cast to a new mould in which personal responsibility took priority over received doctrine 'of the supernatural', he opened a deep theological rift between liberal and orthodox wings of the church. In an influential endorsement of the individualist ethic, he argued that with the language and symbols of Christianity falling into disrepute, with membership falling and influence declining, the church needed a New Morality which took into account changing standards if it was not to lose out 'to all but a tiny religious remnant'.[15] Though it enraged many Christians ('What should happen to an Anglican bishop who does not believe in God?' fumed T. E. Utley in the *Daily Telegraph*), *Honest to God* caught the mood of the times, and sold three quarters of a million copies. Its repudiation of orthodox doctrine, and emphasis on personal love, was also expounded in another influential pamphlet *Towards a Quaker View of Sex*. This was written by a group of radical Quakers, who rejected 'almost completely' the traditional approach of the organized Christian church to morality, 'with its supposition that it knows precisely what is right and what is wrong', its distorted view of the sexual impulse, and its rigid doctrinal constraints. Instead they proposed a sexual ethic founded on individual understanding of the meaning of sex in relationships, that placed love, which 'cannot be confined to a pattern' at its centre.[16]

These were radical statements which spoke eloquently to an audience receptive, at a time of moral confusion, to a re-statement of ethical and spiritual ideals. *Honest to God* divided the church establishment but it also reflected a shift away from doctrinal absolutism, a shift already evident in, for instance, the Church of England's support for the separation of immorality from illegality over the issue of homosexuality in the 1950s and its acceptance of the legitimacy of contraception in *The Family in Contemporary Society* in 1958. In response to increasing pressure from liberal reformers in and outside its ranks, the church abandoned its claim to dictate the Christian standard to a largely secular community, but attempted to retain its influence by modifying doctrine to fit the prevailing libertarian ethic. Having been the chief obstacle to liberal reform, the Church of England, by the late 1950s, had become one of its main agents, a conversion which had repercussions on official attitudes in other areas.

Those institutions charged with controlling the representation of sex were also re-interpreting their public duties. The acquittal of *Lady Chatterley's Lover* in 1960 had seemed to herald a new era in which protection of literary freedom was safeguarded by law.

But almost immediately uncertainty returned in a series of cases which successfully circumvented the protection offered by the Obscene Publications Act. In 1962 the publisher of *The Ladies Directory*, a prostitute contact sheet, was prosecuted on a charge of conspiring to corrupt public morals: *Fanny Hill: Memoirs of a Woman of Pleasure*, a novel written by John Cleland in 1749 had been in free circulation selling at 2 guineas but when it was sold in a cheap edition, it was the subject of a destruction order against a bookseller, under Section 3 of the Obscene Publications Act, which excluded trial by jury. Several witnesses who testified to its historical interest, part of which was its description of an emancipated woman who frankly claimed her right to sexual pleasure, failed to impress (except possibly adversely) the magistrate, Sir Robert Blundell. He took one minute to decide the book was obscene and to order that 171 copies be seized and burned. The decision caused a public and parliamentary uproar which led to the solicitor general giving an undertaking that any publisher or author whose book was seized under Section 3 could insist on trial by jury.

After this the DPP showed increasing reluctance to bring prosecutions against serious literature. The last case against a reputable publishers in the 1960s – Calder and Boyars for the publication of Hubert Selby's *Last Exit to Brooklyn* in 1967 – was initiated not by the DPP but by two Conservative MPs, Sir Charles Taylor (described by Bernard Levin as 'one of those granite survivals from the Jurassic Age which are occasionally to be found sticking up out of the more recent deposits'[17] and Sir Cyril Black, an official of the Public Morality Council who took out a private proseuction after the DPP had refused to take any action over their complaints about the book in the House of Commons. Calder and Boyars were convicted before a magistrate, but refused to cease publication. When the DPP stepped in to prosecute, the publishers elected for trial by Jury. After a nine day trial in November 1967, they were found guilty, but the verdict was overturned on appeal in July 1968 on a legal technicality.

After this, the private prosecution loophole was closed. With changes in the composition of juries (abolishing the property holding and age qualifications of jurors), the decreasing chances of successful prosecution deterred further actions against serious literature. Many more obscenity charges were, however, brought against the proliferating products of the pornography market, and against radical underground publications. This kept the issue of censorship and the boundaries of control of freedom of expression in the forefront of public attention.

Broadcasting organizations, too, responded to the break up of the moral concensus by deliberately adopting a more pluralistic approach. The ethos of paternalism which characterized the BBC of Lord Reith, with its commitment to elevate audience tastes and propogate Christian moral values was changing. The BBC's television monopoly had ended with the coming of ITV in 1956. Under its Director-General Ian Jacob, a new policy emerged, a broadening of the range of programmes to mirror the wider society rather than to elevate taste. 'We are here to reflect the people,' explained Gerald Beadle, Director of Television in 1958.[18] The BBC began to attract a new audience, no longer middle-class and middle-aged, to programmes such as the news magazine *Tonight* and the arts review *Monitor. That was the Week That was* began in 1961, as an outspoken satire show, attracting peak viewing figures for its Saturday night slot.

Hugh Greene, who took over as Director General in 1960, took pluralism further. He encouraged controversy. The BBC's aims were now ' "the breaking down of barriers" so that those of differing views "may come to know and better understand each other's attitudes" . . . in an atmosphere of healthy scepticism.' They were to 'recognize an obligation towards tolerance and towards the maximum liberty of expression';[19] it was 'an important part of our duty to enquire, to question authority rather than to accept it'.[20]

The Broadcasting institutions were bound by Charter and Statute not to include anything 'offensive to public feeling' or which 'offends against good taste or decency'. As the middle ground over what was offensive or bad taste shifted in the 1960s, so those inside broadcasting, the writers and producers who wanted more open exploration of personal and sexual relationships came into conflict with others who preferred the balance shifted back.

The new ethos had attracted new, younger producers and

writers into broadcasting – 'those creative and wayward and surprising talents' as Huw Wheldon described them,[21] 'willing to undertake the adventures of the spirit which must be at the heart of every truly new creative work'. Sir Hugh Greene considered it their duty to 'cultivate young writers who may by many be considered "too advanced," even "shocking" '. What mattered was 'the treatment of the subject', its 'relevance to the audience and the tide of opinion in society', which demanded 'the most careful assessment of the reasonable limits of tolerance in the audience . . . Outrage is impermissible. Shock is not always so. Provocation may be healthy and indeed socially imperative.'[22]

But the provoked struck back. The BBC was sensitive to criticism. The Governors, charged by Charter to look after the public interest, reacted to complaints and pressure by stressing caution. Controversy increasingly focused on drama productions, especially the *Wednesday Play* slot which attracted large audiences to a strand which anchored the personal in a socially realistic setting, and regularly tested the boundaries of acceptability. Bad language caused concern in *'Till Death us Do Part*, but was defended by the BBC, though when Kenneth Tynan first used the word 'fuck' in a 1965 discussion programme about the use of language, the BBC offered no defence. There was a continual stream of attacks on the BBC for lowering standards, explicit sex and 'gratuitous' violence.

Criticism became more organized after Mary Whitehouse, a deeply religious Birmingham housewife and a past supporter of Moral Rearmament, at the time a teacher in a girls secondary modern school, began a campaign to 'Clean Up TV' in 1963. Prompted by disgust at the prominence given to discussion and the portrayal of the New Morality on television and even more by the BBC's apparent refusal to take her protest seriously, she mounted a full scale assault on what she saw as the 'propaganda of disbelief, doubt and dirt' which was belittling and destroying the Christian way of life. Backed up by 365,355 signatures to a Christian manifesto, and the support of a Parliamentary committee of largely evangelical supporters, she launched the National Viewers and Listeners Association on a campaign to restore God 'to the heart of our family and national life'.[23] She was rarely silent from then on.

Her campaign explicitly rejected Greene's pluralism. He in turn defended himself against the 'new Populists' who threatened a 'dangerous form of censorship' by attempting to impose the views of a narrow religious minority – views which were 'anti-intellectual and unimaginative' – on the whole population.[24] ITV, meanwhile, was consistently more responsive to her complaints and they were rewarded. She left them relatively unmolested, even though they adopted a similar balancing act on the middle ground and also extended the boundaries of what was acceptable in taste and decency.

Mary Whitehouse mined widespread anxieties about the apparent loss of a firm sense of moral purpose, and changing meanings for sex which emphasised hedonism at the expense of family values. She attracted a wide constituency of support among Christians and conservative moralists, and helped shape an atmosphere receptive, by the end of the decade, to exaggeration amounting to moral panic about falling standards. This in turn fed an authoritarian backlash against 'permissiveness' in the early-1970s which was to be moulded later into the rhetoric of a return to Victorian moral values.

The film and theatre censorship bodies were also responsive to changing standards. The British Board of Film censors with its dual role – to advise and protect the film industry against the courts and censorship lobbies and protect the public against outrages to taste and decency – had until the war 'considered itself the guardian of public morality, allowing no departure from the accepted code of conduct and behaviour, the protector of the Establishment, the protector of the repute and image of Britain in other countries'.[25] But its paternalism was steadily challenged from the 1950s, and John Trevelyan, its director from 1958 to 1971, was responsive to pressures. He became 'increasingly aware of ferment and change' and of the need to reinterpret the censor's responsibilities, to hold a balance while reflecting intelligent opinion which was variable, not static.[26]

While public opinion was changing, pressure was coming from writers and filmmakers who were broadening the imaginative range of their work and addressing the complexities of love and sexual relations with greater frankness. Censorship institutions which appeared to dictate a single standard of morality in a pluralistic society came under uncreasing attack. They were seen as infringing freedom to explore issues relevant to contemporary morality. The censorship disputes of the sixties hinged on establishing a balance between adults' right to choose what they could and could not see, and the maintenance of controls which could be justified in the public interest.

Under a liberal director, the gauge of the legitimate limits of control altered. Taboos were breached tenatively but steadily. Jack Clayton's film *Room at the Top* was considered a milestone in 1958 for including sex scenes thought sensational not for what was done but because of 'rather more frankness . . . in the dialogue than people had been used to'.[27] From then on directors who portrayed sexual dilemmas as both moral and social issues found they had more room for manoeuvre – Karel Reisz's *Saturday Night and Sunday Morning*, John Schlesinger's *A Kind of Loving*, Bryan Forbes's *The L-Shaped Room*, all thought sensational, were passed uncut. Nudity, previously allowed only in naturist films if no pubic hair was visible but banned in feature films, was passed for the first time (with no sexual connotations) in 1967 in a Swedish film *Hugs and Kisses*. Female pubic hair (flashes of) got its first certificate in Antonioni's *Blow Up* in 1968, although full frontal male nudity had to wait until Ken Russell's *Women in Love* in 1969, while the erect penis was denied a certificate until 1971, when it was awarded an 'X' in Dusan Makaveyevs film *WR. Mysteries of the Organism*.

There were regular skirmishes between film-makers and the censors over the threshold of 'public acceptability'. The two-tier system whereby films refused a BBFC certificate could be submitted to local authorities for licenses, was used as a gauge. If the BBFC 'moves too far in advance of public taste – as reflected in local authorities,' the BBFC President argued, 'they will cease to accept its judgments. If it lags behind, it will lose its influence over the film industry.'[28] But this produced wide discrepancies, even though the system was useful to film producers who could get an exhibition and to the film censor as a means to test opinion. *Fanny Hill*, refused a BBFC certificate in 1965 on the grounds it was salacious rubbish, was submitted to local authorities; 18 gave it an 'X', 44 an 'A' certificate and 4 gave it a 'U' for general family viewing.[29] The BBFC passed it 'X' in 1968. In 1966 several scenes were cut from a Swedish sex comedy *Seventeen*, about the sexual adventures and fantasies of an adolescent boy, but it was passed uncut by the Greater London Council. With Joseph Strick's *Ulysses* (1967) after pre-production script clearance, the BBFC still demanded cuts in the final film, largely because of obscene dialogue. The GLC and 30 other local authorities passed it uncut with an 'X' certificate. In 1970, when the minimum age for 'X' films was raised to 18, it was passed by the BBFC. In 1968, Yoko Ono's film of a large number of bottoms, *Number Four*, was refused a certificate without several cuts. The GLC passed it as 'X' uncut. Birmingham gave it a 'U' certificate.[30]

The Club system, which allowed films an exhibition to a limited audience of members, provided a further loophole for films classed as 'sexploitation', or judged by the BBFC to be too explicit or pornographic. This absorbed the expanding market in obviously pornographic material, already subject to control by customs and excise regulations. Trevelyan supported this useful 'safety valve' for censorship, which enabled sexually explicit but not, in his view pornographic, 'experimental' films to be shown. So much so that in 1970, when police raided a showing of Paul Morissey's *Flesh* at the Open Space Theatre, a reputable theatre club with an Arts Council subsidy patronised by intellectuals, Trevelyan was among the first to rush to the defence of the film, by actually turning up at the club to remonstrate with police. There were few clearer indications of social division than the spectacle of the film censor taking the side of libertarian intellectuals against the Home Office and the moral conservatives.

By the end of his tenure as Secretary, Trevelyan had concluded that the censor's role as custodian of public morals was limited, and that adults were entitled to choose what they wished to see, as they were also entitled to read what they liked.[31] This was not a view shared by those who gathered under the banner of the 'Festival of Light' to mobilise a backlash against explicit sex and violence in the early 1970s. It was, however, the view of a majority in Parliament on the subject of theatre censorship when, in 1968, the Lord Chamberlain was abolished after a decade of sustained conflict.

The impetus for change had come mainly from playwrights who

challenged the theatre censorship system as an anachronism: it hindered playwrights' freedom of expression, retarded innovation, imposed more restrictions on theatre than on any other medium and was destroying the theatre's function to explore and portray issues relevant to contemporary morality. The theatre, they argued, was in danger of falling behind the times when it should be in the vanguard of public opinion. Productions banned in the theatre could be seen or heard on radio or television. Subjects not allowed in the theatre could be freely discussed in the press. Instances like the banning of e. e. cummings *I sing For Olaf* from Royal Shakespeare Company production after it had been read on radio and shown on BBC TV's *Monitor* programme demonstrated the absurdity.

By the late 1950s, playwrights were taking more risks with language and exploring new territory. Several plays had fallen victim to the absolute ban on the representation of homosexual themes, for instance, though some small concessions had been wrung from the Lord Chamberlain when it was pointed out that complete exclusion from the stage seemed hardly justifiable when homosexuality was the subject of public discussion at the time of the Wolfenden Report.[32] Concern grew at the arbitrariness of censorship and its effect on dramatic innovation. This came to a head after a play by Joan Littlewood's experimental Theatre Workshop at Stratford East involving ad-libbing – which was not passed by the censor – ran into trouble, and John Osborne's *The World of Paul Slickey* was severely cut. A group of playwrights, politicians and intellectuals set up a Theatre Censorship Reform Committee to lobby for change, but the first attempt by Dingle Foot MP in 1962 to introduce a Bill into the House of Commons under the Ten Minute Rule to make submission of plays optional was defeated.

Playwrights regularly came into conflict with the Lord Chamberlain's office over subject matter and language. Pressure for reform escalated when the club system loophole, whereby unlicensed plays could be performed to club members, was closed. The club system had become a forum for innovation. Osborne's *A Patriot For Me*, which dealt with, among other things the theme of homosexual relations in the life of an intelligence officer in the Austro-Hungarian Army before the First World War, and which used vernacular language, was refused a license in 1965. Staged as a club production it won the *Evening Standard* award for the best play of the year (1965), but could not be transferred to the West End (at considerable financial loss to both the management and John Osborne.) But in 1966, when the Royal Court turned itself into a club to stage Edward Bond's *Saved* (which had been refused a license unless four letter words and two whole scenes were excised), it was prosecuted for not operating as a genuine Club.

After this no play or theatre could be certain of immunity from prosecution and the club system as a forum for experiment effectively ended.

But opinion was changing. A Joint Committee set up to look into the operation of the censorship in 1967 recommended the Lord Chamberlain be abolished and theatre come under the same legal constraints as literature, where the test of obscenity was the sole basis of censorship. When the incumbent Lord Chamberlain, Lord Cobbold, publicly expressed doubts about whether the censorship should continue to operate through his office, it was clear his days were numbered.[33] He wished to abolish himself. He was widely supported. The Theatres Act 1968, which enacted the Joint Committee's recommendations, passed through Parliament without opposition.

The new freedom was celebrated by a crop of plays which flouted just about every one of the Lord Chamberlain's old guidelines. Kenneth Tynan's *Oh Calcutta* in 1970 broke all the rules of visual and sexual display. It provoked vociferous protest even from former advocates of freedom of expression like David Holbrook, who argued that the limits of tolerance had been breached when sexual intercourse could be represented on stage devoid of any meaning or connection with love. The indignant Holbrook set up the Responsible Society whose aim he claimed, was to reaffirm a Lawrentian reverence for sex, but it became another recruit to the evangelical reaction against 'pornography'.

Impermissible Desires

Behind these institutional changes lay a great shift in attitudes over the issue of the State's power to control private lives, which generated perpetual crisis throughout the 1960s. Divisions between the young and the old widened as protest against established authority escalated into revolt against the State's coercive powers. Tensions over sexual morals were one facet in a wider conflict about the limitations on individual power in an increasingly mechanised, bureaucratic corporate state, a conflict which manifested itself at all layers of sociological and political debate. The moral revolt was a struggle to assert the priority of the personal, to affirm the centrality of individual choice and personal responsibility in the organisation of a new sexual ethic. This libertarian principle steadily gained allegiance.

The young, inheritors of an adult morality which G. M. Carstairs had described as 'a wasteland littered with the debris of broken convictions' were one agent for change. They carried social weight and commanded attention. There were more of them than ever before – a million more unmarried 15–24 year-olds in the mid-1960s than ten years before – and they were better educated, financially better off and more independent than their predecessors. They appeared, as a cohesive group, to embody optimism about change.

The political rhetoric of modernisation in the Opportunity State found its echo in the myths created round the culture of youth – a culture whose style was 'dynamic', modern and 'vital', where former boundaries, particularly class boundaries, seemed to break down as a 'classless' 'new aristocracy' of merit and talent – the much publicised designers, photographers, journalists, painters, pop stars – dislodged the old establishment, and where the barriers which allegedly inhibited the free flow of creativity and imagination seemed to dissolve. By 1964 the tag 'Swinging London' had been invented as the symbol of the dynamic revival of Britain. At its centre was an erotically charged image of, as one American commentator wrote, bold mini-skirted women fearlessly 'upfront' about their sexuality, who 'walk like huntresses, like Dianas', and who 'take sex as if it's candy and it's delicious', of the 'muscular virility' of writers, dramatists, artists and actors, and the 'creativeness and dash' of fashions.[34] These images sold youth very well and they sold a new Britain very well.

Woven into youth culture was an impatience with old forms and an unfocused search for new principles by which to conduct social and personal life. Pop music was one unifying element in the culture; it displaced jazz and folk music as the conduit for dissent and spread a vibrant message of release from 1963. The Beatles began the revival which broke with the past. The Rolling Stones extended its range. Bob Dylan, who began as a folk singer of protest songs, altered the direction of pop music towards a more overt political message. Such singers spoke for a generation and gained the allegiance of the young. The message they delivered about sex was direct and honest. There were few euphemisms; it was explicit. The agonies of adolescent love of the late-1950s charts (*Halfway to Paradise, Only Sixteen, Teenager in Love*) were replaced by a stronger, often more raucous statement about sexual release. Pop music was no longer decorous or restrained. It gave vivid expression to frustration and disillusionment. It was sometimes abut love, though rarely about sentimental love. It was often about emptiness and about betrayal, the emptiness of adult love and the betrayal by society, parents, politicians. It abolished romance and the blurred images of sentimentality, and sharpened the focus on subtleties of feeling, from love to anger.

The aggression was savage, sexual and mostly male. The Rolling Stones music was belligerent, 'cultivated hysteria, using images of dangerous flirtation and dominance. Performance and music were confrontational. There was hardly any sentimentalism; it was *Under My Thumb, Who Wants Yesterday's Papers, Who Wants Yesterday's Girl*, and *I Can't Get No Satisfaction*.

The young were also receptive to the drift of anti-authoritarian intellectual ideas which sought to adjust the power balance within society and explore alternative moral systems. By 1967 dissent had developed into a widespread rejection of dominant cultural and political values. It was fed by political disillusion with the Labour Government's failure to deliver its promises of reform, and influenced by upheavals in America, where opposition to the Vietnam war was forcing sustained cultural and political divisions. On both sides of the Atlantic, disaffected youth participated in the 'great refusal' to be marshalled into established social organisation. The Left, fired by revolutionary ideals of participatory democracy and permanent revolution, engaged in overt confrontation with authority which reached its height in 1968, while the less politicised flower-power hippies and adherents of lifestyle politics rebelled by opting out of and subverting mainstream culture.

The moral revolt in Britain was predominantly a middle-class rebellion against middle-class values which found its voice in the politics of the counterculture. By 1967 among the avant garde there was, according to Jeff Nuttall, 'an unprecedented concern to air all taboos as blatantly as possible, to confess and sing from the rooftops all the most impermissible desires, a strange merging of the titillatory pornographic with the avante-garde absurd'.[35] Playing around with notions of obscenity, going as far as possible to explore and to shock, adopting blatant sexual styles to indicate the distance from the 'straight' world were all forms of provocation which came from a sense of confidence, a consciousness of being part of a moral transformation of society which would clear away what seemed the bankruptcy and hypocrisy of outmoded constraints.

The central intellectual vision of an alternative morality was personal and sexual liberation, achieved by discarding the trappings of conventional morality and adopting alternative lifestyles. Self-realisation, breaking through repression and expanding the frontiers of perception through drugs were the routes to a new moral consciousness and the releases of a new sensibility. Jim Haynes, a prominent activist in the underground, founder of the Traverse Theatre and the Arts Lab recalled: 'We really thought we could change the world. First and foremost it was going to be a world of mutual respect, mutual acceptance. No more prejudice: you could worship who you wanted to worship, how you wanted to worship, wear the clothes you wanted to wear, have the sexual attitudes you wanted . . . You had the right to do that.' [36]

Sexual liberation meant dissolving emotional inhibitions, valuing honesty and openness in relationships, and discarding all the artificial emotional baggage previously brought to the sexual bargain for the sake of a sexual contract in which the pursuit of pleasure, self-realisation and personal fulfilment provided the *raison d'être* and the meaning for sex. Sex for pleasure, for fun, for friendship detached it from the conventions linking it to marriage, the family and the future. This utopian vision was articulated by the advanced avant-garde as a new ethic. It began to command wider support, though it also brought conflict and new moral dilemmas.

Behaviour and attitudes were changing steadily. Despite all the alarms about promiscuity, until the late-1960s young people's behaviour remained conservative, according to surveys. Only 20 per cent of boys and 12 per cent of girls aged 15–19 in Schofield's pre-1965 survey had pre-marital sex, though by 19, a third of boys and 16 per cent of girls had intercourse at least once.[37] In 1969 Gorer found three quarters (74 per cent) of men and 37 per cent of women aged 16–45 had sex before marriage. Attitudes had loosened, but the double standard was still intact; although two thirds (65 per cent) of 21–24 year-olds approved of pre-marital sex for men, under a half (43 per cent) approved of it for women (a shift nevertheless from 1951 when 38 per cent of men and only 14 per cent of women approved of women having pre-marital sex)[38] Another behaviour survey revealed a steady rise in the proportion of women who had sex with their husbands before marriage – from a third of those married in the late-1950s, to 47 per cent married 1961–1965, and 61 per cent of those married in the late-1960s (1966–1970).[39]

The contraceptive pill influenced the steady loosening of constraints, although it was probably not the only factor and its most dramatic impact on behaviour was in the early 1970s; attitudes to pre-marital sex were becoming more flexible in the 1960s before it was widely available to single women. A completely reliable contraceptive satisfied an already established demand. On the market since 1961, its use spread rapidly among married women: by 1967–1968, 28 per cent of women, predominantly middle-class, had used the pill (increasing to 65 per cent by 1973, and 74 per cent by 1975, when its use had spread to all classes.)[40]

It was not so easily available to single women until the Family Planning Act 1967 enabled local authorities to set up or support family planning clinics and for the first time made no distinction between married and unmarried. Before then, the only sources had been the few Brook Advisory Clinics which after 1964 provided advice and facilities to single women over 16, some private gynaecologists and a few more enlightened doctors dealing with students. Some Family Planning Association clinics continued until 1969 to provide advice and facilities only to married couples, and to engaged couples if they had a note from the vicar.

Changes in behaviour among single women before then were not solely linked to pill use. Only 9 per cent of all single women in the 1970 Bone survey had ever used the pill.[41] Another survey found that of those who had pre-marital sex with their husbands, only 7 per cent of women married in 1966, and a fifth of those married 1966–1970, had used the pill before marriage. They concluded pre-marital sexual activity had increased at a faster rate than contraception use. The time when the rise in pre-marital sex was accompanied by rising pill use was in the early- to mid-1970s, when the pill was much more accessible. More than half the women marrying 1971–1975 had used the pill before marriage (an increase from 7 per cent in 1966 to 66 per cent in 1975).[42] By then, a range of influences were bringing about significant changes in the sexual ethic.

Even so, the pill signified an important break with the past. It made contraception – and sex – a more accessible subject for public debate. Dealing with a drug taken in pill form removed embarassing images of 'private parts' (which continued to inhibit public discussion of the sheath); talking about hormones rather than genitals turned contraception into an issue of medicine rather than morality. The pill shifted responsibility for contraception onto women. It gave them autonomous control over their reproductive choices. By releasing women to enjoy sex without fear of pregnancy, it challenged one of the central tenets of the social control of women, that their primary role and fulfilment in life was bound to motherhood. For they now had real choice. It gave women potentially the same freedom as men to explore and pursue sexual desire without penalties. Sex for pleasure, detached from family responsibilites, not related to love or the 'relational needs of couples' was now an option for both women and men. It finally eroded women's support for the double standard. By the early 1970s, only 11 per cent of women in one survey, compared with 40 per cent in 1965, agreed pre-marital sex was OK for men but not for women.[43]

It made possible a heady sense of sexual liberation and validated the embrace of a hedonistic sexual ethic by the avant garde in the late 1960s. But for women this could be more problematic than first appeared. Their freedom was still circumscribed by their inequality in other areas of their lives and by the weight of their cultural conditioning. Moral choices were not necessarily resolved by technology; it created new dilemmas.

Personal Politics

The alternative morality was not concerned with women's equality but with freedom, experiment and breaking down hypocrisy and 'oppressive sexual attitudes'. It was a new ethic for the release of desire, which benefited men more than women. Richard Neville justified his case for a free love ethic without emotional attachment in *Play Power* (1971), in which women were mostly referred to as 'chicks': 'No more tedious "will she or won't she by Saturday?" but a total tactile information exchange, and an unambiguous foundation upon which to build a temporary or permanent relationship. The pot of gold at the end of the rainbow comes first; later one decides whether the rainbow is worth having for its own sake. If the attraction is only biological, nothing is lost except a few million spermatazoa, and both parties continue their separate ways.'[44]

Many young women embraced their freedom to choose and experiment. Andrea Adam, a reporter for *Time* magazine recalled: 'I did fall into bed with the most extraordinary characters, and I think my taste was extremely dubious at times. I took the opportunity to experiment. I felt I owed it to myself. It was part of my growth as a human being, as a woman and as a feminist ... I wanted women to become equal and I wanted permissiveness.'[45] For Michelene Wandor: 'The pretty underground girls with the short skirts and the long hair were a version of the emancipated girl ... It wasn't all oppression by any means. It's true that they were a dolly, but ... they weren't just a decorative dolly, they were a dolly who could make their own choices and not be lumbered with the consequences.'[46]

But there were drawbacks. The pressure to conform to the new conformity was strong, on men as well as women. John Lloyd, editor of the underground newspaper *Ink* recalled: 'We weren't really liberated – all of us had a lot of hang-ups. We had been brought up traditionally, even strictly, and to try to leap out of your own habits and upbringing into this blissful state where there were no hang-ups was of course interesting psychologically but it was completely impossible. And all the jealousies and tensions just grew exponentially.'[47]

Some women believed it was freedom bought at the price of a

new form of coercion. Nicola Lane recalled the pressures: 'There was a lot of misery. Relationship miseries: ghastly, ghastly jealousy, although there was supposed to be no jealousy, no possessiveness. What it meant was that men fucked around. You'd cry a lot, and you would scream sometimes, and the man would say, "Don't bring me down – don't lay your bummers on me... don't hassle me, don't crowd my space." There were multiple relationships but usually in a very confused way; usually the man wanted it.'[48] Student Mary Ingham 'responded to the pleasure principle', believing she was throwing off the hypocrisy of the old values in search of 'purity and honesty within relationships which we equated with freedom and openness', but found the ideal was 'heady and unrealistic... Women, by indulging in the sexual revolution, risked their reputation and security, whereas men simply got what they wanted without the usual attendant fuss and blackmail, manipulation and persuasion.'[49]

Another student living outside London recalled the freedom of being in a mini-skirt, on the pill, and picking up an invitation from a man she'd recently met in 1967: 'I had the feeling there was no pretence any more. No games to be played. No way I could say "be careful with me", or "watch out for my emotions", or worry if I get pregnant, or think of my honour, or that my parents wouldn't like it. I'd offered myself as free... But at nineteen, or twenty, I felt it was tougher for me than him. I was throwing away centuries of breeding, of manners and customs for women. I was putting myself in the rôle of the debased woman but I was also saying "I'm not debased, my currency is as strong as yours." You have to fight your psyche hard not to weaken sometimes.'[50]

Many women ended by feeling let down by liberation. The alternative morality did little to dent traditional female roles; if anything, it reinforced them. The 1960s, Nicola Lane pointed out, 'was totally male-dominated. A lot of girls just rolled joints – it was what you did while you sat quietly in the corner, nodding your head. You were not really encouraged to be a thinker. You were there really for fucks and domesticity. The "old lady" syndrome. "My Lady". So Guinevere-y. It was quite a difficult time for a girl.' Rosie Boycott, who went on to start *Spare Rib* thought the underground only pretended to be an alternative for women:

'there was still a power game going on in that women were typists, men were the bosses, men were the ones who decided what wages people got, whether people had jobs. Women were dependent on men.'[51]

After 1968 a few women active in left-wing politics began to identify their discontents. They found leftist principles of personal and political liberation hardly applied at all to women. Despite social changes which had promised equal opportunity and sexual freedom, inequality and subordination persisted at every level. Women who felt these conflicts in their personal lives increasingly articulated them within a political perspective.

In left-wing organisations, women still played the traditional female role – the corporals to the male lieutanants – servicing the revolution, listening to rather than making the speeches. Their conflicts were invisible. When issues of women's rights were raised, they were invariably deferred by male colleagues as secondary issues, or ridiculed after the fashion of Stokely Carmichael, the charismatic American black leader who declared: 'the only position for women (in the civil rights movement) is prone'.

An intellectual analysis of women's subordination from socialist feminists, like Sheila Rowbotham and Juliet Mitchell, articulated a challenge to patriarchial controls on women and the cultural definitions of their 'femininity' which resonated among women who recognised in it their own conflicts. The waves from America, where women schooled in the politics of oppression in the civil rights and student movements were setting up women's liberation groups to advance demands which had been peripheralised by men, also influenced women to take positive action on their own behalf.

The Women's Liberation Movement was distinctive in its commitment to define women's rights on women's own terms and to organise outside any established political institutions. Early consciousness-raising groups of mostly young married women with families were one forum for women to identify a shared female condition but also to define themselves without the distorting mirror of others' expectations. Naming the discontent was the first step in recognising that personal and sexual relationships lay at the core of the problem of women's political rights. The personal was political. It was through women's rôles as wife and mother and the cultural definitions of their sexuality and 'femininity' that patriarchial subjugation and oppression of women were exercised. To change this was a political question, requiring 'a revolution from below' and demanding a change of consciousness and an entirely different strategy for political mobilisation.

De-mythologising the sexual portrayal of women, re-defining their own sexuality, examining the web of devices by which women were flattered into collusion with passivity and dependence, and asking why women accepted it with their silence was seen as a key to the process of self-identification. The movement mounted a political campaign against the portrayal and exploitation of women as sexual objects; they also voiced the personal conflicts they were experiencing between received definitions of female sexuality and their own sense of sexual identity.

For many women, sexual 'liberation' had not increased their sexual pleasure; often it had simply multiplied the opportunities for failure in a sex act determined by the male prerogative of pleasure in which women were seen, and often saw themselves, in a servicing role, giving pleasure but not making claims to their own fulfilment. By redefining their sexuality and making demands for pleasure, women were attempting to gain control over their bodies and lives. Recent sex research was influential. Masters and Johnson's *Human Sexual Response* published in 1966 had exploded several myths about female sexuality, particularily the hierarchical distinction between the clitoral orgasm, designated since Freud 'immature', and the vaginal orgasm, designated 'mature' (proper) which had over the years generated widespread anxiety among women about their sexual 'inadequacy, as well as sweeping generalisations about women's 'frigidity'. Masters and Johnson raised the status of the clitoris from being an aspect of foreplay to playing the central role by identifying it as 'the primary focus for sexual response in the human female's pelvis'. This conclusion had previously been drawn by Kinsey but had been largely ignored. They reiterated Kinsey's observations on the physiological similarities between men's and women's sexual responses and concluded that not only just a few, as Kinsey had observed, but the vast majority of women were capable of multiple orgasms.[52]

These findings were appropriated by the Women's Movement through Anna Koedt's pamphlet *The Myth of the Vaginal Orgasm*

(1969) which offered a political perspective to women's affirmation of their autonomous sexuality. 'One of the elements of male chauvinism is the refusal or inability to see women as total, separate human beings,' she wrote. 'Sexually, a woman is not seen as an individual wanting to share equally in the sexual act, any more than she was seen as a person with independent desires when she did anything else in society.' It was up to women to 'discard the "normal" concepts of sex' and to 'create new guidelines which take into account mutual sexual enjoyment . . . We must begin to demand that if a certain sexual position now defined as "standard" is not mutually conducive to orgasm then it should no longer be so defined.'[53]

The pamphlet had a disturbing effect on women who recognised in it their own conflicts. 'I don't know why I felt so upset by it, but I do remember just flinging it across the room in an incoherent rage,' recalled Mary Barnes. 'Maybe it was because it showed me that I didn't know my body, but beginning to find out about my body was too dangerous, it was like I knew what it would mean – I would have to take steps to change a relationship in which *I* had always been seen as the problem. Somehow staying that way was less dangerous than showing my husband that *he* was the problem. I wouldn't have known where to start.'[55] Another found it had a positive effect: 'It was my first discovery of my own sexuality. I was sleeping with men and not coming. I was allowing them to be the ones who knew about lovemaking and running the show. And I just kind of joined in.' [55] It would probably have been helpful to a 24-year-old mother, married for six years and waiting for a divorce, who wrote to *Forum* magazine for advice: 'During my marriage I never once reached a climax during intercourse. The only way I could have one was for my husband to manipulate my clitoris. We used to end up having rows over this, with him saying I was frigid and me blaming him for my inability to come. I have now met someone else, and although things went well at first he is now saying that there must be something wrong with me. We have tried everything we can think of to make me climax, but to no avail.'[56]

Women's mobilisation through self-help groups, local organisations, public demonstrations, and subversion of established institutions was to have lasting influence during the 1970s. They forced issues of women's rights onto the agenda: they pressed for radical reform of the institutional controls which governed their lives at work, in the family, in personal relationships, a transformation of the power structure which confirmed male supremacy and women's subordination, and a recognition of women's natural rights to control their bodies. The isolation the women's movement had initially experienced broke down as its influence spread to a wider constituency of women who recognised and began to use the vocabulary of self-determination to challenge patriarchial values and institutional controls.

Permissive Acts

Some issues affecting women's rights had already reached the politcal agenda as part of the 'permissive' legislation which the Labour Government endorsed as libertarianism advanced, and as its economic strategy began to collapse. In this legislative 'package', abortion was legalised, the State took on some limited responsibility for contraception provision, the divorce laws were reformed, and homosexuality was decriminalised. Together they did not eliminate, but re-defined the State's control over private lives.

The reforms acknowledged an ideological shift first signalled by the Wolfenden Report's conclusion in 1957 that the State had only a limited right to intervene in the individual's private morality. Labour backbenchers then proposed law reforms be included in the Labour Party's political agenda as part of a platform designed to widen the party's support base. These proposals never became official Party policy. They remained 'conscience issues', the subject of private member's bills. But by identifying them as social problem areas, which could be adjusted by social engineering, reformers attracted parliamentary and public support.

Until 1966, when Labour was returned with a clear majority of 100, attempts at law reform had met strong opposition from within the ranks of the Labour Party as well as from Conservatives. To the right wing of the party and older members with trades union or religious affiliations, they were vote losers. Prime Minister Harold Wilson would never touch them, dismissing them as 'Hampstead intellectual issues'. But the new intake of MP's after the 1966 landslide was younger, with more members from professional backgrounds who were sympathetic to reform and receptive to libertarian currents in society. Moreover in Wilson's Cabinet there were several sponsors and supporters of previous reform attempts, including Roy Jenkins in the key position of Home Secretary, Anthony Crosland, Douglas Houghton, Kenneth Robinson. Gerald Gardiner, who had defended Penguin Books in the *Lady Chatterley's Lover* trial, was Lord Chancellor, heading the Law Commission, a body set up to review the law. Although the Government was officially neutral over private members' bills, each of which was brought up separately and needed separate constellations of parliamentary support, the Government assisted with extra time for debates and with Home Office drafting of the Bills. This effectively signalled its support, while also giving scope for increasingly restless backbenchers to influence legislation[57]

Opposition to reform was sustained by conservative moralists, paternalists and by religious, particularily Roman Catholic interests. But the strength of extra-parliamentary reform lobbies was a crucial factor in persuading opinion in and out of Parliament towards reform. The Homosexual Law Reform Society, the Divorce Law Reform Union, and the Abortion Law Reform Association, re-activated after the 1963 thalidomide scandal, all became increasingly professional at putting their case. In finely tuned, though sometimes over-cautious, campaigns designed not to alienate moderate opinion they kept the issues in the forefront and, by judicious use of opinion polls, legitimised the argument that the law was out of tune with current practice and beliefs.

The Church of England's conversion to liberalism was crucial. But though its liberal position on homosexual law reform was established in the 1950s it had remained adamantly opposed to any change in the divorce and abortion laws until, forced into direct conflict with wider secular and humanist interests, it was persuaded to compromise on doctrinal orthodoxy. This did not dent opposition from those who believed the State was the instrument for the enforcement of morality, that reducing legal controls in any of these areas would undermine morality and social stability.

Sustained opposition came from those who were convinced that the removal of criminal sanctions would imply that the State condoned homosexuality. Reform attempts had failed in 1965 and

1966. But according to polls public and parliamentary opinion was changing as the issues were exposed to public debate through press and lobbying campaigns. The opposition, which was sustained till the last, was effective in restricting the extent of reforms. The Sexual Offences Act (1968), which decriminalised homosexual acts between consenting adults in private, had several limitations: it excluded the armed forces, and Scotland and Northern Ireland, and the age of consent, 16 for heterosexuals, was 21 for homosexuals – the most reformers thought they could get through at the time. The 'in private' clause became a loophole for prosecution, while sanctions against soliciting and importuning and penalties for gross indecency were actually increased. It was a measure of the law's limitation that, largely because of increased police activity, the recorded incidence of indecency between males doubled, the number of prosecutions trebled, and the number of convictions quadrupled between 1967 and 1976.[58]

Divorce law reformers also faced fierce opposition. Their main proposal was to substitute the old system of proof of matrimonial offence with a new principle of irretrievable breakdown as the sole grounds for divorce. An early attempt by Leo Abse MP in 1963 to reform the law by enabling divorce after seven years separation without an offence having been committed had provoked bitter opposition from religous groups, including the Church of England. Abse, with widespread backing in the press, mounted an attack on the churches for attempting to impose the full Christian standard on a largely secular community. *The Times* joined in pointing out that though church leaders had 'a clear duty to pronounce' on divorce law, 'this is not to say that civil law on divorce should coincide with the law and practice of the churches'.[59]

These signs of public disaffection with the Church of England's rôle helped persuade it to reconsider its position. In 1966 the results of the deliberations of a Committee set up under the Bishop of Exeter to examine the secular law were published in *Putting Asunder*. This concluded in effect that the church could no longer dictate Christian law. It decided the matrimonial offence system 'elicited little to its credit', that the law was 'unjust', 'superficial', 'remote from matrimonial reality' and 'quite simply inept' and supported replacing it with the principle of irretrievable breakdown as the basis for divorce with provisions for reconciliation. The Church Assembly passed it by a majority in 1967 and the Methodist Conference also affirmed its support.[60] When the Law Commission, a body set up to review the law, supported the new principles in its report *Field of Choice*,[61] considerable unanimity was registered.

While this undermined, it did not eliminate resistance from a wider constituency who opposed easier divorce on the grounds that it threatened the institution of marriage and the stability of family life, and that divorce without the consent of one partner after seven years separation introduced an unjust principle which 'allowed defaulters to benefit by wrongdoing'. Others objected there was inadequate financial provision or protection for wives and children – which led Baroness Summerskill to dub it the 'Casanova's Charter'.

It took two reform Bills, presented in 1968 and 1969, to negotiate the details, and it was only after a further Matrimonial Property Act dealing with financial provision had been passed, that the new Divorce Act came into operation in 1971. This enabled divorce on the grounds of irretrievable breakdown after two years and after seven years separation without the consent of one partner. The Act was generally hailed as an improvement on the previous law – the 'jungle of lies, half truths, miserable strategems and ugly publicising', as Leo Abse put it, that the matrimonial offence system had produced. It dismantled the need to allocate guilt and innocence between the parties which it was thought better represented the realities of marital experience, and was judged on balance to buttress rather than undermine the institution of marriage. The result was an immediate rise in divorce, which continued thorugh the 1970s. No attempt was made to amend the law until the 1980s.

The 1967 Abortion Act clarified and liberalised the law relating to the existing practice of therapeutic abortion deemed by reformers unsatisfactory, inhumane, harsh and unjust. Here again, with the exception of outright opposition from Roman Catholics and those who feared it would lead to abortion on demand or undermine morality by taking the punishment out of folly, there was agreement on the basic principle of law reform but considerable negotiation over details. The Church of England, after initial opposition, endorsed reform in its 1966 report *Abortion: An Ethical Discussion*, which introduced the principle that social as well as medical considerations could be taken into account in assessing the risk to the health or physical or mental well-being of the woman.[62] This official support did not prevent individual churchmen opposing the measures. The medical establishment accepted the basic need to legalise abortion but fought long and hard over the 'social clause' and over the professional qualifications required to authorise abortions. Pressure groups on both sides raised the temperature of public debate as they mobilised public opinion. The Abortion Law Reform Association (ALRA) stepped up its campaign for legalised abortion on humanitarian, medical and social grounds, while the Society for the Protection of the Unborn Child (SPUC) set up to fight the Bill, attracted the support of Catholics, some doctors and gynaecologists and 500,000 signatures to a petition opposing it. Dramatic gestures were part of the campaign. Professor Hugh McLaren carried round with him a bottle of foetuses with which he regaled audiences on the iniquities of abortion, while others employed wildly vivid language to condemn it: the Bill 'would out-Herod Herod in his slaughter of the innocents', one opponent claimed.[63]

The immediate result of the Act, which allowed abortion up to twenty-eight weeks with the consent of two medical practitioners and incorporated the new 'social clause' as grounds for abortion, was a rapid increase in the number of abortions – from nearly 24,000 in 1968 to nearly 84,000 in 1970[64] – and continuing controversy which resulted in several attempts to amend the law to restrict the availability of abortion over the next few years. But for many pro-abortionists, the measures had not gone far enough; the inadequacy and lack of uniformity of NHS provision and the discretion given to doctors continued to restrict women's access.

For feminists, neither the Abortion Act nor the Family Planning Act, 1967, satisfied the central principal that women had a right to control their own bodies. Conceived as liberal and humanitarian measures of social engineering rather than from consideration of women's rights, they were limited by their failure to embody all women's right of access to facilities. Although the Abortion Act enlarged women's choices, it was a long way from abortion on demand, allowed doctors too much discretion, and it did not ensure uniformity of provision. The Family Planning Act 1967 established contraception as part of the State's health care policy, but it gave local authorities discretion to decide their own policy. This produced wide discrepancies over the country. Nor was contraception free as part of the National Health Service. Women's organisations and pro-abortionists mounted a campaign to make both abortion and free contraception a right for all women.

Moral Pollution

The Labour Government's legislative reforms re-ordered the State's control over individual morality in the direction of permissiveness and enlarged the areas of private choice, though controls and sanctions were increased, not diminished in some areas. Moral pluralism was enshrined in law. No single moral authority determined the sexual ethic. This major transformation in the control of sexual morals paved the way for a more radical re-assessment of both the sexual code and the meanings of sexuality later in the 1970s.

The limits of 'permissiveness' were also being drawn. The challenge which sections of youth threw down to authority, with their provocations of explicitness, their repudiation of boundaries and the whole rhetoric of liberation, provoked reprisals. 'Permissiveness' was increasingly seen as part of a wider threat to social order represented by all those forces in visible and active dissent from established social and political controls.

The backlash was directed against political dissent, as well as the lifestyle and aesthetic dissent of the counterculture. With drugs, as Stuart Hall has observed, the moral entrepreneurs 'discovered the criminal edge of permissiveness'.[65] In May 1967, in what The Times leader 'Who Breaks a Butterfly on a Wheel?' protested was 'about as mild a drug case as can ever have been brought before the courts'[66] Mick Jagger and Keith Richards of the Rolling Stones were prosecuted – Jagger for possessing four benzedrine tablets authorised by his doctor, and Richard for allowing cannabis to be smoked in his house – and sentenced to three and twelve months imprisonment. The severity of the sentences and the suspicion, confirmed by the judge on appeal, that Jagger's position as a youth idol had influenced his punishment, led many to conclude this was not a question of justice but a case of social revenge.

As political tension erupted in 1968 in civil and industrial confrontation, and fears about the breakdown of social cohesion and order intensified, 'permissiveness' was construed as the moral edge of a conspiracy to undermine the State. James Callaghan, who took over as Home Secretary from Roy Jenkins, had registerd his intention to call 'a halt to the advancing tide of so-called permissiveness' by rejecting, to a chorus of approval in the popular press, two impeccably liberal documents – the Wootton Report on drugs, which recommended a modest liberalisation of the law on cannabis in 1968, and the Arts Council's report on Obscenity which recommended suspending the Obscene Publications Acts for a trial period of five years in 1969.

By 1970 the Conservatives, with an election platform formulated around the restitution of 'law and order', were examining the possibilities of more effective legal meaures, including reactivating the conspiracy laws, to tackle disorder and what was being orchestrated in the press and among organised social purist pressure groups as the moral 'pollution' of society.[67] From 1970 the sex and obscenity laws became the instrument for suppressing the radical underground press in a series of prosecutions which, according to one legal expert, Geoffrey Robertson, gave 'a new and political dimension . . . to a (obscenity) law which was generally thought to guard more against the arousing of emotions than ideologies'. With these prosecutions, the 'apostles of radical change, and not the peddlars of masturbatory fantasies, were indicted as the depravers and corrupters of British youth'. [68]

International Times, set up on October 1966 with a circulation of around 45,000, was the first casualty, when it was convicted in 1970 on a charge of conspiring to corrupt public morals and outrage public decency for printing contact advertisements for homosexuals. The editors were sentenced to eighteen months imprisonment suspended for two years. Legal costs and a £1000 fine broke the paper. Oz, started by Richard Neville in 1967 had been another forum for alternative ideas, using sexually explicit language and playing with visually startling images and cartoons. It flaunted the virtues of guilt-free sex but could hardly be called pornography. It was raided several times before the police prosecuted the *Schoolkids Issue* of June 1970 which the editors handed over to a group of adolescents to edit themselves. Charged with conspiring to corrupt the morals of young children and publishing an obscene libel, the editors – Richard Neville, Felix Dennis and James Anderson – embarked on what become the longest obscenity trial in history.

The defence made it an issue not so much of obscenity as of freedom to dissent from established opinion. It was a case, John Mortimer QC proposed, 'which stands at the cross-roads of our liberty, at the boundaries of our freedom to think and say and draw and write what we please'; it was 'about dissenters; a case about those who are critical of the established values of our society, who ask us to reconsider what they believe to be complacent values, and are anxious, on that basis, to build what they think (and what we may not think) is a better world . . . We are all of us, totally entitled to disagree with their views; but this is a case about whether or not they are also entitled to disagree with us.'[69] The trial became a rallying point for cultural radicals convinced that their lifestyle and beliefs were on trial and it gave new impetus to the anti censorship lobby.

For almost six weeks the magazine was analysed: Would it put ideas into children's heads? What was the meaning of pornography? Did defence witnesses see in it what the prosecution saw in it? 'Is your eyesight normally and reasonably good?' asked the incredulous Judge Argyle of one witness who had failed to notice an incriminating part of a drawing. 'I think that you have to be in a place like a Law Court to look at these things so microscopically,' she replied. And were the *Oz* editors guilty of 'relentlessly promoting certain elements of the new culture, namely dope, rock and roll, and fucking in the streets'?[70]

In the end the defendants were found guilty and sentenced to nine, twelve and fifteen months imprisonment and fined £1000 with costs. Richard Neville, an Australian citizen, was to be deported, and they were all ordered to have their hair cut. This symbolic act, instantly dubbed 'the unkindest cut of all', was in the view of the *New Law Journal*, which questioned several aspects of the trial, 'a monstrous violation of an individual's personal integrity'.[71] The sentences provoked widespread criticism, including in legal circles, and, according to John Trevelyan, 'disturbed even people who thought that the convictions were justified'.[72] Many who found *Oz* unreadable and ineffective, and questioned whether the weapons of revolution were, as Neville had once proclaimed, 'obsenity, blasphemy and drugs', registered their support. The sentences were suspended on appeal.

The trial fuelled the growing backlash against permissiveness and the decline of standards. Sections of the press were delighted at the outcome. 'Most people . . . will be relieved that this latest attempt to subvert the remains of our morality has been hit soundly on the head,' declared Duff Hart Davies in the *Sunday Telegraph*, while a leader in the *Daily Telegraph* lashed out at the Alternative Society as a disease and a cancer striking society: 'Whatever has lifted (man) from the primeval slump, it derides and denounces . . . It is entirely parasitic on society; it flourishes and grows at our expense. We feed it, clothe it, protect it – yet without the protection of the law, which they so obscenely abuse, how long would these drop-outs survive, for the most part so manifestly weak and weedy as they are? Many of them, incidentally, including two of the *Oz* defendants wear spectacles – a visible mark of their dependence on the normal world they despise, as ludicrous in its way as false teeth in the mouth of the noble savage.'[73]

The trial finished *Oz*. In May the same year *The Little Red Schoolbook*, a handbook translated from Danish which dealt mainly with children's rights to question authority, and included twenty-three pages on sex education, was seized by Scotland Yard after Tory backbench pressures to get it banned. It was convicted of obscenity by Lambeth magistrates, though Richard Handyside the publisher was fined only £50 and prosecutions in both Glasgow and Edinburgh failed. Subsequently in 1973 *Nasty Tales* was acquitted by an Old Bailey jury. But the backlash gathered momentum as the attack on permissiveness spread to other areas.

Even so, by the beginning of the 1970s some consensus on moral pluralism was established. In a remarkably short space of time, the sexual code had been re-defined, the State's role reduced, and alternatives were being explored at a personal and political level. Ideals of personal sexual freedom nurtured over half a century by the few now had widespread support and the limited endorsement of the law.

The convulsions of the 1960s were the culmination of social changes which had been steadily altering beliefs and aspirations over two generations. Contraception was established as a routine part of marital expectations by the time the technology of the pill brought about a qualitative change in the meaning given to sex, and particularily to women's sexual freedom. Marriage had been steadily eroticised and sexual fulfilment accorded a central place in marital harmony; with this and a more general sexualisation of the culture, the remaining constraints on premarital sex appeared arbitrary and difficult to justify. The economic priorities of individual choice, no less than instant gratification, were already the foundations for consumer choice before they were appropriated as principles for moral choice. Entrepreneurial innovation, breaking through boundaries to progress had been proclaimed in the political rhetoric of modernisation before it was conscientiously applied by the avant-garde to moral values. Sex had already moved out of the privacy of the marriage bed and onto the billboards before a hedonistic ethic of sexual pleasure became the rallying call for a new sexual code.

The consequence of moral pluralism was a divided society, as the limits to sexual freedom were argued over for the next two decades. The 1960s had paved the way for an individualistic ethic in which sexual freedom was seen as part of personal growth and self development. But it had exposed the extent to which constraints on women limited their opportunities, and generated new tensions which women confronted with programmes for radical change. Simultaneously a backlash against permissiveness was orchestrated by groups concerned at the erosion of Christain values, who yearned for a return to a more stable morality. The 1970s were marked by continuing conflict over sexual morals.

Nine

Alternatives

If there was a 'sexual revolution', it occurred not in the 1960s but in the 1970s, when the ethic of individual choice was democratized. Many sexual boundaries had been crossed during the clamorous call for liberation. The advances were consolidated in quite dramatic alterations in the profile of marriage, in patterns of behaviour and in the meanings given to sexuality. The use of reliable contraception spread, pre-marital sex increased as the sanctions against it diminished, extra marital sex spread as fidelity became less valued as an essential prop to marriage, divorce rose steadily. All polls showed a majority in favour of adults' freedom to see and read what they liked without censorship restrictions. Moral individualism was no longer the prerogative of the avant garde and the rich but the dominant ethic.

Legislation had dismantled some of the apparatus of moral blame and reduced the stigma attached to 'deviancy'. The pill and penicillin had taken the punishment out of folly. They validated a new ethic of 'sex for pleasure', no longer anchored to its private, sacramental place within the marriage bond. According to the expanding counselling and advice industries, sex was now good for you, indeed it was essential to healthy living, the means to personal growth and self realisation.

At the same time, a more radical critique of the sexual code emerged to challenge the structures which controlled sex. Sex moved from being an issue of morality to one of social justice natural rights, economics and power relations. The privacy of sex was invaded by the social meanings attributed to it. For feminists and libertarians, questions of social justice *were* moral issues. To re-negotiate the sexual ethic was to adjust an unequal power balance, to assert the individual's natural rights to self-determination, starting at the site of coercion – in personal relations.

This critique contained a positive assertion of sexual difference, variety, and alternatives, which had a lasting effect on the social fabric. The re-structuring of personal relations has endured, despite attempts to re-draw the boundaries of moral freedom, but it has also brought new dilemmas and social conflicts.

Breaking The Bonds

The profile of marriage and family altered radically from the 'traditional' image. This was as much due to long term social changes which transformed aspirations and expectations as to the enlargement of private moral freedom. In the 1970s society began to address the implications of these changes. Marriage remained popular up till the mid-1970s. More people were getting married than ever before – 95 per cent of women had been married by their late-forties in 1977 compared with 80 per cent in 1931. Most people expected to marry, most expected to have children, most went into marriage expecting it to last, and to satisfy basic needs for love, affection, companionship, stability and family formation within it. By 1976, only 8 per cent of women and 14 per cent of men would not marry.

As the patterns of marriage changed, so its terms and conditions were re-examined. Marriage lasted longer as life expectancy increased. It was now expected to last 50 years whereas in 1901, when men's average life expectancy was 46 years and women's 49, it lasted around 20–30 years. 'There ought to be television commercials about marriage. Famous actors should set aside their coffee beans and ask, "Do you know how long forever is?", Deborah Wood protested to *The Times* in 1981. Disenchanted, she recommended a warning on the marriage certificate: 'Danger! This Marriage Can Seriously Damage Your Health.'[1] People got married later, reversing the 1950s and 1960s trend to younger marriage, as pre-marital sex, accessible contraception and changed material expectations influenced choices. Marriage in the 16–19 age group fell from 27.2 per thousand in 1970 to 17.2 per thousand in 1977.[2]

Expectations had been changing over a long period. A shift

from 'sexual ethics designed to protect the family to sexual ethics based on love and mutual commitment' reflected a move towards the privatisation of marriage and an emphaisis on individual self-fulfilment within it. Already by 1963 Sociologist Ronald Fletcher noted the marital relationship had 'no authoritative "blue-print" in custom, morality, and law of expected family relationships' and depended 'on personal choice and personal responsibility'.[3] By the late-1970s a Home Office study found 'marriage is increasingly required to serve the partners' own personal development'.[4] Children were the most important ingredient in a happy marriage for fewer than a sixth of respondents in a 1981 survey – a long way behind love, understanding each other, and having a good sexual relationship. [5].

Higher expectations also put new stress on marriage. When partners were asked to be 'everything' to each other – lovers, friends, mutual therapists – and marriage was required to be the closest and deepest relationship in life, it was increasingly likely to fail to live up to the emotional demands placed on it. Moreover the criteria for success had changed, as one researcher observed, 'from the accomplishment of known, specific tasks to feeling states, which are much harder to specify and achieve'. Relationships were being re-negotiated 'because individual happiness has become so important: ' "Be your own person", we hear, or "realize your own potential"; become "whole" and "autonomous" we are told. "Grow!".'[6]

Women's changing status had brought about other changes. Legal reforms had reduced some of men's rights over women, social advances had altered their domestic responsibilities. With increased contraception use in all classes family size was down to an average 2.2 children by 1970. Women spent a far smaller proportion of their lives on child-rearing; in 1901 women had spent around fifteen years on rearing children to the age of one while by 1970 this was nearer four years. Machines reduced the time they spent on domestic tasks. As material goals changed, and the economy demanded more women workers, married women went out to work. By 1971, 42 per cent, and in 1981, half of married women were occupied in gainful employment outside the home, the majority in part time work; an increasing number worked while their children were still under five[7]

All this led to complacency in some quarters that women had at last achieved equality. But the real implications of these changes were not fully acknowledged until the 1970s, when women in particular began to examine marriage and the family and call for a thorough review, if not an overhaul. Though the dual-earner family, for instance, had, since the 1950s, been undermining the traditional partnership of breadwinner and housewife, it had not eroded attachment to an ideal as much cherished in family mythology as endorsed in social policy. It had not advanced women's equality since women's work was still seen as secondary, and it had not altered the power structure within marriage. Attempts by optimistic sociologists to detect a new 'symmetrical family' ideal characterized by a less rigid segregation of roles were sabotaged by a close examination of the facts. Willmott and Young in 1973 found only a small amount of de-segregation: 'Division of labour is still the rule, with the husband doing the "man's" work and the wife taking prime responsibility for the housekeeping and the children.' Power had not been equally distributed in more than a few families, they concluded. The description 'egalitarian', 'would not square with the marked differences that still remain in the human rights, in the work opportunities and generally in the way of life of the two sexes'. [8]

Meanwhile the expanding sociology of the 'captive' housewife had uncovered a fundamental incompatability between women's ascribed feminine role as wife/mother, their culturally stimulated aspirations for individual fulfilment, personal ambition and equal citizenship, and the multiplicity of roles they were required to perform in their lives. The 'problem' of women, Hannah Gavron observed in 1966, was the pressure of incompatible beliefs and expectations surrounding "Woman", which was creating a situation of 'conflict and stress'.[9]

When feminists in the 1970s examined the contradictions in the context of women's subjugation, they made visible the reality, rather than the myth, of family life as women experienced it. Far from being the haven of their highest fulfilment, it was most often the site of their oppression, the territory on which coercion and regulation was exercised. Feminists were saying, Bea Campbell recalled, that 'if we can assume that this is some natural order of domestic organization, there's a terrible problem in it. Women go potty. Women are poor. Women are often beaten up in this haven. So its inner life has to be examined, and we all have to take responsibility politically for what goes on in it.'[10] In making a political challenge to the institution of marriage and family and to the laws and cultural assumptions which underpinned their dependent place in it, feminists, and increasingly a wider constituency of women, sought to renegotiate personal relationships on terms which affirmed their rights to sexual equality, independence, and personal growth.

There were other catalysts for change. Accessible divorce after 1971 had acknowledged changed marital aspirations and was seen as an adjustment to its 'realities'. Though it did not dent faith in marriage (it was welcomed as a buttress to the institution) it soon influenced expectations. Most couples expected their marriage to last, but by 1977, 60 per cent of 15–25-year-olds in one survey thought they might divorce.[11] The number of divorces doubled during the 1970s; by the early 1980s, 1 in 3 marriages was liable to be dissolved. Though for moral conservatives this signalled the collapse of marriage, for a wider constituency it indicated its improved quality.

Divorce did not deter partners from marrying again. By the end of the 1970s, a third of all marriages, compared with a fifth in 1970, involved the remarriage of one partner. Around 80 per cent of those who divorced under 30 would remarry.[12] Men – widowed or divorced – remarried at a higher and faster rate than women, an observation which led one researcher, Jessie Bernard, to conclude men not only needed marriage ('Once men have known marriage, they can hardly live without it') but, contrary to popular myth, they benefited from it more than women. Married men enjoyed better mental health than married women, and were happier and lived longer than single men.[13] Wives, on the other hand, expressed more dissatisfaction with marriage and showed a higher incidence of mental and emotional ill-health than married men or single women; they made more adaptations in marriage than men while suffering a diminution in work and social status as they 'are dwindled into a wife', as Congreve put it. [14]

As divorce and remarriage increased, a more complex kinship network of step-families, a new form of extended family, emerged. But since many did not re-marry, another consequence was the significant increase in the number of one parent families, the majority headed by women. In 1974, one family in eleven was a one parent family, rising to one in eight by 1980, totalling 920,000 families, involving one and a half million children.[15] Most were living near the poverty line. The expansion of this group moved the family profile further away from the traditional ideal, while contributing towards another shift – the feminization of poverty, making women as a group among the poorest in the population as a whole.

By the mid-1980s, less than 30 per cent of families conformed to the family profile of breadwinner, housewife and two children in a first marriage, and only around 11 per cent of families relied on a single male breadwinner.[16] Individuals were making adjustments to a variety of different couple and family relationships; the State was endorsing in a haphazard and piecemeal fashion some of these alternative arrangements.

Sexual Pleasures

At the centre of these changing patterns was an ascendant ethic of sexual release. For several decades, sex reformers had proposed that the liberation of the sexual impulse from its artificial constraints would transform social and personal relations. Marriage had been sexualized by the experts who stressed that fulfilment for both partners was essential to a successful and harmonious marriage. Now, with the link between sex and reproduction broken, an ethic of sex for pleasure which would enable the individual to experience their full sexual potential, to grow in self-realization, took hold as the new ideal.

Liberal sex reformers and the pundits and counsellors of the expanding personal advice industries were the conduits for a new message: that a fulfilled sex life was crucial to healthy living and a necessary condition of mature self-development. 'An active and rewarding sex life, at a mature level, is indispensible if one is to achieve his full potential as a member of the human race,' psychiatrist Dr David Rueben confirmed in 1970, in *Everything You Always Wanted to Know About Sex*. 'Those whose sexual behaviour is shrouded in ignorance and circumscribed with fear have little chance of finding happiness in their short years on this planet.' A new orthodoxy developed. 'We are often told that the sex "drive" must be regularily expressed to maintain healthy functioning,' Shere Hite observed in 1977. [17]

Sex was no longer talked about only in marriage. The barriers to sex outside marriage were fast dissolving. Three quarters of women married 1971–1975 had pre-marital sexual intercourse with their husbands. By 1978, American studies found 81 per cent of young women had pre-marital sexual experience, rising, a *19* magazine survey found, to 93 per cent of women aged 20–24 in 1982 in Britain.[18]

According to the ethic of release, sex was for pleasure. Sex was necessary to health. People ought to improve their sex lives. Achievement was measurable. Taking Kinsey's cue, you could measure success (or failure) by orgasm. A new combination of compulsions placed new obligations on individuals. Orgasm became the focus of achievement. Some manuals argued for extensive training programmes to prepare for the sexual success people now owed themselves. Popular newspapers counselled variety and experimentation endlessly. 'To awaken your body and make it perform well, you must train like an athlete for the act of love,' the author of a bestseller, *The Sensuous Woman*, proclaimed in 1970. Though undoubtedly a lot of this information helped some people dismantle their inhibitions, it also succeeded in emphasizing sex as a performance art, akin to gymnastics, as the accomplishments became ever more complicated, or imaginative (depending on the point of view), as well as taxing. Most counsels advised making more effort. Taking more time was also popular. Variety, or variations, usually of positions (frequently illustrated) were proposed as the antidote to sexual failure. It was all a bit mechanical.

Many people, particularly women, felt that new tyrannies had replaced old constraints. The pivot of liberation was alleged to be the release of female sexuality. But already in the 1960s, doubts were being expressed. For sexual freedom, though welcomed as the opportunity to explore guilt-free sex, had not actually released women from their subordinate role in the sex act any more than it had released them from their wider subordination and dependence. While 'an identical morality for both sexes, based on a fundamental revision of our ideas about female sexuality' had developed, one sociologist pointed out, it was 'essentially an adoption by women of the stereotype of sexual behaviour of young men, in which love is not as important as orgasm'.[19] Though it had removed some barriers, and enabled women to see themselves clearly as sexual beings, Shere Hite observed in 1977, the transition had not 'so far allowed much real freedom for women (or men) to explore their own sexuality; it has merely put more pressure on them to have *more* of the same kind of sex'. [20]

Hite was among those who argued that the quality and terms of sexual freedom were still to be renegotiated by women. When women, were expected to enjoy sex as much as men, some women felt they had lost some independence by being pushed into sex they didn't necesarily want – 'they are considered "square" or "frigid" if they don't rush into bed,' one of Hite's respondents pointed out.[21] A *19* magazine survey in 1982 found 70 per cent of respondents had lost their virginity by the age of seventeen, a quarter by sixteen, and over two thirds (69 per cent) thought they were under too much pressure to have sex; just under two thirds sometimes had difficulty finding excuses to say no.[22] Perhaps women had actually lost, rather than gained some of their freedom of choice under the new orthodoxy. Though sex for pleasure was a perceived and acceptable new goal, Hite found almost no woman wanted the kind of spontaneous, no strings attached purely physical pleasure very often, 'although a few thought that they *should*'.[23] In *19* magazine's survey, 87 per cent of young women found sex without affection unsatisfactory. Hite's sample, asked what about sex gave them greatest pleasure, overwhelmingly preferred 'emotional intimacy, tenderness, closeness, sharing deep feelings with a loved one'. Orgasm came second.

Regular checks were kept on the orgasm count, the barometer of sexual success, and it was going up. So was the importance women attached to it. Here was another arena of anxiety, for when Mary Sherfey disclosed that *all* women were capable of multiple orgasms, the pinnacle of achievement moved even further into the distance. Though more women were 'achieving' orgasm, even just the one was by no means universal, and still did not occur every time. Other complications were developing. Many women still faked orgasm in the belief that satisfying their partner was more important than their own satisfaction. There was a hint in some manuals that the point of it all was to give the male partner more pleasure; developing sensual potential was another route in a more demanding climate to holding on to your man. Men were reported to be feeling the pressure too. One medical expert reported men were seeing their partner's orgasm as a reflection of their virility; if women failed, men felt inadequate. Women who failed might also feel inadequate, a new word for frigid. If women succeeded, it was a tribute to male technique.

Feminist sexual politics in the 1970s aimed to define a positive female sexuality around the principle 'our bodies are our own'. But re-negotiating the terms for women's sexual autonomy became the focus of deep conflict and the cause of almost terminal antagonism in the women's movement. For some it meant opting out of heterosexual relationships altogether; some women moved into lesbianism because they discovered their real sexual preferences, others because they took the separatist political view that sex with men was a form of collaboration with the oppressor. Heterosexual women, often struggling with acute conflicts between their learned understanding of 'femininity' and their own desire for a separate sense of sexual self, were forced onto the defensive as they sought a new egalitarian basis for relationships with men.

Some positive alternatives were offered. In 1977 Shere Hite argued that women should choose how to experience their sexuality. The change was 'much deeper than just the idea that "a woman needs an orgasm too".' The definition of women's sexual freedom was not their ability to orgasm 'just like men'. She proposed women move away from the inevitability of intercourse and in particular from 'male orgasm during intercourse as the conclusion of "sex" ', towards varieties of imaginative sensuality which stressed the potential for women's expression of sexual loving, affection and pleasure on terms other than the 'male dominated' sex act. It was one positive strategy in the unresolved struggle to define women's sexual autonomy.

Another strategy was to subvert the structures which entitled men to ownership and possession of women's bodies. The question of adultery and sexual possession became an acute preoccupation, the frontier on which the emotional limits of the new freedoms were explored, as well as the rock on which faith in monogamy began to founder. Within a sexual ethic of release, sexual exclusivity was becoming difficult to justify if personal relationships were to serve the needs of individual self-fulfilment and growth. The majority of both men and women had pre-marital sexual experience with more than one partner. Reassessments were in order.

A tacit tolerance of male adultery was an established part of the double standard. Studies since the war showed a fairly constant 40–50 per cent of men admitting to adulterous affairs. Kinsey estimated around half of married men would have had at least one extra-marital relationship by the age of forty. Shere Hite in 1976 estimated this had increased to 70 per cent, though other studies suggest a figure between 50–65 per cent.[24] The penalties for women's adultery had always been more severe than for men. Gorer in both 1951 and 1969 found men much less tolerant of their wives' adultery than women of their husbands. One of the chief obstacles to women having affairs, sociologist Jessie Bernard suggested, was male jealousy 'with its peculiar violence'; male jealousy was 'the major prop of monogamy'.[25]

At the end of a decade of sexual freedom, attitudes to adultery were ambivalent, but rigid support for monogamy was faltering. Though fidelity was highly valued especially among the young, it was thought less important as a central prop to marriage. Half of 15–24-year olds and almost two thirds of all ages in a 1980 *Sunday Times* MORI survey thought adultery was morally wrong; a third thought it was 'acceptable'.[26] Only 15 per cent of a 1982 sample thought fidelity the most important ingredient of a good marriage, much less valued than being able to talk to each other about feelings, being in love, having a good sexual relationship, and financial security.[27]

The biggest shift in the 1970s was in women's attitude to adultery. It was not only, according to Annette Lawson's sample, that those marrying after 1970 were much more liberal than those marrying before 1960, but women from earlier marriages became more permissive *during* their marriage. Where over 80 per cent of women first married in 1960 thought sex relations outside marriage were always wrong, for 1970s marriages, only a quarter (23 per cent of women compared with 27 per cent of men) now agreed, and over half the older women had altered their attitudes since their marriage. [28]

Behaviour also changed. More married women were having affairs, and they were having affairs earlier in marriage than their husbands. Where Kinsey estimated in 1953 that a quarter of married women would have had at least one extra-marital relationship by the age of 40, a 1973 American survey which found 34 per cent of the 26–30 age group admitted to extra marital affairs, estimated that this would reach 40 per cent by age 40. British surveys by *Woman* and *Woman's Realm* in 1983 and 1985 showed 30–38 per cent of readers having had at least one lover since they married or having 'had affairs'. Hite, in 1987 put the rate of adultery for both women and men in America at 70 per cent.[29]

The narrowing gap between men and women implied a rejection of the double standard, reflecting women's greater sense of their own sexual options. It suggested that the terms of sex were changing because of changed expectations. For both men and women, relationships ordered by feelings placed a higher value on love, personal fulfilment and partners' ability to satisfy their most profound and varied emotional needs. If these were not met, the pursuit of emotional fulfilment justified either in the name of love or entitlement to sexual pleasure meant either breaking the rules or re-defining them.

In the past the rules were broken. In the 1970s they were redefined. This did not sanitize adultery or the passionate feelings it continued to evoke. Adultery remained the focus of moral tension, of fascination and anxiety. Old beliefs did not die; feelings of jealousy and sexual possessiveness could not so easily be reconciled to a new moral order, as Bertrand Russell had discovered two generations earlier. It did not eliminate the deep sense of love betrayed or trust destroyed, which were no less deeply felt by both sexes, perhaps even more painfully when caring, sharing, honesty and integrity were highly valued.

But a more optimistic view was put by advocates of the new sexual ethic. The equal right of both partners to adultery may make a positive contribution to marriage by enlarging their opportunities for self fulfilment. 'Spontaneous sexual feelings and a range of intimate relationships, both sexual and nonsexual, were an important source of growth to both partners,' they argued.

Enforced monogamy in a relationship expected to last up to fifty years was, one research couple suggested, 'a form of emotional and erotic bondage' which, though intended 'to insure social and familial stability against the wild winds of sexual passion' could be self-destructive. Monogamy, as divorce figures and sexual practices were showing 'pushes as many persons apart as it brings together'. With its narrowly defined horizons, it was 'neither realistic nor humane' for it (in the new 'personal growth' language) denied 'the multiplicity . . . of sexual and interpersonal experiences that are available to healthy and mature persons'.[30]

New models for relationships and alternative structures for marriage were advanced on this premise. 'Open marriage' was one – an honest relationship with the commitment to equal freedom or, as one couple put it, 'the right of each to grow as an individual within the marriage'.[31] It was a re-writing of the marriage contract to suit the needs of each individual and provide 'the flexibility they need to grow'. Partners gave each other freedom and independence, aware that one person cannot fulfil all their partner's needs. This might include sexual freedom. Possessiveness, particularily sexual jealousy, was not part of the deal. Affairs which did not threaten the central relationship were seen as enhancing growth. Honesty, so conspicuously absent in adulterous affairs in closed marriage, was valued as a cementing ingredient in open marriage.

Many open marriages worked, though they could also create a certain amount of emotional havoc. Other variations which accommodated openness and sexual variety were tried. Wife-swapping and 'swinging' enjoyed a vogue in the mid-1970s; their therapeutic value as an antidote to the claustrophobia of marital isolation was much proclaimed. Communes were another alternative for breaking down possessive personal ties. Their immediate genesis lay in the sexual liberation politics of the 1960s (when they were presented as the means to opt out of the 'oppressive' and 'alienating' nuclear family.) Because a high value was attached to autonomy and self fulfilment, many were loose and impermanent. The main problems, according to one observer, were 'lack of privacy, jealousy, personality clashes and conflicts over sharing'.[32] Nor did they abolish coupledom and possessive feelings. The commonest worry among women was that their men would leave them. There was not much change in the division of labour either;

women still overwhelmingly carried responsibility for children and household tasks. Those which survived probably worked harder at longer term restructuring.

The most lasting alternative was cohabitation, which by the late 1980s was classed as virtually a majority practice before marriage. It spread rapidly, became socially and morally respectable in a remarkably short space of time, and was soon endorsed in a piecemeal fashion by the State. Where only 3 per cent of women who married between 1965–1970 had lived with their partner before marriage, this had risen to 10 per cent of those married 1971–1975, and by 1979 to a fifth of married women. One in ten single women and almost a fifth of separated or divorced women were cohabiting by the turn of the decade.[33]

It was not always an alternative to marriage. For most it was either convenient at the time because of indecision or because one or other partner was awaiting divorce, or was a form of trial marriage. But as a positive option it offered potentially more freedom to partners and better prospects for achieving an equal partnership than traditional marriage. Couples were under no legal obligations to one another, financially or sexually; they could retain their separate identities and determine their own rules. Women could retain the advantages of their single status – their own identity, separate taxation denied to married women, some tax benefits, control over children, access to some social provision available to unmarried mothers, and freedom in those areas where, even up to the mid-1970s married women could not operate without their husband's consent, such as hire purchase and mortgage agreements, contraception and abortion. What they sacrificed was their right to financial dependence, because men were not legally obliged to support them. All these arrangements might include children. As cohabitation became a stable alternative to marriage, the number of children born out of wedlock who were registered in the joint names of father and mother increased from just over a third (38 per cent) in 1961 to half (51 per cent) in 1976 and to two thirds (63 per cent) in 1984.[34]

Living together became respectable as it became more prevalent. It ceased to be termed 'living in sin'. In 1981, British Rail extended the same travel concessions to cohabiting employees of five years standing as to their married employees, and in the same year the upper class guide to modern respectability, Debrett's *Etiquette and Modern Manners* included advice to hostesses on how to accommodate 'live-in lovers' – a sure sign of their social integration. Seven out of ten respondents to a 1980 poll thought living together was 'acceptable'; only 7 per cent of the 15–24 age group thought it was 'wrong', though a fifth of the total disapproved.[35]

The State endorsed these changes through some legal adjustments which put cohabiting couples on the same footing as married couples – over some social security provisions and entitlement to claim a share of property on separation, for instance. In 1980 a judge trying a tenancy case noted 'a complete revolution in society's attitude to unmarried partnerships' when he decided couples living together in stable relationship could be classed as members of the same family for legal purposes whether they had children or not.[36] But the adjustments were unevenly integrated into social policy. While better-off cohabiting women earned their entitlement to a share of property, lone mothers on social security forfeited their entitlement to supplementary benefit if a man was seen by 'snoopers' to be regularily visiting or cohabiting. Under the 'cohabitation rule' the man was assumed to be financially supporting the women, which disqualified her from benefit. This arbitrary and unjust infringement of the liberties of both the man and the woman was a cause of a continuous protest throughout the 1970s.

Body Rights

The affirmation of alternatives was one outcome of the ethic of individual choice. The terms were affected by the growing influence of the organized feminist movement in re-charting the territory of women's personal and political rights. Feminists put the 'woman question' back on the political agenda on their own terms. Excluded from conventional power structures, they organized outside it, reliant on networks of self-help and collective support groups, on tactics of confrontation and infiltration, and conversions through a change of consciousness rather than conventional lobbying techniques. The transformation which started in their own lives – at the kitchen sink, in the marriage bed – spread to the shop floor, to local committees from trade councils to play-groups, and to the Houses of Parliament.

At all levels they were asserting they had certain natural rights in relation to their economic, social and personal lives; sexuality was an area where those rights also applied. They were rights to equality, to sexual autonomy and independence which could only be achieved through an adjustment of the power balance between the sexes. These were questions of social justice, of personal integrity, freedom and dignity which resonated at every level of women's lives. Their political agenda, a merging of the personal and political, had crystallized by the first national demonstration in 1971 into demands for equal pay, equal education and job opportunities, free contraception, abortion on demand and free nurseries. The agenda expanded as women's influence grew and they captured support from a wider constituency.

The gains were uneven. The revision of women's economic status necessary to women's emancipation never really materialized. When the women sewing machinists at Fords, Dagenham defied their male colleagues and struck for equal pay in 1968, they revitalized an issue which had been peripheralized for over 80 years and galvanized women into action. The equal pay and anti-discrimination legislation which came into force in 1975 established important principles, but were hedged about with qualifications and did not in practice achieve any fundamental restructuring of women's pay or employment opportunities. Equal pay had little impact in those ghettos of 'women's work', the low paid jobs which women were traditionally ushered into (by 1980 57 percent of women were working in only four service industries). Where there was room for dispute over 'work of equal value', there had also been room, in the five years between the Equal Pay Act 1970 and its enactment, for employers to regrade and re-segregate jobs to circumvent the provisions. Even when employers had no argument, as at the Electrolux factory where men were paid more than women for the same job, enforcement was 'difficult'.

The Equal Opportunities Commission, set up under the Sex Discrimination Act, scored a few firsts in discrimination cases but appeared to run out of steam. The number of applications to tribunals fell steadily. Though the differential between men's and women's wages narrowed temporarily – by 1977 women were receiving 75.5 per cent of men's wages – the gains were reversed by the early 1980s when it had dropped back to 70 per cent. Women remained clustered in the lowest paid, least secure sections of the workforce and, as the recession began to bite, were among its first casualties.

It was still not acknowledged that women had a right to work, that their wages frequently made the difference between family security and family poverty, and many were the main or sole breadwinner. Though some inroads were made to narrow the gap between the separate spheres of family and employment, they did not go far. The Labour Government's Employment Protection Act established women's right to paid maternity leave, protection from unfair dismissal and the right to return to the same job after 29 weeks. But a wider recognition of the realities of working women's lives (which women publicized through their growing participation in trade union and other activities) and further provisions such as adequate child care and paternity leave, were resisted, leaving Britain the country in Europe which provided least support for working mothers.

Economics meshed with the larger issue of personal emancipation. Contraception and abortion were, as they always had been, key issues about women's right to control their own bodies and their own lives. Neither had been seen as a right or made freely accessible to all women in the recent 1960s legislation. Feminists called for a free comprehensive contraception service on the NHS as women's right. They swam with an ebb tide: a Birth Control Campaign had been set up in 1971 after Health Minister Sir Keith Joseph had rejected a free service as 'a gratuitous waste of taxpayer's money'; the population lobby, with strong Conservative backing, was also warning that a free comprehensive service was needed to tackle the dangers of global over-population, a view reinforced in 1973 by the official report of the Ross Panel on Population.

The Government was cautious. Although the service was expanded under the NHS (Reorganization) Bill 1974, Sir Keith resisted a free service as a chorus from his backbenches and the tabloid press rose in protest against 'sex on the rates' and other modern day versions of the old argument that contraception would lead to immorality and promiscuity or, as John Stokes MP put it, enable the fornicator and adulterer 'to operate with the aid of . . . a government subsidy'. Prescription charges were retained; it was not until the Labour Government abolished them after its return to power in 1974 that a free and fully comprehensive service integrated in the NHS was achieved. It had taken fifty years for what early feminists had seen as the basic pre-condition for women's emancipation – contraception as part of State health care policy and a right for all women – to be realized.

The rights women had won under the 1967 Abortion Act were soon under threat from the combined pressure of Roman Catholic interests and the pressure groups, the Society for the Protection of the Unborn Child (SPUC) and Life, who harnessed concern about the rising abortion rate and alleged abuses of the system to a series of attempts to restrict the provisions of the Act. Feminists and pro-abortionists banded together to campaign for abortion on demand to overcome the shortcomings of inadequate and patchy NHS provision and the undue discretionary powers available to the medical profession under the Act.

The Government was responsive to pressures. The Lane Committee was appointed to look into the operation of the Act, but came up with a rebuff to both sides which satisfied no-one. In 1974 it rejected both abortion on demand and attempts to restrict the Act. It concluded that any abuses in the private sector were mainly the consequences of NHS shortages, and recommended expanding NHS facilities and improving education to foster a more mature attitude to sexual relations and contraception as a means to reduce 'excessive' abortion demand.[37]

Almost immediately, in 1975, Catholic Labour MP James White launched a campaign to reduce the time limit from twenty-eight to twenty weeks, with measures to cut down 'abuses' of the Act. This met resistance from the National Abortion Campaign which mobilized through the women's movement alongside ALRA with the support of women MP's under the slogan 'A Woman's Right to Choose'. The Bill fell for lack of time, but was followed by further amendments, none successful. (William Benyon's in 1977, Bernard Braine's in 1978 and William Corrie's in 1979.)

By the 1979 Corrie amendment, the pro-abortionists had significantly widened their support base. The Trades Union Congress affirmed its support of abortion on demand after lobbying by women members had convinced male colleagues that abortion was an issue affecting their working lives. A Labour Abortion Rights Committee, Tories for Free Choice, Doctors for a Woman's Choice on Abortion and a Co-ordinating Committee for Defence of the 1867 Act embracing 16 organizations joined with the NAC to oppose it. But it was an altogether colder climate in which to be fighting liberal or radical causes. With a new conservative administration committed to a return to vaguely defined 'Victorian values' and using the stigma of 'permissiveness' as the stick to chastise past governments, the Corrie amendment, which aimed to reduce the time limit from twenty-eight to twenty weeks was the greatest threat to the pro-abortionists so far. It was passed with an overwhelming majority at Second Reading. But with both the professional associations, the British Medical Association and the Royal College of Obstetricians and Gynocologists, opposing the Bill, and opinion polls showing a majority (54 per cent for, 34 per cent against) in favour of the legal availability of abortion to those who wanted it[38], it fell for lack of time in February 1980. As a test of the more conservative climate, it was an early indication the line on 'permissive' liberal legislation could be held. The Government, by allowing it to fall, indicated the limits of its commitment to abortion.

There were other areas where women's rights were negated because a complex web of unchallenged assumptions about 'feminine' behaviour and female sexuality was built into the legal process. When Erin Pizzey set up a refuge for battered wives in Chiswick, West London in 1972, she triggered immediate public attention. The hitherto unmentioned problem of domestic violence was exposed as a widespread phenomenon – that men, regardless of class, frequently beat up their wives in the privacy of their own homes. It provoked closer scrutiny of the way the law treated women. The protection of women in law from assault, it was pointed out, did not extend beyond the threshold of the family home. Police were reluctant to intervene in this 'private' sphere. The controversy exposed underlying assumptions about women's dependence and 'natural' masochism – that they 'invited assault', that the victims were responsible for their attack. It revealed the extent of police reluctance and the lack of seriousness with which they dealt with cases of domestic assault on women. As the issue of male domestic violence was forced to prominence, it was moved out of the private into the public arena. It was no longer considered one of those eventualities women unfortunately had to accept in 'bad' marriages as part of the deal, and keep quiet. Women, with support, could do something to change their situation. Self-help groups mushroomed. By 1974 a Woman's Aid Federation was established with 27 groups all over the country. By 1980 there were 99 groups and 200 refuges, which attracted financial support from government, charities and individual donors.[39]

The issue also attracted parliamentary backing for measures to help women. Jo Richardson's private members measure, the Domestic Violence Act 1976 made it easier for women to get a court injunction to restrain a violent husband or cohabitee. This small step marked a shift towards State intervention to protect women's separate rights *within* the family, for it 'gave priority to a woman's rights to bodily security over a man's rights over his property'. Even so, it did not dent underlying assumptions about the difference between private and public violence, for instance in the 1982 judgment of a man who raped a woman while awaiting trial for the murder of his wife. 'This crime ... so closely resembles the murder of your estranged wife that it may mean you are not just a domestic murderer, but a very dangerous man,' decided Mr. Justice Hodgson.[40]

Rape was another area where women challenged the web of assumptions about female behaviour and sexuality which determined attitudes to sentencing. The persistence of the beliefs that women were essentially masochistic and submissive in their attitudes to coitus, that they were prone to fantasies of rape, and that they were inclined to lie, often as a consequence of shame felt after the act, played a significant part in judicial practice. They were always damaging to women, and were used to undermine women's evidence. Attitudes to the question of consent were just as influenced by cultural definitions of female sexual behaviour: 'Women who say no do not always mean no,' Judge David Wild pronounced in 1982, effectively sympathizing with the defendant, whom he acquitted. 'It is not just a question of saying no, it is a question of how she says it, how she shows and makes it clear. If she doesn't want it she only has to keep her legs shut and she would not get it without force and there would be marks of force being used.'[41]

The belief that women provoked attack by their behaviour, that they 'asked for it', which made them somehow responsible for the assault was also evident. The assumption that assault resulting from men's 'loss of control' over their sexual drive constituted an act of a different order from a criminal act was disturbing. In a 1977 case, a guardsman sexually assaulted a 17-year-old barmaid after she refused him sex and inflicted injuries and swellings to the vulva consistent in the examining doctor's view, with extreme pain during childbirth. Yet his sentence to three years imprisonment was quashed on appeal and substituted with a six month suspended sentence when it was decided by Mr Justice Slynn that: 'It does not seem to me that the appellant is a criminal in the sense in which that word is used frequently in these courts. Clearly he is a man who, on the night in question, allowed his enthusiasm for sex to overcome his normal behaviour.'[42]

Other aspects of procedure and sentencing roused indignation, which intensified after police methods were shown in a Roger Graef TV documentary, *Police* in 1982. Disquiet was expressed about probing the past sexual history and lifestyle, not of defendants but of the women who brought the charges, as evidence of the victim's character; about the police treatment of women who brought charges and their tendency to disbelieve the victim's story which left women feeling it was they who were on trial, and about the leniency of sentencing. After pressure from women's lobbies, some adjustments towards protecting women's rights were made in the Sexual Offence Act 1976. This guaranteed anonymity to the victims and protected them from unnecessary interrogation on their previous sexual experiences. Women again turned to self-help methods. Using the American model, the first Rape Crisis Centre was set up by women in 1976 to provide support for victims of rape and by 1981, a further sixteen centres were established, financed by charitable trusts.

By the early 1980s, loss of faith in the law's ability to protect women was widespread. A clear majority in a *Sunday Times* poll believed the police had too little sympathy for women reporting rape; 70 per cent thought a man accused of rape had a good chance of getting away with it.[43] Though the incidence of reported rape increased from 1,068 in 1981 to 1,336 (in England and Wales) in 1982[44] and of indecent assaults from 10,634 in 1981 to 11,156 in 1982, it was generally believed, including by the police, that the actual incidence was much higher, and that women were deterred from reporting rape because they did not expect fair treatment.

The mishandling of a case in Scotland, when proceedings against three youths were dropped, allegedly because the woman, whose injuries had required 135 stitches, was unable on medical and psychiatric advice to appear in court, caused widespread outrage, compounded by the lenient sentence (a £2000 fine) on a man who raped a hitchhiker. The Lord Chief Justice, Lord Lane, responded with a declaration that all rapists would be imprisoned unless there were exceptional circumstances; a view publicly endorsed by the Prime Minister, Margaret Thatcher who nevertheless rejected calls for an internal inquiry into the operation of the law. In 1984, proposals for a law revision to include rape in marriage, which had been canvassed by women's and civil liberties groups, were turned down by the Criminal Law Revision Committee: 'An extension of the offence to all marriages . . . might be detrimental to marriage as an institution,' it concluded.[45]

Male violence against women and the law's failure to protect women's rights became the focus of vociferous protest. Even before the Yorkshire Ripper seized the headlines, women were claiming the right to live without fear of assault or abuse, in public places and in private. Male violence, in the feminist critique, was identified as part of a wider system of male power and dominance through which women were controlled and kept in their place. The portrayal of women as sex objects and the commercial eroticization of the female body was one facet of this, a perpetual encouragement to see women as sexual 'fair game'. It was not only that women were objectified and de-humanized, it was the reinforcement of male power over the female body which women objected to in their anti-pornography campaigns. The Yorkshire Ripper case crystallized protest into anger. Between 1975 and 1981 thirteen women were murdered and seven seriously wounded at the hands of Peter Sutcliffe. There was little public outcry to begin with, largely because the victims were mainly prostitutes, itself a significant comment on the protection women could expect from the law. With the murder of a 'respectable' woman, the scale of police activities was stepped up. Women in the North of England lived in a state of panic about their safety as a virtual curfew was imposed on their activities after dark. The police failure to solve the murders intensified outrage; all women in the area were vulnerable, forced to see themselves as potential victims and men as potential suspects. After Sutcliffe was arrested in 1981 and sentenced to life imprisonment, the panic diminished. But the Ripper had exposed deep seams of fear and indignation, and left a residue of disturbing questions, not only about police procedure and their inability to trace and identify a man whom they had interviewed on several occasions, but also about the aetiology and nature of male violence and hostility towards women.

Across the board women were challenging the sexual rights men exercised over women through laws, customs and institutional practices. The jeans-clad feminists of the 1970s rebelled against the image of women as fetishized immature sex objects, against accessibility as the price of sexual freedom, against discrimination on the grounds of sex, and against definitions of female sexuality which cramped their opportunities for bodily autonomy, self actualization and pleasure on their own terms. They developed their own forms of resistance to institutionalized oppression, and a new vocabulary to outlaw old habits like sexual harassment and customary forms of 'sexism'. Feminism established a woman-centred voice which refused to be hushed, and echoed through the national debate from then on. In the optimistic climate of the 1970s some gains were made, some structural changes were enacted, and a deeper awareness of the mechanisms of male privilege and female subordination gained currency. But in the 1980s the conservative Government supported neither the policies which would bring about the further advancement of women's rights nor the support system necessary to make them work. Hopes for real change dimmed as most women's economic position deteriorated. Even so gains in personal and sexual freedom were not relinquished easily, and the struggle against coercion was maintained.

Coming Out

In an environment of moral pluralism and changing moral norms, the regulation and constraints on all forms of sexuality were called into question. Just as the rhetoric of sexual liberation nurtured the women's challenge to the construction of female sexuality, so it also informed a radical repudiation by homosexuals of heterosexual norms and the categorizations which defined them as 'deviant' and were used to justify policing them as a threat to morality.

Although the 1967 parliamentary reforms had removed criminal sanctions on some homosexual activities (between consenting adults in private) it did not remove large areas of discrimination nor diminish prosecution of homosexuals for sexual offences (which in fact went up). The emergence of a gay liberation movement in 1970 signalled their resistance to multi-layered forms of oppression – on the one hand, legal persecution and police harassment, restrictions on their personal freedom, discrimination in jobs, housing and child custody, and on the other, forms of self-oppression stemming from guilt about their sexuality and self-hatred built up through internalizing the values of a hostile culture.

The Gay Liberation Front, set up in Britain in 1970, affirmed the validity of a positive gay identity which relied on self definition. It followed the American example of New York gays, who organized after a police raid on a gay bar, the Stonewall Inn under the manifesto: 'We reject society's attempt to impose sexual rôles and simplistic myths. WE ARE GOING TO BE WHO WE ARE.' Several principles were established to achieve this: the importance of 'coming out' with a public assertion of sexual identity; 'coming together' – a declaration of solidarity and strength in collective action; and the idea of 'gay pride'. A theoretical framework evolved for understanding sexuality not as categories in relation to fixed 'norms', but as part of a web of categorizations invented at different times and sustained by professional practices to serve the purposes of social control and regulation. Reconstructing the concept of homosexuality by analysing its historical and social roots, in which the work of the French historian Michel Foucault was influential, was a necessary step to understanding the mechanisms of institutional oppression.

Early consciousness-raising groups were a forum for working

towards self-identification. 'I remember a very, very early meeting when somebody said, "Let's think of reasons why we are glad to be gay", and I thought, "Rubbish, there aren't any, what nonsense," ' Bill Thorneycroft recalled. 'When I actually began to realize that there were advantages to being gay, that changed my whole attitude – up till then I had always thought of it as some-thing to be sorry for, to apologize for. That was the turning-point in my whole attitude to myself.'[46] It was a condition shared by lesbians who, ostracized though not criminally branded for their sexual orientation, were forced into guilt and isolation: 'I lived in secrecy and rebellion,' Elizabeth Wilson recalled of life in the liberated 1960s. 'I lived a double life, in which my womanliness was a masquerade, inhabiting a space between the open rejection of society and an underworld that bordered on prostitution.'[47]

By creating a milieu of openness and affirmation, identifying as a group, and organizing collectively, gays enlarged their personal and political space. By 1972, the Gay Liberation Front was frag-menting because of internal disputes over objectives and a lack of any organizational structure. Lesbians who had actively supported it began to move away, disillusioned by the impossibility of getting their demands on the agenda and by men's sexism. Many found their place in the Women's Liberation Movement. By 1973, the main organizational impetus was coming from the Campaign for Homosexual Equality (CHE), set up in 1969 with more reformist aims and a stress on grass roots organization. It took the lead in parliamentary lobbying for law reform to remove the existing inequalities between gays and homosexuals, age of consent legis-lation, police policies and police harassment.

By then support groups and local organizations were proliferat-ing. More gays were coming out and speaking publicly. Teachers, social workers, medics, students, lawyers, clergymen and other groups were organizing into networks of support around gay rights issues. The main political parties had gay and lesbian groups pressing to put gay rights and issues of heterosexism on the agenda. *Gay News*, set up in 1972 in the wake of the *IT* prosecution reflected the increased visibility of gay issues and a buoyant, cel-ebratory gay culture. By 1976, with a 20,000 circulation, far from being 'furtive and underground', it was providing, one contributor observed, 'some of the uplift of the parish magazine or local community paper, finding an ingenious gay line on a multitude of topics ... It was open, variegated, multi-dimensional, pleasure oriented.'[48] The commercialization of gay culture, with the emergence of gay magazines, films confronting gay issues, theatre groups, and the expansion of meeting places openly catering to a gay clientele all testified to a new confidence built around a positive validation of gay identity and lifestyle. Counselling services expanded and attracted official funds. In 1975 CHE's service, Friend, received £40,000 from Islington Council and the Home Office under the Urban Aid Scheme. Telephone counselling flourished: London Icebreakers was set up in 1973, Gay Switchboard, set up in 1974, provided legal advice, support and information to around 1000 men and women callers a week.[49]

Though there were signs that issues of gay rights commanded wider support by the mid-1970s, it was not difficult to harness blatant hostility in campaigns to vilify and ostracize gays. Mary Whitehouse's successful prosecution of *Gay News* in 1976 for blasphemy over the publication of a poem by Professor James Kirkup, *The Love that Dares to Speak its Name*, was one eruption. The poem described the thoughts of a Roman centurion guarding the crucified Christ on the subject of homo-erotic love. It was the first blasphemy case to come to court since 1921 when John Gott compared Christ to a circus clown – exactly what David Essex was currently doing on stage in the popular musical *Godspell*, as John Mortimer pointed out. There was a chorus of indignation that an outdated law was being resurrected to outlaw the portrayal of homo-erotic love and endorse the belief that homosexuality was abnormal and evil. It was swelled by liberal outrage that the blasphemy law should be used at such a late stage in the twentieth century to control freedom of expression. The judgment provoked volumes of correspondence and several demonstrations, and it polarized opinion. Mary Whitehouse's claim that she intended, not to attack homosexuals' rights but only to prove the words represented 'a radically different set of values and perspectives to those which the traditional Christian would accept as legitimate' cut little ice, even with the church. Church leaders had conspicuously failed to come to her defence, and in the *Church Times* she was criticized for bringing attention to the poem by prosecuting.[50]

Lesbians remained vulnerable to the process of the law and to public ostracism. In 1976, a series of child custody judgments which went against mothers because of their lesbian orientation galvanized women to set up an Action for Lesbian Parents group to campaign for their civil rights and provide support for mothers caught in the position of denying their lesbian identity in order to retain their children, or not concealing it, and losing them. In 1978 the *Evening News* ran a sensationalized story on lesbians who had children through artificial insemination. Two reporters had posed as a lesbian couple, met the doctor concerned, talked to other unsuspecting and supportive couples and then exposed them. It produced an outcry in the press against 'horrific practices' (which did not refer to the journalists' methods), and lengthy debate about medical ethics. The likely damage to children not brought up in a 'healthy and heterosexual environment' was assessed, which revealed deep prejudice against lesbianism, though several articles concluded there was no evidence of harm to children brought up in such an environment. That is, they emerged heterosexual in the end.

Discrimination against homosexuality remained pervasive. When in 1976 a *Charter for Reason*, signed by 170 leading Churchmen, doctors, lawyers, writers and academics argued for homosexual equality by claiming society had reached 'a state of knowledge and compassion when those who hate homosexuals should no longer be able to dictate accepted social attitudes from their own state',[51] the *Daily Telegraph* exploded into opposition: any attempt to treat homosexual love 'by law and by society in general as of equal status with heterosexual love' amounted to 'a sustained campaign for homosexuality as a way of life'.[52]

The churches, under pressure from the Gay Christian Movement and mindful of the publicity surrounding gay clergy coming out, reconsidered their attitude. They set up several committees to examine the issues. Only the Methodists concluded that the basis for moral judgment of homosexual love should be the same as for heterosexual love.[53] The Church of England was equivocal. Their report recommended tolerance and compassion towards those with an unalterable homosexual orientation (which was not blameworthy in itself). But they were unable to distance themselves from expressions of outrage against homosexuality since these derived from convictions based on Christian teaching about the 'proper use of sex'.[54] Thus straddling both sides of the fence, they concluded homosexual relationships could not be considered the moral and social equivalent of heterosexual ones, a view endorsed by *The Times* on the grounds that the 'visible . . . manifestation of (homosexual) activities' may weaken 'the idea of heterosexual marriage as the most reliable way to happiness for most people'.[55] Homosexual activity was to be tolerated if tucked away in private, but not when it was publicly visible, demanding acknowledgement on equal terms. The extent of overt policing and control over 'deviant' sexualities may have lessened, but in crucial areas of life it was still justified on the grounds that gays constituted a threat to morality and the heterosexual monogamous marital ideal.

The most conspicuous victim of his own 'homosexual tendencies' and the ambivalence in public attitudes towards them was Jeremy Thorpe, leader of the Liberal Party. At a time when the law permitted homosexual relations between men in private, when gays were asserting their valid identity and public men were coming out, the scandal of Thorpe's alleged relationship with Norman Scott in 1961 broke Thorpe's career and reputation and removed him from public life. The story was, declared the prosecuting counsel at his trial, 'a tragedy of truly Greek or Shakespearian proportions – the slow but inevitable destruction of a man by the stamp of one defect.'[56]

The machinery of destruction was set in motion when, according to Scott's allegations, an affair between the two men began after Scott, recently discharged from a psychiatric clinic with no job and no prospects turned to Thorpe for help in 1961. The affair lasted into 1962 then cooled. From then on Scott was to repeat to anyone who would listen allegations of an affair with Thorpe which Scott claimed had 'ruined him'. They included the police on several occasions, Thorpe's mother and his wife Caroline, whom he had married in 1968, and a motley collection of landladies and friends whom Scott came across in his roaming and unsettled life.

For Thorpe, public disclosure of his 'homosexual tendencies' presented a grave threat to his public position and his political ambitions. Homosexual activity was illegal in 1962. Exposure might lead to criminal prosecution and would certainly damage irrevocably Thorpe's political career. A close associate, Liberal MP Peter Bessell, claimed Thorpe told him in 1965 that if the truth about his homosexuality were made public he would take his own life rather than face the shame it would bring on him and the Liberal Party.[57] The 1967 reforms did little to alter the stigma attached to homosexuality and the damage it could do men in public life. By then Thorpe had become leader of the Liberal Party.

It was Thorpe's attempts to prevent Scott's allegations becoming public which fashioned the web of intrigue that landed him seventeen years later in the dock with four others on a charge of incitement and conspiracy to murder Scott. During this time, Thorpe responded to Scott's regular pleas for help getting work and financial assistance. Whenever rumours surfaced, he successfully denied them – to an internal Liberal Party Inquiry in 1971, to the Home Secretary, Reginald Maudling, and to the press. Evidence was slender, and Thorpe's public influence undoubtedly protected him. When a reporter tried to sell Scott's story to the *People*, it was turned down: 'It consisted of the incoherent ramblings of a man with a vendetta against Jeremy Thorpe,' Lord Jacobson, chairman of the Mirror Group and a personal friend of Thorpe, decided.[58]

The lengths Thorpe was prepared to go to prevent public disclosure of his 'one defect' became the main issue at his trial. Events had taken a different turn in October 1975 when, on a lonely West country moor, Scott's dog, Rinka, was shot by an airline pilot, Andrew Newton, who at first claimed to be involved in a blackmail case. Though the connection was not immediately made with Thorpe, pressure on him was mounting in other directions; Thorpe's involvement in the London and Counties Securities financial scandal (in which he was cleared of any direct responsibility) and rumours of scandalous mismanagement of Liberal funds kept him in the public eye in a somewhat adverse light. When Scott next retailed details of his alleged affair with Thorpe (whilst being charged with dishonestly obtaining social security payments to the tune of £58.40) it was to a Minehead court packed with reporters.

The next day's papers were filled with the allegations, which Thorpe still denied. Stories about him were multiplying and none of them added up, a sure recipe for continuing scandal. Colleagues who had initially rallied to his support began to peel away. Richard Wainwright lobbied for his removal from the leadership, while Cyril Smith the Liberal Chief Whip, who claimed 'no right thinking person in this day and age would give two hoots about the allegations of a homosexual affair twelve years or more previously' was more disturbed at 'the public disquiet raised by the continuing sickening revelations which, again true or false, nevertheless exposed some undeniably damning machinations by members of the Liberal Party from its very centre, to its ultimate lunatic fringe'.[59] Thorpe's former colleague Peter Bessell, bankrupted and exiled in America, added to the furore by publicly confessing in the *Daily Mail* to lying on Thorpe's behalf. With his colleagues in flight, Thorpe resigned the leadership in May, leaving a jigsaw of deception and intrigue tantalizingly unsolved, and the press in full pursuit.

In October 1977 Newton, the hit man, published (for a large sum of money) the allegation he had been paid £5000 by leading Liberals to shoot Scott. Police investigations were re-opened, and Thorpe was arrested in August 1978. He lost his North Devon seat in the general election; his political career was already at an end by the time he reached court.

In court his 'homosexual tendencies' were almost casually confirmed by both the prosecuting counsel, who declared 'the key and the only key' to the case was the combination of Thorpe's homosexual tendencies and his determined ambition, and by the defence counsel, George Carman QC, who explained: 'Nature so fashioned him that we know that at the time he had the misfortune to ever meet Norman Scott, he was a man with homosexual tendencies.'[60] What now mattered was whether Thorpe's attempts to prevent public exposure had gone as far as incitement and conspiracy to murder. After a skilful defence which managed to discredit all the main witnesses as liars, the jury acquitted all the defendants.

It became clear that whatever had changed in society's attitude to homosexuality, public men could still find themselves vulnerable to allegations involving homosexuality, especially if they went to such lengths to conceal it. 'The proper relationship between the new sexual morality and public life has not yet been resolved,' concluded the *Sunday Telegraph*. 'Until it is, the story of Jeremy Thorpe is a cautionary tale on the dangers of going out in the world with a time-bomb strapped to your chest.'[61]

Ten

Policing Desires

Erotic Compulsions: Public and Private

If sexual freedom generated new areas of ambiguity, it also resurrected old anxieties about the breakdown of traditional moral values. As the frontiers of tolerance shifted, a new battle was joined over the limits of freedom. Pornography was the battleground. For moral conservatives, it provided the scapegoat for wider anxieties about the sexualization of the culture and the loss of moral purpose at the heart of social policy. Pornography violated the boundaries between the public and private; it represented the antithesis of the Christian concept of the private and sacramental meaning of sex and its proper purpose in lifelong monogamous marriage. Moral relativism, moral individualism and the whole ethic of sexual release had, in their view, breached the bounds of tolerance and borne fruit in the 'moral pollution' of society. Their redress lay in the attempt to strengthen the uncertain laws against obscenity, to increase the state's jurisdiction over the boundaries of freedom and bring them into line with Christian moral values.

The problem of where to draw the line preoccupied law makers, law enforcers and Christian fundamentalists, as much as it did libertarians, who were generally interested in reducing interference with individual freedom as far as possible. The problem of pornography was, firstly, one of objective definition, and secondly, of law enforcement at a time of changing standards, increased availability of sexually explicit material, and the wider public acceptance of what were formerly taboo areas. The conflict between the separate interest groups was the loam in which public controversy flourished.

The obscenity laws were thought by all sides to be unworkable and over-complex. Libertarians argued that the difficulties of interpreting the laws with any consistency justified repeal of the Obscene Publications Acts. This was the position taken by the Arts Council Working Party on the Obscenity Laws which argued in 1969 for the repeal of the laws for five years on the grounds that it was not for the State to prohibit citizens from choosing what they may or may not enjoy in literature or art 'unless there were incontrovertible evidence that the result would be injurious to society'. There was no such evidence. Indeed a succession of reports in various countries failed, in the words of the US Presidential Commission on Obscenity and Pornography (1970), 'to establish a meaningful causal relationship or even significant correlation between exposure to erotica and immediate or delayed anti-social behaviour among adults'.[1] The Danes, on the basis of similar conclusions, repealed all existing laws prohibiting pornography; monitoring then failed to reveal any conclusive evidence of its connection with sex crimes. A body of research built up to prove that, on the contrary, it could have therapeutic effects in enabling people to confront sexuality more openly; this was regularly offered as expert evidence for the defence in pornography trials.

The puritan lobby argued that the ineffectiveness of the law justified tightening it to stem the tide of moral pollution. The Festival of Light became the vehicle of protest. It was set up in 1971 by an ex-missionary Peter Hill who had been inspired by a vision of the regeneration of purity to set up a Christian crusade against the forces of darkness, and gathered under its umbrella a collection of religious fundamentalists, Catholics and humanists disturbed at the drift away from Christian values. Malcolm Muggeridge, lamenting the moral and spiritual collapse of the country had already proposed to Mary Whitehouse a form of 'Christian Resistance': 'In these circumstances the only thing Christians can do is to, as it were, go back to the catacombs; to form, as it were, a Christian maquis, or underground resistance movement . . .'[2] Lord Longford another Festival of Light leader envisaged a religious revival comparable to that of the early nineteenth century. A demonstration in September 1971 yielded 35,000 recruits to 'a political, social and evangelist campaign against pornography, obscenity and the so-called permissive society'.[3]

Though marginalized as a minority of extremists, their vociferous public presence helped shape a political climate more favourable to restrictions by the end of the decade. The established
churches distanced themselves from attempts to identify Christian
beliefs with repressive censorship; the Methodists, in their Report
Censorship 1971, warned of the danger of allowing unrepresent-
ative Christian pressure groups to become unofficial cnesorship
bodies.[4] The Conservative Home Secretary, Reginal Maudling,
staked out his liberal position in 1971: stronger action against
permissiveness was not a matter of government compulsion but
of voluntary acceptance of standards and of leadership, 'by academics, the churches, journalists and the mass media'. If there
were a backlash which consisted of a return to Victorian ideas and
morality he would be 'appalled'.[5] The Conservative press also
withheld support. Though the *Daily Telegraph* expressed some
sympathy for their aims, it feared the 'raving lunatics and hysterics'
and the 'self righteous and censorious busybodies' they attracted
to their banner would lead them to advocate all manner of harsh
and injudicious legislation of a kind likely to bring both morality
and the law into disrepute'.[6]

The lobby's main aims were to tighten censorship; in this they
failed. Their much publicized attempts to ban films, notably Ken
Russell's *The Devils* (1971), Sam Peckinpah's *Straw Dogs* (1972)
and Stanley Kubrick's *A Clockwork Orange* (1972) by manipulating local authority film censorship committees provoked fierce
controversy and led to a crisis of confidence in the film censorhip
system but did not succeed in its objectives. Their resort to private
prosecutions against *Blow Out* and *Last Tango in Paris* was no
more successful – although Raymond Blackburn, who established
himself as the scourge of film censorship, scored one success
against *More About the Language of Love*. This loophole was
closed when the Criminal Law Amendment Act 1977 abolished
private prosecutions unless authorized by the Director of Public
Prosecutions and amended the Obscene Publications Act to
include films. The problem of where to draw the line remained,
but it was put back into the hands of the licensing authorities and
the law to decide.

Lord Longford's unofficial inquiry into pornography (the
Government had turned down an official one) generated much

ribald amusement as its members explored the fleshpots of Copenhagen or Amsterdam closely observing their manifold aspects. But it did not advance the cause. Its main recommendation, to replace the test of obscenity (that it may tend to deprave and corrupt) with a far broader definition 'that its effect, taken as a whole, is to outrage contemporary standards of decency or humanity accepted by the public at large'[7] was greeted with caution in even the most conservative circles and turned down by the Home Secretary in 1972 as an even more unworkable legal definition. 'What must be avoided,' said the *Daily Telegraph* 'is using a legal sledgehammer which will smash not only a small, dirty mouse in the corner of the room but some valuable furniture as well.'[8] Mary Whitehouse's continued complaints against television programmes (which now focused on sex education programmes) remained an irritant and perhaps a brake on some 'excesses' under the post-Greene regime. But her attempts to institute a Broadcasting Complaints Body as a forum for public redress and her attempts to extend the provisions of the Obscene Publications Act to broadcasting were specifically rejected by the Annan Committee on Broadcasting in 1977 and made little progress until the Thatcher Government came to power in 1979.

The feminist lobby took an active part in the debate but found itself in a dilemma. The attack on the sexual exploitation and objectification of women was central to their sexual politics. Pornography degraded women, and used them as sex objects. Most feminists brought up in libertarian and liberation politics had supported the enlargement of freedoms which released sex from narrow inhibitions and social controls. The pornography of the 1970s was hardly progress, but a regression endorsing oppressive images of women at least and male violence at worst.

As campaigns against pornography, sex shops and the sexual exploitation of women escalated, sharp divisions developed over whether the suitable weapon of attack was a legal ban, thereby strengthening police powers, or whether stepping up propaganda, confrontation and education was more appropriate. Those who analysed pornography as a fiction constructed around sex argued it was commercially exploitable because it exposed a culture which endorsed the deeper exploitation of women. It revealed rather than caused the conditions of lewd male sexual fantasy. Pornography was the outcome, not the cause, of wider oppressions which were left untouched when all the energies of attack went on the symptoms. In addition, scant attention was paid to the decisions and fate of women who worked in the sex industry, who saw the anti-pornography campaigns as an attack on their livelihood at a time of decreasing work opportunities. Not the least cause for concern by the end of the 1970s was the way feminists were identified with Christian fundamentalists and conservatives whose aims – antithetical to the fundamental aims of feminism – were the denial of women's (and men's) exploration of their sexuality, and the confinement of sex within the narrow constraints of the traditional Christian ethic, which feminists had challenged for over a hundred years.

The beneficiaries of the confusion of the law were the porn merchants, whose trade expanded and flourished. By 1971 profits from hard-core pornography were estimated at £10 million a year; if soft-core and films were included it ran into several hundred millions. Cheap Danish product, imported with the bacon, swelled the market. Hard-core porn amounting to an estimated 10 million articles illegally imported in 1972 remained the most profitable sector; mark-up prices of up to 2000 per cent of production price on illicit material were not uncommon. Far from being 'dirty old men', one marketing survey in 1971 found eight out of ten soft-porn readers were in the free-spending under-45 age bracket, one third earning more than £2000 a year. By 1975, *Men Only* readership was estimated at 1,854,000, *Mayfair* at 1,676,000 and *Penthouse* at 1,661,000[9] A market research firm in 1977 found for its advertizers a £20 million market in men's magazines – 'about the same value as more traditional Mintel markets, like marmalade or lavatory cleansers.' Official figures in 1979 estimated a broad-based readership of 8 million for up-market established magazines. About 4 million adults read one or more porn magazines every month; they were mainly male, mainly under-35, readership was strongest among the skilled working class.[10]

As the market expanded, competition increased, and the boundaries of explicitness shifted rapidly. Where to draw the line, if at all, became more problematic as society endorsed individual freedom of choice. By 1973, polls were showing 74 per cent of respondents agreed 'adults should be allowed to buy whatever indecent erotic books and magazines they like, so long as they are not on public display'.[11] Various rationales justifying pornography gained currency, that it was therapeutic in breaking down inhibitions, that it was a form of sex education (though few believed the newly-rich porn merchants who claimed this). The main arguments against banning it were resistance to the state policing of desire, and defence of freedom of expression, a case tested with success by lawyers in a series of pornography trials.

Police encountered a number of other obstacles when it came to law enforcement. Not the least was the wholesale corruption of officers in the Obscene Publications Squad, the branch of the Metropolitan Police dealing with 'vice', who, it was revealed in 1972, had since the 1960s been virtually running the pornography trade. Through protection rackets operating in the West End vast sums of money – to the tune of £250,000 a year – were paid by large and small operators to police officers of all ranks in the Dirty Squad for the privilege of operating and protection from police interference.[12] This unsatisfactory state of affairs ended after Robert Mark took over as Chief Commissioner with a mission to clean up the 'Met', and eventually led to the conviction of a number of high-ranking police officers in 1977 for bribery and corruption. Searches and seizures of material increased significantly in London's West End from 1972.

But there were other problems about prosecuting. As public opinion became more broad-minded, juries showed increasing reluctance to convict in pornography cases. The problem of the definitions of pornography and obscenity became acute. In 1973 the Chief Commissioner of the Metropolitan Police, complained of the blurred demarcation lines between what was and was not obscene, with the result that half of the contested cases resulted in acquittal.[13] Since 1970 the police had exercized caution over bringing prosecutions in obscenity cases, especially literary cases, partly because of adverse publicity if they failed. This had influenced their approach to 'borderline' cases where the level of pornography was 'exceptionally delicate'.[14] But the boundaries kept shifting. During 1975, several prosecutions which, on previous experience, looked like succeeding, were lost. In one, the jury failed to agree over an American publication containing sado-masochistic material which up to then had been convicted. In another a jury found only certain parts obscene; the depiction of straightforward sexual activity between adults was declared not obscene. The Director of Public Prosecutions was provoked to comment that it was now quite impossible to be certain of a jury conviction even of what he saw as grossly obscene. With the acquittal in 1976 of *Inside Linda Lovelace* the police took the view it was unlikely the law would be invoked against the written word since it was, the judge remarked, 'difficult to imagine what written material would be regarded as obscene if that was not'.[15]

This did not prevent the police asserting their authority in a renewed offensive against porn in 1977. In the first few months over 300,000 copies of magazines were seized. Prosecutions conducted in magistrates courts without juries delivered a higher conviction rate; police switched to forfeiture proceedings against retailers instead of obscenity proceedings against publishers. In Manchester, enforcement was carried out with vigour after James Anderton, who did not disguise his belief that porn was 'sinful', was appointed Chief Constable in 1976. In the first six months of 1977, in 355 raids on newsagents and retailers, including W. H. Smith's, police seized nearly 200,000 items worth round half a million pounds. Proceedings, mainly heard by magistrates, were successful in almost every case. The availability of porn in Greater Manchester was very much reduced.[16] Throughout the country, bookshops and newsagents were reported to be cutting back because of police raids. In 1977, faced with increased police seizures and falling profits, the major pornography producers retrenched. Through a newly set up British Adult Publications Association, agreement was reached to revert to '1976 standards' of explicitness, remain within what the courts agreed was not obscene, cut back on harder core material and issue a trade stamp of approval on all new publications. The number of obscenity cases trebled from 540 in 1976 to 1,679 in 1978, to the point where the police were complaining they could no longer cope with the volume of cases.[17]

Attempts to introduce statutory controls since 1973 had concentrated on display. A 1973 Cinematograph and Indecent Displays Bill aimed to restrict public display was thought by many to be a possible compromise measure, de-fusing some of the worst fears of the Christian lobby while preserving private freedoms. It was in fact more a concession to the views of the puritan lobby, which had recently presented its Nationwide Petition for Decency with 1,350,000 signatures to Downing Street. It contained no proposal to change the definition of obscenity, and made no attempt to define what was meant by indecent display. 'Indecency' was to be left to the courts to decide. It increased police powers, put prosecutions in the hands of magistrates, abolished the defendant's right to trial by jury and the defence of artistic or literary merit, and permitted private prosecutions without authorization by the Director of Public Prosecutions. It was opposed as a significant extension of censorship, which far from clarifying the law led to increased uncertainty. Nor was there apparently wide public support. An Opinion Research Centre poll in 1973 showing 71 per cent of respondents had never been seriously upset by an indecent display, and a further 10% only rarely upset, suggested the silent majority was being pushed by a vociferous minority through their supporters on the Tory benches.[18]

When the Bill fell with the 1974 General Election, the Labour Government did not revive it, arguing that the term 'indecency' had 'no meaningful definition and should not be part of any criminal statute'. There remained the problem of framing a workable law, a task entrusted to a Committee set up in July 1977 under the chairmanship of Professor Bernard Williams, Provost of Kings College Cambridge, to look into the whole question of obscenity and film censorship.

In the meantime, Mrs Whitehouse counted her only parliamentary success, the Child Pornography Act 1976 which tightened controls on the use of under-age children in pornographic material and was passed unopposed even though the available legislation was already adequate to cover offences in this area. On broadcasting, the Annan Committee in 1977 rejected proposals for a Broadcasting Council, arguing that the existing framework of controls was adequate to deal with complaints about taste and decency. The Report steered a mediating and moderate liberal course. Acknowledging that some programmes caused offence to some people, and there was room for improvement in complaints procedures and liaison with the public, they also pointed out that sex and violence were part of the society which boradcasting had a duty to reflect; they were eternal themes in art and literature. More open portrayal of sexual themes might sometimes prove gratuitous but it could also advance understanding. The pursuit of artistic excellence might involve shock which was not necessarily a bad thing. There was a delicate balance which was, it concluded, better preserved through existing procedures than through a 'Tribunal of Taste' set above the broadcasting authorities to police them.[19]

After the Williams Committee reported in 1979, attention shifted back to indecent display as the area most likely to command approval in compromise legislation. The Report bore the stamp of the level-headed sanity of its Chairman, a professor of philosophy, and helped clarify a confused situation. Acknowledging that the central problem was to make obscenity law both rational and workable, it recommended scrapping the existing law and substituting a comprehensive new statute. Its principle objective would be 'to prevent offences to the public at large and to protect young people from indecent material'[20], while not prohibiting material being available for private consumption through licensed outlets which would be restricted to avoid offence to the public in general. In this they used the distinction between public and private, current since Wolfenden, to determine the limits of state intervention. A new film board was recommended to rationalize the functions of the British Board of Film Censors and local licensing authorities. The suggestion that porn shops and blue movies should be officially licensed caused some shock, but the Report met with widespread approval, though Mary Whitehouse dubbed it 'a pornographer's charter'.

Though its recommendations were shelved by the new Conservative Government, it paved the way for a revived Indecent Displays (Control) Bill, a private members' measure which was passed unopposed in 1981 with provisions that shops displaying pornography must have warnings indicating matter was unsuitable for under-18s, displays of an indecent nature should not be visible from outside, and a new criminal offence was introduced, covering books or magazines visible in bookshops or newsagents' windows. Its terms, narrowly confined to the area of public display, did not appear to intervene with individual freedom. But because pornography continued to act as a scapegoat for fears about the commercial exploitation of sex and the sexualization of the culture, it remained controversial in the 1980s.

Rates Of Exchange

The distinction between public annoyance and private acts had also been the rationale for the increased control of prostitution since the Street Offences Act of 1959. Attitudes to prostitution had hardly changed through the 1960s and early 1970s, despite a radical transformation of the sexual ethic particularly in relation to female sexuality. It was not until the late 1970s that it re-emerged as a issue of public controversy. Several factors contributed to this.

The 1959 Street Offences legislation cleared prostitution out of sight, off the streets. It did not aim to eliminate prostitution, nor did it intend to protect prostitute's rights. Inded it increased police powers to control them. It was pointed out at the time the result would be to deprive women further of their civil rights and render them more vulnerable to organized prostitution rackets. Prostitutes remained a stigmatized group more harassed by the law than protected by it.

As the entire sex industry expanded in the late 1960s and early 1970s, work opportunities for women increased – in escort agencies, massage and sauna parlours, 'call girl' organizations, sex clubs and the pornography business. Most were operating on the margins of legality, all were selling sex but fairly discreetly. Prostitution thrived, but out of sight. Public exposure of scandals involving prostitution could still, however, topple public men, just as it continued to be fodder for media titillation. When Lord Lambton's association with Norma Levy, a call girl who ran a network of businesses, was exposed in 1973, it was treated with the utmost seriousness by the Conservative Party (no doubt conscious of echoes of Profumo) and Lambton resigned as Under Secretary of the Ministry of Defence. The press had its usual field day, exposing another Lord (Jellicoe) who had confessed to his Prime Minister, Edward Heath, of his involvement, and causing many who may also have been implicated in practices of an unusual sexual nature to quake in their beds at the possibility of exposure. When it had all blown over, when righteousness was vindicated, and corruption duly rooted out, and the country was again deemed safe, it was apparent that, although the country's morals had changed, men in public positions were still vulnerable if their dirty linen was revealed in public, if not quite as vulnerable as ten years earlier. Although Lord Lambton retired to Tuscany, Lord Jellicoe was subsequently restored to public life.

Prostitution remained the moral boundary, the dividing line between an outlawed and illicit sexual bargain, and 'respectable' sex – even though changing sexual mores had in most other respects transformed the nature of the sexual exchange, and sex was on sale just about everywhere. During the 1970s, what had been seen primarily as a moral problem with an economic dimension became much more an economic and political issue with a continuing moral dimension. The economic and political issue was the position of women and their rights under the law, and the way women, particularly lone mothers and the young unemployed bore the brunt of the recession and public expenditure cutbacks at the end of the decade.

The rights of prostitutes began to be scrutinized mainly because the women began to organize to publicize their case. They exposed their vulnerability under the law, but also the anomalous position of women in the new sexual ethic. Since the earliest days of emancipation, women had challenged the marriage contract as one in which men agreed to support women for life in return for sexual favours. There had been no shortage of people who pointed out the basic contract was not dissimilar to the bargain of prostitution, the main difference being that one was culturally and morally respectable and protected by law and the other was not. The continuing economic disadvantage of women and their cultural subordination served to perpetuate the bargain. The aims of ninteenth-century emancipationists and twentieth-century feminists had been to transform those power relations in the name of equality, freedom and justice. They had continually come up against the dual obstacles of the double sexual standard, and the continuing economic disadvantages of women, chiefly low pay, limited occupational opportunities, the undervaluation of women's work and their expendability in a job market which tended to see women as a reserve labour force, all of which narrow women's choices.

Changes in the sexual ethic from the 1960s had not immediately been accompanied by fundamental alteration in women's status, and there had certainly been no change in the legal status of prostitutes. For one of the first public spokeswomen for prostitute's rights, the new sexual ethic exacerbated women's disadvantage. Helen Buckingham, who became a single mother in her early twenties during the 1960s, was left by her boyfriend and lived on social security after trying and failing for various jobs. She had limited choices as a single mother. 'I was angry at my poverty, angry at the way I had been treated by straight men and above all I was angry that I had no value as a woman. I went on the game as a protest.'[21] She viewed prostitution as an open expression of an accepted bargain between the sexes.

The sexual freedom of the 1960s and 1970s blurred the nature of the bargain for a time. 'In the sixties I think men saw sexual liberation as something that was very nice for them. Women saw it as a chance to be themselves and the women didn't realize they were casualties of this delusion.' An ethos of sexual encounters without attachments did not benefit women, particularly those in Helen Buckingham's position. 'Enormous numbers of women were taken for a very very big ride by the sexual liberation nonsense . . . The sixties had been telling girls to do this sort of thing and some of the girls found they were left with no option but to do it for money and there were people like me that actually said so. I absolutely stunned our own circle. The men said it devalues the currency. It devalues the currency of sex, the beyond-price exclusiveness of sex, their romantic delusions. These were the men who had never offered to marry any of us. In fact they thought marriage was all rather stupid and only rather old-fashioned fuddy-duddy girls were interested in it.'

Women, she believed, paid the price of sexual freedom not only in 'abortions and pills'; but because society, through economic arrangements and conventional discrimination continued to endorse the unspoken bargain: 'People like me called their bluff. I said I do not see I owe men anything more, they owe me their money. Because they can make it, I can't. I'm excluded from most jobs still. I'm excluded from everything that makes money. I cannot even get a council flat because I am a woman. I am discriminated against in the private sector for flats because I am a woman.

I am discriminated against everywhere I go because I am a woman and I cannot ask for the protection of men that I could before because that is now considered old-fashioned and exploitative. So if men want freedom to screw me without any obligations they have to pay for it. People were very stunned by that. I think prostitutes are women who have said no to exploitation.'[22]

To her surprise, she found the vast majority of men who went to prostitutes 'treated us with a lot more respect than a lot of men, who expect sex free and as a right whatever the state of the relationship is, because they paid.' She recalled: 'My anger against men lessened and my anger against the system increased.' She ran a call-girl business at the upper-end of the market, and set up several other businesses, more or less illegal, including a brothel: 'We vetted all the clients ourselves . . . We had plenty of traffic coming through. But it was very discreet. We never annoyed any of the neighbours – we couldn't possibly afford to.'[23]

By the mid-1970s complaints against the sex industry were reaching a crescendo. One result was a crack down on escort agencies which was the initial stimulus for Helen Buckingham to organize on behalf of women's rights. Escort agencies were legal; many offered a 'bent' and a 'straight' list. They gave some protection to women. But whereas formerly they were 'smart outfits run by men who advertised in the glossies', after the clean-up, according to Helen Buckingham, the 'criminal element' began to move in to front them. 'All you got was the man who had ill-gotten gains that needed laundering . . . They were giving up bank robberies and going into running escort agencies. It was a step up the ladder for them . . . We used to keep the men in the background because we realized it didn't look very good when clients came in and saw these rather heavy ex-burglars hanging around.' But women lost a relatively safe venue. Many went back to hostessing in the night clubs – 'just unofficial slavery'. Women invariably weren't paid; they had to encourage men to buy at least two bottles of champagne and forty cigarettes, and pay them for their company. Or there were massage parlours and saunas where women were often kept on low wages so they would be driven to cater for 'extras'.

Prostitutes began to organize for changes in the law to defend their civil rights. Helen Buckingham set up PUSSI (Prostitutes

United for Social and Sexual Integration – later PLAN – Prostitute Laws Are Nonsense) in 1975 to campaign for the abolition of the laws of prostitution, and in Birmingham's Balsall Heath area PROS (Programme for Reform of the law on Soliciting) was set up by prostitutes, social workers and a lawyer to defend the rights of street prostitutes. Around the same time, after French prostitutes had gone on nationwide strike following the occupation of a Lyon church designed to draw attention to the way the law treated women, the English Collective of Prostitutes was set up to campaign for the abolition of imprisonment for loitering and soliciting and to abolish the use of the term 'common prostitute'.[24]

As the recession spread and job opportunities diminished, more women moved into prostitution out of poverty, often at the point of desperation. 'I did work for six years as an office junior and in factories and then I became unemployed. When I was out of work I was at a friend's house when one of her clients called and he said "I like your friend!". I was really desperate and that's how I got into it,' recalled Carol.[25] Margaret, on the game for fourteen years, told of how a girlfriend introduced her to it: 'She had plenty of money, I was always broke. I'd worked as a typist before, but by this time I was divorced with a child. I wasn't getting any maintenance and I had the rent to pay.'[26] Prostitution offered an escape out of poverty. Lack of money to pay the bills, an inability to command a reasonable wage in the market, the difficulties of supporting a family on State benefits, often alone, and the high rewards for prostitution drove many women into it on an occasional or regular basis. An English Collection of Prostitutes estimate reckons around two million women have at some time engaged in full or part-time prostitution. They come 'from all walks of life, from married women supplementing their husband's university grant, to single mothers who find it impossible to feed and clothe their children on supplementary benefit . . . It is impossible to estimate how many families are surviving only because a woman, mother, daughter, wife is "on the game".'[27]

As street prostitution increased at the end of the decade, police activity against prostitutes intensified and prosecutions for soliciting shot up. Prostitution re-emerged as an issue of social and political concern, but this time some of impetus came from prostitute women themselves lobbying in defence of their civil rights. Two attempts to change the law failed. In 1977 Dame Joan Vickers introduced a motion in the House of Lord calling for reform on the prostitution laws, and in 1979 Maureen Colquhoun MP brought in a Bill under the Ten Minute Rule calling for an end to prison sentences for soliciting, the abolition of the term 'common prostitute' which stigmatized women for life, and the replacement of the prostitution laws with one offence to cover persistent street nuisance, with more protection for women. The laws at present constituted, she said, an unjust attack on the civil liberties of women in the name of 'the peculiar sexual hypocrisy of the British'.[28] The Bill got no further.

There was no better example of this hypocrisy than the prosecution in 1980 of Cynthia Payne, on a charge of keeping a brothel in Ambleside Road, Streatham – a leafy London suburb. She was fined a total of £4000 and sentenced to eighteen months imprisonment, (reduced to six months on appeal), by Lord Justice Lawton, who declared, 'this is as bad a case of brothel-keeping as it is possible to imagine . . . This is the sort of conduct that outrages and gives offence to those who have to live in proximity to it.'[29]

Police who kept a close watch on her five bedroomed house for several months in late 1978 (after being tipped off by an anonymous caller) had observed 259 men and 50 women enter it over a period of 12 days. When they raided it in December 1978, they found a Christmas party in progress. 53 middle-aged and elderly men and 13 women were found in varying states of disarray. They were all arrested. Cynthia Payne faced a total of 21 charges including running a brothel and keeping a disorderly house. Peers, judges, vicars, lawyers and MPs were alleged to have been among her clientele. None were charged.

Cynthia Payne was used to running brothels. She had already been fined on several occasions. She had drifted into prostitution in the 1950s. After being let down by several men, she had tried a number of low-paid unskilled jobs, been kept by a man for a time and had several lonely and ghastly illegal abortions. She had run a brothel or two to support herself and the son she decided to keep and bring up alone. Running a brothel was what she did best and she made no bones about being proud of the service she provided. Her service was unique. It catered for older men. For a fee of £25 (originally £15 but it went up with inflation) men were given luncheon vouchers and freedom to consume as much as they wanted of what was available. The women catered to the men's sometimes unusual tastes. As more information emerged about the establishment, – the sex parties, sexual displays, the bank manager who dressed up as a woman, the RAF Squadron Leader who favoured correction, 'Slave' Rodney – Mrs Payne's faithful servant, poached eggs on toast for breakfast and the house-wives who came in from the suburbs in the afternoons to help pay the bills and get home for teatime, it seemed, at the end of a decade of sexual freedom, neither immoral nor corrupt. It was more of a social service. 'Madame Cyn' thrived in the limelight, until the forces of law intervened.

Her sentence provoked an immediate response from some unex-pected quarters. An all party group of thirty MPs tabled a Com-mons motion protesting at its 'unnecessary' severity since she 'poses no threat to the community', and campaigned for her release. Tory MP, John Whale believed the sentence was 'outrage-ous' and concluded 'morality should be moved out of the criminal law'.[30] A *Spectator* leader, 'The Hypocrisy of the Law' decided: 'It is very difficult to discern any justice in this particular case . . . The hypocrisy of the law as it stands could not be better illlustra-ted. Legislators, clergy and lawyers go unnamed and free; the woman who met their demands goes to jail.' The magazine called for a change in the law 'so that what passes privately between consenting adults, corrupts no minors, creates no public nuisance, disturbs no neighbours and frightens no horses is no longer the concern of the law, is no longer a matter for the curiosity of the police and the prurience of the rest of us.'[31] Cynthia Payne emerged from her sentence, a month of which had been spent in the prison hospital, to be greeted with roses from friends and a large Rolls Royce supplied by one of her many loyal clients.

Convictions for loitering and soliciting for the purposes of pros-titution went up as police activity increased on the streets. Convic-tions, running at 3000 a year between 1975–1979 rose dramatically in 1980.[32] Nearly three times as many women were convicted at Clerkenwell Magistrates Court for soliciting in the first quarter of 1980 compared with the same period in 1979.[33] More women were turning to prostitution, their numbers swelled by women coming from the North and Midlands, often on British Rail 'Awayday' tickets. Known as 'Thatcher's Girls' they were mostly unemployed, many without State benefits, many single mothers with children to support, some supporting unemployed husbands, a substantial number of black and immigrant women doubly disadvantaged in a diminishing labour market. One London magistrate, who tried an ex-student of law and politics from Walsall and a young woman from Bristol who had failed to get a job, declared himself disturbed at the social range, at 'how many girls of good education and good character come to London to make a living this way'.[34]

But the rise also reflected a sustained increase in police activity which amounted to saturation tactics particularly in London's King's Cross area. In 1982–1983, the Metropolitan Police set up a special anti-vice squad to deal with prostitution, that is, to bring more women before the law for soliciting. In a blitz on King's Cross in 1982, 220 women were arrested in a fortnight, and fined up to £75. In its first ten weeks of operation the squad made 1000 charges, almost all against women.[35] Some were imprisoned, some bound over to keep away from King's Cross, which meant they could be arrested on sight. Prosecutions soared all over the country. In 1980, 3482 women were proceeded against, in 1981, 4324, rising to 6,062 in 1982 and 10,674 in 1983.[36]

Tensions mounted. Organized groups stepped up their campaign against unjust laws – which they felt had not deterred prostitution, had attacked the civil liberties of all women and had given police wide powers of discretion for proceeding against women. It was almost the only area of the law where a woman, accused of loitering with intent, could be, and frequently was, convicted on the uncorroborated evidence of only one police officer. Once labelled 'common prostitute', a label carried for life, the laws operated to institutionalize prostitution by making it difficult to get off the game. To pay the fines, women had to go on the game again. The laws isolated and stigmatized women. With soliciting and advertising illegal, they fell more easily into the hands of organized crime and dependence on pimps, and then, if they were exploited and beaten up they had no recourse to the protection of the law because of their illegality.[37] In 1982 the English Collective of Prostitutes and their supporters occupied a Church in King's Cross to protest against unjust laws and the treatment and illegal arrest of prostitute women under the saturation policing policies.[38]

Nor did the policing policies work. Women simply moved on to another area. Chief Superintendent Roy Swatman called it 'a Canute situation'. They had arrested 700 prostitutes in 1982: 'The best we can do is kick them from district to district. It doesn't do our professional pride any good.'[39] Residents' associations complained of public nuisance and annoyance. Various remedies were put forward. Westminster City Council proposed a council-run advertizing contact sheet. This roused protests at the misuse of public funds. Legalized brothels were rejected: 'It is unedifying that the State should be concerned with the licencing of people to make money out of sexual intercourse,' declared Lord Justice Lawton.[40] Prostitutes were not keen on the idea either. They tend to be exploitative, Helen Buckingham explained: 'Any recognition of prostitution as respectable brings people in who want to make it cost effective. "If you can screw one man an hour, you can screw two. And if you were to hurry up this and do that you could make it four and if you weren't so fussy you could make it eight. And if you don't mind rapists and murderers you could squeeze in twelve, now come along there are sixty minutes in the hour, why aren't you doing it?".' For prostitutes' women's organizations the remedy was the abolition of all the prostitution laws which criminalized women and the development of social and policing policies which gave women the opportunity to get out of prostitution, instead of institutionalizing it.

One remedy in law, the abolition of imprisonment for soliciting offences, gained support, not least because, it was argued, imprisonment did not serve as a deterrent. It often compounded the problems which had led to the conviction. For example Susan, aged twenty-four, recalled: 'After I got out (three months imprisonment for soliciting and loitering) I was two months behind with my bills. I had £80 debt to come out to. That was money owing on my furniture, TV Insurance and Clubs (hire purchase) besides the £8-£10 a week I give to my mum for my keep. In the end I had to solicit to get the money – I was doing it again within two weeks of coming home.'[41]

After campaigns and lobbying in Parliament, imprisonment for soliciting was abolished by the Criminal Justice Act 1982. It did not solve the problems. Fines went up: in Sheffield in November 1983, a woman was fined a total of £650 after admitting only four offences. Women were then imprisoned for not paying; in the first three months of 1984, more prostitutes were gaoled for defaulting on fines than were sent to prison in 1982 for soliciting.[41]

Pressure increased to adjust the inequality in treatment which criminalized the women and not their clients. The Sexual Offences Act 1985 tackled the demand side; men could be arrested for kerb crawling and fined up to £2000. But the Act was opposed by prostitutes' organizations and others as an extension of police powers which was 'dangerously ill-defined'. The evidence of one police officer was sufficient to convict; it looked like a re-instatement of the 'sus' powers abolished in 1982. 'Very few people actually believe that prostitution itself should be outlawed . . . A more honest approach to prostitution must look at ways and means of decriminalizing the encounter, rather than surrounding it with ever more police powers,' declared the *Guardian*.[43] It did not take the pressure off women. Wider police powers increased their vulnerability. In 1986, 189 men were convicted of kerb-crawling offences, including, (to the evident satisfaction of some) a judge and a senior police officer, while 9,404 women were convicted of soliciting offences. Hypocrisy continued to reign over equality. No inroads were made to adjust the criminality of the encounter or to redress women's legal disabilities. The 'problem' of prostitution was the problem of bad laws, and social policies which reduced women's economic options. Very little was done to adjust either of these.

Eleven

Restraint

By the early 1980s the moral climate was altering fast. Whereas the 1960s and 1970s had been an era of release and exploration, a new set of factors was now encouraging a return to restraint. Disease was re-imported into the sexual arena with AIDS; sex was not only a threat to health, it could mean death. And dissatisfaction with the ethos of performance sex arose as the focus turned to how people relate rather than how they perform. This coincided with an attempt by the Conservative Government to strengthen the family, to make difficult other forms of sexual identity and activity, and to reimpose the values of 'discipline and restraint'. Yet the nation remained largely impervious to a re-adoption of conservative moral values.

After a decade of exhortation, all the indices showed that the libertarian trends of the 1960s and 1970s towards privatization and choice in the formation of relationships continued uninterrupted, indeed accelerated. In fact, the traditional family, allegedly at the heart of Tory Party concerns, was a diminishing proportion of the population, and became one of its most disadvantaged groups. Cohabitation increased, fewer people got married and they married later, more children were born outside marriage, divorce continued at a higher rate, the number of one-parent families rose and their dependence on the State did not diminish. Nor was there much evidence that 'discipline and restraint' were applied to sexual behaviour. The age of first intercourse dropped steadily; sex outside marriage became the common experience of most adolescents and young adults; adultery appeared to increase.

Far from presiding over a return to the traditional family, the Government witnessed its further fragmentation. What did alter, in a climate of renewed moral authoritarianism, were the meanings people gave to sex, the terms on which relationships were conducted, and the nature of controlling influences on sexual behaviour.

Preliminary Cautions

The ethic of sexual release was already being re-assessed before AIDS altered the terms of the debate. Doubts surfaced about the new orthodoxy of 'obligatory', 'performance' sex. Critics pointed out that it had not delivered the promised increase in human happiness and that it was creating more, not less, anxiety. Writer Julian Barnes, who detected in 1982 that 'not to be interested in sex amounts to high treason against the age', suggested new coercions had simply replaced old barriers: the pressure of 'getting it regularily', the 'specific tyrannies – of performance, of orgasm – and then the master tyranny: that of not having any excuse left any more for not having a marvellous time'. Sexual decorum had been reversed – 'where once it was cheap to say Yes, now it is rude to say No'.[1]

Restraint was an option already advanced in the early 1980s. The thriving sex therapy industry was delivering a new message, that sex was no longer about Olympic qualifying standards. 'Doing sex' was not satisfying deeper needs. A more diversified approach was needed, through which sensual and erotic potential could be explored and 'whole-body sensuality' discovered. Restraint was counselled in fashionable therapies; one method banned all genital contact, but directed obligatory touching of every other part of the body to discover its sensual power for a period of weeks, graduating only slowly to genital contact and then intercourse. It was a clear echo of that repudiation of the penetrative model as the main expression of sexuality which feminists had enunciated through the 1970s. Women 'want a wholeness to intimacy that is diffused throughout our sexual lives, in which many acts and sensual expressions share an equal place with copulation,' claimed the authors of For Ourselves. (1981)[2]

Therapists reported that the price of an orthodoxy which detached sex from its anchor in love or affection was a widespread inability to experience intimacy. Failure to express affection was the biggest single obstacle to a successful sex life, according to the new-wave therapists. Where orgasm had been the barometer of success or failure, there was now a new stress on commitment. The quantity of sex was less important than its quality. 'Fewer and deeper relationships' was becoming the received wisdom of the day.

Some people were choosing restraint and caution even before they were forced upon them. Much was made of the rise in virginity among the young. 'Virgins Stage a Comeback,' reported the *Sunday Mirror*, with evidence that half American women undergraduates were now virgins compared with a quarter seven years previously,[3] while only half the female undergraduates at Oxford University had had sex compared with 60 per-cent in 1972. Young women were asserting their right to choose and rejecting the belief that permanent availability was an asset: 'There is more to sex than the good "lay". Sex only matters when partners care,' Sharon Maxwell, former editor of *Isis* reflected. 'It is recognized I have a right to a sex life – if I choose.'[4] Celibacy was advocated by a few as the antidote to the sterility of the new orthodoxy. Journalist Liz Hodgkinson proposed, in *Sex is Not Compulsory* (1986) that celibacy had no medical ill effects, allowed important creative energies to be directed elsewhere, got rid of accumulated anxieties about performance, frequency and so on, and was 'far more life-enchancing and dignified' than living from one sexual adventure to another. Although this view was fashionable among America's radical chic, it did not dent the prevailing British view that celibacy was both unnatural and unhealthy and it attracted much sneering (though not from the current pop idol, Boy George, who announced: 'I'm not interested in sex. I'd rather have a cup of tea and a good conversation.'[5])

There were more compelling reasons for caution. The pre-condition for sexual choice was freedom from the penalties of disease and pregnancy. Uncertainty about both contributed to more cautious attitudes. Liberated sex in the mid-1980s was far from the risk-free activity for women predicted in the early pill days; sex never had been a risk-free activity for women. Although the pill's reliability had symbolized a new sexual order, releasing women to participate in sex on the same terms as men, it was not long before its disadvantages were being widely advertized. Research findings in 1977[6] which revealed the risks of long-term pill-use caused an immediate flight to other less reliable contraceptive methods, particularly by older women. More than half a million women had given up the pill within a year – (a drop from 3.6 million to 3.1 million users).[7] Publicity about the adverse effects of long term chemical dependency also influenced younger women. Accumulating evidence of the association of cervical cancer with early promiscuous sex added to the uncertainty.

Disease re-entered the sexual arena with herpes. It was widely identified as marking the end of worry-free sex. 'Does this contagious, recurrent disease spell the end of the permissive society?' the *Reader's Digest* asked in 1983.[8] A sexually-transmitted virus for which no cure was available, herpes was inaccurately identified in the initial panic of 1982–1983 as a 'killer sex disease' estimated to be affecting between 5 million and 20 million Americans. It did not kill, and though it persisted and was incurable, it was in Susan Sontag's words, 'merely awful, erotically disqualifying'.[9] It brought a new awareness of the risks of sex comparable, according to one British expert, Dr Gordon Skinner, to fears about gonorrhoea and syphilis in the 1940s.

Herpes began to affect attitudes to sex. Guilt was reinstated: 'Some patients think they *should* feel guilty. Every attack is seen as a visitation – a further proof of their sin – which is absurd of course . . . this attitude is very prejudicial to the whole pattern of infection.'[10] For sufferers it encouraged a more open attitude to discussion and some appreciation of the more diffuse expressions of sexuality in non-penetrative or not exclusively penetrative sex. It led to 'a re-evaluation of what sex means to us . . . you realize the importance of warmth, love support, massage and kissing.' Tom Schroeder, an American sufferer, said that he became ' "choosier" about his sex partners, placing more value on the quality of commitment and less on the quantity of sex'. The 'silent carrier', in the panic publicity, was a new spectre haunting the sexual encounter, encouraging a move to fewer partners – 'this promiscuity thing is just too unhealthy – both physically and emotionally', *Cosmo* advised in 1982.[11] Herpes infection in Britain continued at a rate of 10,000 – 12,000 new infections a year, with the total estimate of around 150,000 at the end of the decade.[12] But its impact was soon to be dwarfed by AIDS.

Dangerous Sex

AIDS was first observed in American studies in 1981–1982 of gay
men who were suffering progressive debilitation due to damaged
immunity resulting in two previously rare medical conditions
(Karposi's sarcoma and pneumocystis carinii pneumonia). It was
identified from the start as a disease or syndrome affecting gay
men and this initial diagnosis – the 'gay plague' as it was dubbed
– set the agenda for the public response. In 1982 it was re-classified
(from the original – Gay Related Immune Deficiency (GRID) –
to Aquired Immune Deficiency Syndrome) when it was realized
it did not affect only gay men but could be transmitted through
blood transfusion. It was not until 1984 that the isolation of the
virus HTLV3, later renamed HIV, was made public. The distinction between HIV virus infection and the AIDS syndrome (the
breakdown of the immune system allowing a range of opportun-
istic infections, in themselves not contagious, to take hold) was
glossed over as reporting conflated the virus and the syndrome
into a single disease.

Confusion surrounding the syndrome and ignorance about
transmission and infectiousness contributed to the uncertainty and
distortions which fuelled the AIDS panic. The politicization of
AIDS made it all but impossible to treat it as a purely medical
issue. Because of its powerful associations it was loaded with moral
meanings, which added to popular misunderstanding, exacerbated
prejudice, and tapped intolerance and bigotry against 'deviant'
sexuality. Into the gap created by scientific uncertainty, morality
marched, with its language of fear and retribution, sin and punishment, guilt and innocence. The moral right harnessed AIDS to a
crusade against sexual deviance and 'unnatural' or licentious sexual
behaviour by representing it as a species of divine retribution for
the sins of sodomy, which marked the victims as responsible for
their illness. James Anderton, Manchester's Chief Constable and
a lay preacher, described AIDS as a 'self-inflicted scourge'; its
prime cause was 'degenerate behaviour' and 'obnoxious sexual
practices', people at risk were 'swirling around in a cess-pit of
their own making'.[13] In sections of the press panic-stricken stories
of the 'gay plague' appeared under signs of the skull and cross-
bones, while 'before and after' photos of sufferers emphasised

their guilt and punishment in much the same way as they had been used in the nineteenth century to condemn masturbators for their sins.

Contagion fears were mobilized to separate those labelled 'guilty' from the allegedly 'innocent' heterosexual population. Ghettoization, social isolation, internment, enforced HIV testing, identity cards for those tested HIV positive (branding on the arms and buttocks was suggested in one tabloid) were some of the draconian defensive measures proposed to protect the 'innocent'. In a *News of the World* poll of 12,000 people in 1986, 56 per-cent believed 'AIDS carriers should be sterilized and given treatment to curb their sexual appetite' while 70 per-cent wanted them isolated in hospital, 24.5 per-cent wanted them isolated in camps and 4.6 pr cent on islands. 'Ghettos? A Good Idea' crowed the *Daily Star*.[14] The concept of 'bridging groups' – intravenous drug users, haemophiliacs, bi-sexuals, prostitutes – was epidemiologically a categorization of people at risk of viral infection. 'At risk' soon acquired another meaning which fed growing hostility to 'carriers' especially gays'; it meant those at risk to others. These groups were the route of 'leaks' into the heterosexual population and those most likely to spread infection to the allegedly innocent.

The threat of the 'silent carriers' of a virus whose mode of attack resembled the invasion of the body-snatchers translated easily into a metaphor for attack on the body politic. It was the enemy within – miscoscopic, invisible, incurable and invasive – corroding the nation's moral and physical strength. AIDS emanated from a secretive source, from people living lives of 'lies' and 'shame'. Rock Hudson, the archetypal 1950s beefcake hero, exemplified these fears. His public admission of his illness was treated as an act of betrayal towards the public and his fans. Press reports projected shame and dishonesty onto him: 'Hollywood Made the Legend, Rock Hudson Lived the Lie'; 'He Died a Living Skeleton – and So Ashamed'; 'The Hunk Who Lived a Lie – He Loved Only Mum'[15] The invisibility of 'carriers' was emphasised, for if a legendary macho-man had led the lie, who else was carrying the secret?

But Hudson's death also had the reverse effect. It made AIDS both personal and familiar; his fall from good guy to bad guy, visibly enacted through his physical emaciation, brought the issue before the public imagination, moving it out of the twilight zone populated by the anonymous and insidious 'other' and promoting wider understanding. The Associated Press in the US saluted him as 'a white knight in shining armour' who by acknowledging that he had AIDS 'may be the catalyst that spurs worldwide efforts to find a cure'.[16]

Any rational official response to the medical epidemic was distorted by moral and ideological pressures. The British Government did not take any official action to deal with it as a public health crisis until 1986, when a Cabinet Committee was set up after pressure from medical bodies, and from the voluntary organizations who had taken on responsibility for health education, demythologizing the disease and supporting people with AIDS. Up till then, the Government was in a dilemma; as long as AIDS was marginalized as primarily a disease affecting the gay community, any official commitment to tackle the crisis ran directly counter to its ideological commitment to traditional family values.

In order to introduce any public health initiative, the Government had first to persuade its conservative flank of the need to face the 'reality' of patterns of behaviour of which they might not approve. Then they had to compose 'messages which are effective in alerting people to the risks . . . but in a fashion that does not appear to condone promiscuity or open it to a charge of doing so', and also to override sensibilities by using explicit language and taboo words in the interests of clarity and education.[17] As in the US, it was only when accumulating evidence of heterosexual transmission and the potential scale of the epidemic on the heterosexual population was made clear that the Government provided resources to fund a health education programme and facilities for treatment. In 1986, with 490 AIDS cases, 246 deaths, and estimated 10,000 to 40,000 HIV-positive people – with a projected increase to 20,000 AIDS cases, 10,000 deaths and 2 million HIV-infected by 1990, the Government set aside £2.5 million for an information campaign and a further £20 million to deal with the crisis.[18]

Public health campaigns conveyed the message of conversion, if not to a new set of values then initially to a different set of sexual practices. The pressure from the moral conservatives to coerce the population back into traditional mores with exhortations to chastity and monogamy was turned down on pragmatic grounds, judged ineffective in a population accustomed to sexual activity at a steadily earlier age. Expediency won out over traditional morality. The two-fold message was an encouragement to practise safer sex using condoms, and to cut down on partners.

The campaign ran a narrow line between persuasion, and coercing the population into fidelity through fear. The question of how legitimate it was to invoke fear to persuade, and in the end control, was overridden by the public health imperative to contain the epidemic. At the same time, AIDS provided a pretext to outlaw promiscuity in the name of public safety. Medical campaigners pulled no punches: 'The way not to get AIDS is to restrain your sexual activities,' Dr John Dawson of the BMA warned. 'The promiscuous young are going to be more of a danger than homosexuals, prostitutes and drug addicts all put together,' pronounced West German AIDS expert Hans Dieter Pohle. Health Minister Barney Hayhoe made the message plain – 'the more they can confine their sexual relationships to monogamous or a very stable relationship the better . . . random, casual contacts are to be profoundly discouraged'.[19] The Gothic imagery of the first television campaign conveyed a message of fear and unmentionable threat; icebergs loomed and lowered, tombstones sank dustily into place; drills chiselled into marble inscribing the slogan, 'AIDS – Don't Die of Ignorance'. The concealed part of the iceberg simultaneously hinted at the unknown number of infections and the impossibility of knowing from the surface the risk others might present, while tombstones endorsed potent AIDS fears by the automatic association of infection, but also unwise sex, with death.

The safe-sex message acknowledged casual sexual practices and high rates of partner exchange when it warned of the dangers of unprotected sex. But the Government message of 'if you must do it, use a condom' (and the Health Education Authority came under fire for not being sufficiently moral even on this) contrasted with the attitude of voluntary bodies who were more inclined to portray safer sex as a positive encouragement to sexual variety and imaginative diversity, and to point out that safer sex was not anti-erotic – condoms could be fun. Several independent entrepreneurs moved into a proliferating market with this appeal. 'Jiffi' was marketed through T-shirts with the slogan 'Got a Stiffie? Wear a Jiffie'.

Richard Branson, the Virgin king, with a characteristic blend of flamboyance and benevolence ordered 700 million condoms (more than five times the annual British market of 120 million) to distribute and sell at half price in record shops and cafes rather than toilets (barbers had long since lost their market); profits were to be diverted to AIDS research. His advertising and marketing emphasised eroticism, sexual playfulness and cheerfulness ('Women are only interested in men who are well-equipped'). 'Mates' were successfully aimed at a younger market whose behaviour and attitudes, according to his research, the Government had failed to affect, leaving them 'frightened of the disease and not knowing what to do about it'.[20] The Terence Higgins Trust launched a safer-sex campaign aimed at gays through advertisements which celebrated the erotic possibilities of safe sex, imaginative and diverse sensual play to a constituency which had been practising safe sex for considerably longer than the rest of the population. *Cosmopolitan* recruited women to the cause with a Safe Girls Carry Condoms campaign; designed boxer shorts and filofaxes were equipped with condom pockets. By 1990, according to a report published by Durex, the young preferred sheaths (20 per-cent) to the pill (19 per-cent). Women were buying condoms at twice the rate of five years previously – just under half claimed to have bought condoms at some time.[21]

Public education campaigns were successful in spreading more accurate information about infection, means of transmission and techniques of prevention. Their effect on sexual behaviour remains uncertain. In the gay community significant changes are recorded in the increased use of safe sex techniques (already elaborated in 1983 in a US publication *How to Have Sex in an Epidemic*) and a decline in the rate of partner exchange. These mostly occurred before the Government campaign began. In this group the number of reported new infections began to decline by 1989.[22]

Infections among intravenous drug misusers went up (it was the fastest growing group by 1989) as did heterosexually transmitted infection. However, the numbers in the latter group were so small in Britain by 1989 as to prompt public speculation that the risk of heterosexual transmission in the West for those not also in other high-risk groups (namely intravenous drug users, partners of bisexuals) was minimal. There were clear political implications in publicizing this view. It suggested that the undifferentiated threat in the initial health campaigns may have overstated the case and damaged public credibility. The Government and health groups issued immediate warning of the continuing dangers; any relaxation in vigilance might seriously impair the efforts to control the disease.

Official estimates in Britain showed 5 per-cent of AIDS cases occurred through heterosexual contact. Of the 123 cases of AIDS attributed to heterosexual transmission in the UK up to September 1989, 18 had partners with a known risk factor, such as injecting drug misuse, bisexuality, or infection through blood products. 93 had heterosexual partners from abroad, the majority from countries where heterosexual transmission is the major means of spread, and the remaining 12 reported multiple sexual partners or contact with prostitutes. In the US, which was taken as the model for patterns in the UK, heterosexually acquired cases of AIDS had increased from 1 per-cent in 1983 to over 4 per-cent in 1989. Projections in the UK were unreliable because of the small numbers but it was expected the second wave of the epidemic in intravenous drug abusers would be followed by a third phase of increased heterosexual infection. Sir Donald Acheson, the Government's Chief Medical Officer in 1989 estimated between 3,000–4,000 people either infected by heterosexual intercourse or other means but known to be of a heterosexual habit, and the proportion was increasing.[23]

The unequivocal health message at the end of the decade was that there was no room for complacency about heterosexual infection. At the same time, early projections of the overall spread of the disease were being revised downwards as the rate of HIV infection slowed by the end of 1988 [24] With improvements in management of HIV-infected people and people with AIDS and the use of drugs and antibiotics at different stages, by 1990 the gap between infection and the onset of disease lengthened from an average 8 to an average 10 years and rising, and improvements showed in the life expectancy of people with AIDS.

There was little doubt, however, that the management of the epidemic was affecting attitudes to homosexuality. The AIDS panic was harnessed to a wave of renewed intolerance of gays, targeting them as the carriers of contagion, fanning a climate of opinion favourable to discrimination which reversed the trend to more liberal attitudes of the previous two decades. Almost half (48 per-cent of respondents to a BBC/Gallup survey) thought people with AIDS had only themselves to blame (41 per-cent sometimes thought it was a punishment for a decline in moral standards); 24 per-cent of 'young readers' of the *Sunday Mirror* agreed 'gays deserve AIDS' in January 1986. 62 per-cent of respondents to a *Sunday Telegraph*/Gallup poll thought homosexual acts were 'wrong'; and more than half in a British Social Attitudes Survey believed it was unacceptable for homosexuals to be employed as teachers in any circumstances.[25] Support for stronger social sanctions against gays matched a rise in support for legal controls. Only 48 per-cent questioned in a London Weekend Television poll in 1988 thought consensual acts between homosexuals should be legal, compared with 61 per-cent on March 1985; 43 per-cent thought they should be illegal compared with 27 per-cent in 1985.[26]

The backlash prepared the way for new government initiatives to police gays and confirmed that there was political mileage in being anti-gay. Clause 28 of the Local Government Act by which local authorities could not 'intentionally promote homosexuality' or the teaching of the 'acceptability of homosexuality as a pretended family relationship' was introduced by Lord Halsbury, President of the National Council for Christian Standards in Society. It was a direct attack on the local authority provisions for support of minority rights groups which had expanded during the 1980s. With AIDS in the background 'like Banquo's ghost', anti-gay fears of the corruption of youth were mobilized through a rhetoric which claimed to defend traditional family values against the threat allegedly posed by the positive portrayal of the 'gay lifestyle'.

The provisions of the Clause were dangerously vague and were opposed as an infringement of the rights of minorities likely to lead to increased intolerance and discrimination (already being operated through restrictions in life insurance and mortgage policies). It was argued that they would extend censorship, infringe civil liberties, hinder education in an important area of human life – sexuality, and would have the effect of officially stigmatizing a group by their sexual orientation. 'The country would be in a perilous strait of circumstance if it isolated problems like homosexuality as if they belonged to a category of evil,' Lord Soper warned.[27] But those who feared the positive images of homosexuality were 'insidious and dangerous propaganda', and 'a direct attack on heterosexual family life', triumphed as the Clause passed into law in May 1988.

A spate of violent attacks on gays followed in the wake of the public debate. Gay helplines reported a 30 per-cent increase in gay-bashing, *Capital Gay* offices were burned down in an arson attack in December 1987. A poisonous gas canister thrown into a gay bar in Chatham, resulting in the hospitalization of forty people, was the only one of a number of incidents. Several local authorities threatened to cut off grants to gay counselling organizations. Strathclyde Regional Council warned that student grants would be cut if students refused to disband gay and lesbian societies and stop 'promoting' homosexual equality. The Tory group on Haringy Council passed resolutions to cut off all funds to lesbian and gay groups and 'abolish all references to homosexuality', presumably hoping that by not mentioning it, this dreadful thing would disappear.[28] In this atmosphere the tabloid press launched into some of its worse exposés of gays, usually by paying large sums of money to rent boys, and then hounding the subjects, camouflaging prurience by claiming public interest. When broadcaster Russell Harty, the victim of a previous 'exposure', was dying – not of AIDS – the press invaded the hospital he was in, abandoning any thought for dignity or respect for privacy in pursuit of sensation.

Safer Sex

The explicit aim of health education programmes was to modify behaviour. So far, although there has been a dramatic change in homosexual behaviour, there is insufficient evidence to show any widespread change in heterosexual behaviour, especially amongst 'high-risk' single young people. There are some indications that the association of sex with disease has altered the way people perceive sex. Among gays, there is clear evidence of behavioural changes: a reduction in partner exchange rate (halved from 10.5 to 4.8 per year between February 1986 and February 1987), increase in condom use, and a fall in the proportion reporting casual relationships and high-risk activities such as anal sex, with a fall in the incidence of rectal gonorrhoea to 15–20 per-cent of the levels reported in the early 1980s[29].

The behaviour of young heterosexuals (on which research has concentrated) shows no such dramatic change and continues to reflect the prevalence of intercourse at earlier ages and a high rate of partner exchange. The age of first intercourse continued to fall during the 1980s. Nearly half (47 per-cent) of 16-year-olds in a Somerset survey (1989) had engaged in sexual intercourse, rising to 89 per-cent by age 21. The median age for first female intercourse has fallen from 20 to 16 in two decades, according to the Wellcome Trust pilot study;[30] research in Bristol showed nearly half males and females had intercourse by 16; a fifth of both boys and girls had first experience at 15, rising to 90 per-cent of respondents aged 21-years-old. One survey found more girls (one in two) than boys (one in three) had sex by the age of 16.[31]

The rates of partner exchange were also high. A quarter of 18–24 year-olds had two or more partners in the previous year on one survey, a quarter of 16–21-year-olds in the Bristol survey had had more than four partners in their sexual lifetime (almost a fifth of 16–18-year-olds, 37 per cent of 19–21-year-olds), while a survey carried out for Durex backed by an independent monitor of 5000 adults found 40 per-cent of sexually active young men aged 16–20 had between two and six partners in the past year.[32]

A generally high level of knowledge about methods of transmission which dispelled many early AIDS myths was reported in all research, but nearly half of a BBC/Gallup (1987) survey thought AIDS had nothing to do with them, and only 4 per-cent had changed their behaviour. Although 60 per-cent of young people in the British Market Research Bureau (1986–1987) survey claimed to have changed their behaviour, only a quarter had cut down on partners, cut down casual sex or used condoms more often. Despite massive publicity and increased awareness, only around a third of sexually active young people used condoms on a regular basis. BMRB found that almost half 16–17-year-olds used condoms compared with a quarter of 18–24-year-olds in 1986–1987. In the Wellcome pilot survey published in 1989 nearly a quarter of 16–24-year-olds were ignorant about contraception, but condoms were used in more than half first experiences of sex.

Durex found that more 16–17-year-olds used condoms than the pill as their main method of contraception (31 per-cent compared with 15 per cent pill users, though among 18–24-year-olds, almost a third used condoms, a third the pill), and in the Bristol survey, only 30 per-cent of non-virgins had used a condom during their last sexual encounter.[33]

As the sexual encounter becomes associated with danger and fear, what may be altering more than actual practices are attitudes to sex. 'I grew up with the conviction that there was nothing in the world wrong with sex,' one 23-year-old woman reported. 'But the healthy appetite for, and healthy attitudes towards sex that we inherited from the 1960s now turn out to be unhealthy.' Another woman in her twenties found caution altered the sexual encounter completely: 'If your way of starting a relationship has always been to go to bed with the person on the first or second night and then take it from there, it's very difficult to go back to what amounts to courtship.'[34] The return of 'Romance' had already been proposed in the early 1980s as part of a different set of choices in several articles (mostly by men) which extolled the virtues of anticipation instead of instant gratification, withholding affection, getting to know partners, of wooing and games playing; it now seemed more a necessity than a choice.

The 'safer sex' message may have encouraged variety and imagination in the expression of sexual desire. In 1987, author Rosalind Coward distinguished between the 'anti-sex prohibition' effect of safe sex, and the possibilities it offered for 'radical sexual changes without returning to a conservative morality'. The latter 'challenges the belief that people, especially men, have little voluntary control over their sexual desires' (for instance in attitudes to rape, pornography and prostitution) and 'encourages new meanings for sex which are not focused on intercourse or on necessarily "having an orgasm".'[35] According to new-wave sex therapists, the stress on fewer and deeper relationships highlighted by AIDS was welcomed among individuals reporting isolation and emotional undernourishment and the feeling they had lost the ability to make intimate emotional contact as the consequence of the performance sex ethic. 'Somewhere along the way *sex* and *love* have broken apart . . . We may end up more sexually adept, but we remain emotionally hungry,' American therapist Dagmar O'Connor diagnosed in her best-selling *How to Put the **Love** Back into Making Love*. She argued for a new ethos which would encourage ways to explore sensuality, acknowledge sexual intimacy and experience closeness without fear.[36] It was a theme capitalized on in the successful 1989 movie *When Harry Met Sally* – the theme of people whose sexual relationships had let them down and left them crippled, who sought deeper knowledge of each other in order to discover a range of intimacies, rather than sex, as the basis for love.

Sexual inventiveness was acquiring a longer term perspective. Articles on 'spicing up your marriage' and keeping love alive 'after twenty years' proliferated. After the high adultery figures of the early 1980s, Relate (the former Marriage Guidance Council) reported a dramatic increase in the number of men seeking marriage guidance, particularly the 'unfamiliar figure' of the businessman. Where previously he might have by-passed his marital problems with casual affairs, 'now he feels the risk is too high and has decided against this sort of thing', and is putting more time into relationships at home. One wonders why he did not think of this before, but now therapists were on hand to encourage couples to 'stimulate each other's libido'.[37] Fear could be debilitating; one of O'Connor's clients complained that marriage had become 'a pretty desperate business ... Even fidelity isn't a symbol of love and loyalty anymore, it's just an act of self-preservation.' Another woman found infection fears were invasive: 'I have no trouble being a contented, faithful wife when the fantasy of making it with a tall, dark stranger was still alive, but these days I can't even have a decent extramarital *daydream* without alarms going off in my head ... I can't get off on a fantasy about Russian roulette. So somehow I end up resenting the idea that my husband is the only game in town. "Safe" just feels boring.'[38]

In an ethos of restraint the signals associated with female sexual display changed. Fashion entrepreneurs suggested this marked a different stage in women's sense of their sexual options. 'Look, don't touch, is today's fashion message. Corsets are back, dresses are tight, relationships are monogamous and suddenly it's safe to dress provocatively,' declared a *Sunday Times* Colour Magazine item, 'The Thrill of the Chaste'. The androgynous days of dungarees as a statement of equality were over. Where women turned to the mini-skirt in the 1960s as a statement of confidence in release, they were now adopting it as a statement of power in restraint. Social anthropologist Ted Polhemus saw it as a sign of a new mores: 'What makes provocative dressing in public today different is that it's a safe game. It's understood by all and sundry that it doesn't mean you are looking for a pick-up. We are in the era of safe sex.' Designer Anthony Price agreed: 'The message post-AIDS, is look erotic – but don't deliver.'[39] For women in a decade dominated by style rather than substance, it was almost liberating to be able to don not only power suits but classy little black numbers as well as lipstick and red nail varnish without feeling it made them into objects – even more accessible. It was a transformation accepted, even welcomed, by women. Erotic and sensual dressing in the 1980s signalled that they could be in charge (the current pop icon Madonna showed how it was done) and free to play with sexual messages on their own terms.

Privatized Practice

Although the conservative message of caution, safe sex and fidelity was well entrenched by the end of the 1980s, there was little sign of a return to monogamous marriage patterns and very little evidence that a decade of 'family values' rhetoric had made much impact on the way people conducted emotional and sexual arrangements. Patterns of diversity accelerated as the privatization of personal relationships was consolidated. For many the 'traditional family' was a myth as the focus of social policies. Families with dependent children represented just over a quarter (28 per-cent) of households in 1987 compared to 38 per cent in 1961,[40] and the traditional model of breadwinner and housewife in a first marriage amounted to even less (estimated at around 11–15 per-cent). With one third of marriages ending in divorce by the early 1980s the proportion of families involving an extended network of step-children and parents increased; just over two thirds (70 per-cent) of children were born to women in their first marriage in 1989 compared to 89 per-cent in 1970. The number of lone parent families continued to increase: in 1987 14 per-cent of all families with dependent children were lone parent families compared with 8 per-cent in 1971.[41]

Marriage patterns were also changing rapidly. Though marriage continued to be fixed part of most people's ambitions – 85 per cent of young people still expected to get married (compared to 95 per cent in the 1970s) – the numbers of young people marrying went down (from 56 to 46 per thousand men and from 45 to 39 per thousand women) and the age at marriage went up during the 1980s – from 21.8 to 25.2 among women.[42] One in three women in the age group 25–29 were single in 1987 compared to a fifth in 1980. (At that rate, by aged 50, only 83 per-cent of women would have married compared with 92 per-cent in 1980). Part of this is attributed to the rapid increase in the numbers of cohabiting couples: almost half of women first married in 1987 had cohabited compared with a fifth of women married in the late 1970s (and 7 per-cent at the beginning of the 1970s)[42] By the late 1980s cohabiting before marriage was virtually the norm.

The numbers having children outside marriage also increased with the drift away from marriage. One in four children were born outside wedlock in 1988 compared with 12 per-cent as recently as 1980. Many of their parents were cohabiting – the proportion of births jointly registered rose from 38 per cent in 1961 to half (49 per-cent) in 1975 to over two thirds (68 per-cent) in 1987, and of these, 70 per-cent were by parents living at the same address. But more lone mothers – around a quarter (23 per-cent) – are women who have never married[43], which includes women opting to have children without a steady relationship. Given these demographic patterns of family diversity, the idea of corralling the population into a single concept of the 'traditional family' for political purposes was at variance with the actual experience of most families.

It also ignored the different expectations brought to personal relationships, especially by women. It was no longer accepted that the home was women's sphere, and widely accepted that woman should be free to choose to combine family with outside employment. 41 per-cent of women respondents to a 1983 survey disagreed marriage and family were the only ambition a woman can have, the great majority (86 per-cent) believed women should be able to work if they wished, and 54 per-cent believed women could successfully combine a full time job with running a family (though a third disagreed).[44]

There were deeper changes, some resulting from the long-term effects of feminism. Women were less prepared to accept inequality in relationships. As well as showing less enthusiasm for getting into marriage (by marrying later and some having children outside marriage), they were less prepared to stay in relationships which were unsatisfactory or not fulfilling their needs. By 1975, over two thirds of divorces (72 per-cent) were filed by women – an increase from 67,000 in 1971 to 163,000 in 1985 compared with an increase of husbands filing petitions from 44,000 to 52,000.[45] Women were leaving marriages, according to Christopher Clulow of the Tavistock Institute of Marital Relations, not only for someone else, or because their husbands had left them: 'Something in them snaps. Often the husband has done well at work, leapt ahead and left them behind, taking his wife for granted. Wives feel unnoticed, ignored, the junior partner, providing a service at home. Something trivial triggers them off and they simply walk out, leaving their husbands astounded.' Women, Polly Toynbee observed, were less prepared to accept being treated as inferiors, or to 'tolerate men who expect to dominate, lead, drive, order them about and contribute nothing more than variable sums from salaries'.[46]

Nor were women so ready to accept monogamy and fidelity as necessary terms of the relationship. The gap between the proportions of men and women committing adultery narrowed; around a third of wives admitted to adultery and more women than men were unfaithful in the first four years of marriage. Work, which enhanced women's self worth was the single most important factor conducive to their adultery. A third of Annette Lawsons' mid-1980s sample stressed the sense of independence they found in the liaison; where marriage could make women vulnerable, an affair could restore a sense of power. One, Fanny, recalled: 'I remember consciously thinking, "I am thirty-five – that's half way to threescore years and ten. What have you done with your life?" . . . I was very much aware of being my parent's daughter; my husband's wife; my children's mother – but who was I? There must be more in it, I felt, but for *me*.'[47] Most of her sample felt that regardless of the outcome they had benefited from their liaisons.

Women, particularly younger women, were taking their right to freedom of choice in personal relationships and to some extent equality of opportunity for granted. Freedom of choice was endorsed within a market ethos. Equality of opportunity was selective. In the decade since equal opportunities had been enshrined in law, women's economic position had not improved and for most women it had deteriorated. Women's average earnings still trailed at three quarters of the men's average rate; during the recession their real wages fell. They were still ghettoised in mainly low paid areas, while the proportion of working women had declined, and the proportion of part time jobs had gone up from a third in 1968 to 44 per-cent by 1981. Young women under twenty-five and married women with dependent children were the hardest hit by the recession; almost the only improvement had been for professional women.[48]

The pressures towards equal opportunity had made some inroads into formerly male professions and areas of better paid jobs and adjusted women's aspirations. Women were marginally more visible in public positions – there were more women newsreaders on television (though almost no women in upper management) and more women journalists outside the former ghettoes of the women's pages. In 1986 half of medical school graduates were women, there were more female solicitors (an increase from 1,297 in 1975 to 5,235 in 1985), while 17 per-cent of middle management were women as were a quarter of the self employed.[49] More women were putting off marriage to consolidate jobs or careers. They formed a significant group of independent women (a third of 25–29-year-olds) in charge of their own finances (rather than the household budget) which attracted the attention of the market and the media. In 1983 the financial services started targeting advertizing at women, by then almost equal with men as users of their services. Half of women aged 15–34 had bought or were buying their own homes, while the proportion of women holding building society accounts had gone up from a fifth (21.8 per-cent) in 1974 to nearly half (48.7 per-cent) in eight years, and those holding bank accounts from a third (34.3 per-cent) to two thirds (62.4 per-cent).[50]

The media, ever eager to label and package new phenomena (in this case often itself, since women were now in a better position to speak for themselves) trailed the New Woman, seeking her habitat and habits. She was, in image, an outgrowth of the 1970s

Cosmo woman – independent, single, ambitious with money to spend, sexually predatory and self-oriented: 'we were the first (magazine) to give women permission to be selfish,' claimed *Cosmo* editor Linday Kelsey.[51] She was 'post-feminist' woman, carrying the mark of 'yuppie' culture with its emphasis on power, greed and ambition. She was successful ('burning up the inside track'), high earning, resembling men in most respects including the ability to choose and refuse partners with the power of an income to back it up. 'Superwoman' and her attendant conflicts were dead: 'The whole concept of the Liberated woman is a thing of the past,' one high-flyer claimed, 'women should just get on with their lives and make as much as of a success of them as they can.'[52]

Taking equality for granted, they were putting the old feminist dilemmas behind them, only to encounter new ones. New questions arose about what choices they really had. Evading the guilt of being pulled in all directions, trying to reconcile personal fulfilment with work responsibilities, pushing forward in careers and competing equally with men, some felt they were being 'crucified by the competing demands of intellect and economics, and those of instinct and emotion', as writer Amanda Craig opined. Marriage and motherhood had become 'the great unmentionables in my generation of women'. Unable to reconcile the two, many felt they were again being faced with a stark choice between career and motherhood, even though polls showed most high-earners were in fact managing to divide their priorities equally between careers and personal relationships.[53]

But they did reflect the continuing problem that for women to use their freedom required an alteration in the structure of domestic and work patterns. No government support was forthcoming for such objectives which had been central to the feminist perspective for over a decade. The New Man was one missing link, for a change in women's expectations required a transformation of men's roles. Evidence of his existence continued to be patchy, despite an increased awareness of sexism, attempts to outlaw 'macho man' as socially undesirable, a proliferation of men's consciousness-raising groups during the 1980s and a more general awareness of the feminist case among younger men. Women still overwhelmingly took responsibility for household tasks and parenting.[54] Men's presence at childbirth increased (over 90 per-cent of fathers attended their children's birth by the mid-1980s). But their involvement lessened after that, sabotaged even for the willing by the restrictions of work patterns and the lack of outside support for any changes which would enable and encourage work and family to be seen not as separate spheres but inevitably interdependent.

The drift away from traditional marriage among the young was in part an exercise of freedom of choice based on sound principles (in business enterprise terms) of weighing up its merits. Marriage was one of a range of choices when the values bred by market principles – competition, acquisitiveness, and the right to choice and instant gratification – were applied to it. It had become, one commentator observed in the *Sunday Telegraph*, 'the ultimate lifestyle in consumer terms, with the promise of peak sex lasting the course and of emotional togetherness as every couple's right'.[55] The question, 'is it user-friendly?' seemed just as valid for marriage as for any product in the new ethos.

Family Values

The Conservative Government's emphasis on the 'traditional family' camouflaged a series of contradictions in their policies during the 1980s. Their model bore a decreasing resemblance to the actual diversity of family formation. But a return to traditional values appealed explicitly to the constituency who used the condemnation of 'permissive values' as a rallying point to attack the follies of past governments. It provided justifiction for an authoritarian appeal to restore 'law and order' in the interests of social stability. It also gave moral puritans a new political weight in the national debate.

However, the market principles of the New Right philosophy could apply as well to morals as to economics. Economic policies which promoted self-sufficiency and choice, rejecting state interference and repudiating dependency were more in tune with the steady privatization of personal decisions and the rejection of moral coercion by the State (the direction of change since the 1960s), than with traditional values. In the booming 1960s market forces had opened up new areas of enterprise, dependent for their success on repudiation of old constraints and outworn boundaries, and these had been applied to personal as well as commercial options. It was possible to see the permissive entrepreneurs of the 1960s who had rebelled against constraints on individual freedom, Mick Jagger for instance, as early prototypes of 'Thatcher man'.

The major difference between the moral libertarians of the Left and the New Right libertarianism was their concept of the rôle of the State. The humanist and socialist impetus behind the reshaping of morality on principles of justice, equality and personal freedom demanded state resources to bring about change. The New Right repudiated state intervention in favour of the market. But freedom, like morality, tends to depend on whether it can be afforded.

By the end of a decade of public expenditure cuts, high unemployment and taxation policies which benefited the richer rather than the poorer section of the community, the family unit with dependent children was not only a diminishing proportion of households, but was one of society's disadvantaged groups. The net result of government policies was to increase pressures on the family, to diminish rather than promote its chances of survival. Nor was this helped by the contradictory messages about whether the proper place for women – the pivot of the family – was at home, presiding over the 'nursery of civic virtues', or out at work, helping to sustain the family's self-sufficiency. In the event women were both penalized for staying at home and inadequately supported when they went out to work.

The persistent rhetoric that wealth creation would assist families, free them to make economic choices, enlarge parental responsibility and encourage self-reliance obscured the fact that families with dependent children had benefited less from their policies than other sections of the population. Their living standards as a group declined over 15 years to the point where their income was three quarters of the national average. The combination of public expenditure cuts and taxation policies had worked to discriminate against, rather than for, families with dependent children. 'To act as responsible parents is increasingly difficult and increasingly penalized,' Lord Joseph concluded in a high critical 1990 document, 'Rewards of Parenthood'.[56]

Over twenty years, he pointed out, families had suffered a threefold increase in taxation compared with childless couples, and a fivefold increase compared with single people. The average real income of a childless couple had risen more than twice as fast as for those with dependent children between 1979 and 1985.[57] Discrimination against families increased as child tax allowances were withdrawn, tax thresholds fell and child benefit was frozen. Nor had government policies decreased state dependency. Among lower-income groups which formed the majority of families with dependent children, it increased. For the rising number of lone parent families, little incentive was offered to move out of dependency; the social security system continued to function as a poverty trap.

The proportion of lone parents claiming supplementary benefits had risen steadily from one in six in 1961 to over two thirds in 1987.[58] Even as government spokesmen blamed the increase on the influence of permissive values, the numbers continued to rise inexorably. Nor did the overall direction of government policies help promote family stability for the majority. Though the better off benefited, high unemployment, cuts in public expenditure, and a deterioration of the standard of living amongst the poorest – a 6 per-cent decline compared with a 6 per-cent increase among the richest – compounded strains on family life. Divorce figures remained high during the decade, and three quarters were in the population worst affected by declining living standards.

The position of women, on which family welfare frequently hinged, did not improve, and for the majority deteriorated. The early signals from the Conservatives were that any claims women might make for equality and improvement in their position could be abandoned: 'If the Good Lord had intended us all having equal rights to go out to work and to behave equally, you know he really wouldn't have created man and woman,' Patrick Jenkin, spokesman on Social Services had proclaimed in 1979, and this had been followed by a series of speeches extolling women's place in the home and mothers' crucial nurturing rôle building future generations. Policies which put care back into the community meant women usually took on the increased care responsibilities, while cuts in services also increased pressure on women to stay in the home.

But encouraging women to stay at home was a questionable policy from a government promoting self-sufficiency and attempt-

ing to reduce dependence on the State, since it ignored the importance of women's wages. In up to a fifth of households, women
are the sole breadwinners; without women's wages, the number
of families below the poverty line would increase by half again.[59]

Simultaneously, other policies were stimulating women to go
out to work. Tax allowances favoured working mothers rather
than mothers at home, and families with two earners paid less tax
than those with one earner. Benefit cuts – freezing child benefits,
cuts in maternity allowances, in unemployment benefit, in benefits
to older children dependent on parents all made women and families poorer and increased women's incentive to work. The 'clean
break' provisions of the 1984 Divorce Act forced ex-wives out to
work or to rely on social security.

By 1990, Norman Fowler had changed his approach, perhaps
with an eye on women voters, when he announced the 1990s was
to be the decade of working women – eight out of ten jobs would
go to women because of labour shortages. But even so, little
support was forthcoming for child care. By the late 1980s Britain
had the worst record for child care provision in Europe. Fewer
than 1 per-cent of children had the benefits of state nursery provision.[60] The Government proposed only to encourage voluntary
and employer effort, with no guarantee of take up or uniformity
across the country, rather than offer state commitment.[61]

High divorce rates were cited as yet another product of the
corrosive influence of 'permissive values'. In 1981, the cost of
marriage breakdown was calculated at £1000m by the Society of
Conservative Lawyers in support of their argument the State
should resume responsibility for preserving marriages by making
divorce more difficult. By 1990, the price was estimated to be £1.4
billion (including legal, social security and NHS costs)[62]

Moral conservatives claimed permissive values had removed the
fault from divorce and diminished responsibility in marriage –
though the blame had not in practice been removed from divorce
proceedings; 70 per-cent of divorce petitions cited adultery or
unreasonable behaviour by the other partner as their grounds.[63]
For others the 'unreasonably' high expectations put on marriage
were contributing to high casualty rates. 'Couples look to each
other for a key to the meaning in life in a way that, in previous
centuries, they looked to God,' Maureen Green, author of *Mar-*

riage, surmised in 1984. When marriage had become a means for self realization with high expectations of happiness and closeness, Jack Dominian, Director of the Marriage Research Centre asserted, the gap between expectation and reality was a contributory factor in its breakdown. 'The development of more realistic expectations,' Professor Anthony Clare agreed, was the 'key factor in determining whether marriage survives.'[64]

A shift away from support for the positive aspects of divorce was perceptible. The view that it was not breakdown but breakthrough and that it increased rather than decreased opportunities for human happiness gave way to a stress on its damage and costs, to partners, to children, and to the State. Whereas it had been conventional wisdom since the 1971 Divorce Act that children benefited more from living in a separated than in a warring family, now the damage of divorce to children was being assessed; some surveys showed they fared worse (measured by achievement and delinquency patterns), though the results were inconclusive. Moreover, half of divorced men and 41 per-cent of divorced women in one survey regretted having got divorced, and 37 per-cent of men and a fifth of women wished they were still with their former partner. Nor were second marriages a guarantee of happiness; two thirds of *them* ended in divorce.[65]

Although the social penalties for divorce had been all but eliminated, the financial penalties on men had not. These were eased, however, when the Government, in a contradictory move, passed the 'clean break' Divorce Act (The Matrimonial and Family Proceedings Act, 1984) which required divorced men to support the children of the marriage up to 18 but cut off support for the wife when, in the judge's opinion, she could find the means to support herself. The Act was the product of intensive lobbying by groups of mainly professional middle-class men concerned at the injustice of being obliged to support the divorced first wife while setting up a second household.

It was a curiously anomalous piece of legislation for a government simultaneously exhorting women to stay at home since it encouraged women to go out to work: 'Hang onto your job in case you can't hang onto your man' was the message. It made marriage and motherhood a very precarious occupation, and particularly disregarded the interests of older women who had followed the injunction that a woman's place was in the home, since it flung them onto a market in which women could still command on average only three-quarters of male wages.[66] While it assumed women's ability to become financially independent, no corresponding measures were made to improve women's economic opportunities; re-training opportunities were being cut back with education cuts. The net result, from a government committed to cut public expenditure and reduce state dependency, was to increase both. Although the Act sought to right an injustice on divorced men, it was achieved at the expense of rough justice for their ex-wives.

The spectre of the 'alimony drone' used to justify the changes was a myth, for only a very small proportion of women relied entirely on maintenance – 12 per cent of newly divorced mothers in 1984, and 6 per cent after ten years. Only half maintenance orders were honoured, 90 per cent were under £20 a week and 50 per cent under £5 a week. Most lone parents landed up on social security for lack of maintenance or inability to command a decent wage. (Where 15 per cent of mothers were on supplementary benefit at the time of break up, after six months, 50 per cent were; a total of 70 per cent of lone mothers end up living on social security).[67]

Government proposals in 1989 to enforce the collection of maintenance from negligent fathers were intended to inculcate a sense of responsibility by stressing that 'Fatherhood is for life'. They also had the advantage of cutting the social security bill. Maintenance was to be collected through attachment of earnings with steeper penalties for non-payment. This might benefit some better-off lone mothers, but the complications of the social security system meant that it might not benefit those two-thirds of women on social security. Maintenance was deducted from their social security payments, which threw women back to dependence on men whose unreliability had already been proved, while payments which went through the State, not direct to mothers, did little to encourage a sense of paternal responsibility. Such slight adjustments seemed unlikely to bring about a large scale change in attitudes to family responsibility.

Government proposals for changes in the divorce law resisted pressure from the moral right to tighten up the grounds for divorce by bringing back guilt and innocence into divorce proceedings. They focused on the need to establish more effective conciliation services, giving priority to the interests of children over those of the partners, and delaying the time during which arrangements could be effected. By 1991, however, high interest rates were becoming a more effective brake on divorce than government coercion. With a static house market, couples unable to sell their main asset simply could not afford to get divorced.[68]

Further ambiguities in the Tory attachment to family values were illuminated by the Cecil Parkinson affair. When Mrs Thatcher's Secretary for Trade and Industry confessed in the middle of the Conservative Party's Annual Conference in 1983 that his affair with Sara Keays, who was about to bear his child and whom he had at some time wished to marry, was now terminated and he was returning to his wife, Mrs Thatcher did not condone the usual course of instant resignation. Instead she made clear she considered it was a 'private matter' which in no way affected his ability to do his job. 'The question of resignation does not and will not arise,' she announced. It was an interesting response from the leader of the party promoting the values of discipline and restraint, and one which revealed an attachment to libertarian principles even while exhorting the rest of the population to forego them.

To some it indicated her belief she could get away with anything. Certainly she signalled she had no wish to lose her favoured minister, who, as the former Party Chairman, was credited as the image-maker to the party of 'Victorian values'. This suggested the political calculation (or miscalculation) was that his remaining in office would be less politically damaging than his immediate resignation. He had, after all, taken a course of action appropriate to the party of the family and favoured by Mrs Thatcher and agreed to stay with his wife Ann; and he had already been moved from the chairmanship to the less prominent position in Trade and Industry after news of the impending scandal reached Mrs Thatcher.

The Conservative Conference, following Thatcher's lead, rallied to Parkinson's support. Any criticism of his decision not to resign, on political or moral grounds, was muted until Sara Keays, who had instigated the initial confession in an attempt to head off press exposure, decided to put the record straight. Convinced that support for Parkinson was being mobilized at the expense of blackening her reputation, she published her own account in *The Times*, stressing that the child had been conceived within a long-term loving relationship in which she had been led to believe his promises to marry her.[69] When it was plain she was not willing to be treated like a submissive Victorian mistress, Parkinson's resignation was inevitable.

The Prime Minister had demonstrated a clear preference for separating the private lives of public men from their public position – a wise course in view of the record of other members of her Cabinet. With an almost complete absence of public comment in a less conservative climate of the mid-1970s, her Chancellor of the Exchequer, Nigel Lawson had lived with and made pregnant his mistress before leaving his wife to marry her, and her Home Secretary, Douglas Hurd, had divorced his wife in order to marry his secretary.

But the Prime Minister's position was not shared by those in the Party who were in no doubt that adulterers in the public spotlight were offensive from a moral point of view, or more expediently, that it was stretching political credibility to expect the country to accept the Conservatives as a party of the family if Parkinson was not dismissed from office. In the public and press response there was as much indignation at the 'sheer hypocrisy' of an age which castigates a man in public office just because he has a mistress, as there was condemnation of the judgment that Parkinson could conceivably remain in office. Some were equivocal; instant resignation, one senior politician pointed out, would have meant that this was the particular standard of morality which must prevail, 'and that would have set a standard of hypocrisy which even the Conservative Party could not stomach'.[70] Very little was heard about a return to Victorian values after that.

Although Parkinson was later restored to public office, the mud stuck. Sara Keays was thrown to the wolves. As the figure of the mistress with rights she was prepared to exercise, ambitious (she had put herself up for selection as a Conservative parliamentary candidate), and willing to use the press, she was widely vilified and spent much time defending herself from accusations of revenge and blackmail. Public support went to Ann Parkinson, the main casualty of the affair in the view of almost half (40 per-cent) those polled. (Only 14 per-cent thought Sara Keays had suffered most.) Opinion probes revealed a nation divided down the middle on the moral issue, with half the respondents believing it was legitimate to expect higher moral standards from politicians than they applied to themselves, and 71 per-cent believing adultery was morally wrong. Over half (59 per-cent) believed Parkinson should resign, but a third (and 41 per-cent of Tory supporters following Thatcher's lead) thought he should stay.[71] Clearly, attitudes to morals were still in a state of flux, but no large-scale return to a pre-permissive moral orthodoxy on sexual licence was in evidence.

When the Tory party became involved three years later in a scandal over allegations in two tabloids which linked its Deputy Chairman, Jeffrey Archer, with a prostitute and the sum of £2000, there was no shilly-shallying. Archer resigned immediately, declaring he had been 'silly, very foolish . . . lack of judgement',[72] a promptness possibly also dictated by timing – the Party was in the run-up to an election in which family values was about to figure largely, whereas in the Parkinson case they had only just won an election and had time on their side. Archer sued the *Daily Star* for libel and won after the judge concluded that, with such a 'fragrant woman' as Mary (another independent woman with a career) for his wife, it was unlikely he would ever have to resort to the services of prostitutes. Record damages were awarded.

The Government signalled its intention to address issues specifically affecting women when in 1986, in response to pressures from within and outside Conservative ranks, it set up a Home Office Ministerial Group on Women's Issues to co-ordinate departmental initiatives. The Group's activities reflected government expenditure constraints and an unwillingness to commit state resources to anything which might be achieved by private or voluntary effort. It also demonstrated an inclination to tackle the symptoms rather than the underlying causes of social problems. On child care and maintenance their proposals shifted responsibility away from the State; initiatives for improved child care facilities encouraged employer and voluntary effort but avoided any commitment to a unifed co-ordinated service funded by the State, and their proposals on maintenance increased sanctions on fathers who failed to pay.

On domestic violence, no change of the law to strengthen rights was proposed, though a Law Review was initiated. However new Home Office guidelines were issued to police to take a more positive attitude to complaints of violent abuse, and these were backed by changes in police training methods. Although these shifts encouraged a more sympathetic attitude to complaints, the Government diverted very few resources to the problem, and it was felt that the civil liberties implications in some areas of moral policing could give cause for alarm. Proposals to build up a police 'at risk' register, whereby, as John Patten, Home Office Minister of State, explained, 'every time there is a report of a possible incident, someone hearing shouting and screaming, it is put on a computer with the name and address', met with approval.[73]

Guidelines for a more positive police approach towards rape victims have also been approved. Sentencing, however, continues to vary, and doubts still remain that women will always get fair treatment. But some advances have been made; law review bodies had refused to include rape in marriage as an offence, but the judgment in a case of a women who charged her separated husband with rape went in her favour in 1990, and established for the first time that rape in marriage is an offence.

The public representation of sex fuelled renewed controversy. An explosion of 'sexploitation' journalism in the tabloid press in the mid-1980s was one product of a more competitive climate in the newspaper industry. But exhortations to restore conservative mores gave the press license to deal in sexual 'scandal' in the guise of moralizing on transgressions. This had been the stock in trade of seedier tabloids, such as the *News of the World*, for decades. However the intrusions on privacy dictated by chequebook journalism and justified by competition reached new heights, and provoked public calls to strengthen the laws to protect privacy. Such scandalmongering was only partly checked when, after several court cases, the size of libel damages – an alleged £1 million awarded against the *Sun* to pop star Elton John, £300,000 to Prince Andrew's former girlfriend, Koo Stark, £250,000 to Jeffrey Archer – encouraged serious reflection about the damage wrought not only on newspaper's finances, but on the credibility of the press in general. In 1990 editors set up a voluntary code of practice on privacy to pre-empt the possibility of statutory controls which it was made known the Government was considering.

The Government's hesitation to intervene in press freedom contrasted sharply with their determination to impose new limitations on broadcasting. Two decades of Mary Whitehouse's protests about television sex and violence bore fruit in 1987 when Home Secretary Douglas Hurd, Conservative Party Chairman Norman Tebbit and Mrs Thatcher pledged to clean up TV in a manner which threatened to make Mary Whitehouse the arbiter of public taste. The ground had been prepared during two attempts by Conservative backbenchers in 1986 and 1987, backed by Mrs Whitehouse and given ostentatious support by the Prime Minister, to extend the Obscene Publications Act to broadcasting and widen the definition of obscenity. The second, Gerald Howarth's Bill in 1987, proposed the definition should include material 'a reasonable person would regard as grossly offensive'. When both failed, the leadership's support was converted into the 1987 election manifesto pledge to respond to 'deep public concern over the display of sex and violence on television' with 'stronger and more effective arrangements to reflect that concern.'

This gesture of appeasement to the moral right exposed the deep discrepancy between the Government's market individualism and its enthusiasm for state interferences in moral matters. Though it was argued by professional broadcasters that any further constraints were unnecessary since broadcasting organisations were already restrained by statutory obligations regarding standards of good taste and decency which appeared to satisfy the majority, and that any further constraints were unworkable (a view shared by the Home Office) without a kind of authoritarian policing which threatened to infringe rights to freedom of expression. These views were overridden, however.

The clean-up proposals became enmeshed in the Government's further aim to demolish the existing monopoly structure of broadcasting, to encourage efficiency and market competition and harness technology to an unfettered proliferation of outlets. Opponents pointed out the dichotomy in these proposals: the more diverse the outlets, the more difficult it would be to control progamme content, while increased competition was liable to lower rather than raise standards of programming as the lowest common denominator factor came into play in the race for audiences.

At the end of a long drawn out struggle, the combined efforts of the lobbies, the Home Office and the Government brought forth a multiplication of agencies to police broadcasters. Instead of a single regulator for each channel with codes of practice drawn up in line with its statutory duties, there was now, in addition to a Broadcasting Complaints Commission, a newly-constituted body, the Independent Television Commission, set up to replace the Independent Broadcasting Authority, and a further body, the Broadcasting Standards Council, headed by the former BBC chairman and *The Times* editor, Lord Rees Mogg. Charged with being 'the focus for public concern' the Broadcasting Standards Council was to have a statutory right to intervene and oversee programmes in the area of taste and decency. On top of that, the criminal law was introduced for the first time when the Obscene Publications Acts were extended to cover broadcasting.

The Broadcasting Standards Council turned out to be a mouse. Its guidelines, published in 1989, differed from those already operated by the BBC and the IBA only in the BSC's stress on controlling gratuitous rape scenes and demeaning depictions of women. Otherwise, it followed existing television practice. For instance, nudity and sexual scenes were deemed legitimate in the right dramatic context and as long as no-one was exploited. Swearing should be broadcast only with the approval of senior executives, and the 9 p.m. watershed remained in place. Which raised the question of why the Broadcasting Standards Council had been necessary in the first place if their interpretation of controls coincided so closely with those of the established broadcasting organizations. The answer seemed to be that short term populist pressures had heightened anxieties, but it was found that no radical change was either feasible or necessary in the interests of sustaining a balance between the public interest and broadcaster's responsibilities.

With the removal of Mrs Thatcher as Prime Minister in 1990, the influence of the BSC which had depended on her patronage was further weakened. As 'the focus for public concern', it became the lightning conductor for pressure groups and aggrieved members of the public. But the volume of complaints, particularly about sex, had been diminishing steadily over the years. Aware of the dangers of undermining what authority it possessed, the BSC proceeded cautiously. In the first two months of its operation, it rejected all the complaints it received; by June 1991, it had absorbed 748 complaints from the public but upheld only 10 – and was showing more concern about violence than sex. 'I think we are demonstrating that there's not a great deal that can't be shown,' its Secretary, Colin Shaw, confidently declared.[74]

Nevertheless the complex balance of broadcasting had been disturbed and the most likely casualty was freedom of expression. Professionals were concerned that, faced with so many controlling bodies, broadcasters would become more timid and self-censoring, avoiding controversy and producing bland programmes which would neither offend nor impress. Where television's vitality had depended on harnessing the new talent of writers, dramatists, comedians, it now was more likely to discourage them. 'Even directors of programmes get fed up with the hassle and start dreaming of interviews by Jimmy Young instead of a constant hail of sandbags. Is this what the public really wants?' asked Liz Forgan, deputy head of Channel 4.[75] It could be a high price to pay for concessions to the views of what remained, even after a decade of attempts to engineer a conservative morality, a vociferous minority.

In the late 1980s, broadcasting was at the sharp end of changes which over almost a century had shifted responsibility for sexual order from the public to the private domain. Whereas in 1900 external constraints controlled sex, by 1990 the onus was on the individual to establish private order, though the State still plays a part in shaping codes of conduct.

Since the early years of the century, the belief that an understanding of the individual's sexual nature was the key to a more progressive and civilized society has gradually gained hold, despite resistance from the forces of puritan morality who believed that rules and punitive constraints on sex were necessary to protect society from the chaos of unbridled desire. To early sex reformers, a society whose institutional arrangements were so at variance with human nature was heading for disaster. It not only shaped an immoral, inequitable and inhumane social order, but it denied that desire would invariably defeat rules, and that passion would break through regulations and could not be (and in practice rarely was) confined to a pattern dictated by God or the needs of social order. To maintain institutions which were out of step with changing values would eventually bring them into disrepute and threaten social disruption.

There have been fundamental changes in the sexual order since then. The decline in religious belief has removed the sanction of fear to enforce codes of conduct. Advances in knowledge about sex have broadened understanding of sexual variety and curtailed the powers of those who would keep the public in ignorance the better to control them. Technological advances have diminished the penalties of sex – by controlling disease until recently, by enabling the regulation of fertility, by improving standards of health and by revolutionizing patterns of domestic organization. Changes in the material and economic circumstances of the majority have raised aspirations of marital and family happiness and fulfilment.

Values have changed. The high priority given to personal responsibility, opportunity, choice and gratification of desires, which was endorsed by economic forces and political ideology, has also shaped sexual values. Belief in individual freedom informed the watershed changes of the 1950s and 1960s, when it was acknowledged that the State had limited right to intervene in private morality.

People now claim rights in relation to sex: the right to enjoy sex cleansed of sin and disinfected of guilt; the right to know, and to explore and understand the sexual self, in the belief this is the key to identity and happiness; the right to represent in art and literature the subtleties and complexities of sexual nature as well as the social dilemmas it constantly nurtures; and the right to options in relationships and sexual expression. Women claim the right to sexual autonomy and equality.

The nature of responsibility and duty has also changed. For with the ethic of individual choice emerged a belief that sex serves a higher moral purpose of self knowledge, self identification, and personal growth. In the 1960s, rebellion against sexual taboos was seen as a means of personal revolt, an assertion of self against impersonal rules and religious prohibition, and a celebration of harmony of the self with nature. Since then the ideal of personal growth has become not only a right, but a duty, and a moral responsibility to oneself. As the individual's obligation to conform to externally imposed concepts of moral duty has declined, a sense of moral duty towards self, which may or may not coincide with the community's interests, has increased.

Although responsibility has shifted to the individual, this has not diminished anxiety. The combination of science and social policy has relieved the penalties of sex, but it has not entirely dissolved the accretion of guilt and shame which surrounds sexual feelings. People expect more out of relationships, which multiplies the possibilities for a sense of failure. As the meaning of sex has changed it has ceased to have much to do with morals, very little to do with God, and, for a time, not much to do with love either as the accent shifted to performance and technique. As Malcolm Muggeridge gloomily surmized, the orgasm had replaced the Cross as the focus of longing. One consequence is widespread confusion and a pre-occupation with inability to 'relate deeply', express sexual intimacy and 'get in touch with feelings'. Another is anxiety about living up to new standards of obligatory sex.

More choice brings more dilemmas: a hesitation to make commitments, but also a willingness to opt out of relationships which are not satisfying the high demands placed on them. Few divorcing couples, especially when one partner leaves the other, escape guilt about their conduct which leaves a lasting deposit of moral unease. With one in three marriages ending in divorce, this is perhaps the most fertile source of the era's guilt.

Choice may have given people more freedom. As women have extended their rights within and outside the family, they have fought to improve their sexual rights. Though women's positive sexuality was first recruited to monogamous marriage as an insurance against the wild winds of male passion and later to an ethos of sexual pleasure, the result of the renegotiation of sexual rights initiated by feminists has been to enable women to explore sexuality on their own terms. But the optimistic belief that to discover their true sexual nature and assert their autonomy would empower women and release them from dependency has not been realized. Women have found that they are still subject to the frustrations, dependencies, ambiguities, dissatisfactions as well as the satisfactions of emotional attachment. But insofar as they have carved out some independent status, they are freer to make choices, less constrained by negative prescriptions of their sexual rights and duties, more willing to claim pleasure, and more able to express more openly the range and subtleties of sexual desire, passion, love, lust and delight.

AIDS, on the other hand, has been a brake on freedom. It has changed the meaning of sex, reintroduced fear, reinstated punishment, enforced caution and restraint, and brought back intolerance. It has provided the opportunity to re-assert sexual moralism, and bred a new censoriousness, according to surveys, about 'deviant' sexualities, and about extra-marital affairs. But it may also have encouraged more imaginative sensuality, and a new stress on variety in erotic expression, fantasy and exploration of 'whole body sensuality', which could enlarge rather than diminish the meanings of sex. Ironically it may also provide the perfect justification for the separation of sex from procreation, for the most efficient form of procreative sex – unprotected vaginal penetration – is now deemed the most risky and dangerous form of heterosexual activity. The more diffuse and imaginative the sexual 'intercourse', the safer it is.

Meanwhile the State has not relinquished its powers to censure, coerce, restrain or direct behaviour. It continues to enforce rules of morality. It can intervene at many levels – either in support of freedom, justice and tolerance, or to enforce more restrictive codes, remove support or stigmatize the behaviour of groups or individuals who do not fit prevailing concepts of moral virtue. So far, despite attempts to coerce society back into a conservative morality, the impulse to personal responsibility and private moral freedom of choice has shown itself to be strongly rooted after decades of often painful adjustments to changing sexual norms.

Notes

CHAPTER 1. Introduction

1.   Ed. Michael and Eleanor Brock, *H. H. Asquith. Letters to Venetia Stanley*, Oxford University Press, 1982. p 584–585.
2.   Ibid p 554.
3.   Frances Lloyd George, *The Years That Are Past*, Hutchinson, 1967. p 52, 42.
4.   Ibid p 52.
5.   Brock and Brock, *Letters to Venetia Stanley*, op cit. p 1.
6.   Ibid p 12. Smyth to Archbishop of Canterbury, 11 February 1914. Randall Davidson MSS, Lambeth Palace.
7.   ed. A. J. P. Taylor, *Lloyd George, A Diary of Frances Stevenson*, Hutchinson, 1971. p 110. 28 July 1916.
8.   Ibid p 142. 9 February, 1917.
9.   *Prefaces by Bernard Shaw*, Constable, 1934. *Getting Married*, p 43.

CHAPTER 2. Transition

1.   Havelock Ellis, *My Life*, Heinemann, 1940. p 185.
2.   Ibid p 130–131.
3.   cited Ruth First and Ann Scott, *Olive Schreiner*, Andre Deutsch, 1980. p 141; ed. Richard Rive, *Olive Schreiner, Letters 1871–99* Oxford University Press, 1988. p 141. Olive Schreiner to Havelock Ellis, 1 February, 1887.
4.   Ellis, *My Life* op cit. p 185.
5.   Ed. S. C. Cronwright Schreiner, *The Letters of Olive Schreiner*, Unwin, 1924. p. 90. To Havelock Ellis, 3 January 1886.
6.   First and Scott, *Olive Schreiner* op cit. p 158. Olive Schreiner to Karl Pearson, 6 February, 1886. Pearson Papers.
7.   cited First and Scott, *Olive Schreiner*, op cit. p 141.
8.   ed. Rive, *Olive Schreiner, Letters 1871–99* op cit. p 75. Olive Schreiner to Karl Pearson, 4 April 1886.
9.   cited First and Scott, *Olive Schreiner*, op cit. p 159.
10.   ed Rive, *Olive Schreiner, Letters 1871–99*, op cit. p 124. Olive Schreiner to Havelock Ellis, 1 February 1887.
11.   Ibid p 117. Olive Schreiner to Karl Pearson, 14 December 1886.
12.   cited First and Scott, *Olive Schreiner*, p 172. Charlotte Wilson to Karl Pearson, 17 May 1889. Pearson Papers.
13.   Olive Schreiner, *Woman and Labour*, T. Fisher Unwin, 1911 p 258.
14.   Ibid p 256.
15.   Vera Brittain, *Testament of Youth*, Fontana/Virago, 1979 p 41.

16.   Ed. Norman and Jeanne MacKenzie. *The Diary of Beatrice Webb. 1873–1892.* Vol 1, Virago, 1982. p 21. 19 Sept, 1875.
17.   Ibid p 54. 24 July 1882.
18.   Ibid p 115. 22 April 1884.
19.   Ibid p 17. 13 March 1874.
20.   Ibid p 54, 24 July 1882.
21.   Ibid p 45. 12 Sept 1881.
22.   Ibid p 99. To Mary Playne, October 1883.
23.   Ibid p 104. 12 January 1884.
24.   Ibid p 120–121. 15 October 1884.
25.   Ibid p 122, 16 March 1884.
26.   Ibid p 115–16. 22 April 1884.
27.   Ibid p 118. 9 May 1884.
28.   Ibid p 275. 7 March 1889.
29.   Ibid p 344, To Sidney Webb, December 1890.
30.   Ibid p 345, 1 December 1890.
31.   Ibid p 361, To Sidney Webb, August 1891.
32.   Ibid p 356. 22 May 1891.
33.   Ibid p 357, 20 July 1891.
34.   Ibid p 371.
35.   Beatrice Webb, *Our Partnership*, London, 1948. p 360.
36.   ed. William Coote, *A Romance in Philanthropy*, National Vigilance Association, 1916. p 228, 113.
37.   Winston S. Churchill. *My Early Life*, Thornton Butterworth, 1930. p 66, 71.
38.   cited E. M. Turner, *Josephine Butler. Her Place in History*. The Association for Moral and Social Hygiene. No Date. Fawcett Library.
39.   ed. George and Lucy Johnson, *Josephine Butler, An Autobiographical Memoir*, Arrowsmith, 1909. p 174; E. M. Turner, op cit.
40.   Christabel Pankhurst, *The Great Scourge. And How To End It*, E. Pankhurst, 1913.
41.   General Register Office, Census 1911, HMSO, 1914.
42.   Dr. Mary Scharlieb, *Reminiscences*, William and Norgate, 1924. p 232, 233.
43.   Mary Stocks, *My Commonplace Book*, Peter Davies, 1970. p 113.
44.   Rebecca West, *A Reed of Steel*, in (ed) Jane Marcus, *The Young Rebecca. The Writings of Rebecca West. 1911–1917*. Macmillan/Virago, 1982. p 255–6.
45.   Ibid p 155. *Clarion*, 14 February, 1913.
46.   Ibid p 23. *The Freewoman*, 7 March 1912.
47.   *The Freewoman*, 14 December, 1911.
48.   *The Freewoman*, 23 November, 1911.
49.   *The Freewoman*, 14, 21 December 1911.
50.   cited Ronald Pearsall, *The Worm in the Bud*, Weidenfeld and Nicholson, 1969. p 219: R. Ussher in *Neo-Malthusianism*. 1897.
51.   Ibid p 217.
52.   Ray Strachey, *Millicent Garrett Fawcett*, John Murray, 1931. p 89.
53.   Ibid p 236.
54.   ed. S. C. Cronwright Schreiner, *The Letters of Olive Schreiner*. op cit. p 312. Olive Schreiner to Havelock Ellis, 7 August 1912.
55.   Edward Carpenter, *Love's Coming of Age*, Manchester Labour Press, 1896. p 68–9, *15*.
56.   cited Sheila Rowbotham and Jeffrey Weeks, *Socialism and the New Life*, Pluto Press, 1977. p 116. Robert Blatchford to Edward Carpenter, 11 January 1894. (Carpenter Collection).
57.   cited Jeffery Weeks, *Coming Out*, Quartet, 1977. p 80. Robert Graves to Edward Carpenter, 30 May 1914. (Carpenter Collection).
58.   Dr Richard von Krafft Ebing, *Psychopathia Sexualis*. F. J. Rebman, 1894 edition, p 2.
59.   Havelock Ellis, *My Life*, op cit, p 239.
60.   Ibid p 292.

61. cited Edward Brecher, *The Sex Researchers*, Panther, 1970 p 55.
62. H. G. Wells, *Experiment in Autobiography*, Macmillan, 1934. p 404.
63. Ibid p 400, 406.
64. Anthony West, *H. G. Wells. Aspects of a Life*, Hutchinson, 1984. p 236.
65. H. G. Wells, *Experiment in Autobiography*, op cit. p 399.
66. Ibid p 351, 352–353.
67. Ed. G. P. Wells, *H. G. Wells In Love*, Faber and Faber, 1984. p 56.
68. Ibid p 81.
69. Ibid p 80.
70. Ibid p 82–83.
71. Gordon N. Ray. *H. G. Wells and Rebecca West*, Macmillan London Ltd Press. 1974. p 22 (June 1913).
72. Anthony West, *Aspects of a Life*, op cit, p 5–6.
73. Gordon N. Ray, *H. G. Wells and Rebecca West*. op cit, pp 21–23.
74. G. P. Wells, *H. G. Wells in Love*, op cit, p 176.
75. Ibid p 199–200.
76. *Prefaces by Bernard Shaw*, Constable, 1934. *The Shewing Up of Blanco Posnet*, p 414. 415.
77. *The Westminster Gazette*, 27 May 1895; *St James Gazette*, 27 May 1895.
78. cited Peter Gay, *Education of the Senses*, Oxford University Press, 1984. pp 412–4.
79. Thomas Hardy, *Jude the Obscure*, Papermac, 1966. p v. Preface to the First Edition.
80. Thomas Hardy, Notebooks 17 October 1896. Cited in Michael Millgate *Thomas Hardy : A Biography* Oxford University Press, 1982 p 382.
81. Spectator cited Edward Bristow, *Vice and Vigilance*, Gill and Macmillan, 1977. p 217.
82. Arnold Bennett, *Books and Persons*, Chatto & Windus, 1920. p 33, 13 January 1910; p 138, 26 May 1910.

CHAPTER 3. First World War

1. Vigilance Record, December 1914.
2. Christian Commonwealth, 16 October 1918. cited Joan Lock, *The British Police-woman. Her Story*. Robert Hale, 1979. p 90.
3. *The Times*, 8 October 1914.
4. Imperial War Museum: Women at Work Collection. Emp 44/10. Church Family News, 26.5.1915.
5. IWM Emp 44/1. *The Daily Telegraph*, 29 May 1915.
6. Emp 44/18. *The Weekly Dispatch*. 3 June 1917; Lock op cit, p 59.
7. Emp 42/2/6. NUWW: Woman Patrol Committee. Extracts from Organisers' Reports, August 1915; Emp 42/2/9.
8. Emp 42/2/26. NUWW Woman Patrol Committee. Organisers Reports, July 1917.
9. Emp 43/83.
10. Emp 43/92. The Woman Police Service. An Account of Its Aims. Report of Work Accomplished During the Year 1915.
11. Vigilance Record, December 1914. Letter of Instruction to Police Authorities, Home Office, December 1914.
12. Sylvia Pankhurst, *The Home Front*, Hutchinson, 1932. p 99.
13. Ibid p 101.
14. Vigilance Record, March 1915. Church Quarterly Review, February 1915.
15. Lock, *The British Policewoman. Her Story*, op cit, p 27, 29.
16. IWM. Emp 43/7. Police Women's Work in Grantham: First Annual Report, January 1917.
17. Emp 43/20. Ethel Smith (handwritten) Report for 1917.
18. Emp 43/92. The Woman Police Service. op cit.

19. Emp 43/9. Woman Police Patrols.
20. Emp 44/23. *The Weekly Dispatch*, 22 July 1917.
21. Emp 44/22. *The Weekly Dispatch*, 15 July 1917; Lock op cit p 35.
22. Emp 43/22. Police Chronicle, 22 March 1918.
23. Vera Brittain, *Testament of Youth*, Fontana/Virago, 1979. p 213.
24. C. S. Peel, *How We Lived Then*, The Bodley Head, 1929. p 70.
25. IWM. Emp 45/7. Report on Industrial Welfare Conditions in Coventry in November 1916 by Miss Anderson and Miss Markham, Home Office, 1916.
26. Ibid.
27. IWM. Women's Collection: Mun 14. Memorandum by J. C. Burnham, Superintendent, and Ernest Taylor, Social Manager, H.M. Factory, Gretna Green, August 1919.
28. Lilian Evans, *To Women Workers: Some Homely Advice in Regard to the Maintenance of Their Health and Comfort*, cited Arthur Marwick, *Women at War*, Fontana, 1977. p 130-131.
29. IWM Documents. 83/17/1. O. M. Taylor.
30. Letter from Mrs Elsie Cooper to IWM: *Memoirs of a WAAC*, 23 January 1976. cited Marwick, *Women At War*, op cit, p 95.
31. Commission of Inquiry into Conduct in the WAAC, February 1918, Ministry of Labour, M 40/56. IWM Womens' Collection, Army 3/28.
32. Ibid.
33. Annual Report of the Registrar General for 1916. Cmnd 8869. p xix.
34. Note by Secretary of the War Babies and Mothers League, 1915. IWM Womens Collection B.O.4.
35. Vigilance Record, May 1915.
36. Caroline Playne, *Britain Holds On, 1917–1918*, George Allen and Unwin, 1933. p 240.
37. Sylvia Pankhurst, *The Home Front*, op cit, p 98.
38. cited Marwick, *Women at War*, op cit p 127.
39. C. S. Peel, *How We Lived Then*, op cit, p 69–70.
40. Ibid p 70.
41. Brittain, *Testament of Youth*, op cit, p 131.
42. *The Autobiography of Bertrand Russell: 1914–1944*, Vol 11, George Allen and Unwin, 1968. p 26.
43. C. S. Peel, *How We Lived Then*, op cit, p 68.
44. M. A. Hamilton, in (ed) Ray Strachey, *Our Freedom and its Results, London 1936*, p 251.
45. Eustace Chesser, *The Sexual, Marital and Family Relationships of the English Woman*, Hutchinsons Medical Press, 1956. p. 311.
46. Lawrence Stone, *Road to Divorce*, Oxford University Press, 1910. Table 13.1, p 435.
47. Brittain, *Testament of Youth*, op cit, p 180–181.
48. Ibid p 188.
49. Ibid p 233.
50. Ibid p 182.
51. *The Manchester Guardian*, 25 January 1917, cited Playne op cit, p 239.
52. Charles Edmonds, *A Subalterns War*, Peter Davies, 1929. p 207.
53. Charles Carrington, *Soldier From The Wars Returning*, Hutchinson, 1965. p 160, 163.
54. Ibid p 168.
55. IWM Documents. 87/11/1. Commander R. Goldrich, RN.
56. H. C. Fischer and Dr. E. X. Dubois, *Sexual Life During the War*, Francis Aldor, 1937. p 332, 334.
57. Carrington, *Soldier From the Wars Returning*, op cit, p 164.
58. cited Sir George Arthur, *Life of Lord Kitchener*, Vol 111, Macmillan, 1920. p 27.
59. *cited Edward J. Bristow, *Vice and Vigilance*, Gill and Macmillan, 1977. p 150.
60. Brigadier General F. P. Crozier, *A Brass Hat in No-Man's Land*, Jonathan Cape, 1930. p 50, 51.

61. Ibid 57.
62. Major General Sir W. G. MacPherson, *History of the Great War. Medical Services. General History*, Vol 11. HMSO. 1921. p 340, 346.
63. Report of the Royal Commission on Venereal Diseases, Cmnd 8189. HMSO. 1916. Appendix XII. p 140.
64. Major General Sir W. G. MacPherson, *History of the Great War. Medical Services*, op cit, p 183, 202.
65. Caroline Playne, *Society At War, 1914–1916*, George Allen and Unwin, 1931. p 234.
66. Vigilance Record, September 1916, November 1916; Ibid Playne, p 234; Huntley Carter, *The New Spirit in the European Theatre, 1914–1924*, Ernest Benn, 1925. p 43–44.
67. Lord Bishop of London, *Cleansing London: The Moral Change Required in London*, 20 Sept 1916. (pamphlet).
68. cited ed Harry T. Moore, *Sex, Literature and Censorship*, Heinemann, 1955. p 5.
69. cited Phillip Callow, *Son and Lover*, The Bodley Head, 1975. p 273.
70. ed Harry T. Moore, *Sex Literature and Society*, op cit, p 6.
71. Vigilance Record, December, 1916.
72. Ibid.
73. cited Marwick, *Women At War*, op cit, p 132.
74. Vigilance Record, April 1918.
75. Caroline Playne, *Society at War*, op cit p 237.
76. Vigilance Record, December 1915; E. S. Turner, *Dear Old Blighty*, Michael Joseph, 1980. p 207.
77. Peel, *How We Lived Then*, op cit, p 66.
78. Bristow, *Vice and Vigilance*, op cit, 149.
79. *The Weekly Dispatch*, 2 July 1917.
80. *The Daily News*, 10 August 1918; Vigilance Record, Sept 1918.
81. The Imperialist, 26 January 1918. *The First 47,000*.
82. *The Times*, 5 June 1918.
83. Carrington, *Soldier From the Wars Returning*, op cit, p 227.
84. cited Irene Clephane. *Towards Sex Freedom*, The Bodley Head, 1935. p 204.
85. Edmonds, *A Subaltern's War*, op cit, p 207–8.
86. Ronald Blythe, *The Age of Illusion, 1919–1940*, Hamish Hamilton, 1963. p 16.

CHAPTER 4. Between the Wars

1. Marie Stopes, *Marriage In My Time*, Rich and Cowan, 1936. p 44.
2. Marie Stopes, *Married Love*, A. C. Fifield, 1918.
3. Marie Stopes, *Wise Parenthood*, A. C. Fifield, 1918. p 21.
4. Stopes, Preface to *Married Love*, op cit.
5. cited Ruth Hall, *Marie Stopes. A Biography*. Virago, 1978, p 143. Marie Stopes to Aylmer Maude, 17 May 1918.
6. Ibid p 145. Humphrey V Roe to Marie Stopes, 24 October 1918.
7. Ibid p 243, 128.
8. *Good Housekeeping*, 1938 (p 22), cited Cynthia L. White, *Women's Magazines 1693–1968*, Michael Joseph, 1970. p 107–8.
9. ed. Michael Davie, *The Diaries of Evelyn Waugh*, Weidenfeld and Nicholson, 1976. p 147. 22 November 1921.
10. Irene Clephane, *Towards Sex Freedom*, The Bodley Head, 1935 p 205–6.
11. Ed Davie, *The Diaries of Evelyn Waugh*, op cit, p 202, 1 February 1925.
12. *Eve*, 8 April 1920, cited White, *Women's Magazines 1693–1968*, op cit, p 94.
13. Ibid p 110.
14. Dora Russell, *The Tamarisk Tree*, Virago, 1975, p 173.
15. Ibid p 176.
16. MOH Circular 517, June 1924.

17. Lambeth Conference Report, 1920. Resolution 70, p 161.
18. W. R. Inge, *Vale*, Longman's Green, 1934; *Outspoken Essays*, Longmans Green, 1919.
19. Mary Stocks, *My Commonplace Book*, Peter Davies, 1970. p 161.
20. Dr. Armand Routh. *The Birth Rate*, October 1919. Cited Hall, op cit, p 166.
21. Dr Mary Scharlieb, British Medical Journal, 16 July 1921.
22. The Practitioner, July 1923, p 34–5.
23. cited Hall, *Marie Stopes, A Biography*, op cit p 165.
24. D. Russell, *The Tamarisk Tree*, op cit, p 172.
25. Stocks, *My Commonplace Book*, op cit p 162.
26. ed. Ruth Hall, *Dear Dr Stopes*, Andre Deutsch, 1978. p 24. Mrs HA to Marie Stopes, 13 March 1923.
27. Ibid p 39.
28. Ibid p 39.
29. Elizabeth Roberts *A Woman's Place*, Basil Blackwell, 1984 p 93.
30. Ibid p 88.
31. Ibid p 95.
32. Ibid p 98.
33. Ibid p 99–100.
34. ed. A. H. Halsey, *Trends in British Society Since 1900*, Macmillan 1972. p 55.
35. Encyclical Letter of Lambeth Conference, August 15, 1930. Resolutions of the Conference.
36. E. Lewis Faning, Royal Commission on Population Cmnd 7695 HMSO 1949–50, Papers Vol 1, Ch V, Table 38, p 54.
37. A. H. Halsey, *Trends in British Society Since 1900*, op cit, p 31.
38. Eustace Chesser, *The Sexual, Marital and Family Relationships of the English Woman*, Hutchinson's Medical Press, 1956. p 311, p 313.
39. Eliot Slater and Moya Woodside, *Patterns of Marriage*, Cassell, 1951. p 113, 288.
40. Steve Humphreys, *A Secret World of Sex*, Sidgwick and Jackson, 1988. p 126, 128.
41. Roberts, *A Woman's Place*, op cit, p 71.
42. Humphreys, *A Secret World of Sex*, op cit, p 106.
43. cited Slater and Woodside, *Patterns of Marriage*, op cit, p 111.
44. Cited Jeffrey Weeks, *Sex, Politics and Society*, Longman, 1981. p 211.
45. Janet Chance, *The Cost of English Morals*, Noel Douglas, 1931. p 89–90.
46. * Edward J. Bristow, *Vice and Vigilance*, Gill and Macmillan, 1977. p 147, 153.
47. Chesser, *The Sexual, Marital and Family Relationships of the English Woman*, op cit, p 160, 161, 163.
48. Mass Observation: FR 3110, *General Attitudes to Sex*, April 1949.
49. A. H. Taylor, *Jix. Viscount Brentford*, Stanley Paul, 1933, p 36.
50. Ronald Blythe, *The Age of Illusion*, Hamish Hamilton, 1963 p 36, 37.
51. Bristow, *Vice and Vigilance*, op cit, p 223.
52. Alec Craig, *The Banned Books of England*, George Allen and Unwin, 1962. p 94.
53. D. H. Lawrence, *Pornography and Obscenity*, Faber and Faber, 1929, p 13.
54. D. H . Lawrence, *A Propos of Lady Chatterley's Lover* in (ed) Harry T. Moore, *Sex, Literature and Censorship*, Heinemann, 1955. p 230.
55. D. H. Lawrence, *Pornography and Obscenity*, op cit, p 23.
56. ed Harry T. Moore, *The Collected Letters of D. H. Lawrence*, Vol 11, Heinemann, 1962. p 1046–7. DHL to Harriet Monroe, 15 March 1928.
57. Ibid p 1111. DHL to Lady Ottoline Morrell, 28 December 1928.
58. Ibid p 1047. DHL to Harriet Monroe, 15 March 1928.
59. Richard Aldington, *Portrait of a Genius But . . .* , Four Square, 1963. p 312.
60. ed Moore, *Sex, Literature and Censorship*, op cit, p 18.
61. *Frank Harris on Bernard Shaw*, Gollancz, 1931. p 233.
62. ed Moore, *Sex Literature and Censorship*, op cit, p 21.
63. Aldington, op cit, p 325.

64. Viscount Brentford, (Joynson Hicks), *Do We Need A Censor?* Faber and Faber, 1929. p 23.
65. Rachel Low, *The History of the British Film, 1918–1929*, George Allen and Unwin, 1971. p 63.
66. Ibid, p 59. British Board of Film Censors, Annual Report, 1919.
67. Ibid p 61–63.
68. Th. van de Velde, *Ideal Marriage, Its Psychology and Technique*, Heinemann (Medical Books), 1930. p 144.
69. Chance, *The Cost of English Morals*, op cit, p 36, 37.
70. Ibid p 36, 37.
71. Peggy Makins, *The Evelyn Home Story*, Fontana/Collins, 1976, p 48.
72. Bertrand Russell, *Marriage and Morals*, George Allen and Unwin, 1929. p 182, 249.
73. Irene Clephane, *Towards Sex Freedom*, op cit, p 221–2, 224.
74. Makins, *The Evelyn Home Story*, op cit, 37–38.
75. D. Russell, *The Tamarisk Tree*, op cit, p 157.
76. *The Autobiography of Bertrand Russell, 1872–1914*, Vol 1, George Allen and Unwin, 1967. p 205.
77. D. Russell, *The Tamarisk Tree*, op cit, p 73.
78. Ibid p 69.
79. Ibid p 78.
80. Ibid p 156.
81. Ibid p 148.
82. Ibid p 223.
83. Ibid p 208–9.
84. Ibid p 222–3. Bertrand Russel to Dora Russell, 14 Nov 1929.
85. Ibid p 243.
86. *The Autobiography of Bertrand Russell, 1914–1944*, Vol 11, George Allen and Unwin, 1968 op cit p 192.
87. Kathleen Tait, *My Father Bertrand Russell*, Gollancz, 1976 p 107.
88. Ibid p 103.
89. *The Autobiography of Bertrand Russell, 1914–1944*, Vol II, op cit p 156.
90. White, *Women's Magazines 1693–1968*, op cit, p 99. Womans Life, 10 January, 1920.
91. cited Montgomery Hyde, *The Other Love*, Mayflower, 1972. p 202, 204; Hansard, House of Lords Debates. 46. 15 August 1921.
92. Nigel Nicholson, *Portrait of a Marriage*, Futura, 1974. p 106–7, 27 September 1920.
93. Ibid p 109, 29 September 1920.
94. Victoria Glendinning, *Vita*, Penguin, 1983. p 211.
95. Beverley Nichols, *The Sweet and Twenties*, Weidenfeld and Nicholson, 1958. p 104, 105.
96. Lovat Dickson, *Radclyffe Hall at the Well of Loneliness*, p 140, 124. Una, Lady Troubridge, *The Life and Death of Radclyffe Hall*, Hammond, 1961. p 81.
97. Nichols, *The Sweet and Twenties*, op cit, p 106.
98. *The Sunday Express*, 19 August 1928.
99. Hyde, *The Other Love*, op cit, p 209.
100. Jeffrey Weeks, *Coming Out*, Quarter, 1977. p 158.
101. cited Hyde, *The Other Love*, op cit, p 225.
102. Ibid p 225; Goronwy Rees, *A Case for Treatment; the World of Lytton Strachey*, Encounter, March 1968.
103. Hyde, *The Other Love*, p 224.
104. Ibid p 218–9.
105. cited Dierdre Beddoe, *Back to Home and Duty*, Pandora, 1989. p 4.
106. Ibid p 79.
107. *The Manchester Guardian*, 30 June 1931. Cited Ruth Adam, *A Woman's Place*, Chatto and Windus, 1975. p 123.
108. Beddoe, *Back to Home and Duty*, op cit, p 14.

109. cited Weeks, *Sex, Politics and Society*, op cit, p 205.
110. *Womans Own*, 15 October 1932.
111. Ed. Paul Berty and Alan Bishop, *Testament of a Generation. The Journalism of Vera Brittain and Winifred Holtby*, Virago, 1985. p 127–8.
112. Interim Report of the Departmental Committee on Maternal Mortality and Morbidity, MOH, HMSO, 1930. p 40, para 58.
113. cited Madeleine Simms and Keith Hindell, *Abortion Law Reformed*, Peter Owen, 1971 p 67.
114. Sheila Rowbotham, *A New World For Women*. Pluto, 1977. Appendix 2: F. W. Stella Browne, *The Right to Abortion*, p 114.
115. Chance, *The Cost of English Morals*, op cit, p 59.
116. Interdepartmental Committee of Inquiry, (Birkett Committee), MOH, HO, 1939.
117. Lawrence Stone, *Road to Divorce*, OUP, 1990. Table 13.1, p 435.
118. Hansard, House of Lords Debates, 1937, 105.
119. cited Frances Donaldson, *Edward VIII*, Omega, 1975. p 258.
120. Alistair Burnett, 'The Sorry Wife of Windsor', *The Sunday Times*, 27 April 1986.
121. cited Donaldson, *Edward VIII*, op cit, p 299.

CHAPTER 5. Second World War

1. S. M. Ferguson and H. Fitzgerald, *Studies in the Social Services*, HMSO, 1954. p 3.
2. Susan Briggs, *Keep Smiling Through*, Weidenfeld and Nicholson, 1975. p 20.
3. Ferguson, *Studies in the Social Services*, op cit, p 4.
4. cited Briggs, *Keep Smiling Through*, op cit, p 28.
5. Angus Calder, *The People's War. Britain 1939–45*, Panther, 1971. p 382.
6. Briggs, *Keep Smiling Through*, op cit. p 173.
7. Raynes Minns, *Bombers and Mash*, Virago, 1980, p 48.
8. Zelma Katin, *Clippie*, Gifford, 1944, p 60.
9. cited Calder, *The People's War*, op cit, pp 386–7.
10. Statistical Digest of the War, HMSO. 1951.
11. Briggs, *Keep Smiling Through*, op cit, p 23.
12. Mass Observation Files: MO FR64, *Sexual Behaviour 1939–50*.
13. Ibid, FR64.
14. Ibid, FR64: also MO; US No 9, 29 March 1940.
15. Barbara Cartland, *The Years of Opportunity*, Hutchinson, 1948, pp 147–8.
16. Eliot Slater and Moya Woodside, *Patterns of Marriage*, Cassell, 1951, p 152.
17. Minns, *Bombers and Mash*, op cit, pp 191–2.
18. Mass Observation, *The Journey Home*, John Murray, 1944, pp 37–8.
19. Mass Observation, *People in Production*, John Murray, 1942.
20. Norman Longmate, *How We Lived Then*, Hutchinson, 1971. p 336.
21. Gail Braybon and Penny Summerfield, *Out of the Cage*, Pandora, 1987, p 212.
22. Cartland, *The Years of Opportunity*, op cit, p 223.
23. Ibid p 223.
24. Richard Hillary, *The Last Enemy*, Pan, 1956. p 48.
25. Aidan MacCarthy, *A Doctor's War*, Robson Books, 1979, p 34.
26. Ferguson, *Studies in the Social Services*, op cit, p 99.
27. Cartland, *The Years of Opportunity*, op cit, pp 221–222.
28. cited John Costello, *Love Sex and War*, Collins, 1985, pp 23–25.
29. Lord Hailsham, *A Sparrow's Flight*, Collins, 1990, pp 203–207.
30. Slater and Woodside, *Patterns of Marriage*, op cit, p 152.
31. Minns, *Bombers and Mash*, op cit, p 175.
32. Imperial War Museum Documents. File 106. Miss Robertson.
33. Slater and Woodside, *Patterns of Marriage*, op cit. pp 167, 168, 176.
34. Ferguson, *Studies in the Social Services*, op cit, p 98.

35. Ibid p 20.
36. Ed. Brigadier M. C. Morgan, *The Second World War: Army: Army Welfare*, War Office, 1953, p 31.
37. Ibid Appendix 5, p 217, 'The Soldiers' Welfare'.
38. Ibid p 223.
39. *Army Welfare*, op cit, pp 32, 33.
40. Ibid p 36.
41. Ibid p 37.
42. Ibid, Appendix 5, p 224.
43. Ibid, Appendix 5, p 241.
44. Ed. Squadron Leader S. C. Rexford-Welch, *Royal Air Force: Medical Serivces*, Vol 111, Appendix XXXV, HMSO, 1958; WO 222/12, 'Note to Regimental Officers called upon to lecture on the prevention of Venereal Disease among troops.'.
45. Ibid, ed Rexford-Welch, Appendix XXXV.
46. Ed. Major General Sir Henry Letheby Tide, *Inter-Allied Conference on War Medicine Convened by the Royal Society of Medicine, 1942–5*. HMSO 1947. p 251.
47. Ed. Sir Arthur Salusbury MacNally and W. Franklyn Mellor, *Medical History of the Second World War*, HNMSO, 1968. p 257.
48. Major General Frank M. Richardson, *Mars Without Venus*, Blackwood, 1981, p 43.
49. Dorothy Calvert, *Battledress, Lanyard and Lipstick*, New Horizon (Bognor Regis), 1978, p 14.
50. Costello, *Love Sex and War*, op cit, p 81.
51. WO 222/1300. *Report from Adviser in Venerology, A. G. Johnson AFHQ, 1st Quarter 1945*, 13 April 1945.
52. WO 222/12. *Medical History of the War: Venereal Disease in the British Army*, 3 September 1939- 31 August 1943.
53. Air Ministry Pamphlet 160, September 1943, *Health Hints for Warm Climates*.
54. Ed. Sir Arthur Salusbury MacNally and W. Franklyn Mellor, *Medical History of the Second World War: Medical Services in the War*. HMSO, 1968, p 259.
55. Air Ministry Pamphlet 160. op cit, p 5.
56. Aidan MacCarthy, *A Doctor's War*, op cit, p 21.
57. Air Commodore E. A. Lumley, *Army and Air Force Doctor*. 1971, p 95.
58. Ed. Squadron Leader S. C. Rexford-Welch, *Royal Air Force Medical Services*, op cit, p 214.
59. Ibid pp 415–16.
60. R. C. Benge, *Confessions of a Lapsed Librarian*, Scarecrow Books, 1984, p 52.
61. Ibid p 79.
62. Ibid p 80.
63. Alun Lewis, *In the Green Tree*, George Allen and Unwin, 1948, 93, 104, 105.
64. Benge, *Confessions of a Lapsed Librarian*, op cit, p 84.
65. ed. Brigadier A. B. MacPherson, *The Second World War: Army: Discipline*. W. O, 1950. Appendix 1(a).
66. Costello, *Love Sex and War*, op cit, p 164.
67. George Melly, *Rum, Bum and Concertina*, Weidenfeld and Nicholson, 1977, p 29.
68. Costello, *Sex Love and War*, op cit, p 163.
69. Benge, *Confessions of a Lapsed Librarian*, op cit, p 25.
70. Ibid pp 50–51.
71. IWM Documents, Frederick Bratton Memoirs; Costello, *Sex Love and War*, op cit, p 158.
72. G. F. Green, *A Skilled Hand*, Macmillan, 1980, pp 106–108.
73. Ibid p 114; 14 January 1945, 10 December 1944.
74. Shirley Joseph, *If Their Mothers Only Knew*, Faber, 1945, p 51.
75. IWM Documents. Miss G. Morgan Memoirs.
76. MO: FR1029, 5 January 1942.

77. Slater and Woodside, *Patterns of Marriage*, op cit. p 113; Eustace Chesser, *The Sexual, Marital and Family Relationships of the English Woman*, Hutchinsons Medical Press, 1956, p 311.
78. Minns, *Bangers and Mash*, op cit, p 173, p 178.
79. Costello, *Love Sex and War*, op cit, pp 18–19.
80. Ibid p 137.
81. IWM Documents: Sister A. M. Turner Diaries.
82. Costello, *Love Sex and War*, op cit, pp 97–98.
83. Ferguson, *Studies in the Social Services*, op cit, pp 97–98.
84. Briggs, *Keep Smiling Through*, op cit, p 133.
85. Norman Longmate, *The G.I's*, Hutchinson, 1975, p 157.
86. Calvert, *Battledress, Lanyard and Lipstick*, op cit, p 36.
87. Longmate, *The G.I's*, op cit, p 272.
88. Virginia Wimperis, *The Unmarried Mother and Her Child*, George Allen and Unwin, 1960, p 29. (Mrs Frances P Bolton to US House of Representatives, 6 July 1954.).
89. IWM Documents: Eileen McMurdo, *Memoirs – When We Were Young*.
90. Report of the Committee on Amenities and Welfare Conditions in the Three Womens Services, Cmnd 6384. HMSO, 1942, pp 49–51.
91. Costello, *Love Sex and War*, op cit, p 79.
92. Calvert, *Battledress, Lanyard and Lipstick*, op cit, p 50, p 58.
93. Ferguson, *Studies in the Social Services*, op cit, pp 91–94.
94. Ibid p 91.
95. Annual Report, National Council for the Unmarried Mother and Her Child, 1941.
96. Ferguson, *Studies in the Social Services*, op cit, p 134.
97. Minns, *Bombers and Mash*, op cit, p 184.
98. Mass Observation: Box DR85. Directive Replies, March 1944.
99. Pauline Long, *Speaking Out on Age*, Spare Rib No 82, May 1979; Braybon and Summerfield, *Out of the Cage*, op cit, p 216.
100. IWM Documents: Miss G. Morgan.
101. MO: FR2205. *Sex Morality and the Birth Rate*, January 1945.
102. Ferguson, *Studies in the Social Services*, op cit, p 13, p 15.
103. *The State of Public Health During Six Years of War*, Report of the Chief Medical Officer for the Ministry of Health, 1939–45 HMSO.
104. Neville Goodman, *Wilson Jameson, Architect of Public Health*, 1970. p 90.
105. Hansard, House of Commons Debates, 385. 15 December, 1942; *The Times*, 23 November 1942.
106. MOH. 55/1350; Ed Salusbury and MacNally, *Medical Services in the War*, op cit, p 259.
107. Ibid, *Medical Services in the War*, p 259; *The Times* 8 August 1942.
108. Gladys Mary Hall, *Prostitution, A Survey and a Challenge*. Williams and Norgate, 1933. p 30.
109. Hansard, House of Commons Debates, 385. 15 December 1942.
110. *The Daily Mirror*, 19 February 1943; 22 February 1943.
111. *The Times*, 27 February 1943.
112. David Mace, *The Facts about Venereal Disease*, 1943, p 17.
113. Inter-Allied Conference on War Medicine Convened by the Royal Society of Medicine, 1943–45, HMSO, 1947.
114. MO: FR1542, *Preliminary Report on General Attitudes to Venereal Disease*, 26 December 1942.
115. MO: FR1562. *Public Reactions to the Campaign Against V.D.*, January 1943; FR1633. *V.D. Publicity in the Press*, 20 March 1943.
116. Ferguson, *Studies in the Social Services*, op cit, p 15.

CHAPTER 6. Reconstruction

1. Raynes Minns, *Bombers and Mash*, Virago, 1980, p 199.
2. Barbara Cartland, *The Years of Opportunity*, Hutchinson, 1948. p 222.
3. Minns, *Bombers and Mash*, op cit, p 196.
4. Mass Observation Files: FR2059: Mass Observation. *The Journey Home*, John Murray, 1944, pp 56–64.
5. Mary Ingham, *Now We Are Thirty*, Eyre Methuen, 1981, pp 42–43.
6. Ibid p 46, p 47.
7. Minns, *Bombers and Mash*, op cit, p 200.
8. John Costello, *Love Sex and War*, Collins, 1985, pp 360–361.
9. Susan Briggs, *Keep Smiling Through*, Weidenfeld and Nicholson, 1975, p 251.
10. Cartland, *The Years of Opportunity*, op cit, p 194.
11. P. and L. Bendit, *Living Together Again*, Gramol Press, 1946.
12. Godfrey Winn, *Scrapbook for Victory, 1945*, cited Briggs, *Keep Smiling Through*, op cit, p 250.
13. *The Times*, 26 October 1945.
14. Hansard. House of Commons Debates. 422. 10 May 1946.
15. Denning Committee on Procedure in Matrimonial Causes. Cmnd 7024. HMSO, 1947; Lord Denning. *The Due Process of Law*, Butterworth, 1980, pp 191–192.
16. Hansard, House of Lords Debates,. 169. 23 November 1950.
17. David R. Mace, *Coming Home. A Series of Five Broadcast Talks*, Staple Press, 1945.
18. David R. Mace, *Marriage Counselling*, J and A. Churchill, 1948. p 123.
19. David R. Mace, *Facts About V.D.*, p 23.
20. Edward Griffiths, *Towards Maturity*, 1944, p 136, p 209.
21. Report on Social Insurance and Allied Services (Beveridge Report). Cmnd 6404. HMSO, 1942, p 49.
22. J. Newsome, *The Education of Girls*, Faber, 1948, p 146.
23. Eliot Slater and Moya Woodside, *Patterns of Marriage*, Cassell, 1951. p 183, p 126.
24. Geoffrey Gorer, *Exploring English Character*, The Cresset Press, 1955. G. Gorer, *Sex and Marriage in England Today*, Nasa 1971, 61 p 161, p 125.
25. Ibid p 97, p 87.
26. Slater and Woodside, *Patterns of Marriage*, op cit, p 120, p 168.
27. MO: FR3110. *General Attitudes to Sex*, April 1949.
28. Gorer, *Exploring English Character*, op cit, p 79.
29. Slater and Woodside, *Patterns of Marriage*, op cit, p 181, p 177.
30. Ibid p 210.
31. E. Lewis Faning, *Report on an Enquiry into Family Limitation and its Influence on Human Fertility During the Last Fifty Years*. Papers of the Royal Commission on Population. Vol V. HMSO, 1949. Vol 1, Table 66; p 52, Table 37.

CHAPTER 7. Protest

1. Lawrence Stone, *Road to Divorce*, Oxford University Press, 1990, Table 13.1, p 436.
2. Al Alvarez, *Life After Marriage*, Macmillan 1982, p 21.
3. *Woman's Own*, 21 January 1961.
4. Viola Klein, *Britain's Married Women Workers*, Routledge Kegan and Paul, 1965, p 84; P Jephcott, N. Seear, J. H. Smith, *Married Women Working*, Allen and Unwin, 1962, p 20.
5. Klein, ibid, pp 36–38.
6. Jephcott *et al*, *Married Women Working*, op cit, p 166.
7. Klein, *Britain's Married Women Workers*, op cit, p 65.
8. Jephcott, *et al*, *Married Women Working*, op cit, p 19.
9. *Womans Own*, 28 January 1961.

10. Jephcott, *et al. Married Women Working*, op cit, pp. 165–171; A. Hunt, *A Survey of Women's Employment*, HMSO, 1968. p 185.
11. *The Daily Mail*, 17 May 1962.
12. Alfred Kinsey, Wardell B. Pomeroy, Clyde E. Martin and Paul H. Gebhard, *Sexual Behaviour in the Human Female*, W. B. Saunders, 1953.
13. Eustace Chesser, *The Sexual, Marital and Family Relationships of the English Woman*, Hutchinsons Medical Press, 1956, p 494.
14. Ibid, p 421, p 495.
15. Ibid, p 423.
16. Marie N. Robinson, *The Power of Sexual Surrender*, New America Library, 1962; cited Nena O'Neill and George O'Neill, *Open Marriage*, Abacus, 1975, p 28.
17. Maxine Davis, *The Sexual Responsibility of Women*, Fontana, 1964 (First published 1957), pp 118–119, pp. 130–131.
18. Margaret Mead, *Male and Female*, Pelican, 1962 (First published 1950), pp 269–270.
19. Al Alvarez, *Life After Marriage*, op cit, pp 38–39.
20. Kinsey, *et al, Sexual Behaviour in the Human Female*, op cit.
21. Gorer, *Exploring English Character*, op cit, p 94.
22. Chesser, *The Sexual, Marital and Family Relationships of the English Woman*, op cit, p 312, p 348.
23. John Osborne, *A Better Class of Person*, Faber and Faber, 1981, pp 167–169.
24. Jocelyn Rickards, *The Painted Banquet*, Weidenfeld and Nicholson, 1987, p 27.
25. Mary Ingham, *Now We Are Thirty*, Eyre Methuen, 1981, p 86.
26. Carol Dix, *Say I'm Sorry to Mother*, Pan, 1978, p 41.
27. Ingham, *Now We Are Thirty*, op cit, p 70.
28. Michael Schofield, *The Sexual Behaviour of Young People*, Longman, 1965, p 10.
29. Kenneth Walker and Peter Fletcher, *Sex and Society*, Pelican, 1955, pp 113–114.
30. Mead, *Male and Female*, op cit, p 273, p 293, p 291.
31. Jeff Nuttall, *Bomb Culture*, Paladin, 1970, p 29–30.
32. D. J. West, *The Young Offender*, Pelican, 1968, p 100–101.
33. Ibid p 251–2.
34. Schofield, *The Sexual Behaviour of Young People*, op cit, p 37, p 86, p 130, p 132.
35. Ibid p 11, Table 1.2.
36. R. S. Morton, *Venereal Diseases*, Pelican, 1966, p 36–37.
37. Alex Comfort, *Sex in Society*, Duckworth, 1962, p 101.
38. The Youth Service in England and Wales (The Albemarle Report). Cmnd 929 HMSO, 1960, p 17–18.
39. cited John Montgomery, *The Fifties*, George Allen and Unwin, 1965, p 138.
40. Ed. Tom Maschler, *Declaration*, MacGibbon and Kee, 1957: Doris Lessing, 'The Small Personal Voice'; Walter Allen in *The New Statesman*, 24 October 1953;.
41. cited John Russell Taylor, *Anger and After*, Methuen, 1962, pp 31–32.
42. John Osborne, *Look Back in Anger*, Faber and Faber, 1960.
43. see *The New Statesman*, 2 November 1957: J. B. Priestley, 'Britain and the Nuclear Bombs'.
44. Albemarle Report, op cit, p 29, para 14.
45. Nuttall, *Bomb Culture*, op cit, p 19, p 20.
46. Alfred C Kinsey, Wardell B. Pomeroy, Clyde E. Martin, *Sexual Behaviour in the Human Male*, W. B. Saunders, 1948. pp 650–651.
47. Montgomery Hyde, *The Other Love*, Mayflower, 1972. p 23.
48. Ibid p 239.
49. Hansard. House of Commons Debates. 251. 3 December 1953.
50. Ian Harvey, *To Fall Like Lucifer*, The Quality Book Club, 1971, p 104.
51. News Chronicle, 23 March 1954: Peter Wildeblood, *Against the Law*, Penguin, 1957, p 188.
52. Hansard, House of Commons Debates. 526. 28 April 1954.

53. Report of the Committee on Homosexual Offences and Prostitution. (Wolfenden Report). Cmnd 247. HMSO, 1957. p 9–19 para 13, 14; p 24 para 61.
54. Peter G. Richards, *Parliament and Conscience*, George Allen and Unwin, 1970, p 71; Hyde, *The Other Love*, op cit, p 160.
55. Hansard, House of Commons Debates. 625. 29 June 1960.
56. Wolfenden Report, op cit, Appendix 11, p 143; p 81 para 230.
57. *The People*, 3 Sept 1950.
58. Marthe Watts, *The Men in My Life*, Christopher Johnson, 1960.
59. Hansard, House of Commons Debates. 439. 3 July 1947.
60. Hansard, House of Commons Debates. 596. 26 November 1958; Wolfenden Report, op cit, p 116, p 96.
61. Hansard, House of Lord Debates. 206. 4 December 1957.
62. Hansard, House of Commons Debates, 596. 26 November 1958.
63. Hansard, House of Commons Debates, 23 May 1949.
64. Norman St John Stevas, *Obscenity and the Law*, Martin Secker and Warburg, 1956, pp 112–113.
65. *The New Statesman*, 19 July 1954.
66. *The Times*, 27 October 1954.
67. *The New Statesman*, 6 November 1954.
68. *The Times*, 5 June 1954.
69. *The New Statesman*, July 1954.
70. Ibid, 15 May 1954.
71. *The New Statesman*, 5 November 1960.
72. ed. C. H. Rolph. *The Trial of Lady Chatterley*, Privately printed (and in my edition still bound in plain brown paper) 1961.
73. *The Guardian*, 7 November 1960; *The Sunday Observer*, 13 November 1960. 'Why I Gave Evidence'.
74. *The Sunday Observer*, 6 November 1960.
75. Hansard, House of Lords Debates 14 December 1960; Rolph, *The Trial of Lady Chatterley*, op cit, p 253, pp 269–270.
76. *The Guardian*, 9 November 1960.
77. *The Sunday Times*, 11 December 1960; *The Guardian*, 11 November 1960.
78. *The Guardian*, 6 November 1960.
79. Ingham, *Now We Are Thirty*, op cit, pp 66–67.
80. Roy Jenkins, *The Labour Case*, Penguin, 1959, pp 135–137.
81. Anthony Crosland, *The Conservative Enemy*, Jonathan Cape, 1962, p 162.
82. Anthony Crosland, *The Future of Socialism*, Jonathan Cape, 1956, p 522.
83. *The Tribune*, 10 May 1963.
84. G. M. Carstairs, *This Island Now. The BBC Reith Lectures, 1962*, Hogarth Press, 1963, p 55, p 50, p 51.
85. Alan McGlashan, *Sex on These Islands* in (Ed). Arthur Koestler, *Suicide of a Nation ?*, Hutchinson, 1963, p 210.

CHAPTER 8. Release

1. 'Girl' student interviewed in *The Sunday Telegraph*, 30 November 1969: 'Permissive Britain'.
2. Phillip Knightley and Caroline Kennedy, *An Affair of State*, Jonathan Cape, 1987, p 86.
3. Hansard, House of Commons Debates, 21 March 1963.
4. *The Daily Telegraph*, 7 June 1963; *The Times*, 13 June 1963, 10 June 1963; *The Tribune*, 14 June 1963.
5. *The Sunday Telegraph*, 9 June 1963.
6. *The Times*, 11 June 1963.
7. *The Times*, 13 June 1963.
8. *The Sunday Times*, 16 June 1963.

9. Alistair Horne, *Macmillan 1959–1986*, Macmillan, 1989, p 476: Macmillan Diary, 22 March 1963.
10. Ibid p 495.
11. Ibid p 476: Macmillan Diary 22 March 1963.
12. *The Daily Telegraph*, 7, 10 June 1963.
13. Hansard, House of Commons Debates, 17 June 1963, Vol 679.
14. Phillip Knightley, *An Affair of State*, op cit, p 243, p 255.
15. John Robinson, Bishop of Woolwich, *Honest to God*, SCM Press, 1963, p 7, p 105, p 120.
16. *Towards a Quaker View of Sex*, Friends Home Services Committee, 1963.
17. Bernard Levin, *The Pendulum Years*, Jonathan Cape, 1970, p 302.
18. Michael Tracey, *A Variety of Lives. A Biography of Sir Hugh Greene*, Bodley Head, 1983, p 160.
19. Sir Hugh Greene, *The Third Floor Front*, Bodley Head, 1969, pp 94–95.
20. cited Tracey, *A Variety of Lives*, op cit, p 214. Speech to Commonwealth Broadcasting Conference, May 1963.
21. Huw Wheldon, *Control over the Subject Matter of Programmes in BBC Television* in Report of the Joint Committee on Censorship of the Theatre. H. L. 255, H. C. 503, HMSO, 1967. Appendix 3, pp 113–17.
22. Greene, *The Third Floor Front*, op cit, p 101, 103.
23. Mary Whitehouse, *Cleaning Up TV*, Blandford Press, 1967, p 23.
24. Greene, *The Third Floor Front*, op cit, p 100.
25. John Trevelyan, *The BBFC View*, in *Censorship, The Changing Mood*, Journal of the Society of film and Television Arts, Nos 43–44, Spring/Summer 1971.
26. John Trevelyan, *What the Censor Saw*, Michael Joseph, 1973, p 20.
27. Ibid p 106.
28. Memorandum from Lord Harlech and Stephen Murray to the Longford Committee in *Pornography. The Longford Report*, Coronet, 1972, p 270.
29. Hansard, House of Lords Debates. 272. 17 February 1966.
30. Paul O'Higgins, *Censorship in Britain*, Nelson, 1972. pp 86–87.
31. John Trevelyan, *What the Censor Saw*, op cit, p 229.
32. Report of the Joint Committee on Censorship of the Theatre, op cit, pp 184–185.
33. Hansard, House of Lords Debates, 272. 17 February 1966.
34. *Weekend Telegraph*, 30 April 1965: John Crosby, 'London – the Most Exciting City'.
35. Jeff Nuttall, *Bomb Culture*, Paladin, 1968, p 165.
36. Jonathon Green, *Days in the Life*, Heinemann, 1988, p 129.
37. Michael Schofield, *The Sexual Behaviour of Young People*, Longman, 1965, p 29, 37, 38.
38. Geoffrey Gorer, *Sex and Marriage in England Today*, Nelson, 1971. p 30, p 34, p 35.
39. Karen Dunnell, *Family Formation, 1976*, OPCS, HMSO, 1979. Table 2.4 p 7.
40. Ann Cartwright, *Recent Trends in Family Building and Contraception*, OPCS, 1978. p 4, p 7; Ann Cartwright and Warwick Wilkins, *Changes in Family Building Plans*, OPCS, 1976, p 10.
41. M. Bone, *Family Planning Services in England and Wales*, OPCS, HMSO, 1973, p 58.
42. Karen Dunnell, *Family Formation, 1976*, op cit, p 44–45.
43. Michael Schofield, *The Sexual Behaviour of Young Adults*, Allen Lane 1973, p 194, Table 6/7.
44. Richard Neville, *Playpower* 1971.
45. Green, *Days in the Life*, op cit, p 425.
46. Ibid p 404.
47. Ibid p 424.
48. Ibid p 420.
49. Mary Ingham, *Now We Are Thirty*, Eyre Methuen, 1981, p 176, p 166.
50. Carol Dix, *Say I'm Sorry to Mother*, Pan, 1978, pp 94–95.
51. Green, *Days in the Life*, op cit, p 403, p 409.

52.   William Master and Virginia Johnson, *Human Sexual Response*, Churchill, 1966; Ed Ruth and Edward Brecher, *An Analysis of Human Sexual Response*, Andre Deutsch, 1967, pp 82–87.

53.   Anna Koedt, *The Myth of the Vaginal Orgasm*, (roneo-ed pamphlet), 1969; cited Anna Coote and Beatrix Campbell, *Sweet Freedom*, Picador, 1982, p 219.

54.   Coote and Campbell, *Sweet Freedom*, op cit, p 25.

55.   Ibid p 221.

56.   ed. Micheline Wandor, *The Body Politic*, Stage 1, 1972, p 196.

57.   Political Quarterly, Vol 37, No 3, July–September 1966: 'Not in the Programme'.

58.   Roy Walmsley, Karen White, *Sexual Offences, Consent and Sentencing*, Home Office Research Study No 54, HMSO, 1979; cited Jeffrey Weeks, *Sex, Politics and Society*, Longman, 1981. p 275.

59.   *The Times*, 23 May 1963.

60.   *Putting Asunder; A Divorce Law for Contemporary Society*, SPCK, 1966; Church Assembly, Report of Proceedings, Vol XLVII, No 2, Spring Session 1967.

61.   *Reform of the Grounds of Divorce; The Field of Choice*, Cmnd 3123, Law Commission No 6, HMSO, 1967.

62.   Church Assembly, Report of Proceedings, Vol XLVi, No 1, Spring Session 1966.

63.   Madeleine Simms and Keith Hindell, *Abortion Law Reformed*, Peter Owen, 1971, pp 99–101.

64.   Registrar General's Statistical Review for England and Wales 1969. Supplement on Abortion; Report of the Committee on the Working of the Abortion Act. Cmnd 5579, Session 1974–5.

65.   Stuart Hall, Chas Critcher, Tony Jefferson, John Clark, Brian Roberts, *Policing the Crisis*, Macmillan, 1978, p 240.

66.   *The Times*, 1 July 1967.

67.   Hall et al, *Policing the Crisis*, op cit, p 281, p 286.

68.   Geoffrey Robertson, *Obscenity*, Weidenfeld and Nicholson, 1979, p 292.

69.   Tony Palmer, *The Trials of Oz*, Blond and Briggs, 1971, p 13.

70.   Ibid p 138.

71.   Ibid p 271.

72.   Trevelyan, *What the Censor Saw*, op cit, p 143.

73   *The Daily Telegraph*, 7 August 1971.

CHAPTER 9. Alternatives

1.   *The Times*, 19 June 1981.

2.   Dr Jack Dominion, *Marriage in Britain 1945–80*, Study Commission on the Family, 1980, p 12.

3.   Ronald Fletcher, *The Marriage and Family in Britain*, Pelican, 1966, p 131.

4.   Home Office, *Marriage Matters*, HMSO, 1979, p 21.

5.   *The Sunday Times*, 2 May 1982: 'A Woman's Place'.

6.   Judith M. Barwick, *In Transition*, Holt Rinehart and Winston (New York), 1979, p 121.

7.   R. M. Titmuss, *The position of women*, in R. M. Titmuss, *Essays on the 'Welfare State'*, Unwein University Books, 1958. p 91: CSO. *Social Trends 1971*, No 2. HMSO, 1971, p 61: *Social Trends 1986*, No 16, HMSO 1986, p 63.

8.   Michael Young and Peter Willmott, *The Symmetrical Family*, Routledge Kegan and Paul, 1973, p 31.

9.   Hannah Gavron, *The Captive Wife*, Pelican, 1968, p 145.

10.   cited Phillip Whitehead, *The Writing on the Wall*, Michael Joseph/ Channel 4, 1985, p 318.

11.   *Values and the Changing Family*, Study Commission on the Family, 1982. p 26; McCann Erikson Advertising Ltd, 'You Don't Know Me', September 1977.

12.   Ibid p 11.

13. Jessie Bernard, *The Future of Marriage*, Souvenir Press, 1972, pp 17–24.
14. Ibid Chapter 3.
15. *Values of the Changing Family*, op cit, p 11.
16. Kathleen Kiernan and Malcolm Wuicks, *Family Change and Future Policy*, Family Policy Study Centre, 1990.
17. Shere Hite, *The Hite Report*, Talmy Franklin, 1977, p 336.
18. Karen Dunnell, *Family Formation, 1976*, OPCS, HMSO, 1979. Table 2.4. p 7: Paul Gebhard in (ed) W. Armytage, R. Chester, J. Peel, *Changing Patterns in Sexual Relations*, Academic Press (New York), 1980, pp 45–47; *19* magazine, April 1982.
19. Bardwick, *In Transition*, op cit, p 85.
20. *The Hite Report*, op cit, p 305.
21. Ibid p 311.
22. *19* magazine, April 1982.
23. *The Hite Report*, op cit, p 327.
24. Alfred Kinsey, *et al, Sexual Behaviour in the Human Male*, W. B. Saunders, 1948. p 585; Shere Hite, *The Hite Report on Male Sexuality*, Macmillan (New York), 1978, p 142; Annette Lawson, *Adultery*, Basil Blackwell, 1989, p 75.
25. Bernard, *The Future of Marriage*, op cit, p 102.
26. *The Sunday Times/* MORI, 2 March 1980: 'The Good, the Bad and the British'.
27. *The Sunday Times/* Mori, 2 May 1982: 'A Woman's Place'.
28. Lawson, *Adultery*, op cit, p 74.
29. Alfred Kinsey *et al, Sexual Behaviour in the Human Female*, W. B. Saunders, 1953, p 416; Lawson *Adultery*, op cit, p 76; Shere Hite, *Women and Love*, Viking, 1988, p 856.
30. (ed) James R. Smith and Lynn G. Smith, *Beyond Monogamy*, Johns Hopkins University Press, 1974, p 35, p 33.
31. Nena O'Neill and George O'Neil, *Open Marriage*, Abacus, 1975, p 32.
32. (ed) Lynne Segal, *What Is To Be Done About The Family*, Penguin, 1983, p 49.
33. *Values and the Changing Family*, op cit p 11; Clare Dyer and Marcel Berlins, *Living Together*, Hamlyn Paperbacks, 1982, p 10; Lesley Rimmer, *Families in Focus*, Stucy Commission on the Family, 1981, p 18.
34. CSO, *Social Trends, 1986*. No 16, HMSO, 1986, p 41.
35. *The Sunday Times*, 2 March 1980: 'The Good, the Bad, and the British'.
36. Dyer and Berlins, *Living Together*, op cit, pp 24–25.
37. Report of the Lane Committee on the Working of the Abortion Act. Cmnd 5579, HMSO, 1974.
38. *The Sunday Times*, 3 February 1980.
39. Anna Coote and Beatrix Campbell, *Sweet Freedom*, Picador, 1982, p 41.
40. Polly Pattullo, *Judging Women*, NCCL, 1983, p 13.
41. Ibid pp 20–21.
42. Ibid pp 19–20.
43. *The Sunday Times/* MORI, 24 January 1982.
44. *The Daily Mail*, 10 September 1983.
45. *The Daily Mail*, 18 Jan 1982; *The Guardian* 20 Jan 1982; Criminal Law Revision Committee, 15th Report, *Sexual Offences*, HMSO, 1984, p 20.
46. (ed.) Bob Cant and Susan Hemmings, *Radical Records*, Routledge, 1988, p 158.
47. Ibid p 45, p 46.
48. Jeffrey Weeks, *Coming Out*, Quartet, 1977, p 221.
49. Ibid p 219.
50. Michael Tracey and David Morrison, *Whitehouse*, Papermac, 1979 p 91, p 17 (Church Times, 22 July 1977).
51. *The Guardian*, 20 April, 1976.
52. *The Daily Telegraph*, 31 May 1976.
53. Report of Methodist Division for Social Responsibility, Conference Agenda, 1980. pp 21–22. *The Times*, 5 June 1980.
54. *Homosexual Relationships, A Contribution to Discussion*. Church Information Office, October 1979, p 67.

55.   *The Times*, 5 June 1980.
56.   *The Sunday Telegraph*, 24 June 1979.
57.   Lewis Chester, Magnus Linklater, David May, *Jeremy Thorpe: A Secret Life*, Fontana, 1979, p 310.
58.   Ibid p 159.
59.   *The Observer*, 24 June 1979.
60.   Chester *et al, Jeremy Thorpe: A Secret Life*, op cit, p 347, p 349.
61.   *The Sunday Telegraph*, 24 June 1979.

CHAPTER 10. Policing Desires

1.   *The Obscenity Laws*, Arts Council of Great Britain Working Party, Andre Deutsch, 1969, p 35; Geoffrey Robertson, *Obscenity*, Weidenfeld and Nicholson, 1979, p 148; *Report of the US Commission on Obscenity and Pornography*, Bantam Books, 1970.
2.   cited Michael Tracey and David Morrison, *Whitehouse*, Papermac, 1979, p 179: M. Muggeridge to Mary Whitehouse, 23 July 1967.
3.   *The Guardian*, 21 November 1971.
4.   *The Times*, 10 June 1971.
5.   *The Times*, 3 May 1971. BBCTV, 'The World This Weekend'.
6.   *The Daily Telegraph*, 27 September 1971.
7.   *Pornography, The Longford Report*, Coronet, 1972, p 383.
8.   *The Daily Telegraph*, 21 September 1972.
9.   *The Observer*, 15 August, 1971: Raymond Palmer 'Filthy Rich'; Robertson, *Obscenity*, op cit, p 9; Mintel survey in *Campaign*, 13 August 1971; *The New Statesman*, 30 May 1975.
10.   Report of the Committee on Obscenity and Film Censorship (Williams Committee). Cmnd 7772. HMSO, 1979. pp. 44–45.
11.   *The Sunday Times*/Opinion Research Centre, 30 Dec 1973; 'It Isn't Easy To Shock The British'.
12.   Barry Cox, John Shirley, Martin Short, *The Fall of Scotland Yard*, Penguin, 1977, p 186.
13.   Report of the Commissioner of Police for the Metropolis (1974) Cmnd 5638. HMSO p 21; Robertson, *Obscenity*, op cit, p 5.
14.   Cox *et al, The Fall of Scotland Yard*, op cit, p 170.
15.   Williams Committee, op cit, p 36, p 35.
16.   Ibid p 43.
17.   *The Daily Telegraph*, 28 July 1979.
18.   *The Sunday Times*/ORC, 'It Isn't Easy To Shock The British', op cit.
19.   Report of the Committee on the Future of Broadcasting, (Annan Committee). Cmnd 6753, HMSO, 1977.
20.   Williams Committee Report, op cit, p 130.
21.   *The Express and News*, 16 March 1979.
22.   Personal interview Helen Buckingham with Vivianne Howard, 16 December 1988.
23.   Personal interview, op cit.
24.   English Collective of Prostitutes files, Women's Centre, Kings Cross.
25.   Eileen McLeod, *Working Women: Prostitution Now*, Croom Helm, 1982, p 26.
26.   *Honey*, December 1982.
27.   *The Times*, 28 November 1978.
28.   *The Daily Telegraph*, 7 March, 1979.
29.   *The Guardian*, 16 May 1980.
30.   *The Daily Star*, 24 April 1980; *The Guardian*, 24 April 1980.
31.   *The Spectator*, 26 April 1980.
32.   Criminal Statistics, 1975–79. HMSO.
33.   *Time Out*, 30 May–5 June 1980.
34.   *The Journal*, 14 July 1978.

35. *The News of the World*, 15 August 1982; *The Daily Mirror*, 29 March 1983.
36. Susan S. M. Edwards, 'Prostitution: Ponces and Punters, Policing and Prosecution', in *New Law Journal*, 20 September 1985.
37. English Collective of Prostitutes, *The Laws on Prostitution*, March 1979 (Evidence to House of Commons Committee); ECP, Response to Criminal Law, Revision Committee's Working Paper on Offences Relating to Prostitution and Allied Offences, February 1984.
38. Selma James, *Hookers in the House of the Lords*, in (ed) Joy Holland, *Feminist Action 1*, Battle Axe Books, 1983. pp 189–194.
39. *The Guardian*, 21 November 1983.
40. *The Times*, 10 December 1982.
41. McLeod, *Women Working: Prostitution Now*, op cit, p 97.
42. Edwards, op cit, *New Law Journal*, 20 September 1985; *The Guardian*, 16 August 1984.
43. *The Guardian*, 26 February 1985.

CHAPTER 11. Restraint

1. *The Observer*, 20 June 1982.
2. *The Guardian*, 23 November 1981; *For Ourselves*, Sheba Feminist. Publishers, 1981.
3. *The Sunday Mirror* 4 September 1983.
4. *The Sunday Times*, 23 October 1983.
5. *The Observer*, 6 November 1983.
6. *The Lancet* 1977; ii: 727–30; *The Lancet* 1977; ii: 731–4; *The Lancet* 1983; ii: 926–29; *The Lancet* 1983; ii: 930–4: *The Times*, 31 October 1983.
7. Audrey Leathard, *The Fight for Family Planning*, Macmillan, 1980, p 206.
8. cited, *The Guardian*, 25 June 1987.
9. Susan Sontag, *Aids and its Metaphors*, Penguin, 1988, p 72.
10. *The Guardian*, 25 June 1987.
11. *Cosmopolitan*, July 1982: Sue Blanks of London Self-Help Herpes Group.
12. Interview Dr Gordon Skinner, 5 June 1990, by Paul Wilmshurst.
13. *The Sunday Times*, 14 December 1986.
14. *The News of the World*, 1 March 1986; *The Daily Star*, 2 December 1988.
15. *The Daily Mail*, 24 July 1985; *The Sun*, 24 July 1985.
16. Associated Press, 3 October, 1985.
17. *HIV & AIDS*, Proceedings of Aids Symposium, 24 November 1989, UK Health Departments. Health Education Authority, 1989, p 32.
18. *The Daily Telegraph*, 16 September, 1986; BMJ, WHO Communicable Disease Surveillance Centre, Centre For Disease Control, Atlanta; By 1989, the Government had allocated £43m for AIDS research and £44m for public health campaigns (*HIV & AIDS*, op cit, p 39, Virginia Bottomley, Minister of State for Health.).
19. BBC TV: Nine O'Clock News, 8 August 1986; *The Observer*, 9 November 1986; London Weekend Television: Weekend World, 29 September 1985.
20. *The Independent*, 27 June 1987.
21. *The Independent*, 17 June 1990.
22. Professor Roy Anderson, 'Prospects for the UK. The AIDS epidemic in the UK; Past trends and future projections', in *HIV & AIDS*, op cit, p 27.
23. Ibid pp 14–15. Dr Anne Johnson, *The Epidemiology of HIV in the UK. Sexual Transmission*, p 37. Sir Donald Acheson, Chief Medical Office, *Summary of Presentations*.
24. *The Sunday Times*, 2 October 1988.
25. BBC Broadcasting research, *Public Attitudes to AIDS. A Report on a BBC/Gallup Survey*, February 1987, p 9; *The Sunday Telegraph*, 5 June 1988; (ed.) Roger Jowell, Sharon Witherspoon, Lindsay Brook, *The public's response to AIDS*, British Social Attitudes, 5th Report, 1988–9 Edition, SCPR, p 74.

26. Richard Davenport Hines, *Sex, Death and Punishment*, Collins, 1990, p 364.
27. *The Times*, 2 February 1988.
28. Davenport-Hines, *Sex Death and Punishment*, op cit, p 374; *The Guardian*, 23 May 1988.
29. Anderson, *Prospects for the UK*, op cit, p 27; BMRB, *Aids Advertising Campaign. Report on four surveys during the first year of advertising, 1986–7*, British Market Research Bureau Ltd, July 1987; Brian Evans et al, *Trends in sexual behaviour and risk factors for HIV infection among homosexual men, 1984–7*. British Medical Journal 1989, 298, 28 January 1988.
30. Cameron Bowie and Nicholas Ford, *Sexual behaviour of young people and the risk of HIV infection*. Somerset Health Authority and Institute of Population Studies, University of Exeter. Journal of Epidemiology and Community Health, 1989, 43, pp 61–65; *Nature*, 21 September 1989.
31. Nicholas Ford and Kieron Morgan, *Heterosexual Lifestyles of Young People in an English City*, Journal of Population and Social Studies, Vol 1, No 2, January 1989. p 174; *The Independent*, 12 June 1990: Youthscan Survey, Bristol University.
32. Simon Orton and John Samuels, (1989) *What we have learned from researching AIDS*, ESOMAR Congress 1987. Reprinted JMRS. 30. 1. 1988 p 3–34; Ford and Morgan, *Heterosexual Lifestyles of Young People in an English City*, op cit, p 176; *The Independent*, 17 April 1990.
33. i) BBC Broadcasting Research, *Public Attitudes to Aids*, op cit, pp 9, 10; ii) *Claimed Sexual Behaviour*, in S. Orton and J. Samuels, *What we have learned from researching AIDS*, op cit; iii) *Nature*, 21.9.89; iv) *The Independent*, 17 April 1990; v) Ford and Morgan, *Heterosexual Lifestyles of Young People in an English City*, op cit, p 176. See also John Samuels, Simon Orton, Dominic McVey, *The impact and challenge of Change. An overview of some aspects of the AIDS epidemic in Britain since 1986 with reference to the strategic AIDS monitor*, MRS 1991 Conference Papers, 1991.
34. *The Guardian*, 24 August 1987; *The Guardian*, 28 April 1987.
35. *The Guardian*, 28 April 1987.
36. Dagmar O'Connor, *How to Put the Love Back into Making Love*, Columbus Books, 1989, p 11.
37. *The Sunday Telegraph*, 9 October, 1988.
38. O'Connor, *How to Put the Love Back into Making Love*, op cit, p 104, p 105.
39. *The Sunday Times Magazine*, 5 April 1987.
40. Kathleen Kiernan and Malcolm Wicks, *Family Change and Future Policy*, Family Policy Studies Centre, 1990, p 18.
41. Ibid p 11, p 13.
42. Ibid p 6, p 8: OPCS, Series FM2 No 15, *Marriage and Divorce Statistics*, HMSO, 1988, p 9.
43. Kiernan and Wicks, op cit, p 8, 11, 13; *The Sunday Times*, 8 January 1989.
44. *The Mail on Sunday/ NOP*, 9 October 1983.
45. CSO *Social Trends*, 1987, HMSO.
46. *The Observer*, 10 September 1989.
47. Annette Lawson, *Adultery*, Basil Blackwell, 1988, p 21.
48. *The Guardian*, 17 January 1984 – Heather Joshi, ESRC Centre for Population Studies, 'The New Workers'; *The Guardian*, 18 January 1984 – Vanessa Fry and Nick Morris, Institute for Fiscal Studies, 'For Richer or Poorer'.
49. *The Sunday Times*, 15 March 1987; *The Independent*, 20 June 1988.
50. *Creative Voice*, July-September 1983.
51. *The Sunday Times*, 5 February 1989.
52. *The Independent*, 20 June 1988.
53. *The Evening Standard*, 13 October 1988; (*The Mail on Sunday*/NOP poll) *The Independent*, 20 June 1988; *The Independent*, 13 October 1988.
54. CSO, *Social Trends*, 1987, HMSO.
55. *The Sunday Telegraph*, 12 February 1989 – 'The Hard Lessons of Easy Divorce'.
56. Lord Joseph, *Rewards of Parenthood?*. Centre for Policy Studies, 1990, p 9.

57. Ibid p 9.
58. H. M. Treasury, *The Government's Expenditure Plans 1989–90 to 1991–2.* DHSS. CM. HMSO 1989; Jonathan Bradshaw, *Lone Parents: Policy in the Doldrums*, Family Policy Studies Centre, 1989.
59. *The Observer*, 22 November 1989; Lynne Segal, 'Unhappy Families', *The New Socialist*, July–August 1982.
60. *The Independent*, 28 June 1988.
61. Ministerial group on Women's Issues, Home Office, 11 April 1989, 20 October 1989, 20 February 1990 – *Progress and Plans for the Future.*
62. Society of Conservative Lawyers, *The Future of Marriage*, Conservative Political Centre, 1981; One Plus One, *Partnerships for the 1990s* in *The Times*, 12 June 1988.
63. *The Independent*, 27 May 1988.
64. *The Mail on Sunday*, 15 January 1984; M. Green, *Marriage*, Fontana 1984; *The Sunday Times*, 8 May 1983; *The Sunday Times*, 4 March 1990 – 'Wedded Bliss: Is It A Myth?'.
65. *The Sunday Telegraph*, 12 February 1898. Survey Gwyn Davis and Mervyn Murch, Bristol University, in 'The Hard Lessons of Easy Divorce'.
66. *The Guardian*, 6 March 1985.
67. *The Sunday Times*, 6 November 1983; *The Observer*, 3 September 1989.
68. *The Times*, 6 February 1991.
69. *The Times*, 14 October 1983.
70. *The Observer*, 9 October 1983.
71. *The Sunday Times/ MORI*, 16 October 1985.
72. *The Guardian*, 27 October 1986.
73. *The Guardian*, 12 June 1990; Ministerial Group on Women's Affairs, 20 February 1990.
74. *The Sunday Times*, 16 June 1991.
75. *The Guardian*, 26 March 1990.

Select Bibliography

Abortion, An Ethical Discussion, Church Information Office, 1965

Abse, Leo, *Private Member*, Macdonald, 1973

Adam, Ruth, *A Woman's Place*, Chatto & Windus, 1975

Aitken, Jonathan, *The Young Meteors*, Secker and Warburg, 1967

Aldington, Richard, *Portrait of a Genius But . . .* Four Square, 1963

Alvarez, Al, *Life After Marriage*, Macmillan, 1982

Armytage, W., R. Chester, J. Peel, (ed.) *Changing Patterns of Sexual Behaviour*, Academic Press (New York), 1980

Arthur, Sir George, *Life of Lord Kitchener*, Vol III. Macmillan, 1920

Bardwick, Judith, *In Transition*, Holt, Rinehart and Winston, (New York), 1979

Beddoe, Dierdre, *Back to Home and Duty*, Pandora, 1989

Bendit, P. and L., *Living Together Again*, Gramol Press, 1946

Benge, R. C., *Confessions of a Lapsed Librarian*, Scarecrow Books, 1984

Bennett, Arnold, *Books and Persons*, Chatto & Windus, 1920

Bernard, Jessie, *The Future of Marriage*, Souvenir Press, 1972

Berry, Paul and Alan Bishop, (ed.) *Testament of a Generation. The Journalism of Vera Brittain and Winifred Holtby*. Virago, 1985

Blythe, Ronald, *The Age of Illusion, 1919–1940*, Hamish Hamilton, 1963

Bogdanov, Vernon, and Robert Skidelsky, *The Age of Affluence, 1951–64*, Macmillan, 1970

Bone, Margaret, *Family Planning Services in England and Wales*, OPCS. HMSO, 1973

   The Family Planning Services: Change and Effects, HMSO, 1978

Booker, Christopher, *The Neophiliacs*, Fontana/Collins, 1970

Bradshaw, Jonathan, *Lone Parents: Policy in the Doldrums*, Family Policy Studies Centre, 1989

Braybon, Gail, and Penny Summerfield, *Out of the Cage*, Pandora, 1989

Brecher, Ruth and Edward, *An Analysis of Human Sexual Response*, Andre Deutsch, 1967

Brecher, Edward M. *The Sex Researchers*, Panther, 1972

Brentford, Viscount (W. Joynson Hicks), *Do We Need a Censor?* Faber & Faber, 1929

Briggs, Susan, *Keep Smiling Through*, Weidenfeld and Nicholson, 1975

Brighton Women & Social Science Group, *Alice Through the Microscope*, Virago, 1980

Bristow, Edward, *Vice and Vigilance*, Gill and Macmillan, 1977

Brittain, Vera, *Testament of Youth*, Fontana/Virago, 1979

Brock, Michael and Eleanor, (ed.) *H. H. Asquith. Letters to Venetia Stanley*, Oxford University Press, 1982

Brownmiller, Susan, *Against Our Will*, Bantam, 1975

Butler, Josephine, *Personal Reminiscences of a Great Crusade*, H. Marshall, 1896

Calder, Angus, *The People's War. Britain 1939–45*, Panther, 1971

Callow, Phillip, *Son and Lover*, The Bodley Head, 1975

Calvert, Dorothy, *Battledress, Lanyard and Lipstick*, New Horizon (Bognor Regis), 1978

Campbell, Beatrix, *Unofficial Secrets*, Virago, 1988
>   *The Iron Ladies: Why Do Women Vote Tory?*, Virago, 1987
>   'A Feminist Sexual Politics: Now you see it, now you don't?' in *Feminist Review* Vol 5, 1980

Cant, Bob and Susan Hemmings, (ed), *Radical Records*, Routledge, 1988

Carpenter, Edward, *Love's Coming of Age*, Manchester Labour Press, 1896
>   *The Intermediate Sex*, London, 1908

Carrington, Charles *Soldier From the Wars Returning*, Hutchinson, 1965

Carstairs, G. M., *This Island Now. The BBC Reith Lectures*, 1962. Hogarth Press, 1963

Carter, Erica and Simon Watney, (ed.) *Taking Liberties*, Serpents Tail/ICA, 1989

Cartland, Barbara, *The Years of Opportunity*, Hutchinson, 1948

Cartwright, Ann, *Recent Trends in Family Building and Contraception*, OPCS, 1978:
>   and Warwick Wilkins, *Changes in Family Building Plans*, OPCS, 1976

'Censorship, The Changing Mood.' *Journal of the Society of Film and Television Arts*, Nos 43–44, Spring/Summer 1971

Chance, Janet, *The Cost of English Morals*, Noel Douglas, 1931

Chesser, Eustace, *The Sexual Marital and Family Relationships of the English Woman*, Hutchinson's Medical Press, 1956:
>   *Live and Let Live*, Heinemann, 1958:
>   *Love Without Fear*, Hutchinson, 1941

Chester, Lewis, Magnus Linklater, David May, *Jeremy Thorpe. A Secret Life*, Fontana, 1979

Church of England Moral Welfare Council, *The Problem of Homosexuality*, 1954:
>   *Sexual Offenders and Social Punishment* (Submission to Wolfenden Committee) 1956:
>   Annual Reports, 1947–56

Churchill, W. S., *My Early Life*, Thornton Butterworth, 1930

Clephane, Irene, *Towards Sex Freedom*, The Bodley Head, 1935

Comfort, Alex, *Sex in Society*, Duckworth, 1962:
>   *The Anxiety Makers*, Panther, 1968

Coote, Anna and Beatrix Campbell, *Sweet Freedom*, Picador, 1982

Coote, William, (ed.) *A Romance in Philanthropy*, National Vigilance Association, 1916

Costello, John, *Love Sex and War*, Collins, 1985

Cox, Barry, John Shirley, Martin Short, *The Fall of Scotland Yard*, Penguin, 1977

Craig, Alex, *The Banned Books of England*, George Allen and Unwin, 1962

Cronwright, Schreiner, S. C. (ed.), *The Letters of Olive Schreiner*, Unwin, 1924

Crosland, Anthony, *The Future of Socialism*, Jonathan Cape, 1956:
The Conservative Enemy, Jonathan Cape, 1962

Crozier, Brigadier General F. P., *A Brass Hat in No-Man's Land*, Jonathan Cape, 1930

Davie, Michael, *The Diaries of Evelyn Waugh*, Weidenfeld and Nicholson, 1976

Davies, Christie, *Permissive Britain*, Pitman, 1975

Davis, Maxine, *The Sexual Responsibility of Women*, Fontana, 1964

Denning, Lord, *The Due Process of Law*. Butterworth, 1980

Devlin, Lord, *The Enforcement of Morals*, MacDonald, 1973

Dickinson, R. L., and L. Beam, *A Thousand Marriages. A Medical Study of Sex Adjustment*, Williams and Norgate, 1932

Dickson, R. Lovat, *Radclyffe Hall at the Well of Loneliness*, Collins, 1975

Dix, Carol, *Say I'm Sorry To Mother*, Pan, 1978

Dominion, Dr. Jack, *Marriage in Britain 1945–80*, Study Commission on the Family, 1980

Donaldson, Frances, *Edward VIII*, Omega, 1975

Dunnell, Karen, *Family Formation, 1976*, OPCS, HMSO, 1979

Dyer, Clare, and Marcel Berlins, *Living Together*, Hamlyn Paperbacks, 1982

Edmonds, Charles, *A Subaltern's War*, Peter Davies, 1929

Edwards, Susan M., 'Prostitution; Ponces and Punters, Policy and Prostitution,' in *New Law Journal*, 20 September, 1985:
Female Sexuality and the Law, Martin Robertson, 1981

Ellis, H. Havelock, *My Life*, Heinemann, 1940:
Studies in the Pyschology of Sex, Vol 1, *Sexual Inversion*, Wilson and Macmillan, 1897:
Psychology of Sex, Heinemann, 1933

Feminist Review, (ed.) *Sexuality. A Reader*, Virago, 1987

Ferguson, S. M., and H. Fitzgerald, *Studies in the Social Services*, HMSO, 1954

Findlater, Richard, *Banned!*, McGibbin and Kee, 1967

First, Ruth, and Ann Scott, (ed.) *Olive Schreiner*, Andre Deutsch, 1980

Fischer, H. C., and Dr. E. X. Dubois, *Sexual Life During the War*, Francis Aldor, 1937

Fisher, Seymour, *Understanding the Female Orgasm*, Penguin, 1973

Fletcher, Ronald, *The Marriage and Family in Britain*, Pelican, 1963
For Ourselves, Sheba Feminist Publishers, 1981

Ford, C. S, and F. A. Beach, *Patterns of Sexual Behaviour*, University Paperbacks, 1970

Foucault, Michel, *History of Sexuality*, Vol 1. An Introduction, Allen Lane, 1979

Freud, Sigmund, *Collected Papers*, Vol V, Hogarth Press, 1950:
    Some Psychological Consequences of the Anatomical Differences Between the Sexes Vol XVII (1925):
    Female Sexuality. Vol XXIV (1931):
    On Sexuality, Pelican Freud Library. Vol 7, Penguin, 1977

Friedan, Betty, *The Feminist Mystique*, Penguin, 1965:
The Second Stage, Abacus, 1983

Gavron, Hannah, *The Captive Wife*, Pelican 1968

Gay, Peter, *The Bourgeois Experience. Victoria to Freud*. Vol 1, *Education of the Senses*. Oxford University Press 1984:
    Vol 11. *The Tender Passion*, Oxford University Press 1986

Gillis, John, *For Better, For Worse*, Oxford University Press 1985

Glendinning, Victoria, *Vita*, Penguin, 1983

Gorer, Geoffrey, *Exploring English Character*, The Cresset Press, 1955:
    Sex and Marriage in England Today, Nelson, 1971

Green, G. F., *A Skilled Hand*, Macmillan, 1980

Green, Jonathon, *Days in a Life*, Heinemann, 1988

Green, M., *Marriage*, Fontana, 1984

Greene, Sir Hugh, *The Third Floor Front*, Bodley Head, 1967

Greenwood, Victoria, and Jock Young, *Abortion in Demand*, Pluto, 1976

Greer, Germaine, *The Female Eunuch*, Paladin, 1971:
    Sex and Destiny, Secker and Warburg, 1984

Griffiths, Edward, *Towards Maturity*, 1944

Grosskurth, Phyllis, *Havelock Ellis. A Biography*, Allen Lane, 1980

Haddon, Celia, *The Limits of Sex*, Michael Joseph, 1982

Hailsham, Lord, *A Sparrow's Flight*, Collins, 1990

Hall, Gladys Mary, *Prostitution, A Survey and a Challenge*, Williams and Norgate, 1933

Hall, Ruth, *Marie Stopes. A Biography*, Virago, 1978
    (ed.) *Dear Dr Stopes*, Andre Deutsch, 1978

Hall, Stuart, Chas Critcher, Tony Jefferson, John Clark, Brian Roberts, *Policing the Crisis*, Macmillan, 1978

Halsey, A. H. (ed.) *Trends in British Society Since 1900*, Macmillan, 1972

Hardy, Thomas, *Jude the Obscure*, Papermac, 1966

Harris, Frank, *Frank Harris on Bernard Shaw*, Gollancz, 1931

Hart, H. L. A., *Law, Liberty and Morality*, OUP, 1963:
'Immorality and Treason.' in *The Listener*, 30 July 1959

Harvey, Ian, *To Fall Like Lucifer*, The Quality Book Club, 1971

Herbert, A. P., *The Ayes Have It*, Methuen, 1937

Hillary, Richard, *The Last Enemy*, Pan, 1956

Hines, Richard Davenport, *Sex, Death and Punishment*, Collins, 1990

Hite, Shere, *The Hite Report*, Talmy Franklin, 1977:
    The Hite Report on Male Sexuality, Macmillan (NY) 1978

Woman and Love, Viking, 1987

HIV & AIDS, Proceedings of AIDS Symposium, November 1989, Health Education Authority, 1989

Holland, Joy (ed.) *Feminist Action 1*, Battle Axe Books, 1983

Homosexual Relationships. A Contribution to Discussion, Church Information Office, 1979

Horne, Alistair, *Macmillan, 1894–1956*. Vol 1, Macmillan, 1988: *Macmillan, 1957–1986* Vol 11, Macmillan, 1989

Humphreys, Steve, *A Secret World of Sex*, Sidgwick and Jackson, 1988

Hunt, A, *A Survey of Women's Employment*, HMSO, 1968

Hyde, Montgomery, *The Other Love*, Mayflower, 1972

Inge, W. R., *Outspoken Essays*, Longmans Green, 1919
   Vale, Longmans Green, 1934

Ingham, Mary, *Now We Are Thirty*, Eyre Methen, 1981

'J', *The Sensuous Woman*, Dell (New York), 1969

Jenkins, Roy, *The Labour Case*, Penguin, 1959

Jephcott, P, N. Seear, J. H. Smith, *Married Women Working*, Allen and Unwin, 1962

Johnson, George and Lucy (ed.), *Josephine Butler. An Autobiographical Memoir*, Arrowsmith, 1909

Joseph, Lord, *Reward of Parenthood?*, Centre for Policy Studies, 1990

Joseph, Shirley, *If Their Mothers Only Knew*, Faber, 1945

Jowell, Roger, Sharon Witherspoon, Lindsay Brook, *The Public's Response to AIDS*, British Social Attitudes, 5th Report, 1988–9. SCPR

Katin, Zelma, *Clippie*, Gifford, 1944

Keays, Sara, *A Question of Judgement*, Quintessential Press, 1985

Kiernan, Kathleen, and Malcolm Wicks, *Family Change and Future Policy*, Family Policy Study Centre, 1990

Kinsey, Alfred, Wardell B. Pomeroy, Clyde E. Martin, *Sexual Behaviour in the Human Male*, W. B. Saunders, 1948

Kinsey, Alfred, Wardell B. Pomeroy, Clyde E. Martin, Paul H. Genhard, *Sexual Behaviour in the Human Female*, W. B. Saunders, 1953

Klein, Viola, *Britain's Married Women Workers*, Routledge Kegan and Paul, 1965

Knightley, Phillip, and Caroline Kennedy, *An Affair of State*, Jonathan Cape, 1987

Koestler, Arthur (ed.) *Suicide of a Nation?*, Hutchinson, 1963

Krafft-Ebing, Richard, *Psychopathia Sexualis*, F. J. Rebman, 1894

Lawrence, D. H., *Pornography and Obscenity*, Faber & Faber, 1929
   'A Propos of Lady Chatterley's Lover' in (ed) Harry T. Moore, *Sex Literature and Censorship*, Heinemann, 1955:
   Lady Chatterly's Lover, Penguin, 1960

Lawson, Annette, *Adultery*, Basil Blackwell, 1989

Leathard, Audrey, *The Fight for Family Planning*, Macmillan, 1980

Lee, B. H., *Divorce Law Reform in England*, Peter Owen, 1974

Levin, Bernard, *The Pendulum Years*, Jonathan Cape, 1970

Lewis, Alun, *In the Green Tree*, George Allen and Unwin, 1948

Lewis-Faning, E, 'Report on an Enquiry into Family Limitation and Its Influence on Human Fertility During the Past Fifty Years,' *Papers of the Royal Commission on Population*, HMSO, Cmnd 7695 Vol 1, 1949

Llewellyn Davies, Margaret (ed.) *Maternity Letters from Working Women*, Virago, 1978

Lloyd George, Frances, *The Years That Are Past*, Hutchinson, 1967

Lock, Joan, *The British Policewoman, Her Story*, Robert Hale, 1979

Pornography. The Longford Report, Coronet, 1972

Longmate, Norman, *How We Lived Then*, Hutchinson, 1971
    The G.I's, Hutchinson, 1975

Lord Bishop of London, *Cleansing London, The Moral Change Required in London*, 1916

Low, Rachel, *The History of the British Film 1918–1929*, George Allen and Unwin, 1971

Lumley, Air Commodore E. A., *Army and Air Force Doctor*, 1971

MacCarthy, Aidan, *A Doctor's War*, Robson Books, 1979

Mace, David R., *The Facts About Venereal Disease*, 1943
    Coming Home. A Series of Five Broadcast Talks, Staple Press, 1945
    Marriage Counselling, J. and A. Churchill, 1948

McGregor, O. R., *Divorce in England*, Heinemann, 1957

MacKenzie, Norman and Jeanne, *The First Fabians*, Quartet, 1979

McLeod, Eileen, *Working Women; Prostitution Now*, Croom Helm, 1982

Makins, Peggy, *The Evelyn Home Story*, Fontana/Collins, 1976

Marriage Matters, Home Office, HMSO, 1979

Marwick, Arthur, *Women At War*, Fontana, 1977
    The Deluge. British Society and the First World War, Pelican, 1967

Maschler, Tom (ed.) *Declaration*, MacGibbon and Kee, 1957

Mass Observation: *People in Production*, John Murray, 1942:
    The Journey Home, John Murray, 1944

Mass Observations Files: FR64 *Sexual Behaviour 1939–50*
    FR1542 Preliminary Report on General Attitudes to Venereal Disease, December 1942
    FR1562 Public Reactions to the Campaign Against V.D, January 1943
    FR1633 V.D. Publicity in the Press
    FR2205 Sex Morality and the Birth Rate, January 1945
    FR3110 General Attitudes to Sex, April 1949

Masters, William, and Virginia Johnson, *Human Sexual Response*, Churchill, 1966

Mead, Margaret, *Male and Female*, Pelican, 1962

Melly, George, *Rum, Bum and Concertina*, Weidenfeld and Nicholson, 1977

Minns, Raynes, *Bombers and Mash*, Virago, 1980

Mitchell, Juliette, and Jacqueline Rose, *Feminine Sexuality*, Macmillan 1982

Mitchell, Juliette, *Woman's Estate*, Penguin, 1971
    Psychoanalysis and Feminism, Pelican, 1975

Montgomery, John, *The Fifties*, George Allen and Unwin, 1965

Moore, Harry T., (ed) *Sex, Literature and Society*, Heinemann, 1955 (ed.) *The Collected Letters of D. H. Lawrence*, Vol 11, Heinemann, 1962

Morton, R. S., *Veneral Diseases*, Pelican, 1966

Mount, Ferdinand, *The Subversive Family*, Unwin, 1983

Munro, Colin, R., *Television Censorship and the Law*, Saxon House, 1979

Neville, Richard, *Playpower*, Paladin, 1971

Newsome, John, *The Education of Girls*, Faber & Faber, 1948

Nichols, Beverly, *The Sweet and Twenties*, Weidenfeld and Nicholson, 1958

Nicholson, Nigel, *Portrait of a Marriage*, Futura, 1974

Nuttall, Jeff, *Bomb Culture*, Paladin, 1970

Oakley, Ann, *Subject Women*, Martin Robertson, 1981

The Obscenity Laws, Report of the Arts Council of Great Britain Working Party, 1969

Report of the US Commission on Obscenity and Pornography, Bantam Books 1970

O'Connor, Dagmar, *How to Put the Love Back Into Making Love*, Columbus Books, 1989

O'Higgins, Paul, *Censorship in Britain*, Nelson, 1972

O'Neal, Nena and George, *Open Marriage*, Abacus, 1975

Osborne, John, *A Better Class of Person*, Faber and Faber, 1981

Palmer, Tony, *The Trials of OZ*, Blond and Briggs, 1971

Pankhurst, Christabel, *The Great Scourge. And How to End It*. E. Pankhurst, 1913

Pankhurst, Sylvia, *The Home Front*, Hutchinson, 1932

Pattullo, Polly, *Judging Women*, NCCL, 1983

Pearsall, Ronald, *The Worm in the Bud*, Weidenfeld and Nicholson, 1969

Peel, C. S., *How We Lived Then*, The Bodley Head, 1929

Playne, Caroline, *Society At War*, George Allen and Unwin, 1931
    Britain Holds On, 1917–1918, George Allen and Unwin, 1933
        Putting Asunder: A Divorce Law for Contemporary Society, SPCK, 1966

Pym, Bridget, *Pressure Groups and the Permissive Society*, David and Charles, 1974

Ray, Gordon N., *H. G. Wells and Rebecca West*, Yale University Press, 1974

Reform of the Ground of Divorce; The Field of Choice, Law Commission No 6, Cmnd 3123, HMSO 1967

Reich, Wilhelm, *The Sexual Revolution*, Vision Press, 1961
    The Function of the Orgasm, Panther, 1968

Richards, Peter, *Parliament and Conscience*, George Allen and Unwin, 1970

Richardson, Major General Frank M. *Mars Without Venus*, Blackwood, 1981

Rickards, Jocelyn, *The Painted Banquet*, Weidenfeld and Nicholson, 1987

Rimmer, Lesley, *Families in Focus*, Study Commission on the Family, 1981

Rive, Richard, *Olive Schreiner. Letters 1871–99*. OUP, 1988

Roberts, Elizabeth, *A Woman's Place*, Basil Blackwell, 1984

Robertson, Geoffrey, *Obscenity*, Weidenfeld and Nicholson, 1979

Robinson, John, Bishop of Woolwich, *Honest To God*, SCM Press, 1963

Robinson, Marie N. *The Power of Sexual Surrender*, New America Library, 1962

Rolph, C. H., *The Trial of Lady Chatterley*, Privately printed, 1961
    Books in the Dock, Andre Deutsch, 1969

Rowbothan, Sheila, *Hidden From History*, Pluto Press, 1973
    Socialism and the New Life, Pluto Press, 1977
    A New World for Women, Pluto Press, 1977

Russell, Bertrand, *An Autobiography of Bertrand Russell 1872–1914*, Vol 1, George Allen and Unwin, 1967
    An Autobiography of Bertrand Russell 1914–1944, Vol 11, George Allen and Unwin, 1968
    Marriage and Morals, George Allen and Unwin, 1929

Russell, Dora, *The Tamarisk Tree*, Virago, 1975

Samuels, John and Simon Orton, Dominic McVey, *The impact and challenge of change*, MRS 1991 Conference Papers

Scharlieb, Dr. Mary, *Reminiscences*, William and Norgate, 1921

Schofield, Michael, *The Sexual Behaviour of Young People*, Longman, 1965
    The Sexual Behaviour of Young Adults, Allen Lane, 1973

Schreiner, Olive, *Woman and Labour*, T. Fisher Unwin, 1911

Segal, Lynne, *What Is To Be Done About the Family?* Penguin, 1983
    'Unhappy Families' in *New Socialist*, July-August, 1982

Shaw, George Bernard, *Prefaces of Bernard Shaw*, Constable, 1934

Sherfey, Mary Jane, *The Nature and Evolution of Female Sexuality*, Random House, (New York), 1966

Simms, Madeleine, and Keith Hindell, *Abortion Law Reformed*, Peter Owen, 1971

Slater, Eliot and Moya Woodside, *Patterns of Marriage*, Cassell, 1951

Smith, James R. and Lynn G., *Beyond Monogamy*, John Hopkins University Press, 1974

Society of Conservative Lawyers, *The Future of Marriage*, Conservative Political Centre, 1981

Sontag, Susan, *AIDS and Its Metaphors*, Penguin, 1988

Stevas, Norman, St John, *Obscenity and the Law*, Martin Secker and Warburg, 1956

Stocks, Mary, *My Commonplace Book*, Peter Davies, 1970

Stone, Lawrence, *Road to Divorce*, Oxford University Press, 1990

Stopes, Marie, *Married Love*, A. C. Fifield, 1918
    Wise Parenthood, A. C. Fifield, 1918
    Marriage in My Time, Rich and Cowan, 1935

Strachey, Ray, *Millicent Garrett Fawcett*, John Murray, 1931

Tait, Kathleen, *My Father Bertrand Russell*, Gollancz, 1976

Taylor, A. H., *Jix- Viscount Brentford*, Stanley Paul, 1933

Taylor, A. J. P., (ed.) *Lloyd George, A Diary of Frances Stevenson*, Hutchinson, 1971

Taylor, John Russell, *Anger and After*, Methuen, 1962

Titmuss, R. M., *Essays on the Welfare State*, Unwin University Books, 1958

Towards a Quaker View of Sex, Friends Home Service Committee, 1963

Tracey, Michael, *A Variety of Lives. A Biography of Sir Hugh Greene*, Bodley head, 1983
    and David Morrison, *Whitehouse*, Papermac, 1979
Trevelyan, John, *What the Censor Saw*, Michael Joseph, 1973
Troubridge, Una, Lady, *The Life and Death of Radclyffe Hall*, Hammond, 1961
Turner, E. M., *Josephine Butler. Her Place in History*, The Association for Moral and Social Hygeine, n.d. Fawcett Library.
Values and the Changing Family, Study Commission on the Family, 1982
van de Velde, Th., *Ideal Marriage. Its Psychology and Technique*, Heinemann (Medical Books), 1930
Walker, Kenneth and Peter Fletcher, *Sex and Society*, Pelican, 1955
Walmsley, Roy and Karen White, *Sexual Offences, Consent and Sentencing*, Home Office Research Study No 54, HMSO, 1979
Wandor, Michelin, (ed.) *The Body Politic*, Stage 1, 1972
Watney, Simon, *Policing Desire. Pornography, AIDS and the Media*, Comedia/Methuen, 1987
Watts, Marthe, *The Men in My Life*, Christopher Johnson, 1960
Webb, Beatrice, *The Diary of Beatrice Webb 1873–1892*, Vol 1. (ed.) Norman and Jeanne MacKenzie, Virago, 1982
Our Partnership, London, 1948
Weeks, Jeffrey, *Coming Out*, Quartet, 1977
    Sex, Politics and Society, Longman, 1981
Wells, G. P. (ed.), *H. G. Wells in Love*, Faber & Faber, 1984
Wells, H. G., *Experiment in Autobiography*, Macmillan, 1934
Ann Veronica, (1908), Virago, 1980
West, Anthony, *H. G. Wells. Aspects of a Life*, Hutchinson, 1984
West, D. J., *The Young Offender*, Pelican, 1968
West, Rebecca, *The Young Rebecca. The Writings of Rebecca West 1911–1917*, (ed.) Jane Marcus, Macmillan/Virago, 1982
White, Cynthia L., *Women's Magazines 1693–1968*, Michael Joseph, 1970
Whitehead, Phillip, *The Writing on the Wall*, Michael Joseph/Channel 4, 1985
Whitehouse, Mary, *Cleaning Up TV*, Blandford Press, 1967
    Who Does She Think She Is? New English Library, 1971
Wildeblood, Peter, *Against the Law*, Penguin, 1957
Wilson, Elizabeth, *Women and the Welfare State*, Tavistock, 1977
Wimperis, Virginia, *The Unmarried Mother and Her Child*, George Allen and Unwin, 1960
Wistrich, Enid, *'I Don't Mind the Sex, It's the Violence. Film Censorship Explored*, Marion Boyars, 1978
Woolf, Myra, *Family Intentions*, OPCS. HMSO, 1971
Young, Michael, and Peter Willmott, *The Symmetrical Family*, Routledge Kegan and Paul, 1973

Parliamentary Papers, Government Reports.

General Register Office, *Census 1911*, HMSO, 1914

Report on Industrial Welfare Conditions in Coventry, November 1916, Home Office, 1916

Annual Report of the Registrar General, 1916, Cmnd 8869, HMSO, 1916

Report of the Royal Commission on Venereal Diseases, Cmnd 8189, HMSO, 1916

Commission of Inquiry into Conduct in the WAAC, Ministry of Labour, 1918

History of the Great War. Medical Services. General History, Vol 2, (ed) Major General Sir W. G. MacPherson, HMSO, 1921

Interim Report of the Departmental Committee on Maternal Mortality and Morbidity, MOH, HMSO, 1930

Report of the Interdepartmental Committee of Inquiry on Abortion (Birkett Committee), MOH, HO, 1039

Report of the Committee on Amenities and Welfare Conditions in the Three Women's Armed Services, Cmnd 6384, HMSO 1942

Report on Social Insurance and Allied Services (Beveridge Report) Cmnd 6404, HMSO, 1942

The State of Public Health During Six Years of War. Report of the Chief Medical Officer for the Ministry of Health, 1939–45. HMSO

Report of the Denning Committee on Procedure in Matrimonial Causes, Cmnd 7024, HMSO, 1947

Inter Allied Conference on War Medicine, Convened by the Royal Society of Medicine, 1942–45, (ed.) Major General Sir Henry Letheby-Tide, HMSO, 1947

Report of the Royal Commission on Population, Cmnd 7695, 1949

The Second World War. Army. Discipline, (ed) Brigadier A. B. MacPherson, WO, 1950

The Second World War. Army. Army Welfare, (ed.) Brigadier M. C. Morgan, WO, 1953

Royal Air Force. Medical Services, Vol 111, (ed.) Squadron Leader S. C. Wrexford-Welch, HMSO, 1958

Medical History of the Second World War, (ed.) Sir Arthur Salusbury MacNally and W. Franklyn Mellor, HMSO, 1968

Statistical Digest of the War, HMSO, 1951

Report of the Royal Commission on Marriage and Divorce, (Morton Commission), Cmnd 9678, HMSO, 1956

Report of the Committee on Homosexual Offences and Prostitution, (Wolfenden Committee), Cmnd 247, HMSO, 1957

The Youth Service of England and Wales (Albemarle Report), Cmnd 929, HMSO, 1960

Report of the Select Committee on Obscene Publications (Spens Committee) 1+C 123, 1958

Report of the Joint Committee on Censorship of the Theatre, H.L.255, H.C.503, HMSO, 1967

Registrar General's Statistical Review for England and Wales, 1969

Report of the Committee on the Working of the Abortion Act, (Lane Committee), Cmnd 5579. HMSO, 1974

Report of the Committee on One Parent Families, (Finer Committee), Cmnd 5629, HMSO, 1977

Report of the Committee on the Future of Broadcasting, (Annan Committee), Cmnd 6753, HMSO, 1977

Report of the Committee on Obscenity and Film Censorship, (Williams Committee), Cmnd 7772, HMSO, 1979

Criminal Law Revision Committee, 15th Report, *Sexual Offences*, HMSO, 1984

16th Report, *Prostitution in the Street*, Cmnd 9329, 1984

17th Report, *Prostitution: Off Street Activities*, Cmnd 9688, 1985

C.S.O. *Social Trends*. 1976, 1986, 1987

Newspapers, Journals, Periodicals

British Medical Journal
Campaign
Cosmopolitan
Creative Voice
Daily Mail
Daily Mirror
Daily News
Daily Star
Daily Telegraph
Evening Standard
Feminist Review
The Freewoman – later *New Freewoman*
Guardian (Manchester Guardian)
Good Housekeeping
Honey
Independent
Mail on Sunday
New Socialist
New Society
New Statesman
19
News Chronicle
News of the World
Observer
Parents
Political Quarterly
The Practitioner
People
St. James Gazette
Spare Rib
Spectator

Sun
Sunday Express
Sunday Mirror
Sunday Telegraph
Sunday Times
Time Out
The Times
Tribune
Vigilance Record
Westminster Gazette
Weekly Dispatch
Woman
Woman's Own

Archive Collections

British Museum Newspaper Library
Church of England – Lambeth conference Reports,
      Church Assembly Reports
      Moral Welfare Council, Annual Reports 1947–56
      Board For Social Responsibility, Annual Reports
Conservative Central Office – Conference Resolutions, Campaign Guides
English Collective of Prostitutes Files
Fawcett Library including Josephine Butler Collection.
Hansard, Parliamentary Debates.
Imperal War Museum – Documents Collection,
      Women's Collection,
      Employment Files
Labour Party – NEC Minutes 1959–68, Manifestos 1945–79
Mass Observation Records, University of Sussex
Public Records Office

Index

Nuttall, Jeff 163, 167, 204
nymphomaniacs 160

Obelisk (later Olympia) Press 75
Obscene Publications Act
   (1959) 177–8, 253
  amendment (1977) 254
  extending 301
  suspension recommended 218
obscenity:
  church and 180
  laws against 29, 177–8, 252–3, 254
    suspension recommended 218
  prosecutions:
    distinguishing from
      pornography 257–8
    literature 51–2, 75, 87, 194–5
    press 218–20
    text books 67, 79
Observer 166
O'Connor, Dagmar 284–5
O'Connor, T. P. 3, 74–5
Offences Against the Person Act
  (1861) 93
Oh Calcutta (Tynan) 201
Ono, Yoko 199
open marriage 233–5
orgasm:
  adolescents achieving 161
  clitoral 210–11
  faking 229–30
  as measurement of sexual
    achievement 155–8, 228–9
  in men and women 23
  multiple 210, 229
  mutal 79
  reached by petting 158
  simultaneous 76, 145
  types 210–11
  vaginal 210–11
Oriolo, Giuseppe 76
Orlando (Woolf) 86
Osborne, John 159, 166–7, 200–1
O'Shea, Kitty 2
'Overlord' operation 115
Oxford Union 66
Oxford University: homosexuals
  at 87–8
Oz trial 218–20

Pall Mall Gazette 14
Pankhurst, Christobel 16

Pankhurst, Emily 18
parents:
  control of daughters 71
  influence on children's
    marriage 44–6, 151
Parkinson, Ann 297, 298
Parkinson, Cecil 297–9
Parnell, Charles 2, 3
parties, weekend 70–1
Patriot For Me (Osborne) 200–1
patriotism: moral controls in name
  of 50–7
patrols: women's 33–8, 52, 54
Patten, John 300
Payne, Cynthia 266–7
Pearson, Karl 9–10
Peckinpah, Sam 254
Peel, C. S. 43–4
Pemberton, Max 37
Penguin Books 178–81, 213
People (newspaper) 173, 249
Perfumed Garden 75
permissiveness:
  attack on 218–20
  legislation for 212–17
  limits of 217
personal freedom:
  state supervision of 32–8, 182,
    201–2
  violation of 14, 174, 261
petting 70
  adolescent 158, 160–1
phallic consciousness 75–6
Philanderer (Kauffman) 176
Philips, Marion 66
Pill:
  dangers of 273–4
  influence 186, 205–6, 221
pimps 51
pin money 89
Pitt-Rivers, Michael 170
Pius XI, Pope 69
Pizzey, Erin 239
PLAN (Prostitute Laws Are
  Nonsense) 264–5
Play Power (Neville) 207
plays *see* literature; theatre
Pohle, Hans Dieter 278
Polhemus, Ted 286
police:
  corruption 257
  treatment of women prisoners 34

women: used for moral
    tyranny 34–8
politics:
    disillusion with 203
    dissent in 167
    morality as subject for 291–303
    sex as subject for 185–92
    and women's rights 209–10, 212,
        235–6
pop music 162–3, 202–3
population shift during war 100
pornography 175–82, 195
    authors accused of 51–2
    campaign against 252–61
    degrading women 255
    law against 177
    market for 256
    prosecutions for 257–8
    publications destroyed 175
    women's campaign against 242
    see also obscenity
Potter, Beatrice see Webb, Beatrice
poverty: feminization of 227
Power of Surrender (Robinson) 156
pre-marital sex 70–2, 158–61
    adolescent 271
    effect of war on 44
    statistics 122, 158–9, 205–6, 228
    trends 137
Preddie, Lord 189
Presley, Elvis 162–3
press:
    freedom of 300–1
    libel actions against 300
    obscenity prosecutions 218–20
Price, Anthony 286
Priestley, J. B. 165, 177
prisoners of war: problems on
    return 142
privacy:
    protection 300
    see also personal freedom
Problem of Homosexuality 171
Profumo Affair 81, 175, 185, 187–92
Profumo, John 187–92
promiscuity:
    adolescent 164
    condoned in men 134
    free love and 25–7
    risk of AIDS 278
    war encouraging 47

PROS (Programme for Reform of the
    Law on Soliciting) 265
prostitutes:
    'amateur' 53–4, 72, 134–5
    banned from military areas 33
    child 14
    contact sheet 194
    control of 134
    influence on soldiers 53–4
    laws concerning 171, 172–5
    laws discriminating against 14,
        54–6, 134–5, 174, 261–70
    prosecutions 172–3, 265–70
    rights 262–70
    sex education from 121
    women becoming 265
psychoanalysis 22
psychology:
    influence 61
    scientific studies 5, 31
Psychopathia Sexualis (Ebing) 22
Public Morality Council 74
Publishers' Association 177
pubs:
    closing hours 53
    women in 106
PUSSI (Prostitutes United for Social
    and Sexual Integration) 264–5
Putting Asunder 214

Quakers: and morality 193

RAF 105–6
Rainbow (Lawrence) 51–2, 75
rape 240–3, 300
    in marriage 242, 300
Rape Crisis Centre 241
Reader's Digest 274
Rees, Goronwy 88
Reeves, Amber 26
Reisz, Karl 198
Relate (Marriage Guidance
    Council) 285
religion:
    and abortion 213, 215–16
    and birth control 19, 64–5, 66, 69
    changing attitudes 98
    declining influence 151, 304
    and divorce 95–6, 144, 152, 213,
        214–15
    feminists drawing strength from 15